CHRISTOLOGY

CHRISTOLOGY

*A Biblical, Historical, and Systematic
Study of Jesus*

⁘ ⁘

Gerald O'Collins, SJ

OXFORD UNIVERSITY PRESS

Oxford University Press, Walton Street, Oxford OX2 6DP

Oxford New York

Athens Auckland Bangkok Bombay
Calcutta Cape Town Dar es Salaam Delhi
Florence Hong Kong Istanbul Karachi
Kuala Lumpur Madras Madrid Melbourne
Mexico City Nairobi Paris Singapore
Taipei Tokyo Toronto
and associated companies in
Berlin Ibadan

Oxford is a trade mark of Oxford University Press

Published in the United States
by Oxford University Press Inc., New York

British Library Cataloguing in Publication Data
Data available

Library of Congress Cataloging in Publication Data
Christology: a biblical, historical, and systematic
study of Jesus/Gerald O'Collins.
Includes bibliographical references and index.
1. Jesus Christ—Person and offices.   2. Jesus Christ—History of
doctrines.   I. Title.
BT202.0313   1995   232—dc20   94–32210
ISBN 0-19-875501-5 ISBN 0-19-875502-3 (Pbk)

3 5 7 9 10 8 6 4

Typeset by Selwood Systems, Midsomer Norton
Printed in Great Britain on acid-free paper by
Bookcraft (Bath) Ltd., Midsomer Norton

For Charles and Thérèse

PREFACE

⸖ ⸖

In his recent Christology (*The Way of Jesus Christ: Christology in Messianic Dimensions* (London: SCM Press, 1990)), Jürgen Moltmann points to one of the major 'constraints' in undertaking such a project: 'No contemporary christology is ever completely new. Every christology is part of a grateful and critical dialogue with the christologies of [our] predecessors and contemporaries, setting its own tiny accents in this great dialogue about the messianic secret of Jesus Christ' (p. 38). In other words, to write a satisfactory Christology, you must tell a story that is at least partly familiar and cannot promise to be constantly and startlingly original.

Before presenting my own contribution in the later chapters of this book, I must first engage in some 'grateful and critical dialogue' with my predecessors in the biblical period, the patristic era, and the subsequent history of Christology. Such a critical dialogue necessarily involves being selective. The material from the Bible, the Fathers, and later church history is complex and often controversial. Exegetes, patristic scholars, historians of doctrine, and philosophers will always want to hear more. But this work introduces the biblical, historical, and philosophical contributions with the aim of setting my 'own tiny accents' in a systematic Christology which finds its primary interpretative key in the resurrection of the crucified Jesus and his presence, and not with the aim of writing a complete history of Christology. Like Moltmann and others, I am convinced that one cannot write a systematic Christology without paying attention to and drawing to some extent on what has gone before. Yet writing up the complete history of christological developments would be a quite different and much longer project.

Any 'grateful and critical dialogue' with my contemporaries in Christology also calls for selectivity. In par-

ticular, for the second half of this book, a full critical attention
to all the major alternative positions would mean switching
projects. My purpose is to write a systematic Christology, not
to do something thoroughly worthwhile but quite different—
namely, survey and appraise leading contributions to twentieth-century Christology. In any case the many articles and
books in which I have presented and evaluated the christological views of Karl Barth, Rudolf Bultmann, Walter
Kasper, Hans Küng, James Mackey, Willi Marxsen, Jürgen
Moltmann, Wolfhart Pannenberg, Karl Rahner, John Rob-
inson, Edward Schillebeeckx, Jon Sobrino, and others have
at least established one conclusion: I have not ignored alternative positions. (See e.g. *Interpreting Jesus* (1983); *Interpreting the Resurrection* (1988); *Jesus Risen* (1987); *Jesus Today*
(1986); *What are they Saying about Jesus?* (1983); *What are
they Saying about the Resurrection?* (1978); 'Newman's Seven
Notes', in I. Ker and A. G. Hill (eds.), *Newman after a
Hundred Years* (1990).)

Although the dialogue with my predecessors and contemporaries must be selective, on substantive issues this book
will direct readers to some relevant works and/or major
entries in large dictionaries and encyclopedias. Through
these references interested readers will easily find further
bibliographical information. For some important points, full
or fairly full biblical and other references will be provided.
But, in general, an effort has been made to avoid the massive
footnoting and/or intertextual references which bring some
scholarly books almost to a standstill.

Taking over a phrase from the pioneering work of William
Wrede, Moltmann writes of 'the messianic secret of Jesus
Christ'. Here I would talk rather of 'the messianic mystery
of Jesus Christ'. A secret can be fully revealed once and for
all; a religious mystery invites a lifetime of reflection in which
there cannot really be definitive statements and truly final
conclusions. Both by themselves and in dialogue with others,
workers in Christology, as much or even more than other
theological scholars, find themselves in the 'yes-but' situation. Every significant affirmation will always call for further
qualifications, explorations, and additions. The messianic
mystery of Christ, precisely as mystery, means that we can

never expect to argue everything out in complete and final detail. At the same time, this 'yes-but' situation may never be an excuse for blatantly inadequate or simply inaccurate claims.

I am most grateful to Hilva Martorana for typing much of this book. My special thanks go also to Henry Chadwick, Frank Coady, Monica Ellison, Ernest Fiedler, William Kelly, Catherine LaCugna, Richard McBrien, James Mackey, William Thompson, Bishop Rowan Williams, and a number of Jesuit colleagues (Brendan Byrne, Jacques Dupuis, Kevin Flannery, Andrew Hamilton, Daniel Kendall, Louis Ladaria, J. Michael McDermott, John O'Donnell, Jared Wicks, and John Hickey Wright) for their comments, criticisms, and encouragement. Audiences of students and teachers in Australia, England, Ireland, Italy, Scotland, and the USA helped to sharpen some of the points. I wish to thank very warmly the McCarthy Family Foundation and, specifically, Eugene and Maureen McCarthy for their generous support during my initial work on this book. Lastly, I am particularly grateful to Hilary O'Shea for her help in seeing this book through to publication.

References to verses of the Bible follow the tradition adopted by the NRSV.

Gregorian University, Rome   G.O'C.
16 June 1994

For this revised edition a biblical index has been added, and those errata which have been detected have been corrected.

Gregorian University, Rome   G.O'C.
13 October 1995

CONTENTS

❖ ❖

ABBREVIATIONS

❖ ❖

ABD D. N. Freedman (ed.), *Anchor Bible Dictionary* (6 vols.; New York: Doubleday, 1992)
DS H. Denzinger and A. Schönmetzer, *Enchiridion symbolorum, definitionum et declarationum* (36th edn.; Freiburg im Breisgau: Herder, 1976)
ET English translation
GS Second Vatican Council, *Gaudium et spes*
LG Second Vatican Council, *Lumen gentium*
NJBC R. E. Brown, J. A. Fitzmyer, and R. E. Murphy (eds.), *The New Jerome Biblical Commentary* (London: Geoffrey Chapman, 1989)
NRSV New Revised Standard Version
NT New Testament
OT Old Testament
par(r). and parallel(s) in other Gospel(s)
REB Revised English Bible
Tanner N. P. Tanner (ed.), *Decrees of the Ecumenical Councils* (2 vols.; London: Sheed & Ward, 1990)
TDNT G. Kittel and G. Friedrich (eds.), *Theological Dictionary of the New Testament* (10 vols.; Grand Rapids: Eerdmans, 1964–76)
Th. Inv. K. Rahner, *Theological Investigations* (23 vols.; London: Darton, Longman, Todd, 1961–92)
TRE G. Krause and G. Müller (eds.), *Theologische Realenzyklopädie* (Berlin: Walter de Gruyter, 1977–)

I

Some Major Challenges

❧ ❧

God brought forth the Word . . . as a root brings forth a
shoot, a spring the river and the sun its beam.

(Tertullian, *Adversus Praxean*)

You preach to me God, born and dying, two thousand
years ago, at the other end of the world, in some small
town I know not where; and you tell me that all who
have not believed in this mystery are damned.

(J. J. Rousseau, *Émile*)

In the light of Christian faith, practice, and worship, that
branch of theology called Christology reflects systematically
on the person, being, and doing of Jesus of Nazareth (*c*.5
BC—*c*. AD 30). In seeking to clarify the essential truths about
him, it investigates his person and being (who and what he
was/is) and work (what he did/does). Was/is he both human
and divine? If so, how is that possible and not a contradiction
in terms as being simultaneously finite and infinite seems to
be? Should we envisage his revealing and redeeming 'work'
as having a impact not only on all men and women of all
times and places, but also on the whole created cosmos? In
any case, can we describe or even minimally explain that
salvific 'work'?

In facing and tackling these and other such questions,
historical, philosophical, and linguistic considerations play a
crucial role. They can be distinguished, if not finally separated.

History

How do we know who Jesus was/is and what he did/does?
Not only for those who believe in him but also for those who
do not give him their personal allegiance, obviously the first
answer must be: we know him and know about him from
human history and experience.

The quest for a historical knowledge of Jesus will make us
examine, at the very least, his background in the story of
Israel, his earthly career, his influence on the origins of Christianity, and the subsequent development of christological
thinking and teaching. Those who have attempted to write
the history of anyone or, even more, their own history will
recognize just how difficult it proves to express fully through
a text any human life. To transcribe adequately the story of
Jesus is an impossible dream. As the appendix to John's
Gospel observed centuries ago, 'there are also many other
things which Jesus did. If they were all to be recorded in
detail, I suppose that the world itself could not contain the
books that would be written' (John 21: 25).

Nevertheless, we need to come up with some historical
account of Jesus. Unless it is going to remain outrageously
inadequate, any such account must attend not only to the
events of his life and death to which we have access, but also
to his antecedents in the history of Israel and to the response
he evoked, both in the short term and in the long term,
through his death, resurrection, and sending of the Holy
Spirit. Hence, in pursuing the reality and meaning of Jesus'
person, being, and work, we will examine some themes from
Jewish history and from the origins of Christianity and, in
particular, from the development of christological reflection
and teaching.

As regard the 'things which Jesus did', let me note that he
left no writings and lived in almost complete obscurity except
for the brief period of his public ministry. According to the
evidence provided by the Synoptic Gospels (Matthew, Mark,
and Luke), that ministry could have lasted as little as a year.
John implies a period of at least two to three years.

Such non-Christian sources as the Roman writers Tacitus,
Suetonius, and Pliny the Younger, the Jewish historian

Flavius Josephus (whose testimony suffers from later interpolations), and, later, the Cynic philosopher Lucian of Samosata and the Babylonian Talmud yield a little data about Jesus: he was put to death by crucifixion under the Roman prefect Pontius Pilate during the reign of the Emperor Tiberius; some Jewish leaders in Jerusalem were involved in the execution; his followers called him 'Christ' and regarded him as the divine founder of a new way of life.[1]

The letters of Paul of Tarsus, which were written between 51 and 64 (or 67) and hence before the four Gospels, provide some details: Jesus was born a Jew (Gal. 3: 16; Rom. 9: 5), a descendant of King David (Rom. 1: 3); he exercised a ministry to the people of Israel (Rom. 15: 8); he forbade divorce (1 Cor. 7: 10–11); he celebrated a 'last' supper 'on the night he was betrayed' (1 Cor. 11: 23–5); he died by crucifixion (Gal. 2: 20; 3: 1; 1 Cor. 1: 23; Phil. 2: 8); as risen from the dead, he appeared to Cephas (= Peter), 'the twelve', over 500 followers, James (a Christian leader in Jerusalem), and Paul himself (1 Cor. 15: 3–8; see 9: 1 and Gal. 1: 12, 16).

Other books of the NT occasionally allude to the story of Jesus. These fleeting references mainly concern his suffering and death (e.g. 1 Pet. 2: 24; Heb. 6: 6; 13: 12). For our (limited) knowledge of Jesus' life and work we are almost totally dependent on the Gospels. This book will devote a chapter (Chapter 3) and more to the Gospels.

As regards what I have called 'the response he evoked', the history of Jesus includes not only the emergence of a new community with its NT Scriptures but also all the different items that go to make up the whole Christian tradition: creeds and other official doctrines; liturgical worship in its great diversity; millions of lives which have taken their inspiration from Jesus (and, in particular, the lives of those who teach us by their shining, saintly example); preaching and theological reflection on Jesus (right down to twentieth-century scholars and documents produced by the World Council of Churches and the International Theological Commission); private

---

[1] For details, see C. K. Barrett, *The New Testament Background: Selected Documents* (London: SPCK, rev. edn., 1987), 14–16, 277–9; J. P. Meier, *NJBC* 1317; J. Stevenson and W. H. Frend, *A New Eusebius* (London: SPCK, 1987), 1–3, 18–20, 128–30.

prayer and personal experience of Jesus; the art, literature, plays, and films that have come into existence around him. Let us acknowledge also the response he has evoked in Jews, Muslims, Hindus, and other non-Christians. Those who have volunteered an answer to the question 'who do you say that I am?' (Mark 8: 29) have included not only disciples committed to Jesus but also members of a wider public, others who did not or do not surrender fully to his spell and yet have wanted to say something about his reality and meaning for them.

Philosophy

Putting down this list of historical and experiential sources, in an attempt to summarize where we might go looking for answers to our questions about Jesus' 'being' and 'doing' (including the response they have provoked from the first century right down to the present), raises a whole range of questions of a more or less philosophical nature. What is the status of experiential knowledge? Can it supply any reliable information or evidence about Jesus? Where personal testimonies differ, whose experience counts? The whole Christian tradition about Jesus (and, for that matter, non-Christian traditions about him) can be seen as recording and interpreting various collective and individual experiences of Jesus. But why privilege and emphasize certain voices in that tradition over against others? Why find normative and reliable guides in mainline credal and liturgical texts, as well as in the conciliar teaching of Nicaea I (325), Constantinople I (381), Ephesus (431), and Chalcedon (451), over against what Arius (c.250–c.336), Apollinarius (c.310–c.390), Nestorius (d. c.451), and Eutyches (c.378–454) actually taught or were alleged to have taught?

Elsewhere I have explained what I hold about experience and its evidential status.[2] Likewise, I have offered some guidelines for finding the (reliable and normative) Tradition

---

[2] See my *Fundamental Theology* (London: Darton, Longman & Todd, 1981), 32–52; and C. F. Davis, *The Evidential Force of Religious Experience* (Oxford: Clarendon Press, 1989).

(upper case) within the mass of traditions (lower case), as well as joining Hans-Georg Gadamer and others in recognizing traditional data as an indispensable help for interpreting the biblical texts.[3] Nevertheless, present experience and past (Christian) tradition can never justify refusing to return to the Gospels themselves. What do we know about Jesus from these sources? What level of certainty do we have in our historical knowledge of Jesus? How much do we need to know about him to support our Christian faith and theology (including Christology)? Or, in other words, as believers and theologians what is the nature of our dependence on the historical knowledge of Jesus conveyed primarily through the Gospels?

Some answers here have taken extreme forms. Although obviously they could not face these issues in a modern sense, from the second to the fourth century the authors of the apocryphal, non-canonical gospels responded in a maximalist fashion. They often embroidered and sup-plemented, as well as revising, what the canonical Gospels tell us of Jesus' birth, life, teaching, death, and resurrection. Nineteenth- and twentieth-century 'lives' of Jesus, not to mention sermons and meditations on the Gospels, have encouraged a similar tendency to 'know' too much about the dating and details of Jesus' career, as well as about his motivation, feelings, and whole interior life. Classic films about Jesus like Franco Zeffirelli's *Jesus of Nazareth* have also catered to the desire to 'know' too much about the history of Jesus. Those who in such ways 'enlarge' our available historical knowledge of Jesus can finish up partially depending (in their faith and theology) on what they themselves have produced.

At the other extreme from the maximalists are such writers as Gotthold Ephraim Lessing (1729–81), Søren Kierkegaard (1813–55), and Rudolf Bultmann (1884–1976), who have given minimalist answers to the historical questions about Jesus. Let us examine them in a counter-chronological order.

As a historian Bultmann was by no means a thoroughgoing sceptic. In *The History of the Synoptic Tradition* (German

---

[3] See my *Fundamental Theology*, 208–24, 249–59.

original 1921),[4] *Jesus and the Word* (German original 1926),[5] and *Theology of the New Testament* (German original 1948 and 1953),[6] he accepted quite a range of conclusions about the actual life of Jesus. It was as believer and theologian that Bultmann showed himself a radical reductionist, claiming that we neither can nor should found our Christian faith and theology on any supposedly 'objective' basis in history—apart from one objectively historical event, the crucifixion. We need do no more than affirm the *dass*, the mere fact that Jesus existed and was crucified, without enquiring about the *was*, what Jesus was in his own history. Bultmann argued that he was supported by Paul and John, who both present us with the essential kerygma without entering into the historical detail that we find in Matthew, Mark, and Luke. Apropos of Paul, Bultmann wrote:

Paul proclaims the incarnate, crucified and risen Lord; that is, his kerygma requires only the 'that' of the life of Jesus and the fact of his crucifixion. He does not hold before his hearer's eyes a portrait of Jesus the human person, apart from the cross (Gal. 3: 1), and the cross is not regarded from a biographical standpoint but as saving event. The obedience and self-emptying of Christ of which he speaks (Phil. 2: 6–9; Rom. 15: 3; 2 Cor. 8: 9) are attitudes of the pre-existent and not of the historical Jesus ... the decisive thing is simply the 'that'.[7]

But what would a simple 'that' mean apart from the 'what'? Jesus would be reduced to mere cipher. Why should we find the saving event in the crucifixion of someone about whom we refuse as believers and theologians to 'know' anything further? If no historical detail of Jesus' story matters other than his sheer existence and crucifixion, why should we not look for the saving event in one of the thousands of others who died at the hands of the Romans by this sadistic form of execution?

---

[4] *The History of the Synoptic Tradition*, trans. J. Marsh (Oxford: Blackwell, 1963).
[5] *Jesus and the Word*, trans. L. P. Smith and E. H. Lantero (New York: Scribner, 1958).
[6] *Theology of the New Testament*, trans. K. Grobel (2 vols; London: SCM Press, 1956–8). See also Bultmann, 'The Primitive Christian Kerygma and the Historical Jesus', in C. Braaten and R. Harrisville (eds.), *The Historical Jesus and the Kerygmatic Christ* (New York: Abingdon, 1964), 15–42.
[7] 'The Primitive Christian Kerygma', 20.

As regards Paul, we have seen above how such details about Jesus as his Jewishness and his ministry to Israel do matter to the apostle. Paul's kerygmatic message goes beyond the mere crucifixion of Jesus to include his last supper (1 Cor. 11: 23–5), his burial, and his appearances to Cephas and the twelve (1 Cor. 15: 3–5). As regards its concern to say something about Jesus' human story, John's Gospel is considerably more interested in historical detail than Bultmann would like to admit. Where the Synoptic Gospels seemingly present the ministry as lasting for about a year and including only one (final) journey to Jerusalem, John corrects that impression by reporting that Jesus was active during three Passover feasts, attending two of them in Jerusalem (John 2: 13; 6: 4; 11: 55) and making four journeys there (John 2: 13; 5: 1; 7: 10; 12: 12). Such a prolonged exposure to the Jerusalem public explains more plausibly the hostility towards Jesus shown by the authorities in the capital—something that belongs to John's presentation of Jesus' final destiny. This is just one example among many of how the 'what' matters to John, and not merely the sheer 'that' of Jesus' crucifixion.

After the criticisms mounted by Ernst Käsemann and others, Bultmann's veto against detail from Jesus' human history being relevant for proclamation, faith, and theology has been widely ignored. The wonder is that this veto on historical knowledge was taken so seriously by so many and for so long.[8]

Kierkegaard's classic reduction of the historical knowledge required for faith was phrased as follows: 'if the contemporary generation had left nothing behind them but these words: "We have believed that in such and such a year God has appeared among us in the humble figure of a servant, that he lived and taught in our community, and finally died," it would be more than enough.'[9] Here the incarnation ('God

[8] See my *Foundations of Theology* (Chicago: Loyola University Press, 1971), 176–85; and J. S. Kselman and R. D. Witherup, 'Modern New Testament Criticism', *NJBC* 1137–42. For the nature of Christian faith's dependence on history and historical knowledge, see my *Foundations of Theology*, 65–101, and *Fundamental Theology*, 71–6, 156–60.

[9] S. Kierkegaard, *Philosophical Fragments*, trans. D. F. Swenson (Princeton, NJ: Princeton University Press, 1936), 87. Just as in the case of Bultmann, I do not

has appeared among us') and its hidden character ('in the humble figure of a servant') bulk large. The crucifixion, not to mention the miracles of Jesus, his resurrection, and the sending of the Holy Spirit, is passed over in silence. So too are any details about Jesus' teaching; it is simply stated that he 'taught in our community'. Kierkegaard's reductionism differs from Bultmann's in that it is phrased hypothetically and theoretically ('if'). In fact the contemporary generation via the evangelists in the second generation has left us much more than the words proposed by Kierkegaard. Here, as elsewhere, it seems more profitable to reflect on what we have actually received rather than on what we might possibly have received under different circumstances. In brief, let us begin from matters of fact, rather than from matters of principle and possible alternate scenarios.

Lessing's critique of the role (or rather non-role) of historical knowledge took a general, two-pronged form: 'If no historical truth can be demonstrated, then nothing can be demonstrated by means of historical truths ... Accidental truths of history can never become the proof of necessary truths of reason.'[10] Against this, one can very well argue that, although they cannot be demonstrated by mathematical calculations, repeated scientific experiments, or philosophical logic, historical truths can certainly be established beyond any reasonable doubt. Mathematical calculations cannot demonstrate the existence and career of Alexander the Great in the fourth century BC. But the converging historical evidence would make it absurd to deny that he lived to change the political and cultural face of the Middle East. We cannot 'run the film backwards' to regain contact with the past by literally reconstructing and repeating the assassination of Julius Caesar in the first century BC or the crucifixion of Jesus almost a hundred years later. Such historical events cannot be re-enacted in the way we can endlessly repeat scientific experiments in a laboratory. But once again only

intend to provide here a fully developed and nuanced account of Kierkegaard's position. In the case of both thinkers, I use them to illustrate a minimalist tendency, while granting that there is much more to their thought than what is indicated here.

[10] G. E. Lessing, *Theological Writings*, selected and trans. H. Chadwick (Stanford, Calif.: Stanford University Press, 1967), 53.

the lunatic fringe would cast doubt on these two violent deaths. A priori logic cannot demonstrate the existence of St Augustine of Hippo (354–430). But to deny his existence and massive impact on subsequent European thought and culture would be to exclude yourself from normal academic discussion about the history of Western ideas. The available data let us know a great deal that went on in the past, including the ancient world, even if—from the nature of the case—we cannot (and, in fact, should not try to) demonstrate our conclusions along the lines appropriate to mathematics, the natural sciences, and philosophy. There are very many historically certain truths from which we can argue and draw conclusions.[11]

The main thrust of Lessing's case comes, however, in his second assertion: 'accidental truths of history can never become the proof of necessary truths of reason.' Even if we know with certainty many historical truths, they always remain contingent or accidental. These historical events, the truth of which we have learned and established, neither had to be at all nor had to be precisely the way they were. In principle things could have gone differently in the life and career of Alexander the Great, Augustine, Jesus, and Julius Caesar. As such, historical truths neither enjoy the status of necessary, universal truths of reason, nor can they work to prove such truths of reason. But is that so tragic? In terms of this study in Christology, is it a fatal admission to grant that our knowledge of Jesus' career does not rise 'above' the level of contingent truths? Strictly speaking, he could have done, said, and suffered different things. Only someone like Lessing who was/is bewitched by the pursuit of necessary, universal truths of reason would deplore this (historical) situation. In the strictest sense of the word, '*necessary* truths of reason' are tautologies, mathematical truths, and other a priori deductions that are in principle true always and everywhere without needing the support of any empirical evidence. But how many people would base their lives on such truths? Historical experience and contingent truths have a power to shape and

---

[11] See P. F. Carnley, *The Structure of Resurrection Belief* (Oxford: Clarendon Press, 1987), 104–7, 133–5.

change human existence in a way never enjoyed by Lessing's timeless, universal truths of reason. In particular, 'accidental' truths from the story of Jesus and his most heroic followers have played a crucial role for millions of Christians. They have looked at the life of Jesus and of his more saintly disciples and found themselves awed, moved, and changed. Both within Christianity and beyond, the concreteness of history repeatedly proves far more persuasive than any necessary truths of reason.

In the end, however, Lessing's classic assertion could be usefully modified and pressed into service in this book. For Christology we need both the data and truths of history and the help and truths of philosophical reason. Apropos of our empirical knowledge of the world, Immanuel Kant (1724–1804) observed: 'thoughts without content [= empirical content] are empty, intuitions [= experiences?] without concepts are blind.'[12] This remark might be adapted to read: 'metaphysical thoughts without empirical historical content are empty, historical experiences without philosophical concepts are blind.' Or perhaps it is better not to risk doing violence to the positions of either Lessing or Kant and simply to point out that Christology requires both some historically credible information and some philosophical structure. Right from the second century Christology has rightly drawn on metaphysical reflection, as well as historical experience.

We have just seen how philosophical considerations necessarily turn up when Christology raises questions of hermeneutics (the role of tradition in the work of interpretation) and questions of epistemology (the evidential status of experience and the dependence of Christian faith upon historical knowledge). Yet the contribution of philosophy (as a properly autonomous discipline) to theology in general and to Christology in particular has gone beyond these three tasks.

Where historical claims are tested primarily by the way they correspond or fail to correspond to the available evidence, philosophical clarification comes by testing the coherence of some belief in the light of our most general principles (e.g. those which concern the nature of human and divine

---

[12] *Critique of Pure Reason*, trans. N. K. Smith (London: Macmillan, 1963), 93.

existence). Is it, for example, logically consistent for someone to be simultaneously fully human and fully divine? If we cannot positively justify this conceptually, can we at least show that it is not blatantly impossible? Or is this simply as impossible and blatantly inconsistent as calling someone a married bachelor? To reach a reasoned position here, one needs to clarify the notions of humanity and divinity. What counts as being, in the strict sense of the word, human and/or divine? What do a human nature and a divine nature mean and entail? How could one person be at the same time fully human and fully divine? What does personhood mean?

This last paragraph illustrates the role of philosophy in clarifying concepts and testing possibilities. It is not philosophy's task to say whether some possibility (e.g. a person who is simultaneously fully human and fully divine) has been actualized in history. Philosophy comes into play in hammering out concepts that have a certain clarity, examining whether some claims are coherent, and judging whether some claims are blatantly incoherent to the point of impossibility.

My examples above come from questions about the person and being of Christ. Philosophy has its role also in clarifying concepts and testing coherent possibilities that concern Christ's redemptive 'doing'. How could redemption (e.g. expiation of sins) work? What are the appropriate terms to use here and what could they mean? Sacrifice? Propitiation? Liberation? What does it mean to speak of Christ's representation? How could one person represent the whole human race and have a beneficial effect on all men and women everywhere?

Language

Traditionally the redemptive 'doing' of Christ has been expressed largely through such biblical terms as expiation, love, and conquest, which have been more or (often) less satisfactorily explicated. Much biblical language about Christ's doing and being has been strongly symbolic: he is the bread of life, the good shepherd, the light of the world, the vine, the Suffering Servant, the head of the body, or the last Adam. At times the symbolism can be subtler and less obtrusive as when he is called Lord, Mediator, Messiah, Redeemer, Saviour, Son of God, Son of man, or Word. The primary, biblical language of Christology is analogical and symbolic. The post-biblical language has often been less blatantly symbolic (e.g. one divine person in two natures, the primordial symbol of the Father, the second person of the Trinity, or the Pantocrator), but not always so (e.g. the Sacred Heart).

To recall such terms and titles is to suggest the difficult question of the function, limits, and interpretation of religious language. How far can our language (and, for that matter, our thinking) go in expressing Christ, God, and otherworldly realities? In religious worship, practice, and reflection, language gets used in extended or special ways. We may speak analogically, applying such common terms as bread, light, lamb, shepherd, and priest to Christ, who is both like and unlike the bread, light, lambs, shepherds, and priests of our human experience. His own symbolic language about a lost coin, a lost sheep, and a lost son (Luke 15: 3–32) 'represent' and perceptibly express truths about the invisible God and the divine designs in our regard. As the Book of Exodus tells the story, the crossing of the Red Sea and the making of the Sinai covenant, the roles of Pharaoh and Moses, and the water and manna in the desert work, respectively, as actions, persons, and things that symbolize God's saving purposes. Putting together various particular symbols, the whole Exodus narrative functions as a symbolic story, in which basic truths about God and our existence *vis-à-vis* God get imaginatively expressed. We are guided towards the ultimate realities not only by abstract concepts but even more by symbolic language.[13]

In Christology, as in other branches of theology, we explore the meaning and test the truth of various religious claims in which history, philosophy, or language may be, respectively, more to the fore. But there is this frequent difference. In the area of religious claims of a historical nature, truth will be often a matter of correspondence to the available data. When

---

[13] On religious language see J. M. Soskice, *Metaphor and Religious Language* (Oxford: Clarendon Press, 1985), and my *Retrieving Fundamental Theology* (London: Geoffrey Chapman, 1993), 24–5, 29–30, 98–107.

the claims are of a rather philosophical nature, coherence will be the primary test. In the case of linguistic claims, the truth quality of the language used will be judged by its disclosive, illuminating success. Truth comes across, respectively, as corresponding, cohering, or disclosing.

In this context one should also note how the critical appropriation of tradition and its consensus also leads to truth. Chapters 9 and 14, in particular, will have more to say on this issue, to which, as we recognized above, Gadamer has contributed much.

Talk about truth should not, however, be allowed to encourage a facile optimism in Christology or in the rest of theology. To what extent can history, philosophy, language, and tradition really show us how things are with Christ, God, and the divine–human relationship? We should never claim to know or say too much. Of course, there is the task of clarifying and making sense of things. But at our peril we forget that in Christology, as in other branches of theology, we are dealing with mystery, the mystery of the ineffable God and, for that matter, the corresponding mystery of the human condition. In particular, we should never forget the indirect, analogical, and symbolic character of our biblical, liturgical, and theological language about God. As developed in Eastern Christianity, apophatic theology reminds us of the inadequacy of all attempts to approach the divine mystery. Any affirmation about God has to be qualified with a corresponding negation and the recognition that God infinitely surpasses our human categories. The Western tradition of negative theology insists that we can say more what God is not than what God really is. As the Fourth Lateran Council (1215) pointed out, any similarity between the Creator and creatures is characterized by an even greater dissimilarity (see DS 806). There exists an infinite difference between saying 'God is' and 'creatures are'.

Add too the fact that Christians do not hold that mere language can be rich enough to express everything about Christ, or at least everything that they wish to express about who he is and what he has done. Much of their tradition of christological interpretation has come through various styles of life, commitment towards those in need, public worship's symbolic gestures, music, painting, sculpture, architecture, and other non-verbal forms of communication. Christological language has its undoubted point and purpose. But Christian faith has more to express about Jesus as Son of God and Saviour of the world than can be contained in words, even in the most carefully chiselled theological language.

Content, Emphases, and Context

Thus far this introductory chapter has been limited to more formal considerations about (1) the respective roles and interplay of history, philosophy, language, and tradition in elaborating Christology, and (2) the need to remember the element of mystery and the limits of language. What of the content of this book, its emphases, major themes, and context?

The next chapter will examine something of Jesus' Jewish background and some themes in the OT Scriptures that fed into NT christological thinking. Then we will focus on significant points in the history of Jesus (Chapter 3), before moving to his resurrection (Chapter 4) and the kerygmatic Christ of Paul and early Christianity (Chapters 5 and 6).

During the first centuries of the Church's existence, various heresies and then conciliar responses to these heresies served to develop some clarity about the being of Christ. By the end of the first century two opposite false tendencies had already emerged to mark out for all time the possible extreme positions. On the one hand, the Ebionites, an umbrella name for various groups of Jewish Christians, considered Jesus to be no more than the human son of Mary and Joseph, a mere man on whom the Spirit descended at baptism. This was to assimilate Christ so much to us that he too would need redemption and could not truly function as 'the Saviour of the world' (John 4: 42). On the other hand, the early heresy of Docetism held that the Son of God merely appeared to be a human being. Christ's corporeal reality was considered heavenly or else a body only in appearance, with someone else, such as Simon of Cyrene, suffering in his place. The Docetic heresy, to the extent that it separated Christ from the human race, made him irrelevant for our salvation. The

Johannine literature insisted against Docetist tendencies that Christ had truly 'come in the flesh' (1 John 4: 1–3; 2 John 7) and against any Ebionite tendencies that he was truly divine Lord (John 1: 1; 20: 28).[14]

Chapters 7 and 8 will pick up the trail of the dogmatic Christ, from the end of the first century through to the ninth century and the end of the iconoclastic movement. Those centuries saw the development of the classic, orthodox language about the being of Christ. Chapter 9 will recall some important christological themes which emerged after the patristic age. Chapters 10 and 11 will build on the biblical and historical material provided in the previous chapters to respond systematically to the key questions about Christ's humanity, divinity, personhood, pre-existence, virginal conception, sinlessness, knowledge, and faith.

Chapter 12 will switch to the 'doing' of Christ. What has he done for our salvation? How did/does he save us? What does he save us from and for? Reflection on his salvific work inevitably raises the issue of the absolute and universal scope of his mediation (Chapter 13). Is Christ *the* revealer and redeemer for the whole human race? If so, can we relate him to the various mediators and ways of salvation proposed by non-Christian religions?

The concluding chapter will use the theme of presence to draw together what has been expounded about the being, person, and doing of Christ.

To help readers tune into my text from the start, it seems good to come clean about some emphases and distinctions. The centrality of the paschal mystery will run like a leitmotif through this book. Beyond question, there are other options. 'Earlier' christological mysteries (the creation, the history of Israel, the incarnation, or the life of Jesus culminating in his death on the cross) could serve to organize one's reflections. So too could the 'later' mysteries (the Church guided by Christ's Spirit until his future coming in glory). Nevertheless, historical and liturgical considerations have persuaded me

---

[14] There is something to be said for identifying the first great christological controversy as taking place between Christians and non-Christian Jews over monotheism (John 5: 18; 10: 33); see J. D. G. Dunn, *Christology in the Making* (London: SCM Press, 2nd edn., 1989), pp. xxix–xxx.

to make the resurrection of the crucified Jesus (with the outpouring of the Holy Spirit) the central focus. Historically, it was faith in and the proclamation of the paschal mystery that set the Christian movement going and eventually led to the parting of the ways between the Church and the Synagogue. Second, from the outset the public worship of Christians has maintained the conviction that believers share sacramentally both in the dying and rising of Christ and in the correlative gift of the Holy Spirit (e.g. Rom. 6: 3–11; 1 Cor. 6: 11; 11: 23–6; 2 Cor. 1: 22). If 'the law of prayer establishes the law of belief' (DS 246), the law of christological belief should follow the law of liturgical prayer in centring everything on the paschal mystery. *Dei Verbum*, the 1965 Constitution on Divine Revelation from the Second Vatican Council (1962–5), followed the lead of the previously promulgated Constitution on the Sacred Liturgy (1963) by acknowledging the resurrection of the crucified Jesus (with the gift of the Spirit) as the crowning-point of the divine self-revelation (*Dei Verbum*, 4). Given the way God's 'economy' of revelation is closely integrated with the history of salvation (ibid. 2), the paschal mystery is simultaneously the climax of God's salvific and revelatory self-communication in Christ. Hence the resurrection of the crucified Jesus should be the primary interpretative key for Christology.

Like some other theologians I have long harboured the dream of one day producing a Christology whose standard and clarity no one could question. The unquestionable standard is an impossible dream, above all because Jesus will never find a theologian worthy of him. My clarity can, nevertheless, be helped along by a few distinctions.

The fact of having announced that this book will take shape from Jesus' background and history is tantamount to declaring for a Christology 'from below'—that is to say, a Christology that develops from an examination of Christ's human history, especially as prepared in the OT and presented by the Synoptic Gospels. This Christology has sometimes been called Antiochene, because the school of Antioch, shaped by the martyred St Lucian of Antioch (d. 312), emphasized the full humanity of Christ as does the modern Christology from below. The challenge for this style of Christology is suggested by a further name for it, 'ascending'. How could a human life be and be shown to be that of the Son of God? How could humanity be united with divinity in Christ?

Any Christology 'from below' implies its counterpart, a Christology 'from above', the kind of Christology developed from the theme of the pre-existent Logos or Son of God who descends into our world (John 1: 14). This 'descending' Christology is sometimes called Alexandrian, because the style of theology that began in Alexandria as a catechetical school towards the end of the second century AD focused on the eternal Word being made flesh and the divine nature of the incarnate Christ. The serious challenge for this Christology 'from above' can be expressed by the question: how could the eternal Word of God take on a genuinely and fully human way of acting?

As will emerge in the course of this book, Christologies from below and from above complement each other. Although the Synoptic Gospels suggest an approach 'from below', they do not lack such divine elements 'from above' as the kingdom of God. Although John may begin by focusing on the Word who comes 'from above', that Gospel by no means lacks human elements 'from below'—not least in its realistic account of Jesus' death. In Christology we need both approaches, 'from above' and 'from below', just as the whole Church has been enduringly enriched by the schools of both Alexandria and Antioch.

Talk of a 'Christo-logy' from below or above refers to our knowledge and interpretation ('logos')—the way we move epistemologically from Christ's humanity to his divinity or vice versa. As such, this talk does not refer directly to Christ's order of being—to what happened ontologically when the Word 'descended' by 'being made flesh', or when Christ's humanity 'ascended' towards God by being assumed into the hypostatic union. Yet what happened in the order of being has to be presented, of course, to justify what theologians claim to know and want to say.

Another point to be underlined is that Christologies 'from above' and 'from below' do not by any means necessarily coincide with 'high' and 'low' Christologies. As its name suggests, a genuine Christology '*from* above' begins from the divinity of Christ but it will go on to do justice to his humanity. Vice versa, a true Christology '*from* below' begins from the humanity of Christ but it will go on to do justice to his divinity.

As such, a 'high' Christology acknowledges the divinity of Christ, but the term itself does not indicate what or how much is done to incorporate into a total picture the full humanity of Christ. An early member of the Alexandrian school, St Clement of Alexandria (*c*.150–*c*.215), developed a high Christology of the pre-existent and incarnate Logos, but could say things that cast doubt on Christ's genuine humanity. In his *Stromateis* he claimed that Jesus merely went through the motions of eating and drinking. He had no need to take physical nourishment (6. 9). A high Christology may at times reveal such Docetic tendencies, which fail to do justice to Christ's being fully and genuinely human.

As the term gets used, a 'low' Christology emphasizes one-sidedly the human life of Christ and excludes anything like an appropriate recognition of his divinity. Historically, low Christologies have taken the form of holding that the power of God came upon the man Jesus and adopted him at his baptism or at his resurrection. Often this means mis-interpreting the story of Jesus' baptism, the use of Ps. 2: 7 in Acts 13: 33, or Paul's traditional language about Jesus being 'designated' Son of God (Rom. 1: 4). We will return to these points in Chapter 5.

Whether or not we care to use the distinction high/low Christology, this distinction should not be confused with explicit/implicit Christology. As we shall see, the Synoptic Gospels leave us largely with an implicit Christology—quite different from the explicit statements about Jesus' being and doing we come across repeatedly in John's Gospel. Never-theless, as we shall also see, the implications of what we find in the Synoptics take us beyond any mere 'low' Christology.

A further caution. A high or low Christology should not be immediately attributed to those who observe the distinction between 'high' titles for Jesus (e.g. Logos and Son of God) and 'low' titles (e.g. Son of David and Messiah). The former titles point to the eternal, divine side of things, the latter to the historical, human side. Merely attending to the 'high' or 'low' character of various NT titles for Jesus in no way automatically puts one in the camp either of high or low Christology.

Moreover, the 'low' titles, while they express the earthly functions and at times the humiliation of Jesus, do not in any way exclude all reference to divine transcendence. When Acts calls Jesus 'Servant', it thinks of him as 'Servant *of God*' (Acts 3: 13, 26; 4: 27, 30). Right in the OT itself 'Son of David' also enjoys its divine reference: by being enthroned on Zion where God dwells and by officiating in the temple where God likewise dwells, the Davidic priest-king visibly expresses God. In short, the 'low' titles, as well as the 'high' titles, are all related to God. One should also add that the 'high' titles are not merely high. 'Son of God', for instance, while often pointing to the divine, eternal side of Jesus, is not in any way incompatible with talk about his earthly humiliation and death (e.g. Rom. 8: 32).

Finally, my impulse is to dismiss a further distinction, but reference to it may help the cause of clarity: ontological versus (merely) functional Christologies. An ontological Christ-ology is concerned with who and what Jesus is in himself, whereas a functional Christology focuses on his saving work for us and thus largely coincides with soteriology, or Christ's redemptive activity for human beings and their world. Indis-putably, christological thinking in the NT is somewhat more functional than ontological, while the early centuries of Christianity took a more ontological approach that cul-minated in Chalcedon's teaching about Christ's one person in two natures. Nevertheless, in Christology it would be as mistaken to ignore all the implicit (and sometimes explicit) ontological affirmations in the NT as to deny the strong soteriological interests of the Fathers of the Church and the early councils.

As regards a functional Christology, Philip Melanchthon (1497–1560) classically stated this option: 'to know Christ means to know his benefits, and not ... to reflect upon his natures and the modes of his incarnation.'[15] In various ways

---

[15] P. Melanchthon, *Loci communes theologici*, trans. L. J. Satre and W. Pauck,

Bultmann, Paul Tillich (1886–1965), and others have developed a functional, soteriological approach to Christology. It is doubtful that any of them can propose a *purely* functional Christology, one which attends only to Christ's saving activity on our behalf and refuses to raise any ontological questions whatsoever about who and what he is in himself. According to a classical axiom, 'action follows being' (*agere sequitur esse*). To reflect on the activity of Christ, while denying all knowledge of his being, would be to attempt the impossible. In general, recent Western theology has tried to end any divorce between soteriology and Christology, between systematic reflection on Christ's doing and such reflection on his being.

Lastly, there is the question of context. Clearly, right from its opening pages, this book has situated itself primarily in an academic context. In the light of the Scriptures and later Christian documents, as well as other works of a historical, philosophical, or linguistic nature, it will try to understand and interpret the truth about Jesus' being and doing. Christologies have been valuably developed, however, in two further contexts: a practical and a liturgical one. A Christology can take as its favoured context the world-wide situation of massive injustice, hunger, and deprivation. Such a Christology with and for the poor lets the search for justice and liberation focus its exploration of who Jesus is and what he does. A third possibility is to develop Christology in a context of liturgical worship. Here the primary focus is not on the quest for meaning and truth (first context), nor on the search for justice (second context), but rather on the celebration of the infinite divine beauty through public prayer.

The academic context will inevitably bulk large in this book. But I will try to keep in mind the practical and liturgical

in *The Library of Christian Classics*, xix: *Melanchthon and Bucer* (Philadelphia: Westminster Press, 1969), 21–2. To identify Melanchthon as a functionalist might seem dubious. J. Macquarrie associates him, however, with Luther in producing a Christology 'based on soteriology rather than on metaphysics' (*Jesus Christ in Modern Thought* (London: SCM Press, 1990), 171; see also 296, 332). J. Moltmann prefers the label of 'anthropological christology', interpreting Melanchthon as concerned with the existential, subjective advantages Christ brings us (*The Way of Jesus Christ*, trans. M. Kohl (London: SCM Press, 1990), 58).

concerns that have fed other styles of Christologies. Searching for truth need not mean ignoring the causes of justice and beauty. It is questionable whether academic dialogue alone gives a privileged access to the truth in theology and similar disciplines. It is certainly false to say that such dialogue provides the only access to truth in theology.

Enough has been said to indicate how this book will take shape. Let me now turn to the Jewish background for the NT's presentation of Jesus Christ.

2
The Background
⊰ ⊱

The only-begotten Word, who is always present with
the human race, united and mingled with his handiwork
... is Jesus Christ our Lord.

(St Irenaeus, *Adversus haereses*)

To succumb to a typically Christian temptation and dismiss
the OT Scriptures as 'merely' recording a historical phase in
God's pedagogy would be to risk losing, among other things,
much of what the NT meant and means in presenting Jesus.
To put this positively, the OT is essential for grasping the
NT christological message and its specific identity.

Hans Hübner has rightly insisted on the way the first
Christians fashioned their proclamation and interpretation
of Jesus largely by putting together two elements: on the one
hand, their experience of events in which Jesus was the central
protagonist and, on the other hand, the ready-made images
and concepts they found to be relevant and illuminating in
their inherited Scriptures.[1] To articulate their convictions
about Jesus and his role in fulfilling the divine purposes, they
depended upon the ideas, beliefs, and expectations of Judaism
which we primarily come across in the OT, including the
so-called 'Apocrypha', books written in Greek and Hebrew
mostly after 200 BC, included in the Septuagint, printed in
Roman Catholic bibles, but at times still omitted from other
bibles.[2]

[1] See H. Hübner, *Biblische Theologie des Neuen Testaments*, i (Göttingen: Vandenhoeck & Ruprecht, 1990), 44–70. For an integral Christology based on the OT
and NT see J. A. Fitzmyer, *Scripture and Christology* (New York: Paulist Press,
1986).
[2] *The New Oxford Annotated Bible* (Oxford: Oxford University Press, 1991) gives
full details of the differences between the biblical canons recognized by Catholics,

In the last paragraph I spoke of the OT as the major source quarried by the first Christians for theological language and concepts. But their images and concepts are also illuminated secondarily by other sources from the world around them: for example, the non-canonical Jewish pseudepigrapha (at least those which probably pre-date Christianity), the corpus of writings from Qumran, the Letter of Aristeas, fragments from Hellenistic-Jewish authors, the works of Philo (*c.*25 BC –AD 40) and Josephus (*c.* AD 37–post-100), and the oral rabbinic traditions which were recorded in the Palestinian and the Babylonian Talmud of the fourth and fifth centuries AD, respectively, and some of which may go back to the time of Jesus or even earlier. Middle Eastern literature, Graeco-Roman thought, and non-canonical literature from Hellenistic Judaism can at times throw valuable light on NT ideas. But the major sources from which NT Christians and authors drew their theological notions are clearly the OT Scriptures. To descend to the obvious this is mirrored by the fact that well over 90 per cent of the clear quotations and vaguer allusions in the NT come from the OT books of pre-Christian Judaism. Relatively few come from such pseudepigrapha as Enoch and other non-biblical sources.

If then we wish to appreciate what the first Christians meant about Jesus, we need to examine the inspired Scriptures which we share in common with them and which they quarried for expressions to press into christological service. Their sacred texts, our books of the OT, were indispensable for interpreting their experience of Jesus. A Christology that ignores or plays down the OT can only be radically deficient. Something essential will be missing from what we mean about Jesus, if we ignore his Jewish roots and those of his first followers. The OT Scriptures play their crucial role in interpreting our faith in and experience of Jesus.

Before examining OT images and concepts that fed into the NT interpretation of Jesus' being and doing, it seems important to recall three points. First, affected by the destruction of the Davidic dynasty, the Babylonian exile, later foreign

Greek Orthodox, Jews, and Protestants (pp. xxi-xxiii, xxv-xxvi). See also J. H. Charlesworth, 'Apocrypha: Old Testament Apocrypha', *ABD* i. 292–4; J. A. Sanders, 'Canon', *ABD*: 837–52.

domination, and other watersheds, the use and meaning of
OT religious themes often remained fluid and not very
sharply defined. Over the centuries, in response to new circumstances, key themes could be interpreted, reinterpreted,
emphasized, and marginalized. Hence, one cannot speak, for
example, of clear-cut messianic 'titles' emerging and simply
holding their ground in the OT. Second, when roughly
etched OT images and designations were applied to Jesus,
they could be radically changed in the process. We will see
this at once in the case of 'Christ', a central Christian designation for Jesus which fairly quickly often became simply
his second name.

Third, interpreting his person and work through OT
themes began with Jesus himself. We will see more of this in
the next chapter. Here one example should suffice: that of
relating Jesus to the person of King David and messianic
hopes linked to the name of David. In Mark's Gospel Jesus
invokes David to justify the conduct of his own disciples (2:
23–8). A blind beggar twice calls Jesus 'Son of David' (Mark
10: 46–52). On the occasion of a spectacular entry into Jerusalem, Jesus is associated with David by the crowd (Mark 11:
10). When teaching in the temple, Jesus argues, on the basis
of Ps. 110: 1, that the Messiah, even if descended from David,
is superior to him (Mark 12: 35–7). Unless one wishes to argue
that all this Davidic material derives from the Christian, pre-
gospel tradition or even from the evangelist himself, one
should agree that the interpretation of Jesus' person and work
by aligning him with David began historically in the very
ministry of Jesus himself.

Jesus' Being and Old Testament Language

To illustrate the essential contribution of the OT to the NT
christological message, let me sample a number of descriptive
titles or designations for Jesus: as Christ, High Priest, Last
Adam, Wisdom, and Word.

1. The oldest Christian document shows us Paul repeatedly
calling Jesus 'Christ' in a way that suggests that, within
twenty years of Jesus' death and resurrection, this comprehensive title for Jesus' identity and powers was simply

taken for granted by Paul and his readers, had practically lost its original significance, and was almost his second (personal) name (1 Thess. 1: 1, 3; 5: 23, 28).[3] In a notable pre-Pauline formulation which also goes back to the earliest years of Christianity, 'Christ' seems already to have lost much of its titular significance (or messianic expectations) and to be functioning largely as an alternative name for Jesus (1 Cor. 15: 3). In his letters Paul uses 'Christ' 270 times but never considers it necessary to argue explicitly that Jesus is 'the Christ' whom Israel expected.

The title goes back to the Septuagintal 'Christos' (Hebrew *mashiah*) or 'anointed one'. By a ritual act of anointing, OT kings (and monarchs in ancient and other cultures) were installed: for example, Saul (1 Sam. 10: 1), David (2 Sam. 2: 4; 5: 3), and Solomon (1 Kgs. 1: 34, 39). Hence, a king would be called 'the Lord's anointed' (1 Sam. 16: 6; 24: 6; 2 Sam. 1: 14, 16; Ps. 2: 2) or simply 'the anointed one'. The practice of anointing kings at their investiture was extended to the service for the ordination of the Aaronic priesthood. As in the case of the king, the high priest's head was anointed with oil (Exod. 29: 1–9; Lev. 4: 3, 5, 16; 6: 22; 16: 32). Prophets also could be considered anointed by God, even though no actual rite of anointing is mentioned. Elijah was commanded to 'anoint' Elisha prophet, but in the event simply 'threw his mantle' over him (1 Kgs. 19: 16, 19). A prophetic author knows himself to be empowered by the divine Spirit and sent to encourage the exiled and oppressed: 'The Spirit of the Lord is upon me, because the Lord has anointed me; he has sent me to bring good tidings to the afflicted; to bind up the brokenhearted, to proclaim liberty to captives, and the opening of the prison to those who are bound; to proclaim the year of the Lord's favour' (Isa. 61: 1–2). When their prophetic role was to the fore, the ancestors of Israel could be called God's 'anointed ones' (Ps. 105: 15; see Gen. 20: 7).

[3] Many scholars agree with this observation, but not N. T. Wright, who argues that in Paul's letters 'Christ' is not simply a proper name but can retain its Jewish significance as 'Messiah' (*The Climax of the Covenant* (Edinburgh: T. & T. Clark, 1991), 41–55). See also M. de Jonge, 'Christ', *ABD* i. 914–21; id., 'Messiah', *ABD* iv. 777–88; J. H. Charlesworth (ed.), *The Messiah* (Minneapolis: Fortress Press, 1992).

In what follows I want to concentrate more on the kingly messianic roles and expectations. But in parenthesis one might well observe how the OT anointed ('messianic') king, priest, and prophet provided the ultimate origin for recognizing in Jesus the *munus triplex* (triple office) of anointed prophet, priest, and king. Already present in the writings of the Fathers and medieval theologians, this theme of Christ's 'triple office' was developed by John Calvin (1509–64), many Protestant scholars,[4] John Henry Newman (1801–90),[5] and the Second Vatican Council in its 1964 Dogmatic Constitution on the Church (*LG* 34–6).

OT expectations of a divinely anointed deliverer to come led at Qumran to hopes for a distinct priestly Messiah alongside a kingly Messiah.[6] Expectations also involved the coming at the end-time of a prophet or 'the prophet like Moses', normally identified as Elijah returning from heaven (Deut. 18: 15, 18; Mark 6: 14–16; 8: 28; 15: 35–6; John 1: 21; 6: 14; 7: 40; Acts 3: 22–6; 7: 37). John's Gospel both associates this prophetic figure with kingship (John 6: 14–15) and distinguishes the expectations concerned with 'the prophet' from those concerned with 'the Christ' (John 7: 40–1).

Later in this chapter I will say something about Jesus and OT priesthood. The next chapter will add something on his prophetic role. Here let me simply note how a classic passage in Malachi expects the returning Elijah to bring a moral conversion, and identifies him as the divine messenger who will prepare the day of the Lord's coming in judgement (Mal. 3: 1–4): 'Behold, I will send you Elijah the prophet before the great and terrible day of the Lord comes. And he will turn the hearts of fathers to their children and the hearts of children to their fathers, lest I come and smite the land with

---

[4] In his *Quod unus sit Christus* St Cyril of Alexandria (d. 444) calls Christ 'prophet, apostle, and high priest' (751a); in that christological dialogue he discusses only the first of the three titles (750–751c). For details on the use of this theme by Calvin, his predecessors, and successors, see P. Gisel, *Le Christ de Calvin* (Paris: Desclée, 1990), 131–50.

[5] See M. T. Yakaitis, *The Office of Priest, Prophet and King in the Thought of John Henry Newman* (Rome: Gregorian University Press, 1990).

[6] On this see G. Vermes, *The Dead Sea Scrolls* (London: Penguin Books, 3rd edn., 1987), 53–4, 295; see also Zech. 4: 14; 6: 9–14. On OT priesthood see M. D. Rehm, 'Levites and Priests', *ABD* iv. 297–310.

a curse' (Mal. 4: 5–6; see Sir. 48: 10). Invoking Isa. 40: 3 and Mal. 3: 1, Mark interprets this forerunner as John the Baptist (Mark 1: 2–4; see Mark 9: 11–13)—an interpretation accepted by Matthew and Luke (Matt. 11: 10–14; 17: 10–13; Luke 1: 16–17, 76; 7: 26–7). Thus the prophetic forerunner of 'the Lord' was identified as the forerunner of Jesus himself. Chapter 6 will reflect on this christological development of 'the day of the Lord'.

Let us return to the kingly messianic role, not least because the 'Christos' or 'anointed one' normally denoted the king of Israel. Any kingly Messiah was linked with the divine election of the house of David, and the hope for an everlasting dynasty. Through the prophet Nathan, God was believed to have promised David, 'your house and your kingdom shall be made sure forever; your throne shall be established forever' (2 Sam. 7: 16). Psalm 89 recalls this promise by putting on God's lips the following words: 'I have made a covenant with my chosen one, I have sworn to David my servant: "I will establish your descendants forever, and build your throne for all generations"' (Ps. 89: 3–4). The same psalm goes on to spell out the terms of this eternal covenant (Ps. 89: 19–37; see 132: 11–12). Historically David's dynasty did not prove everlasting. It fell in 587 BC and a king from the Davidic family was not restored to the throne when the exile ended in 538 BC. Even if efforts were made to interpret the governor of Judah (Zerubbabel) as a messianic king on the throne of David (Hag. 2: 20–3; Zech. 3: 8; 4: 6–10), literally the Davidic kingdom was not restored. Davidic messianism, apart from some Jewish circles (see Pss. Solomon and some Qumran texts) and then the Christians, was not a primary idea and expectation.

Nevertheless, the OT contained lyric language (perhaps originally used for the accession of King Hezekiah) which celebrated the ideal messianic king to come. He would exercise divine power ('Mighty God') and a fatherly love ('Everlasting Father'), and would bring peace and prosperity ('Prince of Peace') (Isa. 9: 2–7; see 11: 1–9; Mic. 5: 2–6). The royal or messianic psalms (Pss. 2, 18, 20, 21, 72, 89, 101, 110, 132, 144) witness to the lofty notion of the king and his function for the people. He could even be called God's son

(Pss. 2: 7; 89: 27)—a theme to which we will return in Chapter
5. The OT contained a rich reservoir of language for expressing and developing expectations about a promised ruler from
the line of David who would deliver and shepherd the suffering people (Ezek. 34: 23–4; 37: 24–5). He would free Israel
from foreign domination (Isa. 9: 4), and, through his power
and wisdom, justice and peace would prevail (Isa. 9: 6–7; 11:
1–9). Yahweh himself would be the eschatological king over
all the earth (Zech. 14: 9); the rule of the transcendent God
would be revealed in the rule of the messianic, Davidic king,
who may also possibly be symbolized by the one 'like unto
the son of man' to whom universal and everlasting dominion
would be given (Dan. 7: 13–14).

In pre-Christian Judaism, alongside hopes for a liberating,
warrior Messiah to come, we also find the expectation that
God would simply punish Israel's oppressors and deliver the
people (Isa. 13: 6–16) and the righteous (Wis. 3: 1–9). God
would directly bring such deliverance without any messianic
intermediary being involved. No such agent turns up in the
apocalyptic scenario with which 1 Enoch 91–104 presents
the end-time. The superb hymn that concludes the Book
of Habakkuk celebrates Yahweh who marches in, saves the
people (Hab. 3: 1–19) and their anointed king (Hab. 3: 13),
and does not need any messianic agent to effect this liberation.
It is important to hear such passages and not fondly imagine
that OT expectations of deliverance always imply a messianic
intermediary or royal agent from God.

The first Christians identified Jesus as the promised
Messiah and, as I will argue, Jesus himself interpreted his
person and activity messianically. But both he and his followers massively reinterpreted the messianic figure. Behav-
ing in an unregal and unwarlike fashion (see Mark 10: 42–4;
Luke 22: 24–7), Jesus never promised, let alone tried, to free
the people from foreign domination. Nor did he announce
the imminent lordship of Israel over all the nations (see Isa.
2: 2–3; 25: 6–9; Mic. 4: 1–2). For Jesus the signs of the
kingdom differed from that national hope. Ezekiel's language
about God's promise to care for the flock through a Davidic
shepherd-king to come (Ezek. 34: 23–4; 37: 24–5; see also
Mic. 5: 2–4) found an echo in Jesus' parable of the lost

sheep (Matt. 18: 12–14; Luke 15: 3–7; see Mark 6: 34), and eventually in John's Gospel identifying Jesus as 'the good shepherd' (John 10: 7–16; see 21: 15–17; 1 Pet. 2: 25; 5: 4). But this shepherd would lay down his life for his sheep (John 10: 11, 15, 17–18). Here we reach a major readjustment in the notion of Messiah.

At best we find in the OT only faint traces of a suffering Messiah or a suffering Davidic king to come. One of the psalms speaks of a taunting of the anointed, Davidic king (Ps. 89: 50–5). The final chapters of Zechariah, which were written in the fourth and third centuries BC and hence years after the career of Zechariah himself in the late sixth century, promise a messianic prince of peace (Zech. 9: 9–10) and speak of God's shepherd who will be killed for his sheep (Zech. 13: 7). Second Isaiah contained the four Servant Songs (42: 1–4; 49: 1–6; 50: 4–11; 52: 13–53: 12), which are frequently applied to Jesus and his work by the NT (e.g. Matt. 12: 18–21). The identity of the servant in these songs is by no means clear: the nation of Israel, an individual, or both. Further, the first mention of suffering occurs in 50: 6, well into the third song. (Here I agree with those who do not read 49: 7 as the final verse of the second song.) The final Servant Song tells both of his suffering, death, and burial, and of his exaltation and the vicarious value of his sufferings for the people. Christians found references to Jesus' fate and redemptive work in that song (e.g. Acts 8: 32–3; 1 Pet. 2: 22–5). Nevertheless, possible messianic allusions in the original fourth Servant Song are slight (Isa. 53: 2). To sum up: Jewish messianic expectations hardly show a hint of envisaging a suffering and martyred Messiah, who would be the persecuted and vindicated 'servant' of God (see Acts 3: 13, 26; 4: 27, 30).[7] A crucified (and resurrected) Christ was even more alien to Jewish messianic expectations. It was precisely over that point that the Christian proclamation of a crucified Messiah proved so new,

---

[7] We do not have to modify substantially the judgement of H. H. Rowley, who wrote: 'there is no serious evidence of the bringing together of the concepts of the Suffering Servant and the Davidic Messiah before the Christian era' (*The Servant of the Lord* (London: Lutterworth, 1952), 85). See also Wright, *The Climax of the Covenant*, 60: 'It seems very unlikely . . . that there was a well-known pre-Christian Jewish belief, based on Isaiah 53, in a coming redeemer who would die for the sins of Israel and/or the world.'

strange, and scandalously offensive (1 Cor. 1: 23).

2. From the great reservoir of OT images Christians also called upon that of priesthood to express their experience and evaluation of Jesus. Once again adjustments were made.

The OT Levitical priesthood was set apart to offer sacrifice and mediate in a cultic way between God and human beings. The tribe of Levi became a priestly class, within which Aaron and his sons were distinguished from the other Levites (Exod. 28: 1–5; 32: 25–9; Num. 1: 47–54; 3: 1–51; Deut. 10: 6–9; 18: 1–8; 33: 8–11).

His celebration of the Passover, institution of 'the Lord's supper' (1 Cor. 11: 20), and crucifixion at the time of the Passover soon led Christians to apply sacrificial language to the death of Jesus. Paul, when writing of Christ as 'our paschal lamb' who 'has been sacrificed' (1 Cor. 5: 7) and whose blood expiated sin (Rom. 3: 25; see 1 John 2: 2), apparently took over early, already traditional formulations. Christ was seen as sacrificial victim. But was he also priestly— in his celebration of the Lord's supper and/or in the events of Good Friday and Easter Sunday? Even if he sanctified the people through his own blood, he 'suffered outside the gate' (Heb. 13: 12)—in a profane setting and not in the temple or some other cultic place appropriate for priestly mediation between God and human beings. The setting for his death was no holy place, as was the case with Zechariah, 'murdered between the sanctuary and the altar' (Matt. 23: 35; see Luke 11: 51; 2 Chr. 24: 15–22). Further, unlike his cousin John the Baptist, Jesus was not born into a priestly family and could not claim Aaronic, or at least Levitical, priesthood.

The Pastoral Epistles recognized 'the one mediator' between God and humanity in 'the man Christ Jesus who gave himself as a ransom for all' (1 Tim. 2: 5–6; see Heb. 9: 15; 12: 24). But it was the Letter to the Hebrews which developed an intricate analogy and contrast between Jesus and the role of the Jewish priesthood, especially that of the high priest on the Day of Atonement. As the 'great high priest' (Heb. 4: 14–5: 10), Jesus was not born into the Levitical class but was appointed 'after the order of Melchizedek' (Heb. 5: 6, 10). He enjoyed the two essential qualifications for priesthood: divine authorization (Heb. 5: 4) and the solidarity with those to whom he was sent that was required to represent them (Heb. 4: 15; see 2: 17–18; 3: 1). The story of Abraham's meeting with a mysterious priest-king (Gen. 14: 17–20) allowed the author of Hebrews to argue that Jesus had received an eternal priesthood 'after the order of Melchizedek' (Heb. 7: 1–28; see Ps. 110: 4). The efficacy of his sacrifice, his mediation of the new covenant, the perfect consistency between his human life and cultic activity, his divine identity, and his direct appointment by God made Jesus' priesthood quite superior to the Levitical one (Heb. 6: 20–10: 18).

Priestly language will recur when we turn to examine in detail the background to and reality of Christ's atoning, sacrificial 'work'. The point of these paragraphs was to illustrate how another OT image was pressed into christological service by Christians seeking to describe their experience of Jesus. In comparison with the NT's elaboration of his kingly and prophetic role, the idea of Jesus as priest is—for all intents and purposes—confined to one major document (Hebrews). Nevertheless, the notion of Christ as priest has its biblical roots in completing the picture of his 'triple office'.

3. Christ's sinless solidarity with the human race (Heb. 4: 15) leads us towards the image of him as the last or ideal Adam. Just as in the case of the messianic and priestly titles, calling Jesus 'the last Adam' pointed primarily, albeit not exclusively, to his salvific meaning and function. Here the symbol was full of significance for the entire human race and the whole of its history.

Genesis presents human beings not only as the climax of God's work of creation but also as made in the divine image and manifesting God's rule on earth:

Then God said, 'Let us make human beings in our image; after our likeness; and let them have dominion over the fish of the sea, and over the birds of the air, and over the cattle, and over all the earth, and over every creeping thing that creeps upon the earth.' So God created human beings in his own image, in the image of God he created them, male and female he created them. (Gen. 1: 26–7)

The next two chapters of Genesis repeat (from a different tradition) the story of the creation of humanity, and add a story about Adam and Eve falling into sin.

Subsequent tradition proved both positive and negative about Adam (and Eve). The roll-call of famous persons in Sirach 44–9 ends by praising Adam, who is 'above every living being in creation' (Sir. 49: 16). When the Wisdom of Solomon sets out to show the power and work of wisdom in history, it begins with Adam, 'the first-formed father of the world' (Wis. 10: 1–2). With words to be cited by Hebrews (2: 5–9) and clearly echoing the story of creation, the psalmist celebrates the dignity and power over the rest of creation God has given to Adam and humanity.

> What is man that thou art mindful of him, and the son
>   of man that thou dost care for him?
> Yet thou hast made him little less than God, and dost
>   crown him with glory and honor.
> Thou hast given him dominion over the works of thy
>   hands;
> Thou hast put all things under his feet, all sheep and
>   oxen,
> and also the beasts of the field,
> the birds of the air, and the fish of the sea,
> whatever passes along the path of the sea.
>   (Ps. 8: 4–8)

This positive picture of Adam at the beginning of history led some to postulate an Adam-like figure to appear at the end of the messianic age. Qumran has supplied evidence for this view of Adam which links positively his role in eschatology with that in protology (1 QS 4. 23; CD 3. 20). Some scholars find a pointer to this eschatological function of Adam in canonical Scripture (Dan. 7: 13–14).

The Scriptures also recalled Adam as the one who sinned and brought death to humanity (2 Esd. 3: 6–10; 1 Cor. 15: 21–2). Some biblical passages named Eve as the one primarily responsible for the fall into sin: 'From a woman sin had its beginning, and because of her we all die' (Sir. 25: 24; see 1 Tim. 2: 13–14). But Adam's representative role in originating sin was generally more to the fore (see Rom. 5: 12–14; 1 Cor. 15: 21–3). With almost improbable ease Paul could contrast Adam and Christ as two corporate personalities or representatives (Rom. 5: 12–21; 1 Cor 15: 20–3, 45–9), and see human beings as bearing the image of both Adam and Christ

(1 Cor. 15: 49). Where Adam's disobedience meant sin and death for all, Christ's obedience more than made good the harm due to Adam by bringing righteousness and abundance of grace (Rom. 5: 12–21).[8] As a 'life-giving spirit', the last Adam is risen from the dead and will transform us through resurrection into a heavenly, spiritual existence (1 Cor. 15: 22, 45, 48–9). Thus Paul's Adam Christology involved both the earthly Jesus' obedience (Rom. 5) and the risen Christ's role as giver of the Spirit (1 Cor. 15).

So far we have seen how the NT and, in particular, Paul pressed Adam into service as foreshadowing Christ (Rom. 5: 14) and what Christ was to *do* as a, or rather the, corporate, representative personality. The same symbol was taken up to express Christ's being: he is 'the last Adam' (1 Cor. 15: 45), or the 'second man from heaven', and one not made 'from earth, of dust' (1 Cor 15: 47; see Gen. 2: 7).

Some scholars detect an Adamic reference in several other NT passages: for instance, in the language about 'the glory of Christ, who is the image (*eikōn*) of God' (2 Cor. 4: 4). Perhaps this is an echo of the language of Gen. 1: 26–7 about Adam being created in the divine image. If so, Paul would be thinking here of Christ as the ideal Adam, with his humanity perfectly expressing the divine image. But this exegesis is not fully convincing.[9] One may likewise be less than fully convinced by those who find a reference to Adam in two hymnic or at least poetic passages: Col. 1: 15–20 and Phil. 2: 6–11.

In Col. 1: 15 Christ is called 'the image (*eikōn*) of the invisible God, the first-born of all creation'. In isolation this verse could be taken merely in an Adamic sense as referring to Christ as the first created being, the archetypal human being who visibly reflects God, the invisible Creator. But

[8] J. D. G. Dunn assembles the evidence to show how not only Rom. 5 but also Rom. 1–8 interpret the human condition, at least partly, in the light of the creation and fall narratives of Genesis (*Christology in the Making*, (London: SCM Press, 2nd edn., 1989), 101–5). On the figure of Adam in the OT, intertestamental literature, and the NT see H. N. Wallace, 'Adam', *ABD* i. 62–4.

[9] As the divine *eikōn* or image (2 Cor. 4: 4), Christ reveals God. The 'glory' which becomes visible in the face of Christ is his own glory (2 Cor. 4: 4) or, equivalently, 'the glory of God' (2 Cor. 4: 6). See J. A. Fitzmyer, 'Glory Reflected on the Face of Christ and a Palestinian Jewish Motif', *Theological Studies*, 42 (1981), 630–44.

the context suggests finding the background in personified wisdom, the perfect image of God (Wis. 7: 26) and the agent of creation (Prov. 8: 22–31). The verses which follow speak of 'all things' being 'created through him and for him', of his being 'before all things', of 'all things holding together' in him, and of the plenitude of deity dwelling in him (Col. 1: 16–17, 19). Any parallelism with Adam, who was simply made in the divine image and likeness, gets left behind here.[10] On the contrary, every created thing, including the angelic 'thrones, dominions, principalities, and authorities' (Col. 1: 16), is said to have originated through Christ (as creative agent) and for Christ (as final goal), who likewise is the principle of cohesion in holding the universe together. Further it strains plausibility to argue that a mere Adamic model does justice to the language of 'the fullness of God' dwelling in Christ (Col. 1: 19; see 2: 9).[11]

[10] In his *Jesus Christ in Modern Thought* (London: SCM Press, 1990), 60–1 and 372, J. Macquarrie examines the use of Adam imagery in Paul's Christology, and appeals to 2 Cor. 4: 6 and Col. 1: 15. However, instead of finding in Gen. 1: 26–7 the background to these passages which call Christ 'the image' of God, we should think of the Hellenistic Jewish thought represented by the Wisdom of Solomon and Philo. A classic passage (Wis. 7: 22b–8: 1) describes the nature and works of wisdom, naming among her other attributes the following: 'she is a reflection of eternal light, a spotless mirror of the working of God, and an image of his goodness' (Wis. 7: 26; see Prov. 8: 22–31). In other words, wisdom rather than Adam can very well be the background when the NT calls Christ the 'image (*eikōn*)' of God. At least for Col. 1: 15 an allusion to Adam is, as Dunn observes, 'probably ruled out by v. 16' (*Christology in the Making*, 188). In the hymnic passage from Colossians talk of Christ as the 'image' of God belongs on the divine side, with the eternal Wisdom or the Word enjoying cosmological status and power (Col. 1: 15–17). The sphere of the incarnation and salvation history emerges only subsequently (Col. 1: 18, 20). Talk about the image (*eikōn*) of God is admittedly common to Adam and wisdom traditions. An *eikōn*, however, as a copy derived from a prototype, is not necessarily a perfect copy and full 're-presentation' of the original. Adam is obviously not a full 're-presentation' of God, nor even is Christ that *in his humanity*. Wisdom as the *eikōn* of God opens up the possibility of recognizing such full 're-presentation' on the divine side.

[11] One can read Col. 1: 19 as following on directly from v. 18: also as a consequence of his resurrection Christ is pre-eminent (= 'in him God in all his fullness chose to dwell'). Or one might interpret v. 19 as recapitulating vv. 15–17, whereas v. 20 fills out what has been said in v. 18 about the salvific impact of the crucified Christ's resurrection. On this view the grounds for the cosmological pre-eminence of Christ are run through twice (vv. 15–17 and 19), as are the grounds for his soteriological pre-eminence (vv. 18 and 20). For comments and bibliography on the hymn see M. P. Horgan, *NJBC* 879–80; E. Lohse, *Colossians and Philemon*, trans. W. P. Poehlman and R. J. Karris (Philadelphia: Fortress Press, 1971), 41–61; Wright, *The Climax of the Covenant*, 99–119.

The context of Col. 1: 15, therefore, prompts one to interpret 'the image of the invisible God' as pointing to Christ being on the divine side and being the perfect revealer of God—a thought paralleled by John 1: 18 and 2 Cor. 4: 4. Like the hymn or poem in Colossians, Hebrews also portrays Christ as the exact (divine) counterpart through whom the Father speaks and is revealed, and who is the one that sustains the entire universe: 'He reflects the glory of God and bears the very stamp of his nature, upholding the universe by his word of power' (Heb. 1: 3).

The whole context of Col. 1: 15–20 suggests a more than Adamic and human exegesis of 'the first-born of all creation'. Christ is 'the first-born' in the sense of being prior to and supreme over all creation, just as by virtue of his resurrection from the dead he is supreme *vis-à-vis* the Church (Col. 1: 18). The emphatic and repeated 'kai autos' (and he) of Col. 1: 17, 18 underlines the absolute 'pre-eminence' of Christ in the orders of creation and salvation history, both cosmologically and soteriologically. He through whom the universe was created is the same Christ who formed the Church by rising from the dead. He has been active in both creation and redemption. The context is decisive for interpreting the nature of the genitive in Col. 1: 15 ('of all creation'). The 1989 REB catches nicely its comparative force by translating the passage: 'his is the primacy *over* all creation' (italics mine).[12] The 'firstborn *from* the dead' (Col. 1: 18) is also the 'firstborn *over* all creation' (Col. 1: 15).

In the Philippians hymn any Adamic interpretation that bears precisely on Christ's prior state of being 'in the form of God' and enjoying 'equality with God' (Phil. 2: 6) seems to be made doubtful by what follows. This divine status and mode of existence stand in counterpoint (the emphatic 'but') to the subsequent state of 'assuming the form of a slave', 'being born in likeness of men', and 'being found in human form' (Phil. 2: 7). It is what is said in v. 7 that first puts Christ with the community of human beings and their collective image, Adam. Christ belonged to the eternal sphere of divine

---

[12] For a brief account of the patristic exegesis of 'the first born of all creation', see J. B. Lightfoot, *Saint Paul's Epistles to the Colossians and to Philemon* (London: Macmillan, 1875), 148–50.

existence (Phil. 2: 6), and joined the human (and Adamic) sphere only when he assumed another mode of existence (Phil. 2: 7) which concealed his proper (divine) being. Nevertheless, in talking of Christ as refusing to use for his own advantage or exploit for himself the godhead which was his, v. 6 could also be contrasting his humility (in becoming human and dying the death of a slave) with the presumptuous aspiration of Adam (and Eve) to enjoy illegitimate equality with God and become 'like God' (Gen. 3: 5–6).[13]

Whether we accept the wider circle of references to Adam or limit ourselves to the clear references in Rom. 5 and 1 Cor. 15, the NT used Adamic language to express the being of Jesus and, even more, his task and goal. In post-NT times the symbol of Adam proved a valuable foil for Clement of Alexandria, Origen (d. *c.*254), St Athanasius (*c.*296–373), St Hilary of Poitiers (*c.*315–67), St Gregory of Nazianzus (329–89), St Gregory of Nyssa (*c.*330–*c.*395), and other Church Fathers, when they presented and interpreted the person and work of Christ.[14] St Irenaeus (*c.*130–*c.*200), in particular, did much to elaborate further Paul's antithetical parallelism between Adam and Christ, the latter reversing the failure of the first. In a typical passage of his *Adversus haereses* he wrote: 'The Son of God . . . was incarnate and made man; and then he summed up in himself the long line of the human race, procuring for us a comprehensive salvation, that we might

---

[13] On Phil. 2: 6–11 see Dunn, *Christology in the Making*, 113–21, and Wright, *The Climax of the Covenant*. Against Dunn, Wright convincingly shows that finding elements of an Adam-Christology in the hymn in no way means squeezing everything into a purely Adamic pattern and ruling out a Christology of pre-existence and incarnation: 'The contrast between Adam and Christ works perfectly within my view: Adam, in arrogance, thought to become like God; Christ, in humility, became human' (91; see 90–7). Despite my substantial agreement with Wright's exegesis, I still wonder how closely one may associate Phil. 2: 6–11 with the clear Adam-Christology of Rom. 5: 12–21 and 1 Cor. 15: 20–3, 45–9. Unlike those passages, the Philippians hymn neither mentions Adam by name, nor clearly refers to his creation (out of the earth), his sin, and that sinful disobedience as being more than countered by Christ's obedience. In 1992 Dunn himself acknowledged that 'the majority of scholars' would hardly agree with him in finding an expression of Adam-Christology in Phil. 2: 7 ('Christology (NT)', *ABD* i. 979–91, at 983).

[14] Some of the Church Fathers appealed to various books of the OT and NT when reflecting on the Adam/Christ theme: see L. F. Ladaria, 'Adán y Cristo en los *Tractatus super Psalmos* de San Hilario de Poitiers', *Gregorianum*, 73 (1992), 97–122; and id., 'Adán y Cristo: un motivo soteriológico del *In Mattheum* de Hilario de Poitiers', *Compostellanum* 35 (1990), 443–60.

recover in Christ Jesus what in Adam we had lost, namely the state of being in the image and likeness of God'(3. 18. 1). Interpreting Christ as the 'second' or 'last' Adam, who 'reran' a programme[15] and more than made up what had failed in Adam, has proved a long-lived christological theme, not only in theological teaching but also in liturgical, hymnic, and catechetical texts. To quote John Henry Newman's *Dream of Gerontius*:

> O loving wisdom of our God!
> When all was sin and shame,
> A second Adam to the fight
> And to the rescue came.
>
> O wisest love! that flesh and blood,
> Which did in Adam fail,
> Should strive afresh against the foe,
> Should strive and should prevail.[16]

4. The OT theme of *wisdom* also proved its worth for the first Christians when reflecting on their experience of Jesus. The conceptuality offered various possibilities.

Proverbs vividly personifies the divine attribute or function of wisdom, which existed before the world was made, revealed God, and acted as God's agent in creation (Prov. 8: 22–31; see 3: 19, Wis. 8: 4–6; Sir. 1: 4, 9). Wisdom dwelt with God (Prov. 8: 22–31; see Sir. 24: 4; Wis. 9: 9–10), and being the exclusive property of God was as such inaccessible to human beings (Job 28: 12–13, 20–1, 23–7). It was God who 'found' wisdom (Bar. 3: 29–37) and gave her to Israel: 'He found the whole way to knowledge, and gave her to Jacob his servant and to Israel whom he loved. Afterward she appeared upon earth and lived among human beings' (Bar. 3: 36–7; see Sir. 24: 1–12). As a female figure (Sir. 1: 15; Wis. 7: 12), wisdom addressed human beings (Prov. 1: 20–33; 8: 1–9: 6),

---

[15] See Dunn, *Christology in the Making*, 122–3, for this helpful terminology.

[16] See also J. McAuley, 'By your kingly power, O risen Lord, all that Adam lost is now restored: in your resurrection be adored' (in L. A. Murray (ed.), *Anthology of Australian Religious Poetry* (Melbourne: Collins Dove, 1986), 142). The *Exultet* or Easter Proclamation presents Christ as reversing Adam's failure; see also official church teaching from the 5th to the 20th century (DS 413, 901, 1524, 3915; *GS* 22).

inviting to her feast those who are not yet wise (Prov. 9: 1–6). The finest passage celebrating the divine wisdom (Wis. 7: 22b–8: 1) includes the following description: 'She is a breath of the power of God, and the radiance of the glory of the Almighty. . . . She is a reflection of eternal light, a spotless mirror of the working of God, and an image of his goodness' (Wis. 7: 25–6). No wonder then that Solomon, the archetypal wise person, fell in love with wisdom: 'I loved her and sought her from my youth, and I desired to take her for my bride, and I became enamoured of her beauty' (Wis. 8: 2). Such was the radiant beauty of the wisdom exercised by God in creation and in relations with the chosen people.[17]

In understanding and interpreting Christ, the NT uses various strands from these accounts of wisdom. First of all, like wisdom Christ pre-existed all things and dwelt with God (John 1: 1–2). Second, the lyric language about wisdom being the breath of the divine power, reflecting the divine *glory*, mirroring *light*, and being an *image* of God appears to be echoed by 1 Cor. 1: 17–18, 24–5 (which repeatedly associate divine wisdom with power), by Heb. 1: 3 ('he is the radiance of God's glory'), John 1: 9 ('the true light that gives light to everyone'), and Col. 1: 15 ('the image of the invisible God'; see 2 Cor. 4: 4). Third, the NT applies to Christ the language about wisdom's cosmic significance as God's agent in the creation of the world: 'all things were made through him, and without him nothing was made that was made' (John 1: 3; see 1: 10; 1 Cor. 8: 6; Col. 1: 16; Heb. 1: 2). Fourth, faced with Christ's crucifixion, Paul vividly transforms the notion of divine wisdom's inaccessibility (1 Cor. 1: 17–2: 13). 'The wisdom of God' (1 Cor. 1: 21) is not only 'secret and hidden' (1 Cor. 2: 7) but also, defined by the cross and its proclamation, downright folly to the wise of this world (1 Cor. 1: 18–25; on the hidden, exclusive quality of divine wisdom see also perhaps Matt. 11: 25–7). Fifth, through his parables and in other ways, Christ teaches wisdom (Matt. 25: 1–12; Luke 16: 1–8; see also Matt. 11: 25–30). He is 'greater' than Solomon, the OT wise person and teacher *par excellence* (Matt. 12: 42).

---

[17] On wisdom in pre-Christian Judaism see Dunn, *Christology in the Making*, 168–76; R. E. Murphy, 'Wisdom in the OT', *ABD* vi. 920–31.

Sixth, the NT does not, however, seem to have applied to Christ the themes of Lady Wisdom and her radiant beauty. Pope Leo the Great (d. 461), however, recalled Prov. 9: 1 by picturing the unborn Jesus in Mary's womb as 'Wisdom building a house for herself' (*Epistola*, 31. 2–3).

Up to this point I have been pursuing strands from the OT ideas about wisdom, which, more or less clearly, are taken up (and changed) in NT interpretations of Christ. Here and there the NT eventually not only ascribes wisdom roles to Christ but also makes the equation 'divine wisdom = Christ' quite explicit. Luke reports how the boy Jesus grew up 'filled with wisdom' (Luke 2: 40; see 2: 52). Later Christ's fellow-countrymen were astonished 'at the wisdom given to him' (Mark 6: 2). Matt. 11: 19 thinks of him as divine wisdom being 'proved right by his deeds' (see, however, the different and probably original version of Luke 7: 35).[18] Possibly Luke 11: 49 wishes to present Christ as 'the wisdom of God'. Paul names Christ as 'the wisdom of God' (1 Cor. 1: 24) whom God 'made our wisdom' (1 Cor. 1: 30; see 1: 21). A later letter softens the claim a little: in Christ 'all the treasures of wisdom and knowledge lie hidden' (Col. 2: 3). Beyond question, the clearest form of the equation 'the divine wisdom = Christ' comes in 1 Cor. 1: 17–2: 13. Yet even there Paul's impulse is to explain 'God's hidden wisdom' not so much as the person of Christ himself but rather as God's 'secret purpose from the very beginning to bring us to our destined glory' (1 Cor 2: 7 in REB). In other words, when Paul calls Christ 'the wisdom of God', even more than in the case of other titles, God's eternal plan of salvation over-shadows everything.

At times the Church Fathers named Christ as 'Wisdom'. Thus when rebutting claims about Christ's ignorance, Gregory of Nazianzus insisted that as divine Christ knew everything: 'How can he be ignorant of anything that is, when he is Wisdom, the maker of the worlds, who brings all things to fulfilment and recreates all things, who is the end of all that has come into being?' (*Orationes*, 30. 15). Irenaeus represents

---

[18] On Matthew's identification of Jesus with wisdom see Dunn, *Christology in the Making*, 197–206.

another, minor patristic tradition which identified the Spirit of God, and not Christ himself, as 'Wisdom' (*Adversus haereses* 4. 20. 1–3; see 3. 24. 2; 4. 7. 3; 4. 20. 3). He could appeal to Paul's teaching about wisdom being one of the gifts of the Holy Spirit (1 Cor. 12: 8). However, the majority applied to Christ the title/name of 'Wisdom'. Eventually the Emperor Constantine set a pattern for Eastern Christians by dedicating a church to Christ as the personification of divine wisdom. In Constantinople under Emperor Justinian Santa Sophia ('Holy Wisdom') was rebuilt, consecrated in 538, and became a model for many other Byzantine churches. Nevertheless, in the NT and subsequent Christian thought 'the Word' or *Logos* came through more clearly than 'the Wisdom' of God as a central, high title for Christ. The portrayal of the Word in the prologue of John's Gospel shows a marked resemblance to what is said about wisdom in Prov. 8: 22–31 and Sir. 24: 1–12. Yet that prologue speaks of the Word, not the Wisdom, becoming flesh and does not follow Baruch in saying that 'Wisdom appeared upon earth and lived among human beings' (Bar. 3: 37). The evangelist develops the theme of the Son of God as revealer communicating the divine self-revelation (John 1: 18)[19]—the Logos as spoken word or rational utterance (rather than merely as thought or meaning that remains within the mind). When focusing in a classic passage on what 'God has revealed to us through the Spirit' (1 Cor. 2: 10), Paul had written of the hidden and revealed wisdom of God (1 Cor. 1: 17–2: 13). Despite the availability of this wisdom language and conceptuality, John prefers to speak of 'the Word' (John 1: 1, 14; see 1 John 1: 1; Rev. 19: 13), a term that offers a rich complexity of meanings.

5. Like wisdom, the word is with God from the beginning (Gen. 1: 1; John 1: 1), powerfully creative (Gen. 1: 1–2: 4; Isa. 55: 10–11; Ps. 33: 6, 9; 107: 20; Judith 16: 14), and God's personified self-expression (Wis. 18: 14–16). Like wisdom, the word expresses God's active power and self-revelation towards and in the created world. Solomon's prayer for

[19] As Logos, the Son is associated with revelation, while Matthew's Gospel, by referring explicitly to the Son and implying his identification with wisdom, associates the Son as wisdom with revelation (Matt. 11: 25–30; see Luke 10: 21).

wisdom takes word and wisdom as synonymous agents of divine creation; 'God of my fathers and Lord of mercy, you made all things *by your word*, and *by your wisdom* fashioned man' (Wis. 9: 1–2). Even so, John's prologue does not open by saying, 'In the beginning was Wisdom, and Wisdom was with God, and Wisdom was God' (see John 1: 1).

Despite the fact that, in the literature of pre-Christian Judaism, wisdom, word, and, for that matter, spirit were 'near alternatives as ways of describing the active, immanent power of God',[20] why did John choose word and not wisdom? Several considerations may have told against wisdom and for the choice of word. First, given that *sophia* was personified as Lady Wisdom (e.g. Prov. 1: 20–33; 8: 1–9: 6; Wis. 8: 2), it could have seemed awkward to speak of this female figure 'being made flesh' when Jesus was male. Second, in Hellenistic Judaism the law of Moses had been identified with wisdom (Sir. 24: 23; Bar. 4: 1–4) and credited with many of her characteristics. To announce then that 'Wisdom was God and was made flesh' could have been felt to suggest that 'the Torah was God and was made flesh'. Within a few years Christians were to identify the Son of God and Logos with law or the law (Shepherd of Hermas, *Similitudines*, 8. 3. 2.; Justin, *Dialogue with Trypho*, 43. 1 and see 11. 2). But neither John nor any other NT authors identified Christ with the Torah[21]. Third, Paul, Luke (especially in Acts), and other NT witnesses prepared the way for John's prologue by their use of *logos* for God's revelation through Christ. As Dunn rightly argues, the background for John's choice of 'word' is

---

[20] Dunn, *Christology in the Making*, 196. In pre-Christian Judaism 'basically all three phrases (Spirit, Wisdom, and Word) are simply variant ways of speaking of the creative, revelatory or redemptive act of God … *all three expressions are simply alternate ways of speaking about the effective power of God in his active relationship with his world and its inhabitants*' (ibid. 219; italics his). See T. E. Fretheim, 'Word of God', *ABD* vi. 961–8; T. H. Tobin, 'Logos', *ABD* iv. 348–56. E. Haenchen rightly observes that 'it goes virtually without saying that the hymn in John's prologue could not have used "Messiah" or "Son of man"' (*A Commentary on the Gospel of John*, trans. R. W. Funk, i (Philadelphia: Fortress Press, 1984), 110). Yet the question remains: why 'Logos' rather than 'Sophia'? This is something that not only Haenchen but also Tobin leaves unexplained ('Logos', 353–5).

[21] The closest approach to such identification is found in Gal. 6: 2 ('the law of Christ') and Rom. 10: 4 (if one adopts the more 'positive' translation, 'Christ is the goal of the law').

also to be found in the earlier books of the NT and not just in the OT, Philo, and other such sources.[22]

Both in NT times and later the Johannine 'Word' offered rich christological possibilities. First, the possibility of identification and distinction. On the one hand, words proceed from a speaker; being a kind of an extension of the speaker, they are, in a certain sense, identical with the speaker ('the Word was God'). On the other hand, a word is distinct from the one who utters it ('the Word was with God'). Thus Christ was/is identified with, yet distinct from, Yahweh. Second, God has been uttering the divine Word always ('in/from the beginning'); the Word 'was' (not 'came to be') God. In this context 'Word' opens up reflection on the personal, eternal pre-existence of the Logos-Son, a theme to which we return later. God has never been without the Word.

Third, we did not need John Osborne and other modern playwrights to be reminded of the fact that words reveal their speakers. Shamefully or happily, words express what is in our mind and heart. In the OT 'the word of God' repeatedly

---

[22] Dunn, *Christology in the Making*, 230–9. In his generally fine treatment of the Logos (ibid. 213–50) Dunn curiously argues that the author of the poem (John 1: 1–5, 9–12, 14, 16) behind John's prologue 'did not necessarily intend the Logos in vv. 1–13 to be thought of as a personal divine being'. Dunn suggests that v. 14 marks '*not only the transition in the thought of the poem from pre-existence to incarnation, but also the transition from impersonal personification to actual person*' (ibid. 243; italics his). In a note he insists that it is by no means necessarily true 'that at the pre-Johannine stage the Logos poem envisaged a *personal* Logos prior to v. 14' (ibid. 349 n. 120). Dunn claims that when the fourth evangelist took up the poem he altered its sense by making it clear (through the addition of vv. 6–8) that vv. 9–12 referred 'already to the *incarnate* Logos so that v. 14 becomes more of a resumptive summary of a claim already made' (ibid. 244). For two reasons I find this view unconvincing. First, as Dunn himself suggests, the Logos poem came 'quite probably' from 'the same Johannine circle' (perhaps even from 'the same hand'), and 'not necessarily much before the composition of the Gospel itself' (ibid. 239). If the same circle or even the same author interpreted their/his (her?) own poem as referring in *earlier* verses to the incarnate Logos, that authorial intention does not support Dunn's thesis about a startling transition in v. 14 'from impersonal personification to actual person'. Second, how could a 'poem' (presumably the author of a poem) use 'Logos' as an 'impersonal personification', without being aware that a few verses later he (she?) would use 'Logos' of an 'actual person' (ibid. 243)? Could the author of the poem find himself in such an unexpected transition? Perhaps Dunn is really referring to the readers of the poem then (and now?). Until *they* reach v. 14, they may have been thinking merely in terms of an impersonal personification and then find they have to make a revolutionary transition to an actual person.

denotes the revelation of God and the divine will. John's Gospel can move smoothly from the language of 'the Word' to focus on 'God the only Son who has made the Father known' (John 1: 18). As the Son of God sent from the Father or the Son of man who has come down from heaven, in a unique and exclusive way Jesus reveals heavenly knowledge.[23] At the same time, this Word offers light to everyone coming into the world (John 1: 9), a theme soon developed, with help of Philo, Middle Platonic, and/or Stoic thought, by St Justin Martyr (*c.*100–*c.*165), Origen, and others.

A later chapter will explore the question of Christ's revelatory and salvific role for non-Christians. Yet it may be as well to anticipate here how helpful the Logos Christology quickly proved for this question. In his first *Apology* Justin wrote: 'We have been taught that Christ is the first begotten of God and that he is the Word (Logos) of whom the whole human race partakes. Those who have lived according to the Word are Christians, even though they have been considered atheists: such as, among the Greeks, Socrates, Heraclitus, and others like them' (46. 1–4). Wherever there was the Logos, there was some true light and genuine knowledge of God. Like Justin, Origen acknowledged how this happened beyond and before Christianity: 'It is not true that [God's] rays were enclosed in that man [Jesus] alone . . . or that the Light which is the divine Logos, which causes these rays, existed nowhere else . . . We are careful not to raise objections to any good teaching, even if their authors are outside the faith' (*Contra Celsum*, 7. 17).

Fourth, John's Logos Christology opened the way for Christians not only to recognize the influence of the Logos outside Christianity but also to dialogue with non-Christian thinkers. Those who endorsed Jewish, Platonic, and Stoic strands of thought about the Logos could find a measure of common ground with Christians, who, nevertheless, remained distinctive with their claim that 'the Logos was made flesh'. The notion of 'the Logos' probably offered a more effective bridge to contemporary culture than that of 'wisdom'.

---

[23] Ibid., pp. xxvi–xxviii.

Finally, when NT Christians called the crucified and risen Jesus the Word and Wisdom of God, they were not only expressing his divine identity but also drawing attention to the fact that Christology might not necessarily begin with the incarnation and not even with Jesus' background in the call, history, and religious faith of the Jewish people. By maintaining that the whole world was created through the divine Wisdom and Word (John 1: 3, 10; 1 Cor. 8: 6; Col. 1: 16; Heb. 1: 2), they did more than link Jesus as the last Adam with the high point of creation in the making of human beings. They interpreted him as the divine agent of all creation, which thus right from the beginning carried a christological face.

This chapter has listed and examined five major terms found in pre-Christian Judaism which came to be applied to Jesus. Along the way we have noted how this application called at times for startling readjustments: the notion of a *suffering* Messiah, for example, hardly surfaces before Jesus but became central in the proclamation of 'Christ crucified' (1 Cor 1: 23). Before we leave it, our list invites two comments.

First, it will be supplemented by subsequent chapters when we discuss Jesus' prophetic activity, his use of 'prophetic' and 'Son of man' language (Chapter 3), and his being called Son of God (Chapter 5) and Lord, Saviour, and God (Chapter 6). Even then much more could be said about the way the language of pre-Christian Judaism was pressed into service to interpret who Jesus was and is. Two brief examples should suffice. The NT repeatedly introduces the figure of Moses as an OT type with whom Jesus is sharply contrasted.[24] After the OT compared God with a shepherd, the NT also applies to Jesus this image, understanding his followers and others as the flock to which he dedicates himself.[25]

Second, as we saw, all five terms that we looked at (Messiah, Adam, Priest, Wisdom, and Word) have a strong functional flavour not only in pre-Christian Judaism but also when used

[24] For details see W. Johnstone, 'Moses', in R. J. Coggins and J. L. Houlden (eds.), *A Dictionary of Biblical Interpretation* (London: SCM Press, 1990), 467–9; D. M. Beegle and F. M. Gillman, 'Moses', *ABD* iv. 909–20.
[25] See J. Jeremias, *'Poimēn'* etc., *TDNT* vi. 485–502.

of Jesus himself. In fact speaking about him in such ways often meant saying more about his doing than his being. While they indicated something about his ontological identity 'in himself', these terms highlighted his saving role 'for us'.

A later chapter will address the question of Jesus' redemptive role for all human beings and their world. That chapter will examine and use three characteristic ways for interpreting salvation which come from the NT and have been variously developed through the history of Christianity. First, the *victorious redemption* that *Jesus* effected brings *freedom* from *sin* and *evil*, by a *new exodus* from *death* to *life*. Second, through his *bloody sacrifice*, as *priest* and *victim*, he made *expiation* for us and reconciled us to God. Third, his *love mediated* for us the *mercy*, *peace*, and *blessing* of a *new* and final *covenant* with God.

It may be labouring the obvious. But all the redemptive terms italicized in the last paragraph have their deep roots in pre-Christian Judaism. If we fail to appreciate the ways in which the NT massively appropriated and reread this salvific language in the light of the whole Christ-event, we can hardly expect to describe and explain competently how the first Christians articulated the deliverance Jesus brought them and us. The only significant NT word not italicized in the last paragraph is 'reconciled'. As a helpful notion for expressing some important aspects of Jesus' salvific 'doing', 'reconciliation' (Rom. 5: 10–11; 11: 15; 2 Cor. 5: 18–20; Eph. 2: 16; Col. 1: 20–2) stands practically alone in the NT by not being directly rooted in pre-Christian Judaism.[26]

Almost as much as their experience of Christ himself, the first Christians' rereading of the pre-Christian Scriptures produced the NT Scriptures—in particular, what those Scriptures teach about Jesus' soteriological 'doing' and ontological 'being'. This NT christological appropriation of the Jewish Scriptures has helped to shape not only the way post-NT Christians have understood in particular the salvific work and personal identity of Jesus, but also in general the whole way they read the Scriptures of pre-Christian Judaism. The NT rereading of the Suffering Servant language, for

---

[26] See J. A. Fitzmyer, 'Pauline Theology', *NJBC* 1397–402, esp. 1398–9.

example, has shaped forever Christian interpretation of those passages from Second Isaiah. Here as elsewhere the NT rereading of the pre-Christian Scriptures has decisively influenced ways in which those texts have helped to form the thinking and life of Christians over the centuries.

These considerations should sufficiently justify my decision, when I come to reflect at length on Jesus' saving role, to indicate some of the ways NT (and later) Christians have appropriated and reread OT language in expressing the new life they experienced as mediated through the events of Good Friday and Easter Sunday. Let us turn now, however, to some themes from the life, death, and resurrection of Jesus that assume major importance for a systematic Christology.

3
The Human History
᛭ ᛭

> He was conscious of a vocation from God to proclaim
> this kingdom, and the record shows him as single-
> mindedly devoted to that vocation, even to the point at
> which it brought him to death.
>
> (John Macquarrie, *Jesus Christ in Modern Thought*)

'The Word became flesh and made his home among us' (John
1: 14). We might gloss the climax of John's prologue by saying
that 'the Word took on a human history'. Chapter 1 has
already indicated certain issues connected with our historical
knowledge of Jesus. This chapter aims to develop some
themes about that human history which contribute to our
clarification of his person and work. To begin with, I need to
attend to some preliminaries and show that I am not a victim
of too many assumptions unconsciously adopted.

Some Preliminaries

As was pointed out earlier, our knowledge of Jesus' earthly
life and work is limited and fragmentary. We simply do not
have anything like a reasonably complete picture of his whole
story. Even for the brief period of his public ministry the data
are limited. The fact that, explicitly and for the most part,
Jesus did not proclaim himself but the kingdom of God, as
well as the fact that he left no letters or other personal papers,
makes access to his interior life difficult. (This difficulty will
return in Chapter 11 when we face the question of Jesus'
faith.) But the challenge goes beyond mere limitations in the
data available about someone who lived on earth 2,000 years
ago.

Whenever we seek to know another person, we are grap-
pling with an elusive mystery. Even in the case of those who
live with us today, we would be deluding ourselves if we
imagined that their total personal reality was available for our
inspection. Perhaps we can 'know' characters in some (lesser)
novels and dramas. Real persons as well characters in great
works of literature always remain, at least partly, elusive mysteries. If this holds good for any human beings, whether they
live today or in the past, Christian believers expect it to be
very much more true in the case of Jesus. His question to
Philip 'Have I been with you so long, and yet you do not
know me?' (John 14: 9) can be seen to go beyond a mere
reproach to touch a profound truth about the mystery of his
person. Could anyone ever hope to know him adequately
either then or now?

Let us recall also the way in which knowing other persons
(as much or more than our knowing any reality) is always an
exercise of personal knowledge. This means that we must
reckon not only with the elusive mystery of the other person
but also with the inevitably subjective nature of our own
knowledge, in particular and above all when it is a question
of our experiencing and knowing the reality of other persons.
Admittedly we read the Gospels now with the resources of
modern scholarship; it enriches and clarifies what we know
about the historical reality of Jesus' deeds and words as well
as the events directly connected with him. Yet knowledge of
persons always means, at least minimally, *our knowing
someone*, not simply our knowing about him or her. Our
personal knowledge of the other always goes beyond the
merely empirical and publicly accessible data. Knowing other
persons, whether they belong to the past like Confucius,
Socrates, Martin Luther, or Teresa of Avila or (like our
relatives and friends) share life with us today, is much more
than simply knowing a certain number of 'facts' about them.
Our own (subjective) relationship to and evaluation of those
persons are always necessarily involved. There is simply no
way of knowing any reality and, above all, other persons in a
'purely objective' fashion.[1]

---

[1] The notion of testimony can be illuminating here. Whenever we speak or write

The subjective nature of our knowledge, in particular our historical knowledge and knowledge of other persons, should not be reduced to the mere fact that we are all culturally and historically conditioned. Such conditioning expresses but also conceals the deepest desires (for life, meaning, and love) and primordial questions (about such matters as suffering and evil) which shape our existence but here and now find only fragmentary fulfilment and provisional answers. Inevitably these desires and questions come into play whenever we encounter other persons, all the more so when the encounter assumes some importance for us and the other person is richly significant. Such cases bring the meeting of two mysteries— mine and his or hers.

Gabriel Marcel's classic distinction between a problem and a mystery bears on this point. Getting to know any person and, in particular, someone of world stature and significance is always much more than a mere problem to be solved; it is a mystery to be grappled with. It is at our peril then that we approach our knowledge of Jesus as a problem to be solved by honesty and scholarship rather than as a mystery (or rather *the* mystery) with which to engage ourselves.

To anticipate a theme of Chapters 13 and 14, let me observe here how we are all part of his story and his mystery—whether we realize it or not. This necessary involvement of ourselves in the full, unfolding story of Christ rules out attempts to tackle the history of Jesus as if it were no more than a mere problem 'out there', standing quite apart from our personal existence.

When studying the earthly Jesus, some scholars still limit themselves to applying typically 'scientific' methods modelled on the modern natural sciences or at least on their understanding of them. They take up particular gospel sayings or events and analyse them in an 'objective' fashion, wrenching them apart from the living world of Jesus and his followers and reducing them to their smallest elements. They

about other persons, especially those who are richly significant, we inevitably bear witness to them (and to ourselves). As readers of the Gospels, we are invited by those texts and their authors to experience and interact with a person who, on any showing, was/is extremely significant. What we then say or write about Jesus will necessarily be our way, positively or negatively, of giving testimony to him.

isolate and take apart these sayings and events, as if such separation and reduction were *the* way to know and understand Jesus. All of this insinuates an attempt to dominate him as if he were simply a problem 'back there'. They forget that really knowing another person in depth always demands our participation in and relationship to another personal mystery. Here, if anywhere, appropriate objectivity is gained by involvement, not by artificial attempts to distance oneself.

These reflections about the nature of our knowledge of Jesus should be kept in mind when we move to examine the sources on which we depend for our (limited) knowledge about Jesus' earthly life and work: the Gospels according to Matthew, Mark, Luke, and John. To begin with, why have we inherited four of them in our canonical NT?[2]

One can and should appeal, of course, to the different audiences (with their different needs) for which the four evangelists wrote. One might also remark on the massive nature of the experience into which the first Christians were drawn. Their experience of the earthly and risen Jesus was such that it made it highly likely that they would develop more than one extended account of his human history. Our human experience is essentially conditioned by *history*, being shaped through and through by what we remember from the past and anticipate from the future. Our *religious* experience confronts us with what is most fundamental and lasting for our existence. The historical, religious quality of experience necessarily expresses itself through our human appetite for narrative. Given the extraordinary nature of their experience of Jesus, it was almost inevitable that the early Christians would more than once tell that story as gospels which were eventually to be recognized as the heart of the new Christian Scriptures.

The four gospel 'portraits' can be classified as more representational and concerned with portraying historical details (Mark, Matthew, and Luke), or more (theologically) impressionistic and concerned with characteristic effects

---

[2] On our four Gospels and the apocryphal gospels see G. N. Stanton, *The Gospels and Jesus* (Oxford: Oxford University Press, 1989), 125–35; on the case for a biographical assessment of the canonical Gospels, see R. A. Burridge, *What are the Gospels?* (Cambridge: Cambridge University Press, 1992).

produced by Jesus (John). The first three evangelists at points modify the traditions about Jesus (e.g. the longer form of the Lord's Prayer in Matt. 6: 9–13), occasionally retroject into the lifetime of Jesus traditions which come from the post-Easter period (e.g. Matt. 18: 20), and are largely (but not entirely) responsible for the contexts in which they place the sayings and doings of Jesus. Yet when we make Jesus the object of critical historical research, the Synoptic Gospels, it can be argued, are reasonably reliable in allowing us to reconstruct historically something about Jesus and his activity. In this chapter we shall prefer the evidence from these Gospels over that from John, a Gospel in which years of prayerful and theological meditation have played down features of Jesus' historical ministry (e.g. the preaching of the kingdom, the parables, and his exorcisms) to develop a picture of the eternally pre-existent Word, Son of God, or Son of man who descends from heaven, directly proclaims himself (see the 'I am' sayings which culminate in the 'before Abraham was, I am' of John 8: 58), and returns to the divine glory which in any case he has already manifested during his earthly existence (John 1: 14; 17: 1, 5, 24).

Nevertheless, a too massive contrast between John and the Synoptics would misrepresent the data, as if the latter portrayed Jesus as a purely human teacher while the former let his divinity crowd out his humanity. As we shall see, the Synoptic Gospels convey a high (albeit implicit) Christology. John, for his part, by no means ignores the human dimension of Jesus' earthly history (e.g. John 4: 6; 11: 33, 35; 12: 27; 13: 21), at times may be more historically accurate than the Synoptics, and arguably tells the whole story of Jesus' death on the cross even more realistically than the other Gospels.[3]

Moreover, even in using the Synoptic Gospels, we must

---

[3] On what we can reasonably claim to know about the Jesus of history from our four Gospels, see C. A. Evans, 'Life-of-Jesus Research and the Eclipse of Mythology', *Theological Studies*, 54 (1993), 3–36; J. A. Fitzmyer, *A Christological Catechism* (Mahwah, NJ: Paulist Press, 2nd edn., 1991); J. Gnilka, *Jesus von Nazaret: Botschaft und Geschichte* (Freiburg: Herder, 1990); J. P. Meier, 'Jesus', *NJBC* 1316–28; id., *A Marginal Jew: Rethinking the Historical Jesus* (New York: Doubleday, 1991), 167–95; B. F. Meyer et al., 'Jesus', *ABD* iii. 773–812; E. P. Sanders, *The Historical Figure of Jesus* (London: Penguin Press, 1993).

guard against the illusion that our research could yield a nugget of original, uninterpreted facts about Jesus, historical data which somehow preceded all later 'dogmatic' beliefs and affirmations about him. Human experience (and, as we have recalled above, personal knowledge) is never like that. No one (and no instrument, not even a camera) can ever record and communicate the uninterpreted, unmediated, 'hard' reality of somebody (or, for that matter, of something). Historically there never was an uninterpreted, 'untheological' Jesus. Here, as elsewhere, there was no given that was not yet interpreted. Right from their earliest encounters with him, decades before the Synoptic Gospels were written, the first disciples, and then subsequent disciples, necessarily interpreted Jesus and their experience of him. When Mark, Matthew, and Luke came to put the traditions into gospel shape, they were using material in which, so to speak, the input from Jesus himself and various responses to him were inextricably intertwined. It cannot be otherwise with our human experience of a historical figure. Not even oral reports from the very first meetings with someone can ever give us the 'pure' story of that person, free from any later significance that becomes attached to him or her. No one's reality can ever be captured and exhausted through such initial acquaintance.

Mark, Matthew, and Luke themselves have their personal attitudes towards and relationship with Jesus or at least with the risen and exalted Christ. (There are no good grounds for holding that any of them enjoyed personal contacts with Jesus during his earthly existence.) They write for a Christian community, and as believers share the new life in Christ. Yet this involvement does not disqualify their Gospels as hopelessly compromised by their dedication to the central figure of their works. Composing their story of Jesus 'from the inside', as those who wish to live and share the good news, does not make their versions of Jesus inferior to that of some hypothetical Greek or Roman historian who might have written about Jesus 'from the outside', as a self-styled neutral observer and one 'untainted' by Christian belief. Mark, Matthew, and Luke should be read and interpreted with their involvement in mind. But their commitment, so far from discrediting them, serves to enhance their testimony, in particular for those open to hearing it with faith.[4]

This chapter prioritizes a historical approach through the Synoptic Gospels but in no way wishes to exclude the need to complement such an approach with theological, literary, liturgical, and spiritual reflection. Let me explain. Historical criticism seeks to move from the gospel texts (stage three), through the period of oral or written transmission of the traditions (stage two), and back to the events in which Jesus himself was involved (stage one). This is to use our texts as historical windows which open on to their pre-history and allow us to exercise our imagination in reconstructing the past which led to the formation of these texts. Historical reconstruction goes astray, however, when, in the name of getting at 'the facts behind the texts', it leaves the Gospels in fragments and ignores both the overall theological intention of the evangelists and the literary intention of their texts. The theological and literary whole is greater than the sum of its (historical) parts. Redaction and composition criticism rightly attend to the authorial intentions of the evangelists. What they wish to proclaim and witness about Jesus for their particular readership emerges, however, not just from a mass of specific details but also from the entire scope of their Gospels. At the same time, their texts in their final form are works which have a life of their own, with their own total structure, direction, and characteristics. They are complete narratives to be evaluated also in their own literary right.

The gospel texts function liturgically and spiritually in ways that go beyond 'merely historical' considerations. On the one hand, these texts refer back to Jesus and his earthly reality. On the other hand, however, what they say about him also acts as a mirror for our lives. The stories of Jesus' birth, activity, passion, death, and resurrection have constantly

---

[4] See H. R. Niebuhr's salutary warning about the way in which the interpretations offered by history 'from the outside' can be much inferior to those offered by history 'from the inside': *The Meaning of Revelation* (New York: Macmillan, 1941), 59–73. This chapter or the previous chapter might have included a lengthy digression on the history–faith issue, which I have addressed in earlier publications: *Foundations of Theology* (Chicago: Loyola University Press, 1971), 64–112, and *Fundamental Theology* (London: Darton, Longman & Todd, 1981), 156–60.

evoked in believers and others the 'I was/am there' feeling.
When heard during the Church's liturgy or meditated on
during personal prayer, the gospel stories invite their hearers
and readers to interact imaginatively with them. Thus they
also function as critical mirrors for the ways we view ourselves, the Church, and our world. Just as the evangelists
themselves interpreted the traditions about Jesus 'from the
inside', so contemporary readers and hearers are challenged
to interact with the gospel texts 'from the inside'.

After these preliminaries let us turn to the sense of mission
and of self that the Synoptic Gospels would reasonably
encourage us to recognize in the earthly Jesus. The data are
often difficult to assess and the modern secondary literature
is vast. In what follows I will sketch what appear to be solidly
defensible conclusions about Jesus and his own estimate of
his work and personal identity.

Proclaimer of the Kingdom

Few claims are more historically certain about Jesus than
that he proclaimed a theme which was rare in first-century
Judaism (and, for that matter, would be rare in the NT outside
the Synoptic Gospels): the kingdom or royal reign of God.
Where the OT favoured the language of God ruling as divine
'King' (e.g. Ps. 5: 2; 10: 16; 24: 7–10; 29: 10; 47: 2, 6–7; 48:
2; 74: 12; 84: 3; 95: 3; 98: 6; 145: 1; 149: 2; Isa. 6: 5; 41: 21;
44: 6) over that of the divine kingdom (e.g. Dan. 2: 44; 4: 3;
7: 27; Wis. 6: 4; 10: 10; Ps. 145: 11–13), Jesus never spoke of
God as 'King' but frequently of the divine kingdom, whether
as already present (e.g. Matt. 12: 28 = Luke 11: 20; Luke 17:
20–1), or as to come in the future (Mark 1: 15 = Matt. 4: 17;
Matt. 6: 10 = Luke 11: 2; Mark 9: 1 parr.). Through this
image, Jesus expressed the time and place where the divine
power and will would hold sway. On his lips 'the kingdom'
was practically a way of talking of God as Lord of the world
and God's decisive, climactic intervention to liberate sinful
and suffering men and women from the grip of evil and give
them a new and final age of salvation. The tension that was
apparently there in Jesus' own preaching between the

kingdom as already present and as still to come finds no clear parallel in Judaism.[5] His parables, miracles, and other works were integral to Jesus' message of the present and coming kingdom. The parables (e.g. Mark 4: 1–34 parr.; Matt. 13: 44–50; Luke 15: 3–32) were not merely about the kingdom; they mediated the kingdom with its challenge and grace. Even after the work not only of R. Bultmann, C. H. Dodd, J. Jeremias, and A. Jülicher but also of J. D. Crossan, J. R. Donahue, R. W. Funk, J. Lambrecht, B. Scott, M. A. Tolbert, D. O. Via, and A. Wilder, problems remain about the background and interpretation of the gospel parables. But one cannot fairly dismiss them as peripheral to Jesus' earthly ministry. The parables were challenging addresses and essential events in that ministry for the kingdom—stories that called their hearers to repentance, enacted the divine forgiveness, and mediated religious transformation.[6] The telling of parables was one of the distinctive characteristics of Jesus' work for the kingdom.

All three Synoptic Gospels recall not only that Jesus worked miracles but also that his miraculous deeds were powerful signs of the kingdom, inextricably bound up with his proclamation of the kingdom. His healings and exorcisms were compassionate salvific gestures, the first fruits of the presence of the kingdom which manifested the power of

---

[5] See J. Gnilka, 'Réflexions d'un chrétien sur l'image de Jésus tracée par un contemporain juif', in Commission Biblique Pontificale, *Bible et christologie* (Paris: Cerf, 1984), 197–217, at 213. The pre-Jesus absence of such tension between the present and future reign of God must be seen against the wider fact that prior to him there was little talk of the divine kingdom as such: see D. C. Duling, 'Kingdom of God, Kingdom of Heaven', *ABD* iv. 49–69, at 50. On the OT metaphor of God as 'King', see M. Z. Brettler, *God is King* (Sheffield: JSOT Press, 1989). On Jesus and the kingdom of God see D. E. Aune, 'Eschatology (Early Christian)', *ABD* ii. 594–609, esp. 599–602; G. R. Beasley-Murray, *Jesus and the Kingdom of God* (Exeter: Paternoster, 1986); B. Chilton, *God in Strength: Jesus' Announcement of the Kingdom* (Sheffield: JSOT Press, 1987); Gnilka, *Jesus von Nazaret*, 87–165; M. D. Hooker, 'Kingdom of God', in R. J. Coggins and J. L. Houlden (eds.), *A Dictionary of Biblical Interpretation* (London: SCM Press, 1990), 374–7; G. Lohfink, 'Die Not der Exegese mit der Reich-Gottes-Verkündigung Jesu', *Theologische Quartalschrift*, 168 (1988), 1–15. In the kingdom the 'missing' king is the Father (e.g. Luke 11: 2 par.) of whom more in Ch. 5 below; see I. H. Marshall, *Jesus the Saviour* (London: SPCK, 1990), 224–5.

[6] See J. R. Donahue, 'The Parables of Jesus', *NJBC* 1364–9.

God's merciful rule already operative in and through his person. Matthew edited Q material to present Jesus as saying: 'if it is by the Spirit of God that I cast out demons, then the kingdom of God has come upon you' (Matt. 12: 28; see Luke 11: 20). His exorcisms, in particular, manifested the strength of the Spirit (Mark 3: 22–30) which, according to the Synoptics, empowered Jesus' ministry for the kingdom, right from his baptism.[7]

Both in his preaching and in his miraculous deeds, Jesus himself was inseparably connected with the inbreaking of the divine kingdom. In his person and presence God's rule had come and was coming. As speaker of the parables, for example, he belonged to the kingdom and effected its powerful presence.

Mark, Matthew, and Luke clearly saw Jesus and his activity in that way. A saying about God's kingdom coming with power (Mark 9: 1 = Luke 9: 27) could be easily applied to Jesus himself as the Son of man coming in his kingdom (Matt. 16: 28). High implications about Jesus' function and identity emerge from the way the Synoptic Gospels portray his role for the kingdom.

But how did Jesus himself think of his mission? Did he see himself as fulfilling at least the popular hope for the 'prophet like Moses' (Deut. 18: 15; see Acts 3: 22–6; 7: 37), and as prophetically commissioned and empowered to bring good tidings to an afflicted people (Isa. 61: 1–3; see Luke 6: 20–1 = Matt. 5: 3–6; Matt. 11: 5 = Luke 7: 22)? His audience and contemporaries recognized his prophetic role (Matt. 21: 9–11, 46; Mark 6: 15; 8: 28; Luke 7: 16, 39; 24: 19; see John 6: 14; 7: 40). At times Jesus himself expressed his work in prophetic terms (Mark 6: 4 parr.; Luke 13: 33 par.). Matthew and Luke develop the theme of Jesus as prophet, in particular, by presenting him as empowered by the Spirit and as a

---

[7] See D. Senior, 'The Miracles of Jesus', ibid. 1369–73. To Senior's bibliography one can add: Evans, 'Life-of-Jesus Research', 17–34; H. C. Kee, *Medicine, Miracle and Magic in N T Times* (Cambridge: Cambridge University Press, 1986); R. Latourelle, *The Miracles of Jesus and the Theology of Miracles*, trans. M. J. O'Connell (Mahwah, NJ: Paulist Press, 1988); G. O'Collins, *Interpreting Jesus* (London: Geoffrey Chapman, 1983), 54–9; K. Rahner, *Foundations of Christian Faith*, trans. W. V. Dych (London: Darton, Longman & Todd, 1978), 254–64. R. Swinburne (ed.), *Miracles* (London: Collier Macmillan, 1989).

'Moses-like' prophet.[8] Both these evangelists (using traditions which may well go back to Jesus himself) obviously
did not think of Jesus merely as one prophet among others
(Matt. 12: 41 = Luke 11: 32; Matt. 13: 16–17 = Luke 10:
23–4; Matt. 11: 12–13 = Luke 16: 16). But what sense did
Jesus himself have of his own prophetic commission and
authority? Are there any hints of how he interpreted himself,
his function, and his destiny?

He seems to have conceived his mission as that of one who
had been sent by God (Mark 9: 37 parr.; 12: 6 parr.; Matt.
10: 40 = Luke 10: 16; Matt. 15: 24), to break Satan's power
over the world (Mark 3: 23–7 parr.; Luke 10: 17–18), and to
realize the final rule of God (Matt. 12: 28 = Luke 11: 20).
At times Jesus went beyond a normal prophetic 'I was sent'
to say 'I came' (Mark 2: 17 parr.; Matt. 11: 19; Luke 12: 49).
He presented himself as something 'greater than' a prophet
like Jonah or the classically wise king, Solomon (Matt. 12:
41–2 = Luke 11: 31–2). Despite evidence that he distanced
himself from talk of being the Messiah (e.g. Mark 8: 27–31
parr.; 15: 2 parr.), it is quite implausible to think that Jesus
was oblivious of performing a messianic mission. He gave
some grounds for being seen to have made such a claim (Mark
11: 1–11 parr.). Otherwise it is very difficult to account both
for the charge against him of being a messianic pretender
(Mark 14: 61; 15: 2, 9, 12, 18, 26, 32 parr.) and for the
ease with which his followers began calling him 'the Christ'
immediately after his death and resurrection. Was there no
messianic consciousness betrayed by accounts of his ministry
(e.g. Matt. 11: 2–6 = Luke 7: 18–23), or by his exegesis of
the Messiah being David's lord and hence more than just
David's son by human descent (Mark 12: 35–7)? It is reasonable to trace both Matt. 11: 2–6 (= Luke 7: 18–23) and Mark
12: 35–7 back to the earthly Jesus. On the second text I. H.
Marshall is a reliable guide[9] for those who argue that Jesus
implied something about himself when contrasting the
Davidic descent with the higher status of the Messiah. As
regards the first text, Matthew has shaped the context for

---

[8] See J. D. G. Dunn, *Christology in the Making* (London: SCM Press, 2nd edn.,
1989), 139–40.
[9] See Marshall, *Jesus the Saviour*, 204–6.

Jesus' answer about the expected messianic signs ('the blind receive their sight', etc.), but that does not stand in the way of this Q passage ultimately deriving from Jesus himself. Still active in the background of any discussion of Jesus' messianic activity is the 1901 work by William Wrede (1859–1906). *Das Messiasgeheimnis in den Evangelien* (ET: *The Messianic Secret* (Cambridge: Clarke, 1971)). Wrede argued *inter alia* that the earthly Jesus never made messianic claims. When in the post-resurrection situation the disciples came to believe in Jesus as Messiah and wished to explain why his messianic status had hitherto remained unknown, they created the messianic secret: Jesus had deliberately concealed his messiahship during his ministry. Mark then incorporated into his Gospel this 'explanation', which subsequently turned up also in Matthew and Luke. With all kinds of variations, different scholars have followed Wrede in arguing for (1) the non-messianic character of Jesus' ministry and (2) the centrality of the messianic secret in Mark's Gospel. As regards (2), one should observe not only that parts of this Gospel stress the publicity surrounding Jesus' ministry (from Mark 1: 28 on), but also that Mark's motif of secrecy goes well beyond the messianic question. His theory of hiddenness in relation to Jesus' parables probably reflects the obstacles early Christians experienced in their mission (Mark 4: 1–34). The misunderstanding, shown by the male disciples from Mark 6: 52 on, has to do with Jesus' suffering destiny and the need for the male disciples to be spiritually healed before they can fully receive revelation. Some elements of a messianic secret turn up: in the commands to demons and disciples not to speak about Jesus' identity (e.g. Mark 1: 25; 8: 30) and in the commands to keep silent after a miraculous cure—at least where those commands are apparently obeyed (e.g. Mark 5: 43; 8: 26) and not disobeyed (e.g. Mark 1: 45; 7: 36). All in all, however, any messianic secret is at best a minor motif in Mark and nothing like the sole key to his theology.[10]

[10] See J. L. Blevins, *The Messianic Secret in Markan Research 1901–1976* (Washington, DC: University of America Press, 1981); D. J. Harrington, 'The Gospel According to Mark', *NJBC* 596–8; H. Räisänen, *The 'Messianic Secret' in Mark's Gospel* (Edinburgh: T. & T. Clark, 1990).

This still leaves us with question (1), the actual messianic (or non-messianic) character of Jesus' ministry. In trying to get a fix on how Jesus viewed his mission, there are, as we have seen above, both specific texts (see also Matt. 8: 11) and circumstantial arguments which converge towards the conclusion that Jesus was conscious of his messianic role. Instead of dwelling directly, however, on his awareness of his prophetic and messianic mission, it may be more illuminating to fill out in some detail what realizing the *present* and *final* rule of God entailed for him.

Personal Authority

Jesus so identified himself with the message of God's kingdom that those who responded positively to this message committed themselves to him as disciples. To accept the inbreaking rule of God was to become a follower of Jesus. With authority Jesus encouraged men and women to break normal family ties and join him in the service of the kingdom (Mark 10: 17–31 parr.; Mark 3: 31–5 parr.; Luke 8: 1–3). By relativizing in his own name family roles and relationships, Jesus was scandalously out of conformity with the normal expectations of his and other societies.

The personal authority with which Jesus taught and performed his miracles was blatant. Unlike normal miracle workers in Judaism, he did not first invoke the divine intervention but simply went ahead in his own name to heal or deliver people from diabolic possession. He likewise spoke with his own authority, prefacing his teaching with 'I say to you' (Matt. 5: 21–44 parr.) and not with such prophetic rubrics as 'thus says the Lord' or 'oracle of the Lord'. At times Jesus introduced his sayings with an 'Amen' (e.g. Matt. 5: 18; Mark 3: 28; Luke 4: 24). As an introduction, this use of 'Amen' is rare but attested in pre-Christian Judaism. Even though it is not unique to Jesus, this habit also gave a sense of special authority to the sayings which followed. But it was above all the 'objects' over which he claimed authority that were startling.

Either by what he said or by what he did (or both), Jesus claimed authority over the observance of the sabbath (Mark

2: 23–8; 3: 1–5 parr.), the temple (Mark 11: 15–17 parr.; see
Mark 11: 27–33 parr.), and the law. A unique sacredness
attached to that day (time), place, and code. Let me briefly
recall some aspects of Jesus' attitude towards the law and the
temple.

He took it on himself not only to criticize the oral law for
running counter to basic human obligations (Mark 7: 9–13
par.), but also to set aside even the written law on such matters
as retribution, divorce, and food (Matt. 5: 21–48 par.; Mark
7: 15, 19 par.) It is admittedly difficult to establish much
about Jesus' temple-saying (Mark 14: 57–9 parr.; see Acts 6:
13–14). But it involved some claim that his mission to Israel
was to bring a new relationship between God and the people
which would relativize the central place of their present
relationship, the temple in Jerusalem.

At least on a level with Jesus' astonishing assertion of
personal rights over the central time, place, and rule of Jewish
life was his willingness to dispense with the divinely established channels for the forgiveness of sins (temple offerings
and the priestly authorities) and usurp God's role by forgiving sins in his own name—either by word (Mark 2: 1–12
parr.; 3: 28; Luke 7: 47–9) or by table-fellowship with sinners
(e.g. Luke 15: 1–2).

Thus, in proclaiming the present divine rule, Jesus repeatedly and in a variety of ways claimed or at least implied a
personal authority that can be described as setting himself
on a par with God. After he gave such an impression during
his ministry, one can understand members of the Sanhedrin
charging Jesus with blasphemy; they feared that Jesus was a
false prophet and was even usurping divine prerogatives
(Mark 14: 64 parr.).[11]

What of Jesus and the *final* rule of God? Apparently he
saw his ministry not only as embodying the climax of God's
purposes for Israel (Mark 12: 2–6 parr.) but also as involving

[11] See A. E. Harvey, *Jesus and the Constraints of History* (Philadelphia: Westminster, 1982), 170–1. E. P. Sanders, however, holds that Jesus merely gave the
impression of being ambitious for kingship: *Jesus and Judaism* (London: SCM Press,
1985), 317–18. On some aspects of Jesus' claims to authority, see B. Chilton, 'Amen',
ABD i. 184–6; G. F. Hasel, 'Sabbath', *ABD* v. 850–6, at 854–5; H. Weder, 'Disciple,
Discipleship', *ABD*, ii. 207–10.

his own *uniquely authoritative role* in bringing others to share in the eschatological kingdom: 'I assign to you as my Father assigned to me, a kingdom that you may eat and drink at my table in my kingdom, and sit on thrones judging the twelve tribes of Israel' (Luke 22: 29–30; see Matt. 19: 28). Here Jesus testified to himself as critically significant in the full message of the coming kingdom. His testimony to himself is an essential part of that message. Other such claims to be decisive for our final relationship with God got expressed in terms of 'the Son of man': 'I tell you, every one who acknowledges me before men, the Son of man will acknowledge before the angels of God. But he who denies me before men will be denied before the angels of God' (Luke 12: 8–9 = Matt. 10: 32–3; see Matt. 12: 32). The future and final salvation of human beings was understood to depend on their present relationship with Jesus. Here high claims about Jesus' function and identity were hardly less than explicit. He left us some self-conscious teaching about his own person. At the same time, Jesus (implicitly) recognized that he did not know the time of the end (Mark 13: 32), and (explictly) admitted that to sit at his right or left hand in his coming glory was not a grace that he could grant (Mark 10: 40).

Chapter 5 will examine Jesus' sense of his own unique sonship and his claim that our relationship to him determines our relationship to God as Father. This present chapter will shortly address itself to the question of 'the Son of man'. At this point I wish to emphasize only Jesus' conviction of his own decisive authority for one's relationship to God here and hereafter. This conviction about his authoritative role for human salvation emerges as even more startling, if we agree that Jesus identified himself with the Son of man who was to come 'with the clouds of heaven' (Mark 14: 62), 'with great power and glory' (Mark 13: 26), was to 'send out the angels and gather his elect' (Mark 13: 27), and, sitting upon 'his throne of glory' (Matt. 19: 28; 25: 31), was to judge the nations (Matt. 25: 31–46). This language about the coming Son of man portrays Jesus acting in the final scenario of human salvation as supremely authoritative—in fact, as the divinely authorized judge or even as the divine judge. As we shall see in Chapter 6, the early Church thought of

Jesus as the divine judge to come. But did the earthly Jesus think so and claim this for himself? One can (1) deny that the sayings about the coming Son of man go back to the earthly Jesus, or else (2) join Bultmann in arguing that, in speaking of such a figure, Jesus expected someone distinct from himself, an apocalyptic Son of man for whom he was simply paving the way. Hypothesis (2) lacks plausibility. Who was this distinct figure (with such an awesome role to play) supposed to be? Jesus never gave a hint of playing the forerunner to anyone else except God. Hypothesis (1) will be considered below.

To sum up. Jesus saw himself as *the* prophet and messianic agent commissioned by God to bring about the definitive divine rule. Jesus not only understood the inbreaking kingdom to be inextricably tied up with his presence, words, and works, but he also stated that the way human beings related to him would decide their definitive state before God. He may well have also claimed to be the coming Son of man, who was to enjoy the divine prerogative of judging all people.

Son of Man

Sixty-nine times in the Synoptic Gospels Jesus calls himself (the) 'Son of man', a Greek expression which in its Aramaic (and Hebrew) background could be an oblique way for indicating the speaker's own self (e.g. Matt. 8: 20), or else simply mean 'someone' or 'a human being' (as in Ps. 8: 4, where it is a poetic variant for 'man'). In Dan. 7: 13–14 the 'Son of man' seems to symbolize the angels (perhaps the archangel Michael) and/or the righteous and persecuted Jews who will be vindicated and given authority by God (Dan. 7: 18, 21–2, 27; 10: 13, 21; 12: 1), rather than function as one individual, heavenly figure who represents the people. (For the sake of strict accuracy, we should note that within Dan. 7: 13–14 'the one like a Son of man' is not personally linked with suffering, still less with death.) What is clear from the evidence is that 'Son of man' did not function in pre-Christian messianic expectations as a title for a deliverer expected to come in the last times. It was not even a sharply defined concept, with a specific content and reference.[12]

According to the Synoptic Gospels, Jesus referred to himself as 'Son of man' in three contexts, each with its own circle of fairly distinct meanings. He used this self-designation of (1) his earthly work and its (frequently) humble condition (e.g. Mark 2: 10, 28 parr.; Matt. 11: 19 = Luke 7: 34; Matt. 8: 20 = Luke 9: 58); (2) his coming suffering, death, and resurrection (Mark 9: 9, 12; 14: 21, 41, and, above all, Mark 8: 31; 9: 31; 10: 33–4 parr.); (3) his future coming in heavenly glory to act with sovereign power at a final judgement (e.g. Mark 8: 38; 13: 26–7 parr.; Matt. 24: 27 = Luke 17: 24; Matt. 25: 31–2; see John 5: 27).

These classifications show how 'the Son of man' served as a way of indicating Jesus' importance and even universal relevance. This was especially true of the class (3) sayings. In other words, 'Son of man' was used to say what Jesus did rather than what he was. It was not and did not become a title in the normal sense—at least not on the lips of Jesus himself.

At the same time, the evangelists (and/or their sources) do not always seem to distinguish 'Son of man' sharply from 'Christ/Messiah' or 'Son of God'. In John's Gospel the expression gains a very significant element, not to be found in the Synoptic Gospels for any of the three meanings listed above: 'the Son of man' is a personally pre-existent figure (e.g. John 3: 13; 6: 62).

But what of Jesus himself? Did any or all of the three classes of self-referential sayings derive from what he said in his ministry? Waves of debate have flooded across the issue. A few scholars have even attempted to prove that none of these sayings came from Jesus himself. But there remain good and convergent reasons for maintaining that, while there was some editorial reworking, Jesus did speak of himself as 'Son of man', filled the term with his own meanings, and was responsible for the three classes of 'Son of man' sayings listed

---

[12] On the Son of man see R. E. Brown, *NJBC* 1058; Dunn, *Christology in the Making*, 65–97; J. A. Fitzmyer, *A Wandering Aramean* (Missoula, Mont.: Scholars Press, 1979), 143–60; D. R. A. Hare, *The Son of Man Tradition* (Minneapolis: Fortress Press, 1990); B. Lindars, 'Son of Man', in *A Dictionary of Biblical Interpretation*, 639–42; Marshall, *Jesus the Saviour*, 73–120; Meier, *NJBC* 1324–5.

above. Along with the way he used the image of the kingdom
of God and, as we shall see later, that of God as Father, we
have here the third classic example of Jesus taking an
inherited expression and using it massively but in his own
way.

First, we do not find others ever describing, addressing, or
confessing Jesus as the Son of man apart from four marginal
cases (Acts 7: 56; Rev. 1: 13; 14: 14; Heb. 2: 6). In the last
three cases we are dealing with quotations from the OT; it is
only in Acts 7: 56 that 'Son of man' functions as a title; in the
Gospels themselves other people address and speak about
Jesus in a variety of ways, but never as 'Son of man'. Now if
the early Church had freely created the Son of man sayings,
it would be puzzling that this designation for Jesus is not
found on the lips of others. The puzzle disappears once we
agree that we have here a genuine historical recollection: only
Jesus used the term, and the evangelists and their sources
faithfully recorded that fact.

Second, the Son of man sayings in which Jesus refers to
his earthly activity are attested by both Mark (e.g. Mark 2:
10, 28) and Q (Matt. 8: 20 = Luke 9: 58; Matt. 11: 19 =
Luke 7: 34). The sayings dealing with the coming or apocalyptic Son of man likewise turn up in Mark (8: 38; 13: 26; 14:
62) and Q (e.g. Matt. 24: 27 = Luke 17: 24). This double
strand of tradition or multiple attestation can encourage us
to attribute to Jesus at least class (1) and class (3) of the Son
of man sayings.

Third, there was some Jewish background to Jesus' Son of
man sayings, but there was scarcely any follow-up in the
emerging Church. Later on the Fathers of the Church would
use the term as a way of referring to Christ's humanity as
opposed to his divinity or to his being the Son of God. But
in the first century the designation does not seem to have
been useful in preaching the good news. It does not appear
in credal and liturgical formulas. It was too flexible and even
vague: as we have seen, it ranges from the mysterious heavenly being of Daniel 7 to simply serving as a circumlocution
for 'I'. Linguistically, it was a particularly odd expression for
Greek-speaking people. The fact that the designation was
strange and unsuitable for the early Church's life and ministry

suggests that the Son of man sayings did not derive from groups in the Church but from another source, which could only really be Jesus himself.

Fourth, as we have seen, the sayings about the coming Son of man sometimes imply a certain differentiation between this figure and Jesus. Thus Luke reports Jesus as declaring: 'Every one who acknowledges *me* before men, *the Son of man* also will acknowledge before the angels of God' (Luke 12: 8). Matthew modifies this Q saying to read: 'Every one who acknowledges *me* before men, *I also* will acknowledge before my Father who is in heaven' (Matt. 10: 32). Apparently Luke has preserved the original form of the saying, which indicates a certain unity of function between Jesus himself and the Son of man but at the same time introduces some differentiation between the two figures.

The differentiation makes sense once we recognize that it recalls a turn of phrase actually used by Jesus to distinguish his present preaching from his future judging. The distinction had its point in the historical context of his ministry, but not later in the post-Easter situation where believers acknowledged the personal unity between the risen Jesus and the Son of man to come in glory. Matthew's modification reflects precisely that shift.

Fifth, there are some unusual features about the preservation of the Son of man sayings. The three classes are not blended together. Thus (2) the passion predictions about the Son of man do not go beyond the death and resurrection to include (3) statements about the future coming of the Son of man. Further, the sayings about God's kingdom and, specifically, the parables never introduce the Son of man. As some wit put it, 'the kingdom has no Son of man, and the Son of man has no kingdom'. (A partial exception to this comes in Matthew's story of the final judgement in which the Son of man (25: 31) is also called 'the king' (25: 34, 40).) The absence of a clear and strong connection between the Son of man and the divine kingdom is puzzling. After all Daniel 7 was relevant for the functions of the Son of man and the Danielic imagery had included God's kingdom (Dan. 2: 44; 4: 3; 7: 27).

What are we to make of this curious independence of the three classes of Son of man sayings and the separation of the kingdom sayings from the Son of man sayings? These two features can be explained if we see the Gospels (and the traditions behind them) accurately preserving here distinctions which genuinely went back to Jesus' actual preaching and teaching. If early Christians, however, created the Son of man sayings, why did they not also feel free to blend the different classes of such sayings and also combine them with sayings about the kingdom of God? If they were the real authors of these sayings, why did they stop short in the way they used them?

Self-identity

In short, despite all the debates over the Son of man, it still seems that a good case can be made for holding that the term, with the three classes of sayings attached to it, goes back to Jesus himself. For our purposes here his claim to be the coming Son of man who will exercise the divine prerogative of judging all peoples is the most significant of the three classes of sayings. 'The Son of man' (rather than Messiah or Son of God) was Jesus' characteristic way of referring to himself, just as he characteristically called God 'Father' and characteristically spoke of his mission as being in the service of God's 'kingdom' or rule. Jesus' innovative reinterpretation of 'kingdom', 'Father' (and by implication 'Son of God'), and 'Son of man' sums up much of the thrust of his message.

Any insistence on the Son of man sayings coming from Jesus should not, of course, cloak the fact that he was not concerned to proclaim himself directly. His mission was to announce God and the coming of the divine rule. The present and future kingdom was the immediate theme of Jesus' message, even if that message also involved some astonishing implications about his own person.

As regards the Son of man sayings, even if for argument's sake we were to entertain the quite implausible position that none of them derives from Jesus, we would still be left with the other sayings (and actions) which we have recalled as exhibiting an extraordinary, if mostly implicit, assertion of personal authority in mediating God's present and future rule. Not only through the sayings about the future Son of

man but also in other ways Jesus claimed what can only
be called divine prerogatives. The Gospels, or at least the
Synoptics, do not directly concern themselves with Jesus'
consciousness of his own identity. Nevertheless, his startling
claims about his function for the present and coming kingdom
leave us with the question: who did he think he was?

Chapter 5 will explore what can be recovered about Jesus'
sense of divine sonship. Here let me add that, whatever we
recognize the earthly Jesus to have claimed implicitly or
explicitly about himself, he did not present himself as the
pre-existent Creator of the world.

We have already noted (Chapter 2) and will see more of the
way early Christians attributed to Christ not only the decisive
role in human salvation but also eternal pre-existence and a
share in the very creative power of God (e.g. 1 Cor. 8: 6; Col.
1: 16–17; Heb. 1: 2–3). Christ was/is not only the Saviour of
all but also the Creator of all. We might see such a claim
being already asserted when the earthly Jesus in his own
name healed broken bodies, multiplied food for the hungry,
and in other miraculous ways expressed a power over the
created world. However, there was here at best only an
implied claim to power over creation and no claim at all to
eternal pre-existence. Such claims surface in John's Gospel
(e.g. John 5: 17; 8: 58), but these are later theological reflections rather than historical traditions that reach back to Jesus
himself.

Faced with Death

So far the main thrust of this chapter has been to establish
some conclusions about the way Jesus understood himself
and his mission. What of his passion and death? Are there
indications that he anticipated and interpreted his death in
advance? Did he, for instance, in any way suggest that his
violent end would bring God's final reign and prove salvific
for the human race?

One can put the issue in terms of a possible continuity
between the pre-Easter and the post-Easter situation. Is there
any (even partial) continuity between the early Christian
interpretation of Jesus' death and resurrection (e.g. Rom. 3:

24–5; 4: 25; 2 Cor. 5: 18–19) and what he himself intended as
death closed in?

In trying to determine Jesus' intentions as death loomed
up, we should not wrongly suppose that these intentions—or
rather what we can establish about them—provide the only
criterion for acknowledging that Jesus died to save sinful
human beings and for deciding how that death for others
worked or works. There could have been and can be more
meaning and efficacy in his death than he fully and clearly
realized when he accepted that death. Nevertheless, we normally expect the value of important human actions to stem
at least partly from the conscious intentions of the agent in
question.

First things first. At some point Jesus began to anticipate
and accept his violent death. He saw his ministry as standing,
at least partially, in continuity with the prophets, right down
to John, his prophetic precursor from whom he received
baptism. In his prophetic role Jesus expected to die a martyr's
death and apparently expected that to happen in Jerusalem
(Luke 11: 47, 49–51; 13: 34–5 par.; Mark 12: 1–12). Not only
past history but also contemporary events had their lesson to
teach. The violent death of John, someone who was close to
Jesus, showed how perilous a radical religious ministry was
in the Palestine of that time. Jesus would have been extraordinarily naïve not to have seen the danger.

Before his final Passover in Jerusalem opposition had
already built up against him. The order in which most events
in his ministry took place is lost forever, and we may have
doubts about particular sayings deriving from him. Nevertheless, there is clearly a historical core to the various charges
(of violating the sabbath, working miracles through diabolic
power, rejecting the purity regulations, showing contempt
for the divine law, acting as a false prophet, and expressing
blasphemous pretensions) that are reported as being provoked by his radical mission for the kingdom. Then his entry
into Jerusalem and protest in cleansing the temple, if they
did happen at the end of his ministry (Mark 11: 1–19 parr.)
and not at the beginning (John 2: 13–25), were a final, danger-
ous challenge to the religious authorities in the city and the
power they exercised through the temple.

In the light of such material from the Gospels, we can reasonably conclude that at some point Jesus realized that he would lose his life violently and yet went ahead in obedience to his God-given mission. On the eve of his death, the last supper and the agony in the garden strikingly exemplified this free obedience to the Father's will (Mark 14: 17–42 parr.). There are notorious difficulties in settling the details of those episodes. The Synoptic Gospels, not to mention John and Paul on the last supper, do not provide uniform evidence. Nevertheless, it seems reasonable to accept some historical core for the story of Jesus' agonizing decision to accept his destiny.

All in all, unless we revert to a relentless but unjustified scepticism about our sources, we should agree that death was much more than something which simply overtook Jesus out of the Judaean blue. Besides, a completely unexpected and unwanted death would make Calvary look too much like a meaningless catastrophe turned to the divine purposes by an outsider God. It is not that we need to assert that the value of the crucifixion resided wholly—or even principally—in the conscious intentions behind what Jesus did and suffered. Nevertheless, if we strike out any deliberate purpose on his part, we make him into a totally passive or even unwilling victim, whose execution God picked to serve for the redemption of human beings. Such a thesis maintains an extreme separation between (1) the order of being and (2) the order of knowledge. On the level of what was and what was done, Jesus' death brought salvation to the world. Yet he neither knew nor intended anything of this in advance! Even St Paul, although he usually bypassed any reference to Jesus' mind-set before the crucifixion, could not confine himself simply to the order of being and cried out: 'He loved me and gave himself for me' (Gal. 2: 20). It seems both historically correct and theologically sound to acknowledge that Jesus went willingly and to some extent 'knowingly' to his death.

How far, then, did Jesus intend his crucifixion? Was it a totally premeditated death at which he directly aimed as the only possible way of realizing the kingdom? At the end, did he deliberately go to Jerusalem precisely in order to provoke the religious establishment and political authorities into killing him? Rather it appears that Jesus went up to the capital both to make one last effort at bringing his people to their senses and to keep the Passover like any good Palestinian Jew of that time. He did not wish some of his audience to react by rejecting and killing him, but utter loyalty to his vocation prevented him from escaping, even though his actions set him on a deadly collision course. By continuing his ministry, going to Jerusalem, and facing his opponents, Jesus indirectly brought about the fatal situation. He willed his death by accepting it rather than by deliberately and directly planning and courting it.

Granted the truth of this reconstruction, did Jesus hope to achieve something through his martyrdom and what did he expect would follow that death? It was one thing to remain loyal to his mission and accept death. But it was another to find and give meaning to his being repudiated and killed. Did he understand his death to be salvific? If so, in what sense and for whom? Here we need to scrutinize the evidence with care.

1. To begin with, some of the material which supports the conclusion that Jesus anticipated a violent death says little about what he expected to follow it. Thus the passages in which he aligned himself with the fate of prophet-martyrs say nothing either about his own vindication after death or about the saving significance of his martyrdom (Luke 11: 47–51; 13: 31–4). Likewise the parable of the wicked vine-growers expresses a claim to a special authority, associates Jesus with the violent fate of prophets, but does not attribute redemptive value to his coming martyrdom (Mark 12: 1–9).

2. A circumstantial argument, coupled with the passion predictions, can help us at this point. It would seem almost unaccountably odd if Jesus had never reflected on and applied to himself the Jewish conviction that the righteous suffer but God will vindicate them (Pss. 27, 37, 38, 41, 55, 69, 109). In fact Jesus was remembered as having used in prayer the opening words of Psalm 22, perhaps the classic example of this theme of the righteous sufferer (Mark 15: 34 par.). It is important to observe, incidentally, how in Psalm 22 (and the other psalms) the righteous person does *not* die, but after severe sufferings is delivered and vindicated by God in the

course of this life. Wisdom (2–5) testifies to a further development in the theme which apparently had taken place by the time of Jesus: the just man who suffered would be vindicated by a blessed life beyond death.

The three predictions of the passion which Matthew and Luke took over from Mark associate 'the Son of man' with suffering, death, and a vindication through resurrection. These predictions suggest that the earthly Jesus applied to himself the theme of the righteous sufferer: after a violent death he would be vindicated through resurrection.

The Son of man must suffer many things, and be rejected by the elders and the chief priests and the scribes, and be killed and after three days rise again. (Mark 8: 31)

The Son of man will be delivered into the hands of men, and they will kill him; and when he is killed, after three days he will rise. (Mark 9: 31)

The Son of man will be delivered to the chief priests and the scribes, and they will condemn him to death, and deliver him to the Gentiles, and they will mock him, and spit upon him, and scourge him, and kill him; and after three days he will rise. (Mark 10: 33–4)

Frequently these predictions have been flatly dismissed as prophecies after the event. The precise details from Jesus' passion, especially those in the third prediction, clearly look like post-Easter elements. Nevertheless, we should distinguish between the essential content of the predictions and their formulation. Even if they were to a greater or lesser extent formulated by Jesus' followers, they need not simply be later statements retrospectively attributed to Jesus during his ministry. Some of the content could well derive from the earthly Jesus. In fact, the second passion prediction, the shortest and the vaguest of the three, seems likely to be an authentic saying.

Two further items call for attention here. If the predictions are no more than post-Easter interpretations of Jesus' death and resurrection, one early and pervasive piece of interpretation is missing in these predictions as such. It is *not* stated that 'the Son of man must suffer and be killed for us and for our sins, and then rise again'. That standard reflection from the very early Church which Paul endorses repeatedly does not turn up in any of the three passion predictions. Further, the third prediction may give some details which correspond to the actual course of the passion, but they are hardly very precise if they omit one enormously important detail, the killing by crucifixion. What hangs upon these two omissions? Just this. The omissions encourage the view that the passion predictions are by no means totally free inventions which simply reflect both the actual course of historical events and later theology. The community tradition and the evangelist Mark, here as elsewhere, knew their limits in attributing material retrospectively to the earthly Jesus.

Let me pull matters together. We can conclude that (at least to his core group of disciples) Jesus announced his imminent death and affirmed that his Father would quickly vindicate him through resurrection. Such a conclusion says something about Jesus' view of what that death entailed for himself. But what did he expect it would bring to others?

3. The theme of God's kingdom can help us here. It would take a sceptic with nerves of steel to deny the centrality of this theme in Jesus' preaching. From the outset he announced the divine rule to be at hand. It would be false to separate sharply this proclamation of the kingdom from his acceptance of his own victimhood. Many later scholars have endorsed the true aspect of Albert Schweitzer's original insight into the ministry: Jesus saw suffering and persecution as characterizing the coming of that kingdom which he insistently preached. The message of the kingdom led more or less straight to the mystery of the passion. That message entailed and culminated in the suffering ordeal to come: a time of crisis and distress which was to move towards the day of the Son of man (Mark 13 parr.), the restoration of Israel (Matt. 19: 28 par.), the banquet of the saved, and the salvation of the nations (Matt. 8: 11 par.). Thus his arrest, trial, and crucifixion dramatized the very thing which totally engaged Jesus, that rule of God which was to come through a time of ordeal.

At the last supper Jesus linked his imminent death with the divine kingdom: 'Truly, I say to you, I shall not drink again of the fruit of the vine until the day when I drink it new in the kingdom of God' (Mark 14: 25). It is widely agreed that this text has not been shaped by the eucharistic liturgy of the early Church, but comes from Jesus himself at his last meal with his friends. The argument is this: since Jesus interpreted his death in terms of the coming kingdom, he saw that death as a saving event; for he had consistently presented the equation: the kingdom = human salvation.

Is it enough to maintain here a lesser explanation—Jesus announced that his imminent death would not prevent the coming of the kingdom which he had preached? Despite his death, the kingdom was still to come. This lesser version, however, fails to match a feature of Jesus' message which was noted above: the kingdom was to come through a time of ordeal. Against that background it seems reasonable to conclude that Jesus viewed his death as somehow salvific. He integrated it not only into his surrender to his Father but also into his offer of salvation to human beings. Through those words about the kingdom (Mark 14: 25) Jesus wanted to help his disciples grasp some meaning in his death: it was to effect, not jeopardize, the coming of that kingdom.

It is hardly surprising that Jesus would have made such a positive integration between the coming kingdom and his death. As we have seen, the message about the divine reign was inseparable from the person of Jesus. This essential connection between the message of Jesus and his person meant that the vindication of his person in and through death entailed the vindication of God's kingdom, and vice versa.

Together with the kingdom saying from the last supper, we can usefully consider the intentions conveyed by an episode which apparently took place shortly before Jesus' death: the cleansing of the temple. Beyond question, it is difficult to settle all the details of that action and its intended significance. Likewise the different versions of his saying about the destruction of the temple (Matt. 26: 60–1; Mark 14: 57–9; John 2: 19–22; Acts 6: 13–14; see also Mark 13: 1–2 parr.; Matt. 23: 38 par.) make it hard to state with any kind of assurance all that he originally said. Nevertheless, it seems that the point of both his symbolic action and his temple-saying was to call for a radical break with the past. As his death drew near, he announced that the new age of the divine kingdom was dawning. At the very heart of their religious existence he would refashion God's people. Jesus' mission in life and death was to replace the temple and its cult with something better ('not made by hands').[13]

4. To return to the last supper. The 'words of institution', if taken at face value, show Jesus defining his death as a sacrifice which will not only representatively atone for sins but also initiate a new and enduring covenant with God. But here we must reckon with the question: how far have the sources of Paul, Mark, and the other evangelists been shaped by liturgical usages in early Christian communities? In 1 Cor. 11: 23–5 we read: 'The Lord Jesus on the night when he was betrayed took bread, and when he had given thanks, he broke it, and said, "This is my body which is for you. Do this in remembrance of me." In the same way also the cup, after supper, saying, "This cup is the new covenant in my blood. Do this, as often as you drink it, in remembrance of me." '

In Mark's version of the last supper, however, the repeated instructions to perform the Eucharist ('Do this in remembrance of me', and 'Do this as often as you drink it, in remembrance of me') are missing. And—what is more significant for the issue under discussion—the qualification of 'my body' as being 'for you' is also missing. However, unlike the Pauline tradition, Mark describes the blood as being 'poured out for many'. His version runs as follows: 'He took bread, and blessed, and broke it, and gave to them, and said, "Take; this is my body." And he took a cup, and when he had given thanks he gave it to them, and they all drank of it. And he said to them, "This is my blood of the covenant, which is poured out for many" ' (14: 22–4).

Confronted with the differences between the Pauline tradition (to which, apart from adding, apropos of 'my blood', 'which is poured out for you', and not including, apropos of the cup, 'do this in remembrance of me', Luke 22: 19–20 approximates) and the Markan tradition (which is more or less followed by Matthew 26: 26–8), some writers back away from relying too much on the words of institution as accurate

[13] See J. D. G. Dunn, *The Partings of the Ways* (London: SCM Press, 1991), 37–56.

sources for settling the way Jesus understood his death—at least the night before it happened. Whom did Jesus believe to be the beneficiaries of his death? The 'for you' of the Pauline and Lukan tradition indicates the companions of Jesus at the last supper. Of course, in that case he might well have intended the twelve to represent others. Mark (followed by Matthew) has Jesus speaking of his blood 'poured out for many' (= all). But in that case did Jesus mean not merely all Jews but also all Gentiles?

Some modern writers, however, have not let the difficulties stop them from reaching firm conclusions. Hans Küng, for example, believes that the evidence from the last supper accounts points to Jesus' intention to establish a new covenant through the sacrifice of his death:

In the face of his imminent death he interpreted bread and wine—so to speak—as prophetic signs of his death and thus of all that he was, did and willed: of the sacrifice, the surrender of his life. Like this bread, so would his body be broken; like this red wine, so would his blood be poured out. ... And as the head of the family gives a share in the blessing of the meal ... so Jesus gives to his followers a share in his body given up to death ... and [a share] in his blood shed for 'many'. ... The disciples are thus taken up into Jesus' destiny. The meal becomes a sign of a new, permanent communion of Jesus with his followers: a *new covenant* is established.[14]

Küng's position draws support from the fact that both the Pauline–Lukan tradition ('new covenant') and the Markan–Matthean tradition ('the covenant') report Jesus as speaking of a covenant that is instituted through his 'blood' and as echoing key O T passages (e.g. Exod. 24: 3–8; Jer. 31: 31–4).

5. Ultimately, the pressure on us to establish precisely what Jesus said and intended at the last supper can be eased in three ways: by recalling his *characteristic attitudes*, pointing to *contemporary ideas*, and noting *an implication* in early Christian convictions about Jesus' atoning death.

In general the characteristic ways in which persons act and

[14] *On Being a Christian* (London: Collins, 1976), 324–5. See R. F. O'Toole, 'Last Supper', *ABD* iv. 234–41, at 239–40; F. J. Matera, 'Christ, Death of', *ABD* i. 923–5; H. J. Klauck, 'Sacrifice and Sacrificial Offerings (NT)', *ABD* v. 886–91, at 887–8.

speak can fill their deaths with meaning, even when they have
no chance at the end to express their motivation and make
an explicit declaration of intent. Archbishop Oscar Romero
(1917–80), for instance, was abruptly shot dead when celebrating the Eucharist. He had no last-minute opportunity to
blurt out some statement evaluating and interpreting the
death which confronted him. Nevertheless, all that he had
been saying and doing during his three years as archbishop
of San Salvador served to indicate his basic intentions and
fill his martyrdom with significance.

In the case of Jesus, even if he did not explicitly designate
himself as 'the Servant of the Lord', he consistently behaved
as one utterly subject to his Father's will and completely
available for the service of all those who needed mercy and
healing. His words and actions brought divine pardon to
those who felt they were beyond redemption. He never drove
away the lepers, children, sinful women, taxation agents, and
all those anonymous crowds of 'little people' who clamoured
for his love and attention.

Now it would be strange to imagine that the threat of the
passion abruptly destroyed Jesus' resolution to show himself
the servant of others. Rather, a straight line led from his
serving ministry to his suffering death. Even if the community or Mark himself added the words 'to give his life as a
ransom for many', there was a basis in Jesus' life for the
saying 'the Son of man came not to be served but to serve,
and to give his life as a ransom for many' (Mark 10: 45). He
who had shown himself the servant of all was ready to become
the victim for all. And—as many have insisted—that service
was offered especially to the outcasts and the religious pariahs.
Part of the reason why Jesus' ministry led to his crucifixion
stemmed from the fact that he faithfully and scandalously
served the lost, the godless, and the alienated of his society.
The physician who came to call and cure the unrighteous
eventually died as their representative. His serving ministry
to the reprobate ended when he obediently accepted a shameful death between two reprobates. His association with
society's outcasts and failures led to his solidarity with them
in death. In these terms the passion of Jesus became integrated into his mission as a final act of service. In death, as

in life, he served and sacrificed himself for others. Luke 22: 27 ('I am among you as one who serves') is an authentic pointer to this basic pattern in Jesus' behaviour.

Whom did Jesus take to be *the beneficiaries* of his suffering and death? I have argued that at some point in his ministry he did in fact present himself as the Son of man who was to suffer and bring God's final judgement and kingdom. While Jesus understood his fellow Jews to be the primary beneficiaries of the divine salvation mediated through his mission (Matt. 15: 24; see 10: 5–6), his vision was universal. Although he directed his preaching to the chosen people, he called humanity as such to decision. He addressed his Jewish audience as human beings, not as Jews and still less as a holy remnant, some special group of the saved within Judaism. He spoke to them in parables, the language of everyday and a language which has proved itself capable of communicating to the whole human race. He demanded a realistic love towards other human beings in need, a love which was willing to cross racial frontiers (Luke 10: 25–37) and include everyone, even one's enemies (Matt. 5: 43–8 parr.). He called for a new brotherhood and sisterhood which denied any sacrosanct value to family or tribal bonds within Israel: 'Whoever does the will of God is my brother, and sister, and mother' (Mark. 3: 35 parr.). This statement has a universal ring, which we also find in the parable of the tax-collector and the Pharisee (Luke 18: 9–14). There Jesus asserted that the extent of God's generosity had been hitherto ignored: the divine pardon was offered to all.

By rejecting purity regulations (Mark 7: 14–23 par.) which established and preserved the boundaries between Jews and Gentiles, he implied that this distinction had no ultimate significance before God. Hence Jesus' vision of Israel's future entailed 'many coming from east and west to sit at table with Abraham, Isaac, and Jacob in the kingdom of heaven' (Matt. 8: 11 par.). The restoration of Israel (Matt. 19: 28 par.) or Israel's being superseded (Mark 12: 9 parr.), which was to come through Jesus' ministry, meant salvation for the nations. Having lived and preached such a universal vision, at the end Jesus, one can reasonably suppose, accepted in some sense that he would die for all people.

Secondly, *contemporary ideas* also serve as pointers to his
intentions in the face of death. The experiences of the Maccabean martyrs in the second century BC helped to give rise
to an idea which was in the air at the time of Jesus. The
suffering and violent death of just persons could expiate the
sins of others. The martyrdom of even one individual could
representatively atone for the sins of a group (2 Macc. 7:
37–8; 4 Macc. 6: 27–9; 17: 21; 18: 4). Martin Hengel has
marshalled evidence to show how earlier Greek (and Roman)
literature, history, and customs supported the notion that
someone could die for his city or people and so atone for their
sins. In fact the Jewish conviction to this effect which we find
in the Maccabean texts may have been taken over from Greek
sources.[15]

But my point here is not to discuss questions of provenance,
but rather to recall a relevant belief found at the time of Jesus.
Once the threat of violent death loomed up, it would have
been strange if Jesus had never applied to himself that
religious conviction of his contemporaries. Through his martyrdom he could vicariously set right a moral order disturbed
by sin.

Here I should add a parenthesis on the fourth poem about
the Servant of the Lord from the Book of Isaiah (52: 13–53:
12). Although this material dates from the sixth century BC
and could obviously support reflections on vicarious atonement, the text is never *quoted* either by later works of the OT
or by non-canonical books of the intertestamental period.
Even where *allusions* to this poem about the Suffering Servant
can be detected in subsequent texts, we do not find the notion
of a death which representatively atones for others. Nevertheless, Isa. 52: 13–53: 12 helped to shape early Christian
preaching. Eventually the NT was to include ten literal quotations from this poem and around thirty allusions to it.[16]

What conclusion does this parenthesis point to? We should

[15] M. Hengel, 'The Atonement', in *The Cross and the Son of God* (London: SCM
Press, 1986), 189–284; see N. T. Wright, *The Climax of the Covenant* (Edinburgh:
T. & T. Clark, 1991), 60–1.
[16] Those who are impressed by the prominence in early Christian writings of Isa.
52–3 with its motif of vicarious atonement could argue that the most plausible
reason for the prominence of this motif comes from the fact that it goes back to
Jesus himself and his pre-passion sense of his impending death.

be cautious about invoking the fourth poem on the Lord's
Servant to establish contemporary ideas of vicarious atonement which Jesus could have easily applied to himself. As we
have seen Palestinian Judaism of the first century AD included
the belief that the death of a martyr could representatively
atone for the sins of others. But, curiously enough, this case
cannot be so simply proved for the current interpretation of
Isaiah's fourth song of the Suffering Servant. Certainly we
have no clear text from pre-Christian Judaism which speaks
of the Messiah's vicarious suffering in connection with Isaiah
53. That fact by itself does not, of course, rule out Jesus'
applying to himself the Suffering Servant imagery. Yet it is
one thing for him to envisage his vicarious suffering as
Messiah and quite another thing for him to do so in terms of
the Suffering Servant of Isaiah 53.

Further, we should add that pre-Christian notions of representative expiation never envisaged vicarious atonement
coming through a just person's death *by crucifixion*. Death
on a cross, so far from being a possible form of atoning
martyrdom for others, signified being cursed by God as one
who had violated the covenant (Deut. 21: 23; Gal. 3: 13).[17]
Judaism was not prepared for the atoning meaning of the
cross.

Finally, Paul's letters abundantly document the pre-
Pauline tradition that Jesus' crucifixion was a death 'for us',
which representatively atoned for human sin (e.g. 1 Thess. 5:
10; 1 Cor. 15: 3; Rom. 4: 25; 8: 32). As Hengel rightly argues,
we meet in these formulations from the earliest Christian
tradition a conviction that ran clean counter to the pre-
dominant Jewish beliefs. At the time of Jesus the popular
messianic hopes did not include a suffering Messiah. To talk
of a crucified Messiah was real blasphemy. Hence the early
Christians defended something utterly offensive when they
proclaimed that the crucifixion of someone who was executed
precisely as a messianic pretender was in fact a sacrificial
death which atoned representatively for the sins of all.

[17] See G. O'Collins, 'Crucifixion', *ABD* i. 1207–10; see Dunn, *The Partings of
the Ways*, 120, 122–3, 304 n. 29; Hengel, *The Cross and the Son of God*, 93–185. On
Jesus' crucifixion and other aspects of the passion, see R. E. Brown, *The Death of
the Messiah*, 2 vols. (New York: Doubleday, 1994).

How can we account for this understanding of Jesus' crucifixion as the vicarious atoning death of the Messiah that had
universal impact? Would the disciples' encounters with the
risen Jesus alone have been sufficient to trigger off this
interpretation? It would have been enough to have taken the
resurrection simply to mean that Jesus had been vindicated
by God as a prophetic martyr or an innocent sufferer (Wis.
2–5; Rev. 11: 11–12). But the early Christians went much
further than that in recognizing Jesus' crucifixion to be the
representative death of the Messiah which atoned for human
sin. They could hardly have done so, *unless the earthly Jesus
had already in some way claimed to be Messiah and indicated
that his coming death would have such an atoning value.* They
needed, so to speak, all the help they could get to cope
with the scandalous idea that his death on the cross had
representatively atoned for the sins of all.

Conclusion

This chapter has aimed at establishing some conclusions
about the way Jesus viewed his mission, his own person, and
his death. More than just 'a' or even 'the' prophet of God's
kingdom, he acted out his messianic role with an astonishing
sense of his own authority that was partially but not fully
cloaked by his self-presentation as 'Son of man'. Faced with
death, Jesus interpreted it as a representative and redemptive
service for others.

These conclusions have their importance in demonstrating
some continuity between (1) Jesus' sense of his identity and
sense of what his mission (including his death and subsequent
vindication) was to effect and (2) what his followers were to
proclaim about him as Son of God and Saviour of the world.
This proclamation enjoyed some legitimizing basis in his
human history. The post-Easter image of Jesus was partly
supported by the earthly Jesus' own self-image.

Later chapters will fill out matters, above all, by examining
Jesus' divine sonship and the nature of his atoning work for
the advantage of us all. This present chapter has certainly
not raised every question about Jesus' expectations. To have
argued for the authenticity of at least some of the sayings

concerned with the future activity of the Son of man leads, for example, to the further question: how imminent did Jesus hold the coming of the end and the final kingdom to be? On the basis of some sayings (such as Luke 12: 8–9 par.; 12: 40 par.; 18: 8), it seems plausible to conclude that Jesus expected some interval to elapse after his death and before the parousia.[18] At the same time, at the last supper and in Gethsemane he seems to have faced death as one entrusting himself to a situation and a future that were still to some extent unknown. As we shall see, such limits to his knowledge and foreknowledge are precisely part of his being human and not an ugly imperfection from which Jesus must be miraculously preserved.

The earthly history of Jesus ended with his being barbarously victimized on a cross, the place where God's saving revelation seems conspicuously absent. Left to ourselves, we would not go looking for the divine self-communication when Jesus died 'outside the gate' (Heb. 13: 12). We must now see how with other early Christians the second evangelist could believe that this utterly disgraceful death both manifested Jesus' true identity as Son of God (Mark. 15: 39) and brought salvation for others (Mark 10: 45; 14: 24).

[18] See Marshall, *Jesus the Saviour*, 88–90.

4

The Resurrection

✤ ✤

> The resurrection of Christ has been allegorised and
> volatilised in nearly every imaginable way, but the fact
> remains that neither Jesus himself nor the Christian
> community can manifest a distinctive character or true
> identity apart from the resurrection event itself, where
> faith, hope and love are given their vindication and new
> birthright.
>
> (R. R. Niebuhr, *Resurrection and Historical Reason*)

The resurrection of Jesus supplies us with enough questions
to inspire the writing of at least a generous section for a
theological library. As this subject has already drawn from
me five entire books, several chapters for books, many articles,
and various entries for dictionaries, it is not altogether easy
to select those themes which seem particularly pertinent for
a systematic Christology. Nevertheless, it seems that at least
five questions should be raised and answered. (1) What does
the NT claim about Jesus' fate after death? (2) What were
the experiences which gave rise to that claim? (3) What does
his resurrection reveal about Jesus, God, human beings, and
their world? (4) What does the resurrection say about
redemption? (5) Can we throw any light on the nature of
Jesus' resurrection as *the* great divine interaction with human
history?

Some of these questions or at least subaspects of them will
recur in later chapters. The issue of redemption, for instance,
will take up a whole chapter. The five questions, however,
create challenges that are more than sufficient to fill this
chapter.

The Claim

First of all, what does the NT essentially claim when it talks of Jesus' resurrection? When Paul, for instance, quotes an already traditional, four-part formula about Christ's death, burial, resurrection, and appearances (1 Cor. 15: 3–5), what does he mean when he speaks of the resurrection? (*a*) Does this utterance offer information? If so, about what and/or about whom? (*b*) Or does Paul in no way intend to state facts but merely to encourage a fresh understanding or a new way of looking at things? If we settle for (*a*), are we dealing with an explanation ('Christ has been raised') that rests upon several descriptions (above all, 'he died', 'he was buried', and 'he appeared')? Does the description also include the discovery of an empty tomb?

Whenever we set ourselves to interpret language, there are always complexities and sometimes severe difficulties to be faced. Although they know the legal jargon, tortuous phraseology might at least initially leave even some lawyers wondering what certain new laws mean. During election campaigns the general public may need all the help they can get to decode what candidates for political office are really saying. It may take several years of good teaching before even intelligent students become adept at analysing what poets and their poems mean. Legal, political, and literary authors add fresh terms to our standard vocabulary, stretch the meanings of existing words, and in further ways use ordinary language in a new and odd fashion.

Despite all the difficulties, however, public conventions are always available to help us clarify different kinds of discourse and determine what given writers or speakers want to say. Even when they employ highly 'specialized' language, they use words and form sentences in publicly agreed ways. We can understand, at least to some extent, the meaning of their words and sentences by attending to those public criteria. A purely private language, with its completely individual criteria of meaning, would be a contradiction in terms; it would simply be a non-language.

In the case of religious language a recurrent conventional challenge has asked: does such language ever purport to state

facts or make factual claims? Those who assert that all
reality is limited to the visibly perceptible or at least to the
empirically verifiable must logically hold that religious
language can never state facts involving the invisible and
not (directly) empirically verifiable world of God but must
always mean something else. But what of people who accept
a transcendent divine realm that lies beyond the world of
sense experience? Obviously for them religious language
functions in a variety of ways—to praise and thank God,
subscribe to certain principles of conduct, make requests,
interpret the human condition, express hopes (e.g. 'I believe
in the resurrection of the body'), and so forth. But religious
language can also state facts and offer information, as when
a Christian says, 'Jesus was crucified under Pontius Pilate
and buried by Joseph of Arimathea.' Such an utterance
offers some information about things which are held to
have happened, and does not 'merely' encourage a new way
of interpreting something (e.g. our situation before God).
This is not to deny that these statements not only convey
factual information but also carry a religious meaning. In
the context, speaking about Jesus' death and burial may be
tantamount to confessing the religious truth of his genuinely
full incarnation: right through to death and burial, the Son
of God shared our human condition. Being buried and
sealed in a tomb symbolizes the final helplessness of our
situation into which Jesus entered. Nevertheless, clearly
factual claims (about his death and burial) are also communicated by the utterance. Some things are described: e.g.
Jesus' violent death took place through public crucifixion
under the administration of a Roman official named Pontius
Pilate.

How then might we go about clarifying the way language
is being used, for example in 1 Cor. 15: 3–5, so that we can
detect its meaning and truth? All four verbs found in that
formula ('he died, was buried, has been raised, and appeared')
convey, I want to argue, factual information about what happened to Jesus as well as expressing or at least implying the
religious significance of what happened.

A moment's reflection reveals some religious significance
attaching to the statements about Jesus' death and burial. In

a later letter St Paul refers to an already traditional conviction of early Christians that their baptism meant 'dying' and 'being buried' with Christ, so as to walk with him in newness of life (Rom. 6: 3–4). Death and burial take on here an extended meaning: being plunged into the waters of baptism sacramentally re-enacts Christ's own dying and being buried. This passage from Romans, in highlighting a central aspect of the ongoing religious significance of the first Good Friday, presupposes the facts (Jesus' actual death and burial) claimed by the spare kerygmatic formula cited by Paul in 1 Cor. 15. The kerygmatic assertion of these two facts creates the basis for finding a further, religious meaning in Christ's death and burial.

Just as the factuality of 'he died and was buried' in no way excludes a multi-faceted religious meaning to be found in these events, so the even more obvious religious significance of 'he has been raised and appeared' does not rule out the factuality of the resurrection and the appearances— the factuality of a new, personal, transformed existence for the crucified Jesus who manifested himself alive to certain individuals and groups. In the formula cited by Paul, Christ is the subject of all four verbs ('died, was buried, has been raised, and appeared')—the last two ('raised/appeared') being just as informative as the first two ('died/buried'). In the case of both pairs of verbs, the second verb explains and supports our certainty about what the first claims. We know that Christ died because he was buried; burial is a certain pointer to death. We know that Christ has been raised because he appeared bodily alive (in glory) to a number of individuals and groups; dead persons do not appear like that.

There remains this difference, however, between the way the two pairs of verbs function. In their own way both of the first two verbs 'describe' something, or at least assert something which could be described and is in fact described elsewhere in the NT: Christ's death followed by his burial. In the case of the third and fourth verbs, 'he appeared' provides the major grounds for accepting that a prior event had taken place: 'he has been raised.' That event explains why it was possible for him to have appeared. But the canonical NT never attempts to describe the actual event of the resurrection in the way that it tells the story of various appearances of the risen Christ (in Matthew, Luke, John, and Acts).

Thus far we have attended to the essential claim made in the kerygmatic formula of 1 Cor. 15: 4—that Christ has been personally raised or, in terms of the practically dead metaphors behind the verb *egeirō*, 'woken from the permanent sleep of death' or 'set upright'. We should take the form as a 'divine passive', understanding the unspoken agent to be God (e.g. in Rom. 4: 25 where we should complete the clause 'was raised again for our justification' and add 'by God'). Paul himself, as well as the very early tradition behind him, also explicitly states the resurrection claim as 'God raised Jesus' (e.g. Rom. 10: 9; 1 Cor. 6: 14; 15: 15; Gal. 1: 1; 1 Thess. 1: 10). Another (less frequently used) verb which conveys the same claim, *anistēmi* ('to set erect, make to stand up'), is clearly a dead metaphor: Jesus was raised up or rose, in the sense of being put back on his living feet (e.g. Acts 2: 24; 13: 33; 1 Thess. 4: 14; Mark 9: 9, 10, 31). But in this case the extended usage and meaning (of new life after death) has clearly left behind the original metaphor.

The NT, in particular the Pauline letters, frequently applies resurrection language to Jesus' final destiny and situation. Here the Christian Scriptures go well beyond the canonical OT, which employs relatively little resurrection terminology. The non-canonical literature of pre-Christian Judaism (e.g. the Ethiopic Apocalypse of Enoch and the Psalms of Solomon) speaks somewhat more of resurrected life after death, albeit in a variety of ways. The Easter experience of the first Christians greatly developed and dramatically reshaped the old wineskins of the available resurrection language.[1] One major shift affected the traditional expectation

---

[1] See G. W. E. Nickelsburg, *Resurrection, Immortality and Eternal Life in Intertestamental Judaism* (Cambridge, Mass: Harvard University Press, 1972); P. Perkins, *Resurrection* (London: Geoffrey Chapman, 1984), 37–56; D. Kendall and G. O'Collins, 'Christ's Resurrection and the Aorist Passive of *egeirō*', *Gregorianum*, 74 (1993), 725–35. For bibliographies of recent writings on the resurrection see G. Ghiberti and G. Borgonovo, 'Bibliografia sulla resurrezione di Gesù (1973–92)', *La scuola cattolica*, 121 (1993), 171–287; J. Nolland, *Word Biblical Commentary*, xxxv: *Luke 18: 35–24: 53* (Dallas: Word Books, 1993), 1168–73.

of a *general* resurrection. The NT radically modified this tradition by proclaiming that one *individual* (Christ) had been raised from the dead to enjoy a glorious, eschatological existence which actualized in anticipation the final end of others.

Before leaving the basic NT claim about Jesus' own resurrection, we should note how it is conveyed through a variety of idioms: for example, pre-Pauline kerygmatic and confessional formulas (e.g. Rom. 4: 25; 10: 9; 1 Cor. 15: 4); a new (Christian) attribute for God (e.g. Gal. 1: 1); the Easter narratives of the Gospels; a long, reflective argument developed by Paul (1 Cor. 15: 12–58); and missionary speeches in the Acts of the Apostles which centre on Jesus' resurrection (e.g. Acts 2: 31–2; 3: 15; 4: 10; 13: 30, 37). The NT complements these claims about Jesus' personal resurrection by also speaking of his being 'alive' (e.g. Luke 24: 5, 23; Rom. 14: 9), 'exalted' (e.g. Phil. 2: 9) to God's 'right hand' (e.g. Acts 2: 33; Rom. 8: 34; Col. 3: 1; Heb. 8: 1; 10: 12; 12: 2; 1 Pet. 3: 22), or his 'entering' or 'being assumed into glory' (e.g. Luke 24: 26; 1 Tim. 3: 16). Whether it uses resurrection or exaltation language, the NT's primary claim concerns Jesus' own living and glorious destiny after death.

In my *Jesus Risen* I took issue with those like Gordon Kaufman, Rosemary Ruether, and Paul Winter who alter the essential Easter claim and reduce it to this: the NT may appear to be speaking about Jesus and his personal resurrection, but 'really' the early Christians were not talking about Jesus himself but merely referring to some event in their own lives, their new life in the Spirit. Their language about the 'resurrection' should be decoded that way, and in fact made no claim about the post-mortem destiny of Jesus.[2] A couple of years after that book appeared, Robert F. Scuka built on James Mackey and came up with an even more emphatic assertion that the NT resurrection message has

[2] See my *Jesus Risen* (London: Darton, Longman & Todd, 1987) 103–7; id., *What are they Saying about Jesus?* (Ramsey, NJ: Paulist Press, 2nd edn., 1983), 44–51 (on J. Mackey's reduction of the basic Easter claim); and id., *The Resurrection of Jesus Christ: Some Contemporary Issues* (Milwaukee: Marquette University Press, 1993), 1–11. On various challenges to the resurrection claims see S. T. Davis, *Risen Indeed: Making Sense of the Resurrection* (London: SPCK, 1993).

ultimately nothing to do with a presumed event in Jesus' own personal story.[3]

What controls Scuka's reductionism is his theology of grace, according to which through creation God has offered grace always and everywhere, in such a way that everything is given in and with human existence itself. Hence affirming Jesus' resurrection as an event which manifests God's 'special activity' and conveys an 'additional and distinct salvific grace' makes no sense (81–3). In 1 Cor. 15 Paul was simply mistaken in claiming something about Jesus' own post-mortem destiny (92 nn. 7, 8).

En route to this 'explanation', even if three times he allows himself to speak of 'the in-breaking' of God's kingdom, Scuka assures us that by proclaiming the kingdom Jesus was simply drawing attention to the fact that the divine grace is 'present in every here and now' (86–7). (So much for Jesus bringing anything new in his ministry, let alone announcing any future decisive action on the part of God!) The 'coming of the kingdom of God' is not 'to be conceived as an event in time, but instead designates a dimension of the reality of God's presence' (94 n. 23). In the name of his own 'systematic, theological' position, Scuka simply claims this, quite consciously prescinding from what Jesus himself might have 'said', 'meant', or 'believed' (94 n. 24).

As well as refusing to face up to what Jesus actually proclaimed about God's present *and future* kingdom, Scuka also tampers with what the NT announces about the consequences for us of Jesus' resurrection: justification here and eternal life hereafter. He acknowledges the special character of divine grace according to St Paul. But the apostle should have known better and grasped that 'grace is given in and with the conditions of human existence'. 'This is what Paul's doctrine should be understood to mean', Scuka concludes,

---

[3] R. F. Scuka, 'Resurrection: Critical Reflections on a Doctrine in Search of a Meaning', *Modern Theology*, 6 (1989), 77–95. References to this article will be made within the text. Interpretation of biblical (and other classical) texts should keep in mind and work with at least seven factors: the traditions drawn upon, the final authors and their intentions, their audience and context, the text itself, the history of its reception in various traditions, the contemporary contexts, and the contemporary readers. As we shall see, Scuka reduces everything to the last factor (as understood in his own way).

'*regardless of whether he himself recognized this as its implicit meaning*' (95 n. 26; italics mine). Hope for eternal life is dismissed as a (or even the) sinful 'form of self-pre-occupation'. Jesus, John, and Paul are pressed into service as 'implicitly' supporting our author's view that NT and Christian talk about our 'future' resurrection life simply points to the new quality of meaningful existence we can enjoy here and now (88–9).

At the end of the day, all this talk about what Jesus, John, and Paul 'implicitly' understood or 'should' have understood amounts to Scuka himself wanting them to have said, written, or meant something different from what we actually have from them. This wish comes right out into the open when he speaks of 'what the claim concerning Jesus' resurrection *should* be understood to mean, regardless of what the New Testament may have said, or meant' (91–2 n. 4). It would be outrageous to apply this principle to contemporary works in history, law, philosophy, psychology, sociology, and other disciplines: this is what these authors 'should be understood to mean, regardless of what they may have written or meant'. It is just as outrageous to apply the principle to ancient authors, be they Plato, Aristotle, Julius Caesar, Seneca, Josephus, or the authors of the NT. Scuka and other reductionists would not be pleased if this 'method' of interpretation were applied to their own texts: '*this* is what these authors should be understood to mean, regardless of what they may have written, or meant.' The 'regardless-of-what-they-may-have-written-or-meant' principle gives us the licence to find what we want in the work of such reductionists and play fast and loose with what they intend to say.

Some years ago, Renford Bambrough put his finger on the motive which often seems to lie behind the reductionism of Scuka and others. When discussing Matthew Arnold's version of Christianity, Bambrough wrote:

What he [Arnold] does say is that what is usually thought to be meant by the propositions of the Christian religion is unverified and unverifiable, and that therefore those propositions must mean something else that he *can* believe. This is a gross *non sequitur*, but it is not a rare aberration, not an idiosyncratic lapse on the part of

Arnold. It is a common response to the predicament that Arnold found himself in.[4]

In these terms, the title of Scuka's article could be adjusted to read: 'Resurrection: Critical Reflections on a Doctrine in Search of [what I will admit to be a verifiable] Meaning'. He dismisses as 'a theological straightjacket' the normal exegesis of what Christians mean when they affirm Jesus' resurrection (85). But his own doctrine of grace, rigidly based on creation alone ('sola creatione'), operates as a strait-jacket stopping him from recognizing what the NT authors meant when they wrote about Jesus' new, resurrected life after his death and burial. Scuka is sure they cannot possibly mean that by what they are saying. He 'knows' better than the NT authors what those authors meant when they wrote what they did.

Here one can spot a startling difference between modern reductionists like Scuka and traditional sceptics like Celsus (who wrote *The True Discourse* around AD 179) and David Hume (1711–76). Those sceptics acknowledged the *meaning* of the NT assertions, but in the name of reason and common sense they rejected the *truth* of Jesus' resurrection. The reductionists, however, tamper with the meaning of those assertions, and then accept the truth which they have fashioned for themselves.

Grounds for the Claim

Describing the central Easter claim of the NT inevitably raises the question: although we can know what the first Christians were saying about Christ's resurrection, how did they know that what they were saying was true? What grounds did they have for making their claim about the transformed personal life and activity of Jesus after death? New experiences, received and interpreted in the light of factors already effective in the disciples' lives, gave rise to the claims. The new experiences comprised the appearances of the risen Jesus, the discovery of his empty tomb, and the gift of the Holy Spirit. The prior factors through which the first Chris-

---

[4] R. Bambrough, *Reason, Truth and God* (London: Methuen, 1969), 79.

tians interpreted these events came from their Jewish faith, sacred Scriptures, and memories of the earthly Jesus.

As regards the post-resurrection appearances, my stated aim in this present book does not include expanding what I have already published on the subject.[5] My reading of the evidence suggests that a summary of what I have written elsewhere should mention at least the following features of those appearances.

The NT records appearances to individuals and to groups (e.g. 1 Cor. 15: 5–8; Luke 24: 34; Acts 10: 40–1; 13: 30–1; John 20: 11–18). (1) These encounters depended upon the initiative of the risen Jesus (he 'appeared' or 'let himself be seen' rather than 'was seen by' someone). (2) There is a notable 'ordinariness' about the Easter appearances, as reported very briefly by Paul and narrated by the Gospels. Unlike other communications from God, they do not take place during ecstasy (e.g. Acts 10: 9–16; 2 Cor. 12: 2–4), nor in a dream (e.g. Matt. 1: 20; 2: 12–13, 19–20, 22), nor by night (e.g. Acts 16: 9; 18: 9; 23: 11; 27: 23–4). The appearances occur under 'normal' circumstances and without the traits of apocalyptic glory which we find elsewhere (e.g. Mark 9: 2–8; Matt. 28: 3–4). The one exception comes in the way Acts describes Paul's experience on the Damascus Road when he faces 'a light from heaven, brighter than the sun' (Acts 26: 13; see 9: 3; 22: 6, 9). But there is no mention of this phenomenon when Paul himself refers to his encounter with the risen Christ (1 Cor. 9: 1; 15: 8; Gal. 1: 12, 16).

3. The appearances were episodes of revelation (e.g. Gal. 1: 12, 16) which called the recipients to faith (e.g. John 20: 29), in (4) a special experience which (5) corresponded to their special and non-transferable mission and role in being with Christ founders of the Church, and which (6) had something visually perceptible about it.

As regards (4) and (5), those disciples who had been with Jesus during his ministry recognized the risen Christ as being identical with the master whom they had known and followed: 'It is the Lord' (John 21: 7). No later group or indi-

---

[5] See *The Easter Jesus* (London: Darton, Longman & Todd, new edn., 1980), 3–38; *Interpreting the Resurrection* (Mahwah, NJ: Paulist Press, 1986), 5–52; *Jesus Risen*, 107–9, 112–21.

vidual believer, not even Paul, could duplicate this aspect of those first post-resurrection meetings with Christ. Peter, Mary Magdalene, and other disciples are presented as bridge persons who linked the period of Jesus' ministry with the post-Easter situation. In that way their experience of the risen Lord was unique and unrepeatable. Yet more should be added about their 'once only' experience and its aftermath.

Peter, Paul, and other apostolic witnesses who meet the risen Christ are understood to have the mission of testifying to that experience and founding the Church. These witnesses have seen for themselves and believed. In proclaiming the good news and gathering together those who have not seen and yet are ready to believe, these original witnesses do not need to rely on the experience and testimony of others. Their function for Christianity differs from that of any subsequent believers, inasmuch as they alone have the once-and-for-all task of inaugurating the mission and founding the Church. Others will bear the responsibility of continuing that mission and keeping the Church in existence. But the coming-into-being of the Church and its mission cannot be duplicated. The way in which that unique function (5) implies some difference between the experiences of the founding generation and all subsequent believers is expressed by John's classic distinction between those who have seen and believed, the persons covered by (4), and all those who are 'blessed' because they 'have not seen and yet believe' (John 20: 29).[6]

As regards point (6), in reporting or referring to the encounters with the risen Christ, the NT heavily privileges the language of sight.[7] He 'appeared' to some people (e.g. 1 Cor. 15: 5–8; Luke 24: 34) and they 'saw' him (e.g. 1 Cor. 9: 1; Matt. 28: 17; John 20: 18, 20). Occasionally in the NT the Greek 'see' (*horaó*) can be used of intellectual perception, just as blindness is a metaphor for incomprehension. Thus 'for those outside everything is in parables, so that they may indeed see but not perceive, and may indeed hear but not

---

[6] See D. Kendall and G. O'Collins, 'The Uniqueness of the Easter Appearances', *Catholic Biblical Quarterly*, 54 (1992), 287–307, at 289–93.

[7] On the visual vocabulary used to express the risen Christ's appearances see J. Hug, *La Finale de l'Évangile de Marc* (Paris: J. Gabalda, 1978), 53–61; Hug also has a useful section on the vocabulary for the resurrection itself (ibid. 40–5).

understand' (Mark 4: 11–12). But normally 'seeing' and 'appearing' include some visual component (e.g. Mark 9: 4; Luke 5: 12; John 1: 29; Acts 2: 3). Instances like Mark 4: 11–12 deal with the intellectual perception of some truth or the failure to comprehend some truth. One can 'see' truth in a purely interior, non-corporeal way. But with the Easter encounters we are dealing with a claim about a bodily resurrected person appearing to other persons who exist within our space-time world and see him. In that case it is difficult to imagine how a purely spiritual, interior seeing could be reconciled with the NT terminology of the appearances. This is not to argue that, when the risen Jesus appeared, he was an exterior object to be perceived by any who happened to be present, irrespective of their personal dispositions. Further, one must admit that Paul and the evangelists show little interest in describing and explaining in detail the nature of the appearances. In any case their (partly) unique and unrepeatable nature would rule out the possibility of fully conceptualizing these experiences and expressing them according to the canons of ordinary fact-stating discourse. Here I wish simply to point out that some visual component seems implied by the NT language for the encounters with the risen Jesus. Unlike the OT prophets, the apostolic witnesses to Easter typically saw the risen Lord rather than heard his word.

Before leaving the account I have offered of the Easter appearances, let me note that there are a few partial exceptions to the pattern of the seven features I have outlined. There is the case of the two disciples on the Emmaus road (Luke 24: 13–35) and the more than 500 believers (1 Cor. 15: 6). They are recalled among those to whom the risen Jesus appeared, but seemingly they were not specially commissioned and authorized to become foundational, apostolic witnesses as Peter, Paul, and others like Andronicus and Junia (Rom. 16: 7) were (see point (5) above).

The discovery of the empty tomb served as a secondary sign, which was ambiguous by itself but which taken with the appearances served to confirm the reality of the resurrection. The gospel stories of one or more women finding Jesus' tomb to be mysteriously open and empty contain a reliable

historical core. The arguments mounted to support that conclusion in my *Easter Jesus* (38–45), *Jesus Risen* (121–6), and
elsewhere convince me as much as ever.[8]

Two traditions report the empty tomb story: the Markan
tradition (followed by Matthew and Luke), and that somewhat different tradition which entered John's Gospel. Early
polemic against the message of the resurrection supposed the
tomb was known to be empty. Naturally the opponents of the
Christian movement explained away the missing body as a
plain case of theft (Matt. 28: 11–15). What was in dispute
was not whether the tomb was empty but why it was empty.
We have no early evidence that anyone, either Christian or
non-Christian, ever alleged that Jesus' tomb still contained
his remains.

Furthermore, the central place of women in the empty
tomb stories speaks for their historical reliability. Women
were central: Mary Magdalene (John 20: 1–2) and perhaps
other women with her (Mark 16: 1–8 parr.) to their aston-
ishment found Jesus' tomb to be open and empty on the
first Easter Sunday. If these stories had simply been legends
created by early Christians, they would have attributed the
discovery of the empty tomb to male disciples, given that
in first-century Palestine women were, for all intents and
purposes, disqualified as valid witnesses. Legend-makers do
not normally invent positively unhelpful material.

One could add fresh items and refinements to the case for
the empty tomb. Paul, for instance, quotes the kerygmatic
tradition about Christ's burial and resurrection (1 Cor. 15: 4)
and goes on to repeat six times the same verb (in precisely
its same perfect, passive form—*egēgertai*), twice speaking of
Christ's being raised 'from the dead' (1 Cor. 15: 12–20).

---

[8] See G. O'Collins, 'Resurrection Belief: A Note on a Recent Book', *Gregorianum*,
70 (1989), 341–4. Reviewing Hans Küng's *Credo: The Apostles' Creed Explained for
Today* (London: SCM Press, 1993) in *Tablet* for 5 June 1993 (722–3), I pointed out
its merits and various questionable features, which include the claim that 'the
majority of biblical exegetes' have argued that 'the stories about the tomb are
legendary elaborations of the message of the resurrection' (*Credo*, 104–5). I referred
to the many exegetes listed in my *Jesus Risen* (123) who recognize a historical
nucleus in the empty tomb stories and do not accept the thesis of mere 'legendary
elaborations'. To that list one could add the names of other such exegetes as J.
Gnilka, C. Rowland, and P. Perkins. Readers can decide what to make of Küng's
reply in *Tablet* for 19 June 1993 (787).

Several times elsewhere the apostle uses the same verb (*egeirō*) and predicate ('from the dead') in what many scholars hold to be formulaic traditions that he has taken over (Rom. 10: 9; Gal. 1: 1; 1 Thess. 1: 10). That, for Paul and the tradition, the addition 'from the dead' points to Christ's empty tomb or *resurrection from the grave* is suggested by Paul's citing the kerygmatic announcement of Christ's burial (1 Cor. 15: 4). The resurrection 'from the dead' entailed a rising from the tomb. Furthermore, Matthew, Luke, and John use the same verb (*egeirō*) and predicate ('from the dead') in reference to Jesus' own resurrection (Matt. 27: 64; 28: 7; Acts 3: 15; 13: 30; John 2: 22) and to the case of Lazarus (John 12: 1, 9, 17). Here they unquestionably mean a raising from the grave and an empty tomb, just as John 20: 9 and Acts 10: 41 do when they use *anistēmi ek nekrōn*. One might argue that they are adding specific meaning to the vaguer, traditional language which they adopt (*egeirō* plus 'from the dead'). But Paul's use of this language, in close proximity to his citation of the kerygmatic tradition about Jesus' burial, makes it more likely that resurrection 'from the dead' (*ek nekrōn*) implies resurrection from a grave. In any case, as many have remarked, for a Pharisaic Jew like Paul a resurrection which did not involve an empty tomb would have been inconceivable.

The next section of this chapter will ask: what did Jesus' resurrection reveal? Here we have been putting the prior question: What factors conspired to reveal and interpret the resurrection? How was it made known?

The short answer as we have seen is: the Easter faith and claim occurred only because the appearances of the risen Jesus occurred and his tomb was found to be empty. In the circumstances, the appearances were the necessary condition for the rise of Easter faith. Yet even the appearances cannot be regarded as the one and only cause of the Easter faith and claim. We may and indeed should single them out, but several other factors jointly contributed to the result: the knowledge-in-faith of Jesus' resurrection.

To their encounters with their risen Jesus the first disciples brought their Jewish faith in God. Through this faith they presumably shared with the Pharisees a hope for a general resurrection to come at the end of time (see also Mark 12:

18–27; Acts 23: 6–8). Even if the resurrection of Jesus proved a massively new thing (bringing, as it did, the idea of the final glorious resurrection of one person in real anticipation of the end of all history), nevertheless, the notions of resurrection and of final resurrection to glory were apparently already familiar to the disciples.

What of the sacred Scriptures which recorded and interpreted the disciples' Jewish faith? Did they contribute to the genesis of the disciples' knowledge-in-faith of Jesus' resurrection? The NT emphasizes that the resurrection happened 'according to the scriptures' (1 Cor. 15: 4). Those who knew the Scriptures should have been ready to expect Jesus' resurrection (Luke 24: 25–7, 32, 44–6; John 20: 9). It seems, however, that it was only after they came to know Jesus' resurrection that the first (and then the second) generation of Christians looked to their inherited Scriptures to support and interpret the Easter faith they already enjoyed (e.g. Acts 2: 25–36; 13: 33–7). This subsequent search for scriptural passages to illustrate and confirm Easter led Matthew, for instance, to extend the meaning of Jesus' talk about Jonah and his effective preaching in Nineveh (see Luke 11: 29–30, 32; Matt. 16: 4). Jonah's three-day stint in the great fish became a sign of Jesus' three days in the grave (Matt. 12: 39–40)—alongside the contrast which Jesus had originally drawn between the defective audience response to his preaching and the positive response to that of Jonah (Matt. 12: 41). It does not seem that reflection on the Scriptures contributed as such to the rise of Easter faith. Rather it came into play subsequently and with some difficulty to confirm and, for various purposes, to illustrate a belief in Christ's resurrection that was already firmly held.[9]

In opening themselves up to and interpreting the central

---

[9] C. F. Evans points out that, although it quickly 'became part of the church's apologetic' that Jesus' resurrection, like the cross, was 'according to the scriptures' (1 Cor. 15: 4), 'the church was hard put to substantiate this claim. Thus, in contrast to the passion narratives, which are laced with Old Testament quotations and echoes ... the resurrection narratives are almost entirely free from such, and those Old Testament passages which came to be used in apostolic preaching to argue the resurrection of Jesus are plainly being forced into service, and are made to bear a sense other than the original.' *Resurrection and the New Testament* (London: SCM Press, 1970), 11–12; see 12–14.

signs of Jesus' resurrection (his appearances and the discovery of his empty tomb), the disciples were helped by two
other factors: (1) their memories of what the earthly Jesus
had said and done, and (2) the new gift of the Holy Spirit.
First they had to face the extreme theological crisis of the
cross. Jesus had called God 'Abba' and had associated himself
in a quite extraordinary fashion with the divine cause. Nevertheless, his life had ended in a death that, humanly and
religiously speaking, was utterly disgraceful. But then the
catalyst of the Easter appearances put a dramatic end to the
disciples' theological crisis. They now knew that Jesus had
been divinely vindicated, and their memory of his words and
deeds never dimmed. In particular, some things that he had
done and said helped to root in the past their new experience
of him as risen from the dead (see Luke 24: 8; John 2: 22; 12:
16). According to John it was through the prompting of the
Holy Spirit that they now remembered and finally understood the testimony of the earthly Jesus (John 14: 26; see also
16: 12–13).

The Resurrection as Revealing

One profitable way of reading Paul's letters is to note how
the apostle progressively explores the revelatory significance
to be found in the resurrection of the crucified Jesus. In his
earliest letter Paul attends largely to what the resurrection
discloses about the future of Christian believers (e.g. 1 Thess.
1: 10; 4: 13–18). By the time he writes the Letter to the
Romans, his vision of what is revealed by the Easter mystery
spans not only the believers' new life of grace here and now
(e.g. Rom. 4: 25–5: 11; 8: 9–17) but also the future of Israel
(Rom. 9–11) and indeed of the whole world (Rom. 8: 18–25).

The Acts of the Apostles, especially through the
speeches/sermons of Peter and then of Paul, offer their
version of the revelatory power of Jesus' resurrection. The
Gospels themselves, in presenting the resurrection, do not
limit its disclosive significance to their closing chapters; the
Easter mystery throws a new and final light on the whole
story of Jesus and his mission.

What did and does the resurrection of the crucified Jesus

reveal not only about him but also about God, human beings,
and their world? Let me summarize here some important
themes. Later chapters will fill out the picture, especially
about Jesus and his redemptive work.

Let us begin with Jesus. His rising from the dead vindicated his certainty in the powerful future of the kingdom
of God (Mark 14: 25). The presence of the kingdom, manifested in the preaching and miracles of Jesus' ministry, had
suffered apparent defeat through his condemnation and crucifixion. But now its power was reasserted in a much more
striking way through his resurrection and the gift of the Holy
Spirit. This denouement fully justified the personal authority
with which Jesus had spoken of the kingdom and which
he had claimed over the sabbath, the temple, the law, the
forgiveness of sins, final judgement and human salvation.
The resurrection showed that, so far from being cursed by
the God whom he called 'Abba' (see Gal. 3: 13), Jesus had
been divinely vindicated in himself, in his teaching, and in
that utter fidelity to his vocation for which he sacrificed
everything, even life itself. The resurrection disclosed that
his self-sacrifice had been accepted and that, instead of being
a mere messianic pretender as the title on the cross asserted,
he was/is the Messiah and that his crucifixion had truly been
the death of the Messiah. In short, the resurrection fully and
finally revealed the meaning and truth of Christ's life, person,
work, and death. It set a divine seal on Jesus and his ministry.

To say all this is not to lapse back into the discredited
apologetic about his resurrection being the miracle proving
Christ's claim to divinity. First, instead of anachronistic talk
about 'proof', I wish to associate myself with the themes of
vindication (Acts 2: 36; 3: 14–15; 4: 10) and revelation (Gal.
1: 12, 16) which Luke and Paul, respectively, develop in their
interpretation of the resurrection. Second, far from being
reduced to a mere miracle, even the 'greatest' of the miracles,
the resurrection is presented by the NT as something qualitatively different—the beginning of the end of all things (e.g.
Rom. 8: 29; 1 Cor. 15: 20). In calling the resurrection 'the
paschal mystery', the closing section of Chapter 1 wished to
avoid studiously any hint of miracle-language. Third, past
apologetic often misrepresented the (largely implicit) claims

made by Jesus during his ministry, taking them in individual isolation as if he were simply and boldly asserting 'I am God'. The modern stress on his 'Abba-consciousness' has the merit of reminding us that Jesus' claims were claims-in-relation. By much of what he said and did he made claims to stand in a unique relationship to the God whom he called 'Abba' and with whom he shared authority over the temple, the sabbath, the law, the forgiveness of sins, and the eschatological judgement. Jesus' assertion of divinity is distorted if it is plucked out of its historical context as a claim-in-relationship.

Besides its revelatory importance for Jesus' person and historical activity, his resurrection also manifested the transformed being which the glorified humanity of Jesus now enjoyed. His human life or total embodied history rose with him and was transfigured into a final mode of existence.[10] This revelation of Jesus' new and definitive way of existing radically changed the value of what was remembered and recounted from his earthly history. The early traditions and then the Gospels offered much more than a mere record from the past. They challenged their hearers and readers with words and deeds, the value and truth of which were now fully disclosed. These were/are the words and deeds of the risen Son of God, their living Lord.

We have seen above how the NT weaves the wider language of exaltation into its account of Jesus' new life. Even more than the language of resurrection, 'exaltation' bespeaks the post-death revelation of Jesus' status and dignity. A royal psalm which came up for debate during Jesus' ministry (Mark 12: 35–7 parr.) opens as follows: 'The Lord says to my Lord: "Sit at my right hand, till I make your enemies your footstool"' (Ps. 110: 1). Finding here an OT prophecy of Jesus' exaltation, the first Christians also saw fulfilled in the resurrection a promise that Jesus apparently made at his trial before the Sanhedrin: 'You will see the Son of man seated at the right hand of the Power and coming with the clouds of heaven' (Mark 14: 62).[11] We noted earlier how widely the NT employs the image of the exalted Jesus' being seated not near

[10] See my *Jesus Risen*, 182–7.
[11] See I. H. Marshall, *Jesus the Saviour* (London: SPCK, 1990), 203–9; T. Prendergast, 'Trial of Jesus', *ABD* vi. 660–3.

the divine throne but at the very right hand of God.

Nothing illustrates more clearly than one hymn how the early Christians used the language of exaltation to express the revelation of Jesus' divine status that calls for the worship of the whole world. Publicly exalted to the glory which he already possessed in his pre-existent divine state of 'equality with God' and into which, in his humanity, he entered for the first time, Jesus is worshipped and confessed as divine Lord (Phil. 2: 6–11). Through his resurrection he is disclosed as the exalted Lord who merits worship—a point clearly made also by three evangelists in their Easter stories.

In Matthew's final chapter, first the female and then the male disciples worship Jesus (Matt. 28: 9, 17). Luke (Luke 24: 3, 34) and John (John 20–1 *passim*) recognize Jesus' divine lordship manifested in his new life. The risen Jesus' promise to be with the disciples right to the end of time (Matt. 28: 20) clearly hints at the revelation of his status as 'God with us' (Matt. 1: 23). Through the ascension motif Luke (Luke 24: 51; Acts 1: 9–11) and John (John 20: 17), among other things, associate the risen Jesus with the 'place' now known to be his—heavenly glory.

Lastly, as we have seen in Chapter 2, for the first Christians Jesus' resurrection from the dead threw definitive light on 'the fullness of God' which was in him (Col. 1: 19). The hymn cited in Colossians confesses his divinity immediately after it speaks of him as being 'the first-born from the dead' and immediately before it celebrates his reconciling death on the cross. The very same hymn not only recognizes Christ's divinity manifested in the new creation, which was his resurrection from the dead, but also celebrates his role in the original creation of the world and its conservation (Col. 1: 16–17). The Easter revelation of Christ's divine status quickly led his followers to acknowledge him as agent of creation, sharing in an essential property of God as creator of the universe (see 1 Cor. 8: 6; Heb. 1: 2–3; and eventually John 1: 3).

With the crucifixion and resurrection, Christians grew also into a fresh understanding of God. The first Good Friday and Easter Sunday revealed God in suffering, new life, and unconditioned divine love. This is not to say that pre-Christian Judaism failed to associate these themes with God. Even a rapid reading of the Psalms, Isaiah, Jeremiah, and Hosea would give the lie to that. But, in a startlingly different way, through these themes, Jesus' destiny focused and fixed the specifically Christian doctrine of God.

First, suffering. In developing the opening ideas of 1 Corinthians, Paul nine times brings God together with the 'word of the cross' (1 Cor. 1: 18–25). Left to their own devices, the vast and mysterious disgrace of crucifixion was the last place where Jews or others might expect to find God. Paul is not exaggerating when he calls it a scandal and a folly to recognize in the atrocious and shameful death of Jesus the high point of divine revelation and salvation (1 Cor. 1: 18, 23–5). But with the resurrection the disclosive power of the cross comes into play, and shows that the weak, the despised, and the suffering—those who become fools for God's sake—can serve as special mediators of revelation (and salvation).

The next chapter will examine Jesus' divine sonship, a claim that was simply offensive and quite unacceptable to the strict monotheism of first-century Judaism. What Christians found revealed in the resurrection made things even worse. It was uniquely and weirdly offensive to see the face of a crucified man as the human face of God.[12]

Above I referred to the resurrection as a new divine attribute, in the sense of God now being 'defined' not simply as the Raiser of the dead but specifically as the Raiser of the dead Jesus. In pre-Christian Judaism the hope had emerged for a general resurrection at the end of world history. But many Jews did not share this hope (e.g. the Sadducees), and at best it remained one aspect in their vision of God, expressed by the second of the Eighteen Benedictions but not by the Shema.[13] The language Paul took over from the tradition of early Christians shows how the resurrection of Jesus essentially shaped their vision of God (e.g. Rom. 8: 11; 1 Cor. 6: 14; 2 Cor. 4: 14; Gal. 1: 1). God was the Resurrector, the God who had raised Jesus and would raise the other dead to new life. The OT consistently illustrates how the Jews named

---

[12] See my 'Crucifixion', *ABD* i. 207–10.
[13] See R. Martin-Achard, 'Resurrection (OT)', ibid. v. 680–4; G. W. E. Nickelsburg, 'Resurrection (Early Judaism and Christianity)', ibid. 684–91.

'life' as a key attribute of God.[14] The resurrection of Jesus led his followers to enlarge radically this notion and worship God as the One who not only gives life but even raises the dead to new life. Paul drew the conclusion: those who failed to acknowledge God as the Resurrector of the dead were essentially 'misrepresenting' the deity (1 Cor. 15: 15).

The OT has much to say about the initiatives of the divine love.[15] Yet these initiatives are enacted through others, above all through such prophetic emissaries of God as Jeremiah, Ezekiel, and Hosea. In the story of Jesus' crucifixion and resurrection, Christians perceived the initiative of self-giving love which led God to be personally involved in our sinful history (Rom. 8: 3)—even to the extent of an appalling death on the cross: 'God shows his love for us in that while we were yet sinners Christ died for us' (Rom. 5: 8). This prior and unconditioned divine love towards human kind caused God to send for our redemption his Son (Gal. 4: 4–6), whose free and obedient acceptance of a violent death at the hands of a wicked world revealed as nothing else could God's loving self-giving on our behalf (Rom. 8: 31–2; see 2 Cor. 5: 18–19; 1 John 4: 10). This divine self-giving, manifested supremely in the events of the first Good Friday and Easter Sunday and communicated through the Holy Spirit (Rom. 5: 5), eventually drew forth the lapidary statement: 'God is love' (1 John 4: 8, 16).

Such then in summary is what is meant by claiming that the resurrection of the crucified Jesus disclosed God in a fresh and startling way—through the focus of suffering, new life, and unconditional love. With this triple focus of the Easter revelation we come to its trinitarian face.

Even before John told the story of Jesus' passion, death, and resurrection in terms of the Father, Son, and Holy Spirit, Luke and Matthew, in their different ways, had already drawn attention to the trinitarian face of Christ's dying and rising. Matthew chose to insert into the setting of the solemn encounter of the eleven disciples with the risen Jesus the later formula of baptism, 'in the name of the Father and of the Son

---

[14] See G. von Rad, G. Bertram, and R. Bultmann, '*Zaō, zōē*', etc., *TDNT* ii. 843–61.
[15] See K. D. Sakenfeld, 'Love (OT)', *ABD* iv. 375–81.

and of the Holy Spirit' (Matt. 28: 19). Matthew found it appropriate to interpret the Easter revelation in a trinitarian key. According to Luke the risen Christ communicated to his disciples 'the promise of my Father' that they would be 'clothed with power from on high' (Luke 24: 49)—a promise which was realized in the coming of the Holy Spirit at Pentecost (Acts 2: 1–4), an event interpreted in a trinitarian fashion as Christ being 'exalted at the right hand of God', receiving 'from the Father the promise of the Holy Spirit', and 'pouring out' on believers the visible and audible effects of the Spirit (Acts 2: 33).

Years before any of the evangelists wrote, Paul ended a letter to the Corinthians by citing a formula about 'the grace of the Lord Jesus Christ', 'the love of God' the Father, and 'the fellowship of the Holy Spirit' (2 Cor. 13: 14). In an earlier letter to the same community, a letter which began with Christ's crucifixion (1 Cor. 1: 18–25) and reached its climax with his resurrection (15: 1–28), Paul wrote of the Spirit, the Lord (Jesus Christ), and God (the Father) (1 Cor. 12: 4–6). The apostle had most to say about his own revelatory encounter with the risen Jesus and its missionary consequences when writing to the Galatians. That letter began with God the Father (1: 1) and his Son (1: 16; 2: 20), and then added talk about the Holy Spirit (3: 2–5, 14; 4: 6, 29; 5: 5, 16–25; 6: 1, 8), while continuing to speak of the Father and the Son (e.g. 4: 4–6). In other words, Paul gave a strongly trinitarian tone to a letter which, to say the least, had much to say about and draw from the crucifixion and resurrection of Jesus.

To be sure, applying 'trinitarian' to the revelation communicated through the resurrection of the crucified Jesus could be misleadingly anachronistic. It was to be centuries before the divinity of Christ was officially clarified at the First Council of Nicaea (325) and the divinity of the Holy Spirit at the First Council of Constantinople (381). Nevertheless, John, Matthew, Luke, Paul, and the pre-Pauline tradition had already discerned what can only be described as a trinitarian pattern in the events of Christ's dying and rising.

The revelatory impact of his resurrection from the dead extends beyond new light on Jesus and God. Easter showed that God had already initiated the resurrection of human beings and their world (Rom. 8: 29; 1 Cor. 15: 20, 23; Col. 1: 18). In raising and transforming Jesus in his human existence, God was seen to have begun the work of finally transforming the rest of creation and the rest of history. In the time between Easter and that end, Jesus' dying and rising had brought into existence the community of the Church (Eph. 5: 25–7). With these remarks about the Church and the world, we reach the work of redemption, the essential co-ordinate of revelation. If the resurrection of the crucified Jesus is essentially and massively revelatory, it is also necessarily redemptive and brings communion with God and Christ through the Holy Spirit. When fresh light is thrown on God, our human condition, and our future destiny, that must be salvific. We now turn to say something about the redemptive impact of Easter—a topic which will be more fully elaborated in Chapter 12.

Resurrection as Redemptive

What then does the resurrection of the crucified Jesus indicate about human redemption and his role in/for it? His shameful death on the cross, followed by his startling vindication through resurrection, forced the first Christians to rethink their Jewish view of the divine plan for human salvation.

What Jesus had taught during his ministry about the law, the sabbath, the temple, the forgiveness of sins, and, in general, about the kingdom of God had already challenged them to modify and radicalize their concepts of the nature and mediation of salvation. In particular, he had invited his audience to accept the disconcerting reality that their relationship to him was determinative for their state before God here and hereafter. In the event, he was executed at the time of the Passover feast, after he had first defined his imminent death as instituting a 'covenant' (Mark 14: 24 par.) or 'new covenant' (Luke 22: 20; 1 Cor. 11: 25).

The resurrection of the crucified Jesus made the early Christians go beyond their Jewish faith that the deliverance from Egypt (with the subsequent Sinai covenant and entrance into the promised land) was *the* act of divine redemption.

Now, with 'the end of the ages' (1 Cor. 10: 11), they became aware that the events of Good Friday and Easter Sunday, together with the coming of the Holy Spirit, constituted God's decisive and final act of salvation—the new exodus (see Luke 9: 31; Acts 7: 17–39; 1 Cor. 5: 7; 10: 1–11; Heb. 11: 22–31) and the new day of atonement (Heb. 9: 6–10: 10). Christ himself, without ceasing to be the same person and without being replaced by another, had been delivered from death, was transformed in glory, and had become for others the last Adam (see Chapter 2 above), life-giving Spirit (1 Cor. 15: 45), powerful Son of God, and Saviour (see the next chapters). In the words of Hebrews, 'being made perfect he became the source of eternal salvation to all who obey him' (Heb. 5: 9).[16]

For obvious reasons, a fuller systematic discussion of Christ's redemptive function will come later. Here let me simply note two authors (Luke and Paul) who exemplify the NT conviction about the universalist nature of the salvation mediated through Christ's death and resurrection. In the name of the risen Lord the mission for the forgiveness of sins must go out to all the nations (Luke 24: 47). This proclamation of universal salvation begins in Luke's scheme of things from the Jews and in Jerusalem, the central location of the salvific events. At Pentecost the disciples encounter the Jews of the diaspora who link Jerusalem with the rest of the world and represent all the nations. The use of Joel makes it clear that the Holy Spirit and salvation are available for everyone: 'I will pour out my Spirit upon all flesh . . . and it shall be that whoever calls on the name of the Lord shall be saved' (Acts 2: 17, 21).

Paul teaches emphatically that faith and baptism into the risen Christ are open to all. This faith transcends all pre-existing religious, social, and gender distinctions or barriers: 'In Christ Jesus you are all sons of God through faith. For as many of you as were baptized into Christ have put on Christ. There is neither Jew nor Greek, there is neither slave nor free, there is neither male nor female; for you are all one in Christ Jesus' (Gal. 3: 26–8). In another letter, by repeatedly underlining the saving power of the risen Christ over 'all'

---

[16] See my article 'Salvation', ibid. v. 907–14.

persons and 'all' things, Paul builds up a sense of the total
and universal consequences of the resurrection (1 Cor. 15:
20–8). Christ's rising from the dead has inaugurated the end
for all things (Rom. 8: 18–23), the beginning of God's making
all things new (see Rev. 21: 1–5).

God's Activity

Up to here, this chapter has kept close to the NT in spelling
out the basic claim about Jesus' resurrection, the original
experiences which gave rise to and interpreted that claim,
and the resurrection's revelatory and redemptive impact. To
carry out our stated aims we end by taking up the challenge of
attempting to clarify somewhat the resurrection as a specific
divine act or rather as the divine act *par excellence*.

Western thinking about divine causality, or the active
relations between God and the world, has been deeply
affected for several centuries by the deist temptation, which—
expressed in the light of the modern big bang theory—would
mean that God created the universe and put it on automatic
pilot about fifteen billion years ago. This would mean that no
specific divine action lies behind any particular occurrence.
There would be only one (initial and perhaps ongoing) divine
act and no divine subacts, whether miraculous or providential. What if we reject this reduction of divine causality
to one initial act and insist on maintaining infinitely many
divine subacts, which would include both 'extraordinary'
subacts like the call of the Jewish people, the incarnation,
Jesus' miracles, and his resurrection, and the 'ordinary'
subacts which constitute the exercise of God's providence
according to the normal laws of the universe and in the
life of every individual? How can we conceive the divine
interaction, whether extraordinary or ordinary, with all the
physical objects, living beings, and rational beings that make
up the created realm?

First things first. Since the time of David Hume the difficulty of establishing causal connections and offering causal
explanations has at times been exaggerated. Even if it can be
hard both to trace many effects back to their causes and to
analyse successfully the nature of causation itself, never-

theless, we can demonstrate some causal ties and say something about causation.

How then should we conceive divine causality in general? This question must be considered once we name Christ's resurrection as a (or even the) divine act. To begin with, we must part company with many empiricists who, if they do allow the question to come up, then go on to present God simply as a cause (or even the cause) among other causes. God's action is not an action alongside other (created) actions. Events caused by God are not events alongside other (created) events. Between the divine first cause (and the way it produces effects) and secondary causes there is far more difference than likeness.

1. Unlike created, secondary causes, God is neither spatial nor temporal. Nevertheless, while being timeless or eternal and non-spatial God is intimately related to time and present to space—the inmost ground of all being. (2) After its creation the world remains radically dependent on God. At every moment God is responsible for the world's persistence and continually active in sustaining in existence the things that have been created. Neither the entire universe nor anything within it is or can be fundamentally self-sustaining. Unsustained by God, things cannot continue in existence, just as they could not in the first place bring themselves into existence.

3. What follows then for created, secondary causes, if from moment to moment they are all fundamentally dependent upon God's active support for their continued existence? They have only a relative autonomy, and can operate only if directly supported by God. Even if they possess and exercise the causal powers proper to them, God is necessarily and intimately involved in their activity. Hence every effect and phenomenon in the world has God as its primary or first cause. We would be wildly astray if we pictured uncreated and created activity as the operation of two quite separate agents.

All of this means that God must be conceived of as a radically different kind of agent from created agents. At times the Bible puts together God and human beings as being co-responsible for some decision and/or action (e.g. Acts 1: 15–

26; 15: 28). In the practice of their religious faith, believers
think of themselves as being in personal interaction with God:
in their prayer, in the enlightening and life-giving thoughts
which come to them, and in the providential ordering of
their lives. But just as divine causality is radically unlike any
created causality, so God is a very different kind of personal
agent from ourselves.

Above we noted how God is timeless (or beyond any temporal succession) and non-spatial, that is to say, incorporeal
and immaterial. When we add further divine attributes and
recognize God as being all-powerful, all-knowing, and all-
perfect, we may well ask ourselves: what kind of action concepts apply to such an agent? How many of our notions about
personal, human actions and their mechanism can we transfer
to God? When, for example, we do something in the external
world, bodily movements must come into play. Such activity
outside ourselves does not promise to be very enlightening
about the actions of God who is incorporeal.

We may find more help from two analogies, the first at the
intrapersonal level—from the way our mind or conscious
centre controls our bodily actions. To observe how the mental
affects and guides the material need not mean lapsing into
the dualistic explanation of the mind–body relationship
offered by Descartes—with the human soul as an immaterial
substance controlling a machine-like body. Our analogy
simply suggests that divine action could be seen to be something like human action within, something like the interaction
of mind–brain or mind–body within a human person. We
experience ourselves as agents when our thoughts affect our
bodies—an experience that offers an 'intimate' analogy to
God's action on us and our world. The other analogy that
promises to throw light on the divine action can be drawn
from the interpersonal sphere—from the way human beings,
often unconsciously and even very mysteriously, have influences on one another. The impact of human persons on other
human persons, especially those of a loving and life-giving
kind, could offer some action concepts that might be transferred to God and the divine actions.

A further general issue to be mentioned before we come to
the specific case of the resurrection concerns the great variety

of free divine actions in human history to which the Bible bears witness. How is it possible for the supreme Being, who both is beyond time and space and is the intimate ground of all being, to be 'more' or differently engaged 'here' rather than 'there'? In any case how could we tell that this supreme Being is 'more' engaged in this or that particular slice of space and time? The chance of answering both questions positively opens up, once we admit that love and freedom radically characterize God's exercise of causality. The personal spontaneity of love allows for endless variation in the God–world relationship and, in particular, for effects that are qualitatively distinct from God's 'ordinary work' in creating and then sustaining creation. We can know God to have acted in special ways, when the events or effects (e.g. Jesus' new life after death) differ from what would normally have happened otherwise (e.g. Jesus' remaining dead and his body corrupting in the grave). The quality and nature of the effects point to God's special activity.

Thus far I have obviously been stating, rather than offering any detailed argument for, positions I hold on divine causality. What then of the divine act in the resurrection of Jesus? Three principles can help to clarify matters a little.

First, both in biblical history and in general, it is easier to grasp and talk about effects rather than causes. The effects are often blatant; causes and their precise nature can remain shadowy and to a degree mysterious. The Jewish people, for example, understood and lived their call, the deliverance from Egypt, the Sinai covenant, the Mosaic law, the sabbath rest, the kingship, their religious feasts, their holy Scriptures, the challenges of the prophets, the return from Babylonian exile, and much else besides as all coming from God. When they experienced these realities, they did not take them to be self-explanatory but to be effects of God's activity on their behalf. From the effects, including their very messianic existence as a people, they knew in faith the divine cause. Their early creeds show how the Israelites gave a causal explanation to thoroughly concrete features of their history, naming God as *the* agent even if the precise way God brought these things about remained somewhat mysterious (e.g. Josh. 24: 2–13; Deut. 26: 5–11).

For us today the question obviously arises: do we successfully explain the history of the chosen people, if we name God's special activity on their behalf as the major cause of that history? But my point here is not to mount arguments to bolster the plausibility of this reading of Israel's story. Rather it is simply to use examples from biblical history to illustrate how effects are clearer than causes, even (or especially?) when it is a matter of claiming the presence of special divine activity.

An even more basic example than those from biblical history is creation itself. We all see created reality every day. But we never directly observe the cause of this effect, the very act of creation (and conservation). At best we see God's creative action only in and through its effects. Genesis beautifully symbolizes this point by speaking of Adam being plunged into 'a deep sleep', so that he would not observe the creation of Eve (Gen. 2: 21–2).

Second, the traditional adage about 'every agent bringing about something similar to itself' (*omne agens agit sibi simile*) reminds us that efficient causes are also exemplary causes. Effects reflect the 'form' of their causes. Children resemble their parents, not only through their common humanity but also genetically and in other ways. In their colour, shape, and scent, new roses will take after the bushes from which they have been grown. Causes leave their impression on their effects. They are thus present in their effects, which participate in them. Hence the observer can recognize the imprint and image of the cause in its effect(s).

Applied to God, this means that whatever is brought about will resemble and reflect its divine cause. God leaves a divine impression on all creation and, above all, on created human beings (see Gen. 1: 27). God is always and necessarily present in whatever is effected. All the divine effects, albeit in varying ways and degrees, participate in God and share the divine life.

Israelite history illustrates a third characteristic of divine activity. God's different acts on behalf of the chosen people took place in view of a future completion. Together they formed a dynamic movement towards a final goal, a progressive assimilation to God which aimed at full participation in the divine life and presence. To be sure, God often had to write straight with crooked lines. Human freedom and human dissidents saw to that. Nevertheless, God's acts were/are never disconnected, still less arbitrary. Paul can read off a final divine unity in God's ceaseless activity for the salvation of Jews and Gentiles (Rom. 9–11), even if the apostle must admit the deep mystery of this unfolding story (Rom. 11: 33–5). Israel's special history wrote large what very many spiritually sensitive and committed people continue to experience. God's providential activity for each one moves progressively towards its final goal: the fullest possible assimilation to God and participation in the divine presence.

If there is nothing wildly unfamiliar or substantially unacceptable about these reflections on the divine causality, how do they fare when applied to the resurrection of the crucified Jesus? To begin with, it is better not to speak of it as a/the divine intervention. Like military 'inter-ventions' in various parts of the world, this language can too easily suggest an outsider, in this case an outsider God coming actively on the scene for the first time—a kind of meddlesome God. But, as we have recalled above, God is always intimately present everywhere and in every situation, from moment to moment sustaining in being everything that is and standing behind/under every effect as its primary or first cause. The God who is always and everywhere the very ground of being acted with loving and life-giving power in Jesus' resurrection.

Here the first principle stated above is dramatically exemplified. Mary Magdalene, Peter, and the other Easter witnesses saw the primary and immediate effect of the resurrection appearing to them, the living Jesus himself. They gave their causal explanation, 'he has been raised', but never claimed either to have witnessed the divine cause in action (the very resurrection itself) or to understand how it worked in itself. In faith they knew the cause, the resurrecting power of God, but, unlike the effect, that cause remained shrouded in mystery.

Second, in the resurrection the divine agent brought about something *sibi simile*. God's resurrecting power left its impression on the effect, Jesus' raised and glorified humanity. In his transformed human existence Jesus became even more like unto God, as the Son in whom one can recognize even more fully the image of his Father (see Rom. 1: 3–4). His risen humanity reflects and resembles to the ultimate extent possible its divine cause. In the highest degree possible, through his risen life he participates in God (see Rom. 6: 10).

Finally, the third principle we detected in divine activity towards human beings is realized *par excellence* in the case of Jesus' resurrection. The divine activity at work from the incarnation on formed a dynamic movement towards its future completion: Christ's full participation in the divine presence when he sits at God's right hand (e.g. Rom. 8: 34) after he has subjected all things to God (1 Cor. 15: 20–8).

The closing section of this chapter has aimed to give some brief answer to questions about divine causality and Jesus' resurrection. Here, if anywhere, philosophical considerations are needed to clarify a little what the NT claims and to some extent describes about the foundational Christian experiences.

We have been examining data from the NT about the resurrection of the crucified Jesus. Both in the light of his new life and guided by the Spirit and their memory of the earthly Jesus, how did the early Christians understand his identity and being? To that issue we now turn.

5
The Son of God

❖ ❖

One is tempted to say that more happened [in Christ-
ology] in this period of less than two decades than in the
whole of the next seven centuries, up to the time when
the doctrine of the early church was completed.

(Martin Hengel, *The Son of God*)

The Gospel of Mark illustrates two possible extremes in
presenting the sonship of Jesus. He can be interpreted in
totally human terms. Many of those who hear him in the
Nazareth synagogue demand testily: 'is he not the carpenter,
the Son of Mary?' (Mark 6: 3). Other passages suggest that
he can be interpreted as a heavenly being who for a brief
period appears as a 'guest' on earth. An unclean spirit in the
country of the Gerasenes shouts at him, 'What do you want
with me, Jesus, Son of the most high God?' (Mark 5: 7).
These two interpretations, a merely human or a merely divine
sonship, mark the two extremes between which the christological debates of the early Church take place.

In general, divine sonship means (1) belonging or being
related to God in some special way, and (2) being commissioned by God to fulfil some vocation. The mere title
'Son of God' as such leaves matters open. What kind of
relationship to and vocation from God are we talking about?

Through the first centuries, when reflecting on and
attempting to express the identity of Jesus, the Church made
considerable use of christological titles. To begin with, the
incarnate 'Logos' competed with 'Son of God' as the major,
high christological title. From the time of the Arian controversy, 'Son of God' entered into its own as the principal title

lodged in the Apostles' Creed, the Niceno-Constantinopolitan Creed, and other universally used Christian prayers and texts. To clarify the origin and meaning of this title is obviously thoroughly important for those who wish to understand NT and post-NT Christology.

This chapter sets itself to explore and answer some basic questions (which to a degree inevitably overlap) about Jesus' title 'Son of God'. (1) How early was the title used of him? Was it introduced by the Hellenistic Church in the 40s (for example, at Antioch)? Or does it go back to Palestine in the 30s and even to Jesus himself? Practically identical with the question of dating is that of origin. Where did the title come from? From Graeco-Roman sources, from Christianity itself, or from pre-Christian Judaism? (2) What was meant by it? That Jesus' humanity made him God's son like Adam (Luke 3: 38)? That Jesus was a righteous person (Wis 2: 13, 16, 18)? That he was totally open to be led by God's Spirit (Rom. 8: 14) and was *the* peacemaker (Matt. 5: 9) who loved his enemies (Luke 6: 35; Matt. 5: 45)? Was this title merely an alternative way of speaking of Jesus as Messiah? Was it simply functional (e.g. he was Son of God because he revealed God)? (3) What led early Christians to call Jesus 'Son of God'? Simply his resurrection and exaltation (see Rom. 1: 3–4; Acts 13: 33) and their experience of the Spirit (Gal. 4: 6)? Or did Jesus' own (implicit) self-description also play a role?

Before tackling these questions two cautionary observations are in order. First, this chapter does not intend to endorse a purely 'titular' Christology, as if everything important about Jesus and everything believed about Jesus in the early Church could be gleaned from a mere examination of key titles. The fact that this treatment of the Son of God title comes after an extensive reflection on his life, death, and resurrection should give the lie to any suspicion of 'titular' reductionism.

The complete picture of how Jesus thought of himself and how others thought of him goes beyond the question of his titles. At the same time, the titles are also valuable pointers to what others thought of Jesus and possibly to what he thought of himself. Second, this chapter concentrates on the Son of God title. But that is in no way meant to imply that our NT sources always and everywhere sharply distinguish it from such other designations for Jesus as Lord, Christ, and Son of man.

Before plunging into historical details, it can do no harm to underscore the relational nature of the title that takes over this chapter. Being a son or daughter necessarily implies a vertical relationship (to one's father and mother) and the possibility of a horizontal relationship (to brothers and sisters). Hence to name Jesus 'the Son of God' obviously involves a vertical relationship (in this case to the God whom in a startling fashion he called 'Abba'), and opens up the possibility of a horizontal relationship with those who through him could become (adopted) sons and daughters of God. Later in this chapter we will recall in detail how Jesus himself, Paul, and John presented this wider, horizontal relationship. Lastly, talk of sonship necessarily raises the question of its inauguration and possible subsequent enhancement. Did Jesus' divine sonship exist from all eternity? Or was it understood to have begun at his (human) conception, baptism, or resurrection from the dead? Did his baptism and/or his resurrection bring an enhancement of an already existing sonship? When and how did his horizontal relationship begin with other (adopted) sons and daughters of God?

The last paragraph has shown, if it needs to be shown, that a discussion of Jesus' divine sonship inevitably involves the question of his eternal pre-existence. The issues may be distinguishable but are not finally separable. This chapter will, however, concentrate on the Son of God question, leaving for a later chapter that of Jesus' pre-existence.

Dating the Title[1]

The later Johannine literature frequently calls Jesus 'Son' and 'Son of God' (e.g. John 1: 34, 49; 3: 16–18, 36; 11: 27; 1 John 4: 15; 5: 12; Rev. 2: 18). The stated purpose of John's

---

[1] See J. A. Fitzmyer, 'Paul's Christocentric Soteriology', *NJBC* 1388–402, esp. 1393–4; id., '4Q246: The "Son of God" Document from Qumran', *Biblica*, 74 (1993), 153–74; J. Fossum, 'Son of God', *ABD* vi. 128–37; M. Hengel, *The Cross and the Son of God* (London: SCM Press, 1986), 1–90.

Gospel is to bring its readers to believe in Jesus as the Son of God or at least to maintain them in that faith (John 20: 31).

But the title had already entered Christian usage decades earlier. The oldest Christian document calls Jesus God's Son (1 Thess. 1: 10), and subsequently Paul continues to introduce that title—often at key places in his letters (1 Cor. 15: 28; 2 Cor. 1: 19; Gal. 2: 20; 4: 4; Rom. 1: 3–4; 8: 3, 32). Altogether he speaks of Jesus seventeen times as God's Son. It is significant that Paul himself never tries to prove that Jesus is the Son of God; he takes it for granted that this belief is simply shared by the early Christians to whom he writes. Further, in some cases when Paul calls Jesus by that title he draws on earlier formulations which take us back to the opening years of Christianity (e.g. 1 Thess. 1: 10; Gal. 4: 4; Rom. 1: 3–4).

Not only the data from Paul, our earliest Christian writer, but also the Semitic nature of some gospel sayings about the Son (e.g. Mark 5: 7; Matt. 11: 27) rule out the thesis that the Son of God title had a later, Hellenistic source. When used in the Synoptic Gospels, the title betrays its Palestinian, Jewish character. But, before examining the evidence from the Synoptic Gospels, something should be said about the title's background in pre-Christian Judaism.

In the OT divine sonship was attributed to a range of subjects: in particular, angelic beings, the chosen people, and their king. Since they were understood to share in the heavenly life of God, angels could be called 'sons of God' (Job 1: 6; 2: 1; 38: 7; Pss. 29: 1; 89: 6; Dan. 3: 25).

The divine choice and deliverance begot Israel (Deut. 32: 5, 15, 18) as a people and made Israel God's children (Isa. 45: 11), God's 'first-born son' (Exod. 4: 22–3), and God's 'sons and daughters' (Deut. 32: 19; see 14: 1; Isa. 1: 2; 30: 1; 43: 6; Jer. 3: 22; 31: 9, 20; Ezek. 16: 20–1; Hos. 1: 10; Wis. 9: 7; 18: 13). Later applied to Jesus himself (Matt. 2: 15) but originally referring to the whole people, Hosea's classical words about divine sonship stated: 'When Israel was a child, I loved him, and out of Egypt I called my son' (Hos. 11: 1). Eventually the collective divine sonship based on God's act in electing and adopting the people was to be listed by Paul as Israel's first privilege (Rom. 9: 4). It was the destiny of

God's (collective) son, Israel, that Matthew saw fulfilled in Jesus.

Within the OT people as a whole, certain individuals could occasionally be called 'sons of God'. Although a sense of collective sonship dominated in pre-Christian Judaism, righteous and royal persons were also at times singled out. In the wisdom tradition a righteous person could be called God's 'child' or 'son' (Wis. 2: 13, 16, 18; 5: 5). The man who cares for widows and orphans 'will be like a son of the Most High' (Sir. 4: 10).

In ancient Egypt and elsewhere rulers were styled 'sons of God'. Given the way the person of the monarch was considered divine in the ancient Middle East, it is not surprising to find that God's promise through Nathan about an everlasting Davidic dynasty mentions Solomon, David's son and successor, in these terms: 'I will be his father, and he shall be my son' (2 Sam. 7: 14; see also 1 Chr. 17: 13; 22: 10; 28: 6). The royal psalms reflect the belief that the anointed king is deemed to be God's son: 'you are my son, today I have begotten you' (Ps. 2: 7). This refers to the day when the king is crowned as the people's God-given leader. The king is understood to rule by God's choice, through God's power, and in fulfilment of God's purpose. Another royal psalm, recalling the divine covenant with David (Ps. 89: 3–4, 19–37), presents God as saying of the Davidic king: 'he shall cry to me, "Thou art my Father, my God, and the Rock of Salvation." And I will make him the first-born, the highest of the kings of the earth' (Ps. 89: 26–7). Being enthroned on Zion where God is believed to 'dwell' (Ps. 2: 6), the royal son of David is legitimated by God—God's son in that sense but not in the sense of physical sonship (being literally God's offspring), nor in the sense of being divinized or literally made divine.

Having noted the connection between kingship and divine adoption, one should also observe the limited messianic role that divine sonship played in pre-Christian Judaism. Messianic expectations were expressed in terms of Davidic sonship, while the Davidic king received the royal title of 'God's son'. Yet 'son of God' hardly entered messianic expectations and was not an OT messianic title. Evidence from

Qumran suggests that it might have been just emerging at
the time of Jesus.[2] To put the puzzle in bold terms, if David
= God's son and if the Messiah = David's son, why not
draw the conclusion: the Messiah = God's son? But this was
not clearly done. By association the anointing of David (Ps.
89: 20) could have implied the anointed Messiah to come,
who like David would be God's son (Ps. 89: 26–7). But the
implication was not obviously drawn out. Luke 1: 32–5
should not seduce us into imagining that 'the son of the Most
High' or 'the son of God' was a firmly established messianic
title in pre-Christian Judaism. To speak of the people collectively as God's son or children was one thing. To use 'son
of God' as a messianic title was another. Such a title for the
future messianic king could have been felt to threaten Jewish
monotheism.

Before moving on from this sampling of sonship according
to pre-Christian Judaism, something must be added about
the correlatives of sonship: fatherhood and motherhood.
Although the OT uses 'father' (Hebrew *ab* = LXX *patēr*)
around 1,180 times in a normal, 'secular' sense, it calls (or
addresses) God as 'Father' only fifteen times. As we saw
above, the king of Davidic line cries out to God, 'You are my
Father' (Ps. 89: 26). But on the few occasions that God is
called 'Father', this is normally in reference to the people of
Israel (Jer. 31: 9), and rarely in reference to an individual (in
particular, the king) or to the whole of human kind. Here the
OT differs sharply from the ancient, non-Jewish world. El,
the Ugaritic god, was called 'the father of humanity' or 'the
father of gods and human beings'. Sin, the Babylonian moon-
god, was honoured as 'the father and begetter of gods and
human beings'. Among the Greeks, from the time of Homer
Zeus was known as 'the father of human beings and of gods'.
Let us see the OT usage in a little detail.

To encourage fidelity to the divine covenant, Malachi

---

[2] See 1QSa 2. 11–12; 4QFlor 1. 10–11; J. D. G. Dunn, *Christology in the Making*
(London: SCM Press, 2nd edn., 1989), 15–16; J. A. Fitzmyer, *A Wandering Aramean*
(Missoula, Mont.: Scholars Press, 1979), 102–7. On the question of the king as
God's son, see K. W. Whitelam, 'King and Kingship', *ABD* iv. 4–48, at 45. The
NT used 'Son of God' also in a somewhat messianic way (see not only Luke 1: 32–
5 but even John 1: 49; 11: 27).

appeals to the blessing of God's fatherhood enjoyed by Israel: 'Have we not all one Father? Has not one God created us?' (Mal. 2: 10). Deuteronomy has Moses making a similar appeal to a perverse people: 'Is not he [the Lord] your Father, who created you, who made you and established you? (Deut. 32: 6; see 32: 18). Tobit's song of praise blesses God 'because he is our Lord and God, he is our Father forever' (Tob. 13: 4).

In denouncing those who trust idols to bring them and their ship safely across the seas, the Book of Wisdom turns to God and confesses: 'It is your providence, O Father, that steers its [the ship's] course, because you have given it a path in the sea and a safe way through the waves (Wis. 14: 3; see 2: 16). Sirach elaborately addresses God as 'Lord, Father, and Ruler of my life' (Sir. 23: 1) and, with slight variation, as 'Lord, Father, and God of my life' (Sir. 23: 4). In an appendix, echoing Ps. 89: 26, the same book tells us: 'I appealed to the Lord, the Father of my Lord' (Sir. 51: 10). (Possibly this passage from Sirach reads: 'Lord, you are my Father'; so NRSV). Yahweh behaves as a father does towards his children (Ps. 103: 13; Prov. 3: 12; Mal. 3: 17).

In direct prayer to God, 'our Father' turns up twice in Second Isaiah. The patriarchs Abraham and Israel (= Jacob) are dead but God always remains powerfully present to deliver the people: 'You are our Father. Though Abraham does not know us and Israel does not acknowledge us, you, Lord, are our Father; our Redeemer from of old is your name' (Isa. 63: 16). A little later the prophet pleads with God on behalf of desolate Jerusalem and the ruined temple: 'Yet, Lord, you are our Father; we are the clay, and you are the potter; we are all the work of your hand' (Isa. 64: 8).

These two prayers to God as 'our Father' are based on the deliverance from Egypt which created the people and their divine sonship. Before making these prayers, the prophet has just portrayed God as saying, '"Surely they are my people, sons who will not deal falsely." And he became their deliverer in all their troubles. No envoy, no angel, but he himself delivered them, redeemed them in his love and pity. He lifted them up and carried them through all the days of old' (Isa. 63: 8–9).

This passage links up with those we cited above—on God's choice and deliverance bringing forth the people and making them his children. What can seem puzzling here is the asymmetrical nature of the language. The OT readily speaks of the people as God's children but rarely names or addresses God as 'Father' or 'our Father'. Probably the OT avoids applying this title (or that of 'Mother') to Yahweh, because such usage could suggest the 'natural', procreative activity attributed to El, Asherah, and other gods and goddesses of the Near East. Far from being that kind of biological, physical parent, Yahweh had no consort. The divine fatherhood (and the Israelites' corresponding status as God's sons and daughters) was understood to result from the free divine choice and intervention in the history of salvation. Perhaps the image of God as 'husband' to the people of Israel (e.g. Isa. 54: 4–8; Jer. 2: 2; Ezek. 16: 1–63; Hos. 2: 7, 19) also functioned to inhibit talk about God as 'Father'.[3]

So much for the divine fatherhood. What of Yahweh's motherhood? Although never in the OT directly addressed or spoken of as anyone's 'Mother', in the context of salvation God is compared to a woman in childbirth (Isa. 42: 14). The divine love is like that of a woman for her children (Isa. 49: 15). As a mother does, God wishes to comfort the suffering people (Isa. 66: 13). Less directly the OT speaks of God as conceiving and begetting the chosen people (Num. 11: 12; Deut. 32: 18; see Deut. 32: 15).

The official OT prohibition of divine images witnessed to the sense that God was/is neither male nor female, and is simply beyond creaturely images. At the same time, the material we have just reviewed shows how members of prophetic circles and other Israelites acknowledged that God embodies in a perfect way the best characteristics of both men and women—the fullness of fatherhood and motherhood. Like our metaphors, their metaphors for God had to include both the male and the female. In a passage in the Thanksgiving Hymns from Qumran the motherly and fath-

---

[3] See A. Strotmann, *'Mein Vater bist Du!' (Sir 51,10): zur Bedeutung der Vaterschaft Gottes in kanonischen und nichtkanonischen frühjüdischen Schriften* (Frankfurt: Verlag Josef Knecht, 1991). J. Sievers has contributed a valuable review of this important book in *Biblica*, 74 (1993), 420–3.

erly images for God come together beautifully: 'For Thou art a father to all [the Sons] of Thy truth, and as a woman who tenderly loves her babe, so dost Thou rejoice in them; and as a foster-father bearing a child in his lap, so carest Thou for all Thy creatures.'[4]

When we turn from OT origins to the Synoptic Gospels, the evidence makes it clear that Jesus understood his relationship to God as sonship. Since it was/is a relationship with God that automatically means we are dealing with a divine sonship. But what kind of divine sonship did Jesus imply or lay claim to? A somewhat distinctive one? Or a divine sonship intimate to the point of being qualitatively different and radically unique? To prevent things from becoming confused and confusing when examining the Synoptics, it could be useful to distinguish between what Jesus said or at least is represented as saying about his divine sonship and what others say about him in this connection.

We come across Jesus speaking absolutely of 'the Son' but never 'the Son of God'. In an important passage, heavy with wisdom language (Matt. 11: 25–30; see Luke 10: 21–2), Jesus refers to the Father, identified as 'Lord of heaven and earth', and claims that a unique and exclusive (salvific) knowledge of 'the Father' is possessed by 'the Son' who is tacitly identified as 'me': 'All things have been delivered to me by my Father; and no one knows the Son except the Father, and no one knows the Father except the Son and anyone to whom the Son chooses to reveal him' (Matt. 11: 27).[5] Then Mark 13: 32 (followed probably by Matt. 24: 36) also has Jesus referring absolutely to 'the Son' and (implicitly) acknowledging limits to his knowledge over against 'the Father' with respect to the end of the age: 'Of that day and of that hour no one knows, not even the angels in heaven, nor the Son, but only the Father.' Thirdly, a parable of the vineyard and the wicked tenants reaches its climax with the owner sending

---

[4] G. Vermes, *The Dead Sea Scrolls in English* (Harmondsworth: Penguin Books, 3rd edn., 1987), 192 (= 1QH 9, 34–5).

[5] On Matt. 11: 26–7 see W. D. Davies and D. C. Allison, *The Gospel According to Saint Matthew*, International Critical Commentary 2 vols. (Edinburgh: T. & T. Clark, 1988, 1991), ii. 271–87. On *huios* and *huiothesia*, see W. von Martitz *et al.*, *TDNT* viii, 334–99.

to the tenants 'my son' and their killing this 'beloved/only
son' (Mark 12: 1–12 parr.). Mark or the pre-Markan tradition
has evidently added 'beloved/only' (see Mark 1: 11), but the
substance of the parable, with its clear, 'allegorical' reference
to his own violent death, appears to derive from Jesus. One
should note also that sense of his mission as the eschatological
climax of God's saving interventions (the 'finally' of v. 6). Yet
neither here nor elsewhere in the Synoptic Gospels does Jesus
ever come out into the open to say, 'I am the Son of God' (see,
however, Matt. 27: 43). Curiously he does not do so even in the
baptismal formula ('. . . and of the Son') 'quoted' by the risen
Jesus at the end of Matthew's Gospel (Matt. 28: 19).

Three times the Synoptic Gospels present Jesus as referring to the divine sonship enjoyed by others here and hereafter: 'Blessed are the peacemakers, for they shall be called
sons of God' (Matt. 5: 9); 'love your enemies . . . and you will
be sons of the Most High' (Luke 6: 35 = Matt. 5: 44–5);
'they cannot die anymore, because they are equal to angels
and are sons of God, being sons of the resurrection' (Luke
20: 36). One might argue that the promise of divine sonship
to peacemakers and those who love their enemies goes back
very probably to the preaching of Jesus. The verse about the
risen sons of God seems to be Luke's addition to a pericope
on the resurrection he has taken over from Mark 12: 18–27.

All in all, even if every one of these references to 'son(s) of
God' in the Synoptic Gospels comes from Jesus himself, we
are faced with less use of the divine sonship theme than we
find in the OT, which, while not often but in a way that is
widely spread, names the whole people and/or the Davidic
king 'children/sons/daughters of God'. The situation comes
across, however, as the opposite with God as 'Father'. We
saw above how rarely the OT calls God 'Father', especially
in prayers addressed to God. Jesus seems to have changed
that situation.

Mark's Gospel five or six times calls God 'Father'—most
strikingly in Jesus' prayer in Gethsemane: 'Abba, Father, all
things are possible to you; take this cup from me. Yet not my
will but yours' (Mark 14: 36). Even if 'Abba' was not a child's
address to its male parent, Jesus evidently spoke of, or rather
with, God as his Father in a direct familial way that was

unique, or at least highly unusual, in Palestinian Judaism. In other words, 'Abba' was a characteristic and significantly distinctive feature of Jesus' prayer life (Mark 14: 36; in Matt. 6: 9; 11: 25–6; 16: 17; Luke 11: 2; and perhaps other passages in Matthew and Luke, 'Father' stands for the original 'Abba').[6] Jesus' example, at least in the early years of Christianity, encouraged his followers to pray to God in that very familiar way (Gal. 4: 6; Rom. 8: 15). As Dunn points out, 'the clear implication' of these passages is that Paul regarded the 'Abba' prayer 'as something distinctive to those who had received the eschatological Spirit'—in other words, 'as a distinguishing mark of those who shared the Spirit of Jesus' sonship, of an inheritance shared with Christ'.[7]

Altogether in the Synoptic Gospels (excluding simply parallel cases) Jesus speaks of 'Father', 'my (heavenly) Father', 'your (heavenly) Father', or 'our Father' fifty-one times. Sometimes we are dealing with a Father-saying which has been drawn from Q (e.g. Matt. 11: 25–7 = Luke 10: 21–2), or else with a Father-saying attested by Matthew alone (e.g.

---

[6] When reporting Jesus' prayer in Gethsemane, Matthew and Luke do not reproduce the Markan 'Abba', just as they drop other Aramaic expressions Mark records (Mark 3: 17; 5: 41; 7: 11, 34; 15: 34). The only Markan Aramaisms that survive in either Matthew or Luke are 'Hosanna' (Mark 11: 9–10 = Matt. 21: 9) and 'Golgotha' (Mark 15: 22 = Matt. 27: 33). See J. Ashton, 'Abba', *ABD* i. 7–8; J. Barr, ' "Abba" isn't Daddy', *Journal of Theological Studies*, 39 (1988), 28–47; Davies and Allison, *The Gospel According to Saint Matthew*, i. 600–2; J. A. Fitzmyer, *'Abba* and Jesus' Relation to God', in *A cause de l'Évangile*, Lectio Divina 123 (Paris: Éditions du Cerf, 1988), 15–38; U. Luz, *Matthew 1–7: A Commentary*, trans. W. C. Linss (Edinburgh: T. & T. Clark, 1990), 375–7; E. Schuller, '4Q372: A Text about Joseph', *Revue de Qumran*, 14 (1990), 352–5, 362–3. M. R. D'Angelo has argued that using 'Abba' or 'Father' of God or in prayer to God cannot be traced back to Jesus with certainty. She finds it significant that 'Father' is so used 'only' nine times in Q and 'only' four times in Mark (who also reports Jesus as using 'Abba' once): see her 'Theology in Mark and Q: *Abba* and "Father" in Context', *Harvard Theological Review*, 85 (1992), 149–74, at 157 and 162. Set, however, these statistics over against the entire OT, where God is called or addressed as 'Father' only fifteen times: that is to say, in a corpus at least thirty-five times longer than Mark and Q (together) there are only slightly more occurrences of this usage. Qumran has yielded three texts which address God as 'Father' or 'my Father' (see D'Angelo, 'Theology in Mark and Q', 151–3), and this occurs also in the prayer of Eleazar from 3 Macc. 6: 3–4, 7–8. But there are no other texts calling on God as Father which can be confidently dated to pre-Christian Judaism. John Ashton's conclusion seems to remain justified: 'the personal sense of the fatherhood of God was a typically Christian development of the Judaic tradition, and . . . this probably originated in a recollection of Jesus' teaching and of the example of his own prayer' ('Abba', 7).

[7] Dunn, *Christology in the Making*, 27.

Matt. 16: 17) or by Luke alone (e.g. Luke 22: 29) that seems
to be an authentic saying of Jesus, even if the original setting
for that teaching may well have been lost. Matthew shows a
liking for 'heavenly', and at various points has added the
adjective to sayings that originally spoke only of 'your Father'
or 'my Father' (e.g. Matt. 6: 32).[8] The same evangelist may
at times have inserted 'Father' into his sources (e.g. Matt. 6:
26; 10: 29, 32–3; 12: 50; 20: 23; 26: 29). Even discounting a
number of examples as non-authentic, it is clear that Jesus
spoke fairly frequently of God as Father.

Further, Jesus seems to have called those who did God's
will 'my brother, and sister, and mother' (Mark 3: 31–5 parr.).
But being his brothers and sisters did not put others on the
same level with him as sons and daughters of God. Jesus
apparently distinguished between 'my' Father and 'your'
Father, a distinction upheld by Matthew. At least no saying
has been preserved in which Jesus linked the disciples with
himself, so that *together* they could say 'Our Father'. When
he encouraged the disciples to pray to God as Father, the
wording 'Our Father' (Matt. 6: 9, unlike Luke 11: 2, where
there is no 'Our') was for the disciples only. If Jesus did
actually say *'Our* Father', it was in a prayer he proposed for
others ('Pray then like this'—Matt. 6: 9). He invited his
hearers to accept a new relationship with God as Father, yet
it was a relationship that depended on his (Luke 22: 29–30)
and was distinct from his. When Jesus spoke in a startlingly
new way of 'my Father', was he conscious of being 'Son' in a
distinctive way? Was he conscious of a unique divine sonship?
We will return to this point shortly.

In the Synoptic Gospels, it should be added, others speak
of Jesus or even address him as the Son of God. The disciples
do so (Matt. 14: 33; 16: 16), as does the centurion after the
death of Jesus (Mark 15: 39 = Matt. 27: 54). At the hearing
before Caiaphas Jesus is charged with claiming to be the Son
of God (Mark 14: 61 par.). He is mocked on the cross for
making the same claim (Matt. 27: 40, 43). From the other
world, an angel announces his birth as that of the Son of God

---

[8] While 'heavenly' is used of God as Father only twice in Mark and Luke (Mark
11: 25; Luke 11: 13), Matthew uses the qualifier thirty-one times.

(Luke 1: 32–5). Evil spirits tempt Jesus or name him under that title (Matt. 4: 3, 6; Luke 4: 3, 9, 41; Mark 3: 11; 5: 7; Matt. 8: 29). At his baptism and at the transfiguration a heavenly voice recognizes Jesus as 'my beloved Son' (Mark 1: 11; 9: 7 parr.). Lastly, the evangelist Mark calls Jesus 'the Son of God' (Mark 1: 1).

How much of all this actually goes back to the ministry of Jesus? Did his disciples (and a Roman centurion) acknowledge him then as Son of God? Was there a voice from heaven at his baptism and transfiguration? If so was it significant and how was it significant for Jesus' own self-understanding and sense of communion with the Father? Was Jesus in fact charged and mocked for claiming to be the Son of God? Did Satan tempt him over his divine sonship? It is not the place here to make a huge digression and tackle these questions. It is enough to note that, whereas they never represent Jesus as using the title 'the Son of God' (see, however, Matt. 27: 43 where his taunters recall, 'he said, "I am the Son of God"', even though Matthew's Gospel never reports Jesus saying just that), the Synoptic Gospels portray others as calling or addressing him by that title. At the very least that reflects what Christians were doing in the 60s, 70s, and 80s (when Mark, Matthew, and Luke wrote their Gospels) and even earlier (wherever the evangelists drew on already existing sources in applying 'the Son of God' to Jesus).

The Title's Meaning

We saw above that pre-Christian Judaism characteristically used 'son/children of God' collectively of the whole people and that in the OT no individual ever addresses God as 'my Father'. (Even the one partial exception to that universal negative does not have the Davidic king directly saying to God 'you are my Father' (Ps. 89: 26). Rather this is a prayer which God puts in the mouth of the king.[9]) What Jesus did

[9] The targum to Ps. 89: 27, however, has the messianic king address God as 'Abba'; see B. Byrne, *'Sons of God'—Seed of Abraham*, Analecta Biblica 83 (Rome: Biblical Institute Press, 1979), 222–3. With respect to Jesus' sonship (as well as the wider sonship of believers), Byrne makes the helpful suggestion that a 'formerly hidden/now revealed' progression operates in the continuity between the earthly and post-resurrection life of Jesus (ibid. 197–211).

with the language of divine sonship was first of all to apply it
individually (to himself) and to fill it with a meaning that
lifted 'Son of God' beyond the level of his being merely a
human being made like Adam in the image of God, his being
perfectly sensitive to the Holy Spirit (Luke 4: 1, 14, 18), his
bringing God's peace (Luke 2: 14; 10: 5–6) albeit in his own
way (Matt. 10: 34 = Luke 12: 51), or even his being God's
designated Messiah.

Above we noted how, according to the Synoptic Gospels,
Jesus referred to himself obliquely as 'the Son' and even more
significantly spoke of God as 'my Father' (Matt. 11: 27 par.;
16: 17; Luke 22: 29). He not only spoke like 'the Son' but
also acted like 'the Son' in knowing and revealing the truth
about God, in changing the divine law, in forgiving sins, in
being the one through whom others could become children
of God, and in acting with total obedience as the agent for
God's final kingdom. This clarifies the charge of blasphemy
brought against him at the end (Mark 14: 64 par.); he had
given the impression of claiming to stand on a par with God.
Jesus came across as expressing a unique filial consciousness
and as laying claim to a unique filial relationship with the
God whom he addressed as 'Abba'.[10] Even if historically he
never called himself 'the only' Son of God (see John 1: 14,
18; 3: 16, 18), Jesus presented himself as Son and not just as
one who was the divinely appointed Messiah (and therefore
'son' of God). He made himself out to be more than just
someone chosen and anointed as divine representative to fulfil
an eschatological role in and for the kingdom. Implicitly
Jesus claimed an essential, 'ontological' relationship of
sonship towards God which provided the grounds for his
functions as revealer, lawgiver, forgiver of sins, and agent of
the final kingdom. Those functions (his 'doing') depended
on his ontological relationship as Son of God (his 'being').

Jesus invited his hearers to accept God as a loving, merciful
Father. He worked towards mediating to them a new relation-
ship with God, even to the point that they too could use
'Abba' when addressing God in prayer. Yet Jesus' consistent

---

[10] It should be emphasized here that Jesus' consciousness of such divine sonship
is one thing, whereas (human) consciousness of divine pre-existence would be quite
another.

distinction between 'my' Father and 'your' Father showed that he was not inviting the disciples to share with him an identical relationship of sonship. He was apparently conscious of a qualitative distinction between his sonship and their sonship which was derived from and depended on his. His way of being son was different from theirs.

In their own way John and Paul maintained this distinction. Paul expressed our new relationship with God as taking place through an 'adoption' (Gal. 4: 5; Rom. 8: 15), which makes us 'children of God' (Rom. 8: 16–17) or, alternatively, 'sons of God' (Rom. 8: 14; Gal. 4: 6–7). John distinguished between the only Son of God (John 1: 14, 18; 3: 16, 18) and all those who through faith can become 'children of God' (John 1: 12; 11: 52; and 1 John 3: 1–2, 10; 5: 2). Paul and John likewise maintained and developed the correlative of all this, Jesus' stress on the fatherhood of God. Over one hundred times John's Gospel names God as 'Father'. Paul's typical greeting to his correspondents runs as follows; 'Grace to you and peace from God *our Father* and the/our Lord Jesus Christ' (Rom. 1: 7; 1 Cor. 1: 3; 2 Cor. 1: 2; Gal. 1: 3; Phil. 1: 2; 2 Thess. 1: 2; Philem. 3).

If he distinguished between our graced situation as God's adopted children and that of Jesus as Son of God, what did Paul understand the latter's 'natural' divine sonship to entail? First of all, he speaks of God 'sending his own Son in the likeness of sinful nature and to deal with sin' (Rom. 8: 3). In a similar passage Paul says that 'when the fullness of time had come God sent his Son, born of a woman, born under the law' (Gal. 4: 4). Does Paul think here of an eternally *preexistent* Son coming into the world from his Father in heaven to set us free from sin and death (Rom. 8: 3, 32) and make us God's adopted children (Gal. 4: 4–7)?

Our answer will (1) partly depend on the way we interpret other Pauline passages which do not use the title 'Son of God' (2 Cor. 8: 9; Phil. 2: 6–11). These latter passages present a pre-existent Christ taking the initiative, through his 'generosity' in 'becoming poor' for us and 'assuming the form of a slave'. Our answer will (2) also depend on whether we judge 1 Cor. 8: 6 and Col. 1: 16 to imply that as a pre-existent being

the Son was active at creation.[11] It should be noted that 1
Cor. 8: 6, without mentioning as such 'the Son', runs: 'There
is one God, the Father, from whom are all things and for
whom we exist, and one Lord, Jesus Christ, through whom
are all things and through whom we exist.' Naming God as
'the Father' moves us toward talk of 'the Son'. In the case of
Col. 1: 16, the whole hymn (Col. 1: 15–20) does not give Jesus
any title. However, he has just been referred to (Col. 1: 13) as
God's 'beloved Son'.

3. Third, it should be observed that the language of 'sending' (or, for that matter, 'coming' with its stress on personal
purpose (Mark 10: 45 par.; Luke 12: 49, 51 par.)) by itself does
not necessarily imply pre-existence. Otherwise we would
have to ascribe pre-existence to John the Baptist, 'a man sent
from God', who 'came to bear witness to the light' (John 1:
6–8; see Matt. 11: 10, 18 = Luke 7: 27, 33). In the OT,
angelic and human messengers, especially prophets, were
'sent' by God, but one should add at once that the prophets
sent by God were never called God's sons. It makes a difference that in our Pauline passages it was *God's Son* who was
sent. Here being 'sent' by God means more than merely
receiving a divine commission and includes coming from a
heavenly pre-existence and enjoying a divine origin. (4) In
their context, the three Son of God passages we are looking
at (Rom. 8: 3, 32; Gal. 4: 4) certainly do not focus on the
Son's pre-existence but on his being sent or given up to free
us from sin and death, make us God's adopted children, and
let us live (and pray) with the power of the indwelling Spirit.
Nevertheless, the apostle's soteriology presupposes here a
Christology that includes divine pre-existence. It is precisely
because Christ is the pre-existent Son who comes from the
Father that he can turn us into God's adopted sons and
daughters.

Other Son of God passages in Paul centre on the crucifixion
and resurrection of Jesus and their (immediate and final)
salvific consequences. The death of God's Son has 'recon-

[11] In Ch. 2 we have seen the reasons for interpreting Phil. 2: 6 and Col. 1: 16 in
terms of divine pre-existence. In Ch. 6 we will look at the implications of 1 Cor. 8:
6. In Ch. 1 we saw how Rudolf Bultmann had no difficulty about taking 2 Cor. 8: 9
(and Phil. 2: 6–9) to express 'attitudes of the pre-existent' Christ.

ciled' us with God (Rom. 5: 10) and called us into 'fellowship'
with God's Son (1 Cor. 1: 9). We have been made God's
adopted children and heirs with Christ (Rom. 8: 14–17; Gal.
4: 6–7) to await in hope the final resurrection of the sons of
God (Rom. 8: 19–25). All these saving graces coming through
God's Son can be summed up as being 'conformed' to his
'image' (Rom. 8: 29). As always, *redemption* goes hand in
hand with divine *revelation* (and its correlative, human faith).
The revelation of God's Son brought Paul's call to preach
him among the Gentiles (Gal. 1: 16; see Acts 9: 20). Through
the spiritual power of the risen Son, Paul has been enabled
to 'bring about the obedience of faith among all the nations'
(Rom. 1: 4–5; see 2 Cor. 1: 19–20). Preaching the 'gospel' of
God's Son (Rom. 1: 9) is Paul's service of revelation. But,
in general, the *salvation* which reached its climax with the
crucifixion and resurrection of God's Son (rather than the
divine self-*revelation* which also came then to its climax) is
more to the fore when Paul speaks of Jesus as God's Son. In
a personal passage Paul recalls the crucifixion of 'the Son of
God, who loved me, gave himself for me', and now 'lives in
me' (Gal. 2: 20). Christian life means 'waiting for' God's 'Son
from heaven' and the deliverance he will bring (1 Thess. 1:
10). At the end the risen Son will destroy all enemies, even
death, and effect the entire subjection of all things to God (1
Cor. 15: 20–8). These passages highlight the Son of God's
redemptive and revelatory impact on Christian believers, on
Paul's ministry and life, and on the entire universe. The Son
can have this impact because of what he is and because of
what he became (through his crucifixion and resurrection
from the dead). He is the 'post-existent' Son, existing and
acting as risen from the dead. To put matters equivalently,
Christ's sonship is seen eschatologically as post-existence
(not pre-existence). He is not so much directly described in
his relationship to his Father but in terms of what, as sent by
his Father, he has achieved and will achieve for human beings
and their world. In other words, when Paul speaks of Jesus
as God's Son, he thinks more of his soteriological (and
revelatory) doing than of his christological being.

Beyond question, Christ's resurrection from the dead is
the major focus in Paul's presentation of his divine sonship.

One passage in which the apostle draws on traditional, credal material could be interpreted as going much further and proposing that Christ became Son of God through his resurrection, not having been that before. In other words, the resurrection could have been the moment of his adoption as God's Son. On two levels (human and 'spiritual') the passage describes the 'content' of Paul's preaching as 'the gospel concerning his [God's] Son who was descended from David according to the flesh and declared Son of God in power according to the Spirit of holiness by his resurrection from the dead' (Rom. 1: 3–4). All of this might suggest that, just as his human conception and birth made Jesus (in the historical, earthly order) the messianic son of David, so his resurrection from the dead made him Son of God (in the heavenly, divine order). However, Paul does not intend to allege that Jesus was, so to speak, found 'suitable' and thus *became* God's Son for the first time at the resurrection. The passage itself calls Jesus God's 'Son' *before* it goes on to speak either of his descent from David or of his designation as Son of God. Moreover, the same letter twice names Jesus as the Son of God before he was 'sent in the likeness of sinful flesh' and 'given up for us all' in his death (Rom 8: 3, 32). In another letter Paul calls Jesus Son of God when he was 'sent' to 'redeem those who were under the law' and when he 'gave himself up for me' (Gal. 2: 20; 4: 4–5). When he came and was crucified, Jesus already was the Son of God; his divine sonship, while fully deployed with power for us from the time of his rising from the dead, did not simply stem from the resurrection. What he had been before (Son of God) was now definitively realized, confirmed, and given clearer definition by his passage from his earthly state to his risen state. The resurrection showed that Jesus, born of the house of David on the human level, was/is God's Son on the divine level. (See Phil. 2: 11; Eph. 1: 20–3; Heb. 1: 1–13; 2: 5–9 for other examples of the revelatory power of Jesus' resurrection/exaltation.)

If we agree that Paul himself did not want to say that Jesus received divine sonship for the first time as a result of the resurrection, what of the tradition he used in Rom. 1: 3–4? Did the early Christians whose faith was expressed by that formula think that Jesus was first made Son of God at his resurrection? Two reasons suggest an answer in the negative. First, the Jesus-traditions which were in circulation from the 30s and fed into the Synoptic Gospels testified clearly to his 'Abba-consciousness'. Christians could hardly have preserved those traditions while refusing to recognize him as already God's Son during the ministry. Second, some scholars detect echoes of pre-Pauline material behind the 'sending' and 'giving up' of God's Son in several of the passages which we cited above from the apostle (Rom. 8: 3, 32; Gal. 4: 4–5). If this derivation is correct, the early Christians echoed by Paul recognized Jesus as already being the Son of God prior to his crucifixion and resurrection.

Luke-Acts raises a problem similar to the one thrown up by Rom. 1: 3–4. In a speech by Paul located in Pisidian Antioch and probably reflecting an early christological theme, Acts quotes Ps. 2: 7, interpreting it as a divine promise and 'prophecy' fulfilled by Christ's resurrection: 'We bring you the good news that what God promised to the fathers, this he has fulfilled to us their children by raising Jesus, as also it is written in the second psalm, "You are my Son, today I have begotten you"' (Acts 13: 33). Somewhat like Rom. 1: 3–4, the context of these words on Jesus' resurrection refers to King David (Acts 13: 22–3, 34, 36), and the claim is made: from David's 'posterity God brought to Israel a Saviour, Jesus, as he promised' (Acts 13: 23). Without using the title 'Christ', verse 33 speaks of Jesus in messianic terms. Paul's speech goes on to add that in the death of Jesus the people and rulers of Jerusalem unwittingly fulfilled all the prophecies, evidently messianic prophecies (Acts 13: 27–9). Thus the whole passage brings up the question: is Acts saying here that Jesus was Davidic Messiah during his lifetime and was made Son of God for the first time through his resurrection from the dead, Ps. 2: 7 helping the author to see that the resurrection was analogous to the begetting or the birthday of a child? Only by ignoring the whole context of Luke-Acts could we answer in the affirmative. Way back in the infancy narrative Luke has already spoken of the child to be born of Mary as God's Son (Luke 1: 32, 35). Likewise Luke recognizes Jesus as already being 'the Son' during his ministry

(Luke 10: 22; 20: 13). Hence, instead of first creating it, the resurrection vindicates and manifests the status which Luke (and his source(s)) have recognized from the beginning and which Jesus has already claimed for himself.[12]

The problem raised by Acts 13: 33 could remind us of Acts 2: 36, where Peter says, 'Let all the house of Israel know assuredly that God has made him both Lord and Christ, this Jesus whom you crucified.' In isolation this verse might suggest that his resurrection from the dead made Jesus for the first time 'Lord and Christ'. Luke, however, is not going back on what he has said about the new-born Jesus being already 'Lord and Christ' (Luke 2: 11). The resurrection is confirming and manifesting the status Jesus enjoyed from the very outset. He who was ontologically 'Lord and Christ' from his conception became functionally so after his resurrection from the dead.

Thus far, in exploring the significance of the Son of God title, we have concentrated on how Jesus himself understood his divine sonship and then on what Paul associated with the title. Instead of pausing to examine the characteristic ways other NT authors (in particular, Mark, Matthew, and the author of Hebrews) profiled the title, I want to jump ahead to John. Although in his massive use of the title (twenty-two or twenty-three times in the Gospel) John fills 'Son of God' with a certain new content, in various ways he is only developing themes that go back to the Synoptic Gospels and Jesus himself.

In the Fourth Gospel Jesus is the eternally pre-existent

---

[12] Like some others Dunn argues, largely on the basis of its appearance in Acts 13: 33, that Ps. 2: 7 was associated with Jesus' resurrection in 'early Christian apologetic' and that 'primitive Christian preaching seems to have regarded Jesus' resurrection as the day of his appointment to divine sonship, as the event by which he became God's son' (*Christology in the Making*, 36). Heb. 1: 5 and 5: 5 quote Ps. 2: 7 in connection with Jesus' exaltation, but Mark 1: 11 echoes the verse in connection with his baptism. In any case the last few years have seen a number of scholars more aware of the problem of identifying 'primitive christological emphases' (ibid.) in the speeches of Acts. Finally, Dunn mitigates the 'became God's Son' when he goes on to say about the first Christians: they '*regarded Jesus' resurrection as introducing him into a relationship with God* [that was/is] *decisively new, eschatologically . . . different from what he had enjoyed before* (before and after birth was the imagery used)' (ibid.; italics his). Such a change in relationship is one thing, *becoming* God's Son is another. The imagery of birth is instructive here; before birth I already was my mother's son.

Son who was sent from heaven into the world by the Father (e.g. John 3: 17; 4: 34; 5: 24, 30, 37). He remains conscious of the divine pre-existence he enjoyed with the Father (John 8: 23, 38, 42). He is one with the Father (John 10: 30; 14: 7) and loved by the Father (John 3: 35; 5: 20; 10: 17; 17: 23–6). The Son has the divine power to give life and to judge (John 5: 21–2, 25–6; 6: 40; 8: 16; 17: 2). Through his death, resurrection, and ascension the Son is glorified by the Father (John 17: 1, 5, 24), but it is not a glory that is thereby essentially enhanced. His glory was not only already there from the time of the incarnation to reveal the Father (John 1: 14) but also pre-existed the creation of the world (John 17: 5, 24). Where Paul and the author of Hebrews picture Jesus almost as the elder brother or the first-born of God's new eschatological family (Rom. 8: 14–17, 29; Heb. 2: 10–12), John insists even more on the clear qualitative difference between Jesus' sonship and that of others. Being God's 'only Son' (John 1: 14, 18; 3: 16, 18), he enjoys a truly unique and exclusive relationship with the Father.

Some at least of these themes go back to Jesus himself. Although we have no real evidence for holding that he was humanly aware of his eternal pre-existence as Son, his 'Abba-consciousness' revealed an intimate loving relationship with the Father. The full Johannine development of the Father–Son relationship rests on an authentic basis in the Jesus-tradition (Mark 14: 36; Matt. 11: 25–6; 16: 17; Luke 11: 2). Second, Jesus not only thought of himself as God's Son, but also spoke of himself as sent by God. Once again, John develops the theme of the Son's mission, which is already present in sayings that at least partly go back to Jesus (Mark 9: 37; Matt. 15: 24; Luke 10: 16), especially in Mark 12: 6, where it is a question of the sending of a 'beloved Son'. Third, the Johannine theme of the Son with power to judge in the context of eternal life finds its original historical source in the sayings of Jesus about his power to dispose of things in the kingdom assigned to him by 'my Father' (Luke 22: 29–30) and about one's relationship to him deciding one's final destiny before God (Luke 12: 8–9). Fourth, albeit less insistently, when inviting his audience to accept a new filial relationship with God, Jesus, as we have seen, distinguished his own relationship to God from theirs. The exclusive Johannine language of God's 'only Son' has its real source in Jesus' preaching. All in all, Johannine theology fully deploys Jesus' divine sonship but does so by building up what we already find in the Synoptic Gospels and what, at least in part, derives from the earthly Jesus himself.

Naming the Son of God

The last question this chapter has set itself to answer is: what led the early Christians to call Jesus 'Son of God'? 'Memory' and 'experience' pull together the major strands of their motivation.

First, the memory of that personal sense of filiation which came through Jesus' prayer, teaching, and other activity played its part. The Synoptic Gospels witness to the way in which Christians kept alive the memory of Jesus' filial consciousness: his conviction of radical obedience towards, authorization by, and specific relationship to the God whom he called 'Abba'. That sense of filial consciousness helped to fuel deadly opposition but was vindicated by Jesus' resurrection.

Second, believers experienced Jesus' post-existent activity as the Saviour (see the next chapter) and the Son of God, who with the Father had sent the Holy Spirit (see the next chapter). They experienced the risen Jesus as the one who made it possible for them to join him in praying to God as 'Abba' (Rom. 8: 15; Gal. 4: 6). They recognized that in and through the living Jesus they had come to share in his divine filiation. That experience underpinned their new faith in the fatherhood of the God of Israel, who, in the first place, is/was 'the God and Father of our Lord Jesus Christ' (e.g. Rom. 15: 6; 2 Cor. 1: 3; 11: 31).

The obviously relational nature within the life of God of the titles 'Son of God' and 'Word' gave these titles their special prominence in the christological and trinitarian debates that flourished during the first few centuries of the Church's existence. Paul along with other early Christians, however, showed a marked preference for 'Lord' (and 'Christ') as designations for the risen Jesus. (Matthew,

Hebrews, and especially the Johannine literature show more interest in the Son of God title.) The prominent way the NT called Jesus 'Lord' suggests devoting the next chapter to this and some related titles.

In the end much of the importance of the Son of God title lies in its being rooted in Jesus' earthly ministry (as well as in its OT background), and in its being intimately related to the strong sense of God's loving and life-giving fatherhood promoted by Jesus and reflected in Paul's letters.

At the same time, even before developing the topics for the next chapter, we should recall that the recognition of Jesus' divinity did/does not stand or fall with the Son of God title, its antiquity, and its meaning. In Paul's typical greeting to his addressees, 'God the Father' and 'our Lord Jesus Christ' are named together as the source of 'grace and peace'—that is to say, of integral salvation (e.g. Gal. 1: 3). Such a divine prerogative as the work of creation was, as we have seen, quickly attributed to the risen Jesus. In the making of Paul's apostolic vocation, Christ stands on the divine side, not on that of human beings (Gal. 1: 1). The next chapter will investigate further how NT Christians explicated their faith that 'the fullness of divinity' dwelt/dwells in Jesus (Col. 2: 9), who had for them the same religious value as God.

6

Lord, Saviour, God,
and Spirit

❖ ❖

It was their [the Christians'] habit on a fixed day to
assemble before daylight and recite by turns a form of
words to Christ as God.

(Pliny the Younger, *Letter* 10)

Those who wish to acquire a more adequate sense of how NT
Christians evaluated Jesus' being and doing rightly examine
other high christological titles like 'Lord', 'Saviour', and
'God'. Such titles exemplify further what Paul, John, and
other NT witnesses held to be important about Jesus.

Lord

One of the oldest (and briefest) Christian prayers turns up in
a closing benediction from Paul: 'Maranatha' (1 Cor. 16: 22).[1]
Transliterated into Greek from two Aramaic words, in this
context 'Maranatha' probably means 'Our Lord, come!'
rather than 'Our Lord has come.' The Bible ends with the
same prayer (but in Greek): 'Come, Lord Jesus!' (Rev. 22:
20). In this way Christians prayed that the risen and exalted
Jesus would come to them in his post-Easter glory. As we saw
in Chapter 3, Jesus was remembered as speaking of himself
as the Son of man who would come in glory at the end to

[1] J. A. Fitzmyer, 'New Testament *Kyrios* and *Maranatha* and their Aramaic
Background', in *To Advance the Gospel* (New York: Crossroad, 1981), 218–35; id.,
'The Semitic Background of the New Testament *Kyrios*-Title', in *A Wandering
Aramean* (Missoula, Mont.: Scholars Press, 1979), 115–42. Like many other scholars
nowadays, Fitzmyer supports a Palestinian, Semitic religion origin for the *Kyrios*-
title.

judge. Yet the early Christians did not pray 'Come, Son of man,' but 'Come, Lord Jesus.'

Applying the title 'Lord' to the crucified and risen Jesus began very early in Christianity. Our oldest Christian document, 1 Thessalonians, calls him by that title twenty-four times. In a passage which parallels the Synoptic Gospels' language about the apocalyptic Son of man's future descent from heaven at the parousia, Paul does not use that designation but six times writes of the coming Christ as 'Lord' (1 Thess. 4: 13–5: 3). Elsewhere in the same letter he also gives Christ the title of *Kyrios* in an eschatological context (e.g. 2: 19; 3: 13). Altogether Paul uses that title for Jesus around 230 times and does so sometimes in passages that derive from a pre-Pauline tradition (e.g. Rom. 10: 9; 1 Cor. 12: 3; Phil. 2: 11). The mark of a Christian was the confession of Jesus as Lord (Rom. 10: 9).

Paul maintained Jesus' own practice by speaking of God as 'Abba' (Rom. 8: 15; Gal. 4: 6), 'the Father' (e.g. Gal. 1: 1; Phil. 2: 11), or the 'Father of our Lord Jesus Christ' (e.g. Rom. 15: 6; see 2 Cor. 11: 31). But then, as we saw in the last chapter, Paul's typical greeting to his correspondents ran as follows: 'Grace to you and peace from God our Father and the Lord Jesus Christ' (e.g. Rom. 1: 7). Here the apostle set Christ on a par with Yahweh—without, however, identifying him with Yahweh since he was not 'Abba'.

Paul even split the Jewish confession of monotheism in the Shema (Deut. 6: 4–5), glossing 'God' with Father and 'Lord' with Jesus Christ to put Jesus as Lord alongside God the Father: 'For us there is *one God, the Father*, from whom are all things and for whom we exist, *and one Lord, Jesus Christ*, through whom are all things and through whom we exist' (1 Cor. 8: 6). Here the title 'one Lord' expanded the Shema to contain Jesus. Using the classic monotheistic text of Judaism, Paul recast his perception of God by introducing Jesus as 'Lord' and redefining Jewish monotheism to produce a christological monotheism.[2] By and large, Paul reserved 'God' for 'the Father', whereas he used 'Lord' (or 'Son of God') of

[2] See N. T. Wright, *The Climax of the Covenant,* (Edinburgh: T. & T. Clark, 1991), 120–36.

Jesus. In its highest religious sense 'Lord' referred to Jesus more often than to the Father in the Pauline letters.

Paul's redefining of Jewish monotheism also involved acknowledging Christ as agent of creation ('through whom are all things and through whom we exist'). To speak of Christ in such terms was to attribute to him a divine prerogative, that of creating human beings and their universe. To be the agent of salvation (or God's final kingdom) was also to be the agent of the new creation (2 Cor. 5: 17; Gal. 6: 15). What held true at the end must be true also at the beginning; eschatological claims about Christ led quickly to protological claims about his involvement in the divine act of creation. Back in Chapter 2 we examined, among other things, two OT personifications of God's activity in creating, sustaining, and relating to the world: Wisdom and Logos or Word. Our earliest Christian writer (Paul), in applying to Christ the name of 'Wisdom', was in fact expressing his divine identity, just as one of the last Christian writers (John) did when he gave the name of 'Logos' to Jesus of Nazareth. John quite explicitly associated the Logos with the divine work of creation (John 1: 3, 10). Paul, although he both attributed to Christ the divine prerogative of creation (1 Cor. 8: 6; Col. 1: 16) and called him the 'Wisdom of God' (1 Cor. 1: 17–2: 13), did not quite clinch matters by writing of 'the Wisdom of God, Jesus Christ, through whom all things exist'.

Before pursuing further these reflections on the way Paul and other early Christians applied to Jesus the title of 'Lord', it may be as well to recall a few 'lexical' facts. In biblical Greek *Kyrios* (somewhat like the Italian *signore*, the Spanish *señor*, and the German *Herr*) spans a wide range of meaning: from a polite form of address ('Sir') right through to God as the One who has absolutely sovereign rights and full control over human beings and their world. In the Septuagint the (Hebrew) divine name of Yahweh (not pronounced out of reverence but replaced by *Adonai*, 'Lord') was rendered *Kyrios* or 'Lord', and, especially in the prophetic books, God could be called 'the Lord of hosts'. The NT applies to Jesus this name for the one true God.

Let us review the range of usage for this term in the entire NT. (1) *Kyrios* could be simply a respectful way of addressing other people (e.g. Matt. 21: 30; 25: 11; 27: 63; John 4: 11; 12: 21; Acts 16: 30). (2) It could be a way of addressing a 'teacher' or 'rabbi' (Matt. 8: 25; see Matt. 17: 15; Mark 4: 38; 9: 17). (3) The designation can suggest authority, in the sense of one with power to perform mighty works (e.g. Matt. 8: 25). (4) *Kyrios* may denote the owner of property (Mark 12: 9; Luke 19: 33) or the master of slaves (Luke 12: 42–7; Eph. 6: 5; Col. 4: 1). In some parables 'the master' or *kyrios* is a metaphor for Jesus (e.g. Matt. 25: 18–24, 26). (5) Because of their power, political rulers (Matt. 27: 63) could lay claim to a certain divinity and as 'lords' even demand worship (see Acts 25: 26). (6) 'Lords' might also refer to so-called gods who were supposed to have rights over human beings (1 Cor. 8: 5). (7) Finally, the NT speaks not only of God (e.g. Matt. 5: 33; 11: 25; Mark 12: 29–30; Acts 2: 39; 4: 26; Rom. 4: 6–8; 11: 2–4) but also of Jesus as *Kyrios* and often does so in a way that raises him above the merely human level (e.g. Mark 12: 36–7; Luke 19: 31; John 13: 13–14; Phil. 2: 11; Rev. 22: 20–1).

'The word of the Lord', to which OT prophets and prophetical books so often appeal, becomes the word of (or message about or from) the Lord Jesus (1 Thess. 1: 8; see 2 Thess. 3: 1; Acts 8: 25; 12: 24; 19: 10, 20). Where deliverance has been promised to those who 'call upon the name of the Lord' (Joel 2: 32 = 3: 5 in Hebrew text), Christians 'call upon the name of our Lord Jesus Christ' (1 Cor. 1: 2). Passages in the OT which call God *Kyrios* are referred to Christ: Rom. 10: 13 cites Joel 2: 32; Phil. 2: 10–11 echoes Isa. 45: 23–4; Heb. 1: 10–12 cites Ps. 102: 25–7. In the other words, these three NT passages intend to read as applying to Jesus or being fulfilled in Jesus OT passages which speak of God as 'Lord'.[3]

Christ alone, and not any 'deified' emperor, merits the title 'Lord of lords' and 'King of kings' (Rev. 17: 14; see 19: 16). His lordship is superior to that of all the greatest political rulers. What is implied by reapplying to Jesus the OT name

---

[3] In Rom. 14: 10–12 Paul uses two OT passages (Isa. 45: 23; 49: 18) when writing of God and judgement by God. That 'Lord' in Rom. 10: 13 means the risen Jesus is made clear by the context, in particular by Rom. 10: 9. Fitzmyer calls Rom. 10: 12–13 'an eloquent witness to the early church's worship of Christ as *Kyrios*' ('The Letter to the Romans', *NJBC* 859).

for Yahweh is made quite explicit when Thomas calls him
'my Lord and my God' (John 20: 28). Not surprisingly then
in many places, even in Paul's letters, it is not always clear
whether the NT means God or Christ when it speaks of the
Kyrios (e.g. Acts 9: 31; 1 Cor. 4: 19; 7: 17; 2 Cor. 8: 21).

Christ is understood to share God's lordship over all
created beings 'in heaven and on earth or under the earth'
(Phil. 2: 10). In particular, Christ's lordship makes him sovereign over all angelic beings in heaven (Col. 1: 16–17; 2: 8–
10; 1 Pet. 3: 22). Over and over again the two opening chapters
of Hebrews (Heb. 1: 1–2: 16) insist that Christ is superior to
the angels. Unlike them he 'bears the very stamp' of God's
nature, upholds 'the universe by his word of power' (Heb. 1:
3), and has 'the world to come' subject to him (Heb. 2: 5).
No wonder then that the angels also bow down before Christ
in worship (Rev. 5: 11–14). As divine Lord, Christ merits the
adoration of all.

To fill out the NT account of Christ's lordship, it is helpful
to note how the first Christians also appropriated to Jesus the
rubric of 'the day of Yahweh (the Lord)'. They acknowledged
Christ as Lord not only of all space (being worshipped by the
angels and all creatures in heaven, on earth and under the
earth) but also of all time and history.

The day of Yahweh was the day when God was to intervene
decisively in judgement against the wickedness of Israel (Jer.
17: 16–18; Amos 5: 18–20; 8: 9–10; Ezek. 7: 1–27; Zeph. 1:
14–18; Joel 2: 1–2), of Babylon (Isa. 13: 6, 9), or of Egypt
(Ezek. 30: 3). On this doomsday God would judge sinners
and manifest the divine glory (Isa. 2: 11–12). Jeremiah (30:
5–9) and later prophets came to fill the phrase with a somewhat more positive sense, which had not been totally lacking
in earlier usage. 'The day of the Lord' would bring Israel's
restoration in a time of final conflict and final victory (Zech.
14: 1–21). This doomsday of judgement was to destroy evil-
doers and spare the good (Mal. 3: 13–4: 3). In essence to talk
of that day was to see God as the awesome future of history,
not only for the chosen people but also for all nations.

The NT took the term and reapplied it to Christ's parousia
or final coming (1 Thess. 5: 2), 'the day of our Lord Jesus
Christ' (1 Cor. 1: 8; 5: 5; 2 Cor. 1: 14; Phil. 1: 6, 10; 2: 16), or

the day of the Son of man (Luke 17: 24, 30; see Matt. 24: 42–4). The day of God's final and decisive intervention in judgement was understood to be the day of Christ's final and decisive intervention in judgement. Christ was to carry out the future function of God. The expectation of doomsday associated God and Christ to the point of their becoming interchangeable.

'The day of the Lord' Jesus Christ (2 Pet. 3: 10) functioned synonymously with 'the day of God' (2 Pet. 3: 12).[4]

By taking over the OT language of 'Lord' and 'the day of the Lord', the NT puts Christ in his doing and being on a par with God. This 'reading' of Christ in OT terms for God shows up in yet another example. Second Isaiah, with its strong sense of God as both the Creator of the world and final Lord of history, calls Yahweh 'the first and the last' (Isa. 41: 4; 44: 6; 48: 12). The closing book of the NT picks up this language when it calls God 'the Alpha and the Omega' (Rev. 1: 8; 21: 6). But at once it has Christ also identify himself as 'the first and the last' (Rev. 1: 17; 2: 8), and in its final chapter has him most emphatically say: 'I am the Alpha and the Omega, the first and the last, the beginning and the end (Rev. 22: 13).

For all the emphasis of the latter (third) example from Revelation, the context of the first example in the opening vision of the risen and exalted Christ (Rev. 1: 9–20) shows him clearly being merged with God. The 'one like a son of man' (Rev. 1: 13; a direct allusion to Dan. 7: 13) is described as having hair and a head 'white as white wool, white as snow' (Rev. 1: 14), a description taken from Daniel's vision of God as the Ancient of Days (Dan. 7: 9). When the exalted Christ proceeds to call himself 'the first and the last' (Rev. 1: 17), he makes the same claim as the Lord God does in Rev. 1: 8. Christ is not only the Lord of history and eschatological judge ('the last') but also the Creator of all things ('the first' in the language of Second Isaiah).[5]

Such applying to Christ of the OT language for God's creative (and conserving) power turns up in the hymn from

---

[4] See R. H. Hiers, 'Day of Christ', *ABD* ii. 76–9; id., 'Day of the Lord', ibid. 82–3.
[5] See M. G. Reddish, 'Alpha and Omega', ibid. i. 161–2.

Colossians: 'in him all things hold together' (Col. 1: 17). This
echoes what Sirach says of the glory and creative/conserving
power of God revealed in nature: 'by his word all things hold
together' (Sir. 43: 26). Perhaps the most spectacular example
of this christological use of OT language for God comes in
the opening chapter of Hebrews, which reads a hymn of praise
to the eternal God and Creator (Ps. 102: 25–7) as applying to
Christ as Son: 'By you, Lord, were earth's foundations laid
of old, and the heavens are the work of your hands. They will
perish, but you will remain; like clothes they will all wear
out. You will fold them up like a cloak, and they will be
changed like any garment. But you are the same, and your
years will have no end' (Heb. 1: 10–12; REB). It is hard to
see how an NT writer could have been clearer and more
explicit than this in recognizing and praising in Christ a
creative power and an eternal existence that sets him on a par
with Yahweh ('Lord').

Before passing on to see how the NT also designates
Jesus as 'Saviour' and 'God', it would be well to take stock
of the masculine quality of the titles which we have just
been examining (Son of God and Lord) and of some titles
which have turned up earlier (e.g. Messiah/King, Priest,
Prophet, and Last Adam). Given the fact of Jesus' maleness,
the NT could not term him 'Queen', 'Priestess', 'Proph-
etess', or 'Last/Second Eve'. However, it did name him in
neutral ways such as 'the Word' and 'the Alpha and the
Omega'. Even more to the point, it applied to him the
female image of Lady Wisdom. In the OT she had personified the divine activity of creating, sustaining, and
interacting with the whole universe.

Here we can rightly spot the need to recognize a certain
'feminine' aspect of Jesus. The last chapter noted how the
OT used feminine as well as masculine imagery when speaking of the divine relations with Israel. God, of course, simply
transcends sex and gender in a way that is not true of Jesus
in his maleness. Nevertheless, Paul, other NT writers, and
post-NT Christians knew that they were employing a thoroughly feminine image when they expressed Jesus' divine
identity as 'the Wisdom of God'. In doing so, whether they
remembered this or not, they were taking a cue from Jesus

himself. Among other striking images for his saving mission, he had chosen to compare it to the action of a mother hen gathering and protecting her chickens under her wings (Luke 13: 34 par.).[6]

Saviour and God

The exodus, the return from the Babylonian captivity, and other profound religious experiences convinced the Israelites that Yahweh is the God who saves. Despite Isa. 43: 11 ('I am the Lord and beside me there is no saviour'), at times human beings could be called 'saviour' (e.g. Judg. 3: 9, 15, 31). In the NT, however, only God (eight times) and Christ (sixteen times) are called 'Saviour'.

Sometimes the NT puts together 'Lord' and 'Saviour' when speaking of Christ. Thus 2 Peter writes of 'the know-ledge of our Lord and Saviour Jesus Christ' (2 Pet. 2: 20; see 1: 11; 3: 2, 18). In Luke's infancy narrative the angel tells the shepherds: 'Today there has been born to you in the city of David a Saviour who is Christ the Lord' (Luke 2: 11). Paul does the same at least once: 'We are citizens of heaven, and from it we await a Saviour the Lord Jesus Christ' (Phil. 3: 20). From his birth to his future parousia Christ shows himself to be 'Lord and Saviour'.[7]

As we have just seen, 2 Peter four times links 'Lord' and 'Saviour' when speaking of Christ. The dyad once turns up as changed into 'God and Saviour'—in the letter's address to

---

[6] J. D. G. Dunn maintains that 'the picture of a protective mother is wholly familiar from the OT' and refers the reader to Deut. 32: 11; Ruth 2: 12; Ps. 17: 8; 36: 7; 57: 1; 61: 4; 63: 7; 91: 4; and Isa. 31: 5. He adds: 'Since the imagery usually [surely always?] describes God's protectiveness, he who used it for his own concern [= Jesus] thereby claimed to have been divinely commissioned and to embody the "steadfast love" of Yahweh for Israel' (*Christology in the Making* (London: SCM Press, 2nd edn., 1989), 203). But the OT imagery is not that of a 'mother hen': Deut. 32: 11 evokes a mother eagle; Ruth 2: 12 speaks of the protecting divine 'wings' without specifying what bird it has in mind; the passages in the psalms likewise remain non-specific, when invoking the 'shadow' or 'shelter' of God's wings. The simile in Isa. 31: 5, of 'birds hovering overhead', leaves behind earth-bound hens. There are two astonishing features of Jesus' use of the imagery: first, he applies to himself an OT picture which seems to have been used only of God; second, he gives the image a very homely twist by representing himself not as a mighty eagle but as a farmyard hen.

[7] See my 'Salvation', *ABD* v. 907–14, at 910–11.

'those who have obtained a faith of equal standing with ours in the righteousness of our God and Saviour Jesus Christ' (2 Pet. 1: 1). Possibly the last phrase should be rendered 'of our God and of the Saviour Jesus Christ', thereby distinguishing between 'our God' and 'the Saviour Jesus Christ'. A similar slight doubt affects the translation of Tit. 2: 13 which encourages Christians to look forward to 'the appearing of the glory of our great God and Saviour Jesus Christ'. It is also possible but again less likely that the phase should be rendered 'the appearing of the glory of the great God and of our Saviour Jesus Christ'.

The balance of probabilities really shifts, however, in the case of Rom. 9: 5. Paul concludes his list of Israel's special privileges with a brief prayer of praise: 'God who is over all be blessed forever. Amen.' Another possible punctuation would present Paul's list as ending with a confession of Christ's divinity: 'Christ, who is God over all, blessed forever. Amen.' For three reasons this translation looks less likely. First, while expressing the divinity of Christ, in a variety of ways (e.g. through the titles of Lord, Son of God, and Wisdom), Paul reserves the title of 'God' to 'the Father'. If *theos* (admittedly not *ho theos*) here in Rom. 9: 5 refers to Christ, it would be, together with Phil. 2: 6, an exception in the authentic Pauline letters. Second, the apostle directs his doxologies to God the Father (e.g. Rom. 11: 36; 16: 27) and not directly to Christ (as does Heb. 13: 21). Third, to name Christ as being 'over all' would differ from his being usually 'subordinated' to God the Father in the Pauline scheme (1 Cor. 3: 23; 11: 3; 15: 27–8). He is 'sent' by the Father (Rom. 8: 3; Gal. 4: 4), who in Deutero-Pauline language is 'above all' (Eph. 4: 6).[8]

Two quite unambiguous attributions of 'God' to Christ occur in John's Gospel. The prologue celebrates 'the Word' who in the beginning was not only 'with God' (*pros ton theon*) but was 'God' (*theos*) (John 1: 1). At the end Thomas confesses Jesus as 'my Lord and my God' (*ho kyrios mou kai*

---

[8] On Rom. 9: 5 see not only J. D. G. Dunn, *The Partings of the Ways* (London: SCM Press, 1991), 203–4, but also Fitzmyer, 'The Letter to the Romans', *NJBC* 856; id., *Romans*, The Anchor Bible 33 (New York: Doubleday, 1993), 548–9.

ho theos mou) (John 20: 28).[9] The NT was willing to speak of Jesus as 'God', but obviously preferred to limit that name to the One whom he had called 'Abba', expressing Jesus' divinity through various titles (Word, Wisdom, Son of God, Saviour, and, especially, Lord) and appropriating to him the OT language for Yahweh.

More should be added about the divine language used of Jesus. The NT speaks of the risen and exalted Jesus as sitting, not near or under the divine throne, but at God's right hand (Mark 16: 19; Eph. 1: 20; Heb. 1: 3, 13; see also Mark 14: 62; Acts 7: 55–6; 1 Pet. 3: 22). He is the Lamb who shares the divine throne (Rev. 7: 17; 22: 1).

The exalted Jesus who now sits at God's right hand will come as the Son of man 'with the clouds of heaven' (Mark 14: 62), 'in the glory of his Father' (Mark 8: 38), 'with great power and glory' (Mark 13: 26; see Tit. 2: 13), to 'send out the angels and gather his elect' (Mark 13: 27). He will sit in final judgement upon 'his throne of glory' (Matt. 19: 28; 25: 31–2; see John 5: 27). The OT associations of this language about 'clouds', 'heaven', 'glory', 'power', 'angels', and 'throne' imply that Jesus is more than merely the final judge; he is the divine Judge (see Sir. 17: 15–24). The scenario for this future, definitive judgement with all the angels and for all nations simply does not square with a judge who is thought of as merely human: 'When the Son of man comes in his glory, and all the angels with him, then he will sit on his throne of glory. Before him will be gathered all the nations, and he will separate them one from another as a shepherd separates the sheep from the goats' (Matt. 25: 31–2).

The NT regularly attributes 'doxa' ('praise' or 'glory') to God (the Father) (e.g. Luke 2: 14; Rom. 11: 36; 1 Cor. 10: 31; Phil. 2: 11; Rev. 19: 7). But, given the various ways early Christians came to evaluate Jesus in divine terms, it is in no way surprising to find them attributing 'glory' also to Christ

[9] In 1 John 5: 20 'the true God' may possibly refer to 'Jesus Christ'; John 1: 18 calls Christ 'God the only begotten Son', according to some strong manuscript evidence which is followed by the NRSV. Heb. 1: 8–9 addresses to Christ as God's Son those words of Ps. 45, which begin: 'Your throne, o God, is forever and ever.' In this passage Hebrews wants to stress primarily the reign of the pre-existent Son, who was active in creation and is now enthroned at God's right hand. Yet the fact remains that the name 'God' is here applied to the Son.

(1 Cor. 2: 8; 2 Cor. 4: 6; Heb. 1: 3; Jas. 2: 1) and saying of him: 'To him be *glory* both now and to the day of eternity' (2 Pet. 3: 18). A classic passage associates Christ (as 'the Lamb who was slain') with the praise and glory the whole universe offers God: 'I heard every creature in heaven and on earth and under the earth and in the sea, and all therein, saying, "To him who sits upon the throne and to the Lamb be blessing and honour and glory and might for ever and ever!"' (Rev. 5: 13; see 5: 11–14). Worship of the Lamb matches what has been said about the worship of God (Rev. 4: 8–11; see 7: 10).

Not only Revelation (Rev. 4: 10; 14: 7; 19: 4) but also other NT books (e.g. Matt. 4: 10; John 4: 20–1, 23–4; Acts 24: 11; 1 Cor. 14: 25) point to worship and the giving of adoration (*proskuneō*) as the appropriate posture before God. In the case of Jesus this verb may at times denote little more than the respectful action of someone seeking a favour from him (Matt. 8: 2; 9: 18; 15: 25; 20: 20). But there remain some instances where Matthew obviously means more than merely adopting a reverent attitude in making a request. The wise men come 'to worship' the new-born Jesus (Matt. 2: 2, 8, 11); later on, those in the boat, when he comes to them across the waters, 'worship' him as 'the Son of God' (Matt. 14: 33). After his resurrection from the dead, first female and then male disciples 'worship' him (Matt. 28: 9, 17). Matthew's Gospel obviously holds that right from his conception and birth, as 'Emmanuel' or 'God with us' (Matt. 1: 23), Jesus deserves the adoration appropriate to God.[10]

Spirit

At the end of his Gospel Matthew puts on the lips of the risen Jesus a formula about baptism 'in the name of the Father and of the Son and of the Holy Spirit' (Matt. 28: 19). Christians began by baptizing 'in the name of Jesus' (Acts 2: 38; 10: 48; Rom. 6: 3; 1 Cor. 1: 13, 15; 6: 11). Then at

---

[10] On the question of NT prayer and worship directed to Jesus see R. Bauckham, 'Jesus, Worship of', *ABD* iii. 812–19; L. W. Hurtado, *One God, One Lord: Early Christian Devotion and Ancient Jewish Monotheism* (London: SCM Press, 1989); Dunn, *The Partings of the Ways*, 204–6.

some point they introduced the tripartite formula which has remained normative ever since. Another such formula turns up (much earlier) as a concluding benediction at the end of one of Paul's letters. It maintains the Holy Spirit in the third place but changes the order of the first two figures, names them differently ('Lord Jesus Christ' instead of 'the Son' and 'God' instead of 'the Father'), and speaks not of their 'name' but of 'grace', 'love', and 'fellowship', associated respectively with the first, second, and third figures: 'the grace of the Lord Jesus Christ and the love of God and the fellowship of the Holy Spirit be with you all' (2 Cor. 13: 14). In earlier teaching Paul speaks in a different order and more succinctly of 'Spirit', 'Lord', and 'God' (an order which reverses the first and third figures in Matthew's baptismal formula), and insists that spiritual gifts come from the one ('the same') divine source and should contribute to 'the common good' (1 Cor. 12: 7). 'There are varieties of gifts, but the same Spirit; and there are varieties of service, but the same Lord; and there are varieties of working, but it is the same God who inspires them all in every one' (1 Cor. 12: 4–6).

These texts from Paul and Matthew (which certainly in the case of Matt. 28: 19 and probably in the case of 2 Cor. 13: 14 draw on a previous tradition) set Jesus as 'the Son' or 'the Lord' alongside (1) 'the Father' or 'God' (*ho theos*) and (2) 'the Holy Spirit' or 'the Spirit'. The last chapter explored something of what the NT has to say about the Father–Son relationship. This chapter began by examining what is involved in calling Jesus 'Lord'. Let us now turn to the association of 'the Son' or 'the Lord' with 'the Spirit' or 'the Holy Spirit'.

When dealing with God's spirit (Hebrew *ruah*; Greek *pneuma*), the OT highlighted its power as 'wind', the breath of life, or the divine inspiration that comes upon prophets. In pre-Christian Judaism 'word', 'wisdom', and 'spirit' were practically synonymous ways for speaking of God's manifest and powerful activity in the world. In celebrating God's creative power the psalmist uses 'word' and 'breath' (or 'spirit') as equivalent parallels: 'By the *word* of the Lord the heavens were made, and all their host by the *breath* of his mouth' (Ps. 33: 6; see Ps. 147: 18). The work of creation can be expressed in terms of God's *word* (Ps. 33: 6, 9; see Gen. 1: 3–31) or in terms of the divine *spirit*, as Judith's thanksgiving to God also illustrates: 'Let your whole creation serve you; for you spoke, and all things came to be; you sent out your spirit and it gave them form; none can oppose your word' (Judith 16: 14 REB; see Ps. 104: 29–30). 'Spirit' and 'wisdom' are likewise identified: when God gives 'wisdom', this is equivalent to sending 'the holy Spirit' (Wis. 9: 17; see 1: 4–5; 7: 7, 22, 25). In short, like 'word' and 'wisdom', the 'spirit' was a way of articulating the divine activity and revelation in the world. But Dunn has rightly argued that, at the time of Jesus, the divine 'spirit' or 'Spirit' was not yet thought of in Judaism even as a *semi*-independent divine agent.[11]

The evidence marshalled by Dunn also establishes that the Synoptic Gospels envisioned Jesus during his ministry as being driven, inspired, and empowered by God's Spirit.[12] For Luke, in particular, Jesus was the paradigmatic Spirit-bearer (e.g. Luke 4: 1, 14, 18–21; 6: 19). Probably Jesus himself was conscious of the Spirit in such terms (Mark 1: 12; 3: 22–9; also perhaps 13: 11). But he never seems to have unambiguously pointed to his deeds as signs of the Spirit's power. In any case he is not credited with an awareness of the Spirit of anything like the same intensity as his consciousness of the God whom he called 'Abba'. In other words, the Synoptics (and Jesus himself) described the divine Spirit in a fairly normal Jewish way: the dynamic power of God reaching out to have its impact on Jesus and through him on others. It took Jesus' resurrection and exaltation to initiate a new, characteristically Christian way of thinking about the Spirit and the relationship of Jesus to the Spirit.

First of all, the relationship between Jesus and the Spirit was understood to be transformed by the resurrection. Jesus now shares in God's prerogative as sender or giver of the Spirit. Paul speaks of the risen Christ as having become 'a life-giving Spirit' (1 Cor. 15: 45). Yet he never quite says that Christ has sent or will send the Spirit. Luke and John say

---

[11] Dunn, *Christology in the Making*, 132–6.
[12] Ibid. 136–41.

just that. Exalted 'at the right hand of God and having received from the Father the promise of the Holy Spirit', Christ pours out the Spirit with its perceptible effects (Acts 2: 33; see Luke 24: 49). According to John, the Spirit comes from Jesus, is sent by Jesus, or is bestowed by Jesus (John 7: 39; 15: 26; 19: 30, 34; 20: 22; see 4: 10, 14). At the same time, neither for Luke nor for John does the sending or giving of the Spirit become merely Jesus' gift. He receives 'from the Father' the promised Holy Spirit before pouring it out (Acts 2: 33). John also talks about the Father giving the Spirit (John 14: 16–17) or sending the Spirit (John 14: 26), albeit, respectively, in response to Jesus' prayer and in Jesus' name. Even when John has Jesus promise to send the Spirit, the words 'from the Father' feature prominently: 'when the Advocate comes, whom I shall send you from the Father, even the Spirit of truth, who proceeds from the Father, he will bear witness to me' (John 15: 26).

When referring to the bestowal of the Spirit, Paul picks up formulaic traditions to say that 'God has sent the Spirit of his Son into our hearts' (Gal. 4: 6; see 3: 5; 1 Cor. 2: 10). He also uses a divine passive which does not explicitly name the divine Giver or Sender: 'the Holy Spirit has been given to us' (Rom. 5: 5); to each Christian 'is given' some manifestation of the Spirit (1 Cor. 12: 7, 8). Or else Paul writes of Christians 'receiving' the Spirit without stating from whom they receive it (Rom. 8: 15; 1 Cor. 2: 12, 14; Gal. 3: 2).

Nevertheless, Paul speaks not only of 'the Spirit of God' (Rom. 8: 9; 1 Cor. 2: 11, 12, 14), but also of 'the Spirit of Christ' or 'the Spirit of God's Son' (Rom. 8: 9; Gal. 4: 6; see Acts 5: 9; 1 Pet. 1: 11). The genitive is exquisitely ambiguous; it can be read either as a genitive of origin (the Spirit which comes from God/Christ) or as a genitive of identity (the Spirit which is God/Christ). This latter possibility leads to a further major reflection on the post-resurrection function and understanding of the Holy Spirit.

Second, even though both Luke and John identify the Spirit as sent by the risen and exalted Jesus, they do not draw here a sharp distinction between the sender and the sent. Luke can move from cases of guidance by the ascended Lord (Acts 9: 10–16; 18: 9–10; 22: 17–21) to cases of guidance by the Holy Spirit (Acts 8: 29; 10: 19; 16: 6), without distinguishing very clearly between them. In fact, he reports at least once guidance by 'the Spirit of Jesus' (Acts 16: 7). (Does he mean 'the Spirit which comes from Jesus' or 'the Spirit who is Jesus'?) In John the coming of the Spirit (John 14: 16–17, 25) seems to merge with the return of Christ himself (John 14: 3, 18, 23, 28).

In Paul's letters the Spirit is not only characterized by its relationship to the risen and exalted Christ but in the experience of believers is almost identified with Christ (= the Spirit which is Christ or which is the presence of Christ). The Spirit witnesses to Jesus as divine Lord (1 Cor. 12: 3). The Spirit 'in us' (Rom. 5: 5; 8: 9, 11, 16; Gal. 4: 6) is practically synonymous with talk about our being 'in Christ' (Rom. 6: 3, 11, 23; 16: 11; 1 Cor. 1: 30; 3: 1; 4: 15; Phil. 3: 1; 4: 1–2). Christians' experience of the Spirit merges with their experience of the risen Christ (1 Cor. 6: 11). The Spirit of God dwelling 'in you' (Rom. 8: 9, 11) is, for all intents and purposes, equivalent to 'having the Spirit of Christ' or Christ being 'in you' (Rom. 8: 9, 10). This near functional identity allows Dunn to say not only that for Paul 'the Spirit is the medium for Christ in his relation' to human beings, but even that *'no distinction can be detected in the believer's experience between exalted Christ and Spirit of God'.*[13]

Nevertheless, and this is my third point regarding NT thinking about the relationship Christ–Spirit, it is patent that neither Paul nor others finally identify Christ with the Spirit. Jesus was conceived through the power of the Holy Spirit (Matt. 1: 20; Luke 1: 35)—a statement which cannot be reversed. It was the Word, and not the Spirit, that became flesh (John 1: 14). It was the Son, and not the Spirit, who was sent 'in the likeness of sinful flesh' to deal with sin (Rom. 8: 3), and who was not 'spared' but 'given up for us all' (Rom. 8: 32). Through his resurrection Christ, and not the Spirit, became 'the firstborn' of a new eschatological family (Rom. 8: 29) and 'the first fruits of those who have fallen asleep' (1 Cor. 15: 20).

It is the indwelling Spirit that helps us to pray 'Abba' and

---

[13] Dunn, *Christology in the Making*, 146.

witnesses to Christ (Rom. 8: 15–16; Gal. 4: 6; 1 Cor. 12: 3), and not an indwelling Christ who makes us pray like that and who witnesses to the Spirit. Finally, unlike the Spirit, it is Christ who was crucified and resurrected, who at the end will subject all things to his Father (1 Cor. 15: 24–8).[14] The NT's story of Christ's mission, conception, death, resurrection, and its aftermath distinguishes him from the Holy Spirit.

Trinity

The last section of this chapter has taken us beyond christo-logical titles to NT formulas and other passages linking Jesus with the Father and the Spirit, the most striking being the closing benediction of 2 Cor. 13: 14 and the baptismal formula of Matt. 28: 19. Although we certainly do not find here (or elsewhere in the NT) anything like the later, full-blown doctrine of God as three (Father, Son, and Holy Spirit) in one and one in three, nevertheless, the NT data provide a foundation and starting-point for that doctrinal develop-ment. To conclude these chapters on the biblical material, let me add some brief observations on the 'trinitarian' pres-entation of Jesus in the NT to supplement what Chapter 4 has already indicated under the rubric of the revelatory quality of Christ's resurrection from the dead.

In the final verse of 2 Corinthians it seems that Paul has expanded his more usual farewell benediction to quote or produce a triadic benediction that invokes 'the grace of the Lord Jesus Christ', 'the love of God', and 'the fellowship of the Holy Spirit'. In a summary of salvation history that can take different forms elsewhere in the Pauline correspondence (e.g. Gal. 4: 4–7), Christ is here associated with 'God' and 'the Holy Spirit' in bestowing spiritual blessings. 'Grace' and 'love' have characterized the divine dealings with human beings, who through faith and baptism share in the new fellowship created by the Holy Spirit.

Like the baptismal formula in Matthew, Paul's closing benediction names the Holy Spirit in third place, but differs both by not speaking of the Father and the Son and by

---

[14] On the Spirit see F. W. Horn, 'Holy Spirit', *ABD* iii. 260–80.

placing 'the Lord Jesus Christ' before 'God'. Presumably the apostle's sense of the historical mediation of revelation and salvation through Christ led here to his placing in first place 'the Lord Jesus Christ'.[15]

The order and the names (the Father, the Son, and the Holy Spirit) found in Matthew's baptismal formula became and remained standard for Christian faith. Yet even that formula does not clarify anything about the relationship between the Father, the Son, and the Holy Spirit. To speak, on the one hand, of 'the Father/the Son' and, on the other, of 'the Holy Spirit' ('Holy' obviously through being 'the Spirit of/from God') is to offer a very minimal identification of the Father, the Son, and the Holy Spirit in their relationship to each other. In its own setting the Matthean baptismal formula is no less concerned than the Pauline benediction with the blessings that have come through Christ. The soteriological motif remains to the fore, as we shall also see, in the story of subsequent christological reflection and debate.[16]

---

[15] On 2 Cor. 13: 14 see V. P. Furnish, *II Corinthians*, The Anchor Bible 32 A (New York: Doubleday, 1984), 583–4, 587–78; R. P. Martin, *Word Biblical Commentary*, xl: *2 Corinthians* (Waco, Tex.: Word Books, 1986), 491, 495–7, 503–7.

[16] See further J. M. Bassler, 'God in the NT', *ABD* ii. 1049–55, at 1055.

7

To the First Council of Constantinople

❖ ❖

Our Lord Jesus Christ, the Word of God, of his boundless love, became what we are that he might make us
what he himself is.

(St Irenaeus, *Adversus haereses*)

My immediate purpose in this and the next two chapters is
to prepare the way for the heart of the book: the systematic
chapters on Christ's being and saving work. Over the last two
millennia various church teachers and writers have addressed
in depth most of the central christological issues. It is at our
peril that we neglect their discussions and conclusions. We
have something, or rather much, to learn from those councils
and theologians before raising the crucial issues for ourselves.
At the same time, however, in our retelling of the story of
developments in christological thought, teaching, and terminology, we will mention only the major points and try not
to lose sight of the systematic discussion to come.[1]

To approach the heart of early christological developments,
one can usefully ask: on what basis did (or could) these

---

[1] On the early history of Christology see A. Grillmeier, *Christ in Christian Tradition*, 2 vols. (London: Mowbrays, 1975 and 1995); R. P. C. Hanson, *The Search
for the Christian Doctrine of God* (Edinburgh: T. & T. Clark, 1988); J. N. D. Kelly,
Early Christian Doctrines (London: A. & C. Black, 5th edn., 1968); R. Williams,
'Jesus Christus II', *TRE* xv. 726–45. On individual writers and themes see the
relevant articles in F. L. Cross and E. A. Livingstone (eds.), *The Oxford Dictionary
of the Christian Church* (Oxford: Oxford University Press, 3rd edn., forthcoming),
and in A. di Berardino (ed.), *Encyclopedia of the Early Church*, 2 vols. (Cambridge:
James Clarke & Co., 1992). For the teaching of councils and their contexts, see the
bibliographical information provided by N. P. Tanner (ed.), *Decrees of the Ecumenical
Councils*, 2 vols. (London: Sheed & Ward, 1990).

Christians believe or say this or that about Jesus? This question breaks up into four further queries. (1) What experiences fuelled their insights and assertions about Jesus? (2) How important for them was the task of interpreting the scriptural testimony to Jesus? (3) What contextual factors put a pattern on their christological understanding? (4) What language did they reach for when interpreting their convictions about Jesus' being and doing? Question (1) has already threaded through Chapters 3, 4, 5, and 6. Questions (2), (3), and (4) obviously hearken back to issues briefly outlined above in Chapter 1. Expounding the biblical texts (2), in particular those which make up the NT, necessarily involved subsequent Christian believers in questions of history, no matter whether they were fully aware of this or not. Cultural, religious, and, in particular, philosophical currents (3) massively shaped the context of the Mediterranean world in which christological interpretation developed. Struggles with questions of terminology (4) marked not only the first period of christological debate but also later centuries. The debate over *homoousios* and other terms witnessed to the wide Christian concern that their official language about Jesus should not take a wrong turn.

Before reviewing relevant themes from St Ignatius of Antioch (d. *c.*107) to the First Council of Constantinople (381), it seems useful to develop these four queries. They can help to put a pattern on the story of Christology as it unfolded.

Four Queries

1. Right from the outset the driving force behind theological inquiry and official teaching about Jesus was clearly the experience of salvation. Having experienced through him the forgiveness of sins, the gift of the Holy Spirit, and the new life of grace in community, Christians asked themselves: what questions does this experience of salvation raise about Jesus, his being, and his identity? What did/does he have to be as the cause, in order to save us in the way that we have experienced (the effect)? What does 'Christ experienced by us/me' say about Christ-in-himself and Christ-for-God?

The overriding concern for salvation and their experience of it led Christians to maintain that two basic conditions make it possible for Jesus to do this for them: he must be truly human and truly divine to function as their effective Saviour.

Irenaeus classically expressed the salvific reason for divinity and humanity being united in Christ:

If a human being had not overcome the enemy of humanity, the enemy would not have been rightly overcome. On the other side, if it had not been God to give us salvation, we would not have received it permanently. If the human being had not been united to God, it would not have been possible to share in incorruptibility. In fact, the Mediator between God and human beings, thanks to his relationship with both, had to bring both to friendship and concord, and bring it about that God should assume humanity and human beings offer themselves to God. (*Adversus haereses*, 3. 18. 7; see 3. 19. 1)

Without the incarnation of the *Son of God*, divine redemption would be impossible. Yet without a genuine *incarnation*, the battle against the diabolic forces of evil would not be won from the inside.

The Adam/Christ contrast elucidated what Irenaeus understands by 'rightly overcoming the enemy': 'As it was through a man's defeat that our race went down to death, so too through a man's victory we rise up to life' (ibid. 5. 21. 1).

One basic and persuasive conviction about the conditions for salvation was then that, to have healed and saved us/me, Jesus must be truly and fully human. This conclusion, current from the time of Irenaeus, Tertullian, and Origen in the second and third centuries, received its classical formulation from Gregory of Nazianzus in the fourth century: 'the unassumed is the unhealed' (*Epistola* 101. 32). His friend St Basil of Caesarea (*c.*330–79) wrote of Christ needing to take on true humanity if he were to do what we know him to have done—namely destroy the power of death and sin:

If the Lord did not come in our flesh, then the ransom did not pay the fine due to death on our behalf, nor did he destroy through himself the reign of death. For if the Lord did not assume that over which death reigned, death would not have been stopped from effecting his purpose, nor would the suffering of the God-bearing flesh have become our gain: he would not have slain sin in the flesh. We who were dead in Adam, would not have been restored in Christ.[2]

A century later Leo the Great (d. 461) insisted that Christ had taken through Mary the same human nature as the first Adam to whom he was traced in Luke's genealogy (Luke 3: 38). Unless Christ had truly assumed our humanity, the redemptive 'battle' would have 'been fought outside our nature' and we would not have experienced what we have experienced, deliverance from the power of evil:

If the new man, made in the likeness of sinful flesh, had not taken our old nature; if he, one in substance with the Father, had not accepted to be one in substance with the mother; if he who was alone free from sin had not united our nature to himself,—then men would still have been held captive under the power of the devil. We would have been incapable of profiting by the victor's triumph if the battle had been fought outside our nature. (*Epistola* 31. 2)

The passage from Basil quoted above also expresses the other basic conclusion to which deliverance from the power of sin and death through Christ brought believers: he has to be the divine Lord; his flesh is 'God-bearing'. To have effected our salvation, he must be truly divine. As Gregory of Nazianzus put it, for sinful human to be 'fashioned afresh', this needed to be effected, 'by one who was wholly man and at the same time God'.[3]

From Irenaeus (*Adversus haereses*, 3. 19; 4. 20) and Athanasius, through to its high point in the writings of Gregory of Nazianzus and Gregory of Nyssa, and beyond in the teaching of Augustine of Hippo, Cyril of Alexandria, Leo the Great, and others, the experience of becoming 'godlike' or being 'deified' through Christ in a 'wonderful exchange' (*admirabile commercium*) underpinned the conviction about his identity: 'It was God who became human that we humans might become divine.' Cyril asks in one of his christological dia-

---

[2] *Epistola* 261. 2; trans. H. Bettenson, *The Later Christian Fathers* (Oxford: Oxford University Press, 1972), 70
[3] *Epistola* 101. 15; Bettenson, *Later Christian Fathers*, 107.

logues: if Christ had only received his own divine filiation by gift without possessing it by natural right, how could he bestow on others the power to become children of God (*Quod unus sit Christus*, 738c, e; 762c; 768c–769a; 771c; 773a)? It takes a divine 'Insider' to grant such a gift. Centuries later in his *Summa theologiae* Thomas Aquinas makes what amounts to the same point, but in terms of the universal redemptive scope of the incarnation: 'the goodness of someone who is merely a man cannot be the cause of good for the entire race' (3a. 2. 11. *resp.*). It was because in the person of Jesus Christ God had really assumed human nature and entered our history that we could experience what we do experience, that sharing in the divine life which salvation has brought us (see 2 Pet. 1: 4). In brief, so the argument ran, we are truly divinized (our experience) because the Son of God truly became man. His assumption of humanity is the condition of our/my sharing in divinity.

Through the notion of a 'new creation', Athanasius expressed the same belief. The saving work of Christ has brought us a 'new creation'. But creation is God's exclusive prerogative. Hence Christ must be divine in order to bring about the new creation. Athanasius' argument rests on a parallel or really a continuity between creation and redemption (conceived as new creation). It was through the Word that God created at the beginning. Likewise it was through the same divine Word, who now assumed human nature, that God effected human renewal in the new creation (*De incarnatione Verbi*, 1. 1, 4).

If the experience of salvation made early Christian writers draw the conclusion that Christ must be truly divine, they also at times drew a similar conclusion under the rubric of revelation. To be the revealer of God (as they knew him to have been), he had to belong on the divine side. Irenaeus wrote: 'no other being had the power of revealing to us the things of the Father, except his own proper Word' (*Adversus haereses*, 5. 1. 1). Here the patristic argument for the revealer being divine paralleled the argument for the saviour being divine. The parallelism was completed when it was argued that the revealer must also be humanly visible in order to reveal God to us. Thus Cyril of Alexandria (d. 444) explained that the Word of God was 'begotten of a woman according to the flesh, inasmuch as, being God by nature' and so 'invisible and incorporeal', it was not possible for him to make himself visible 'to the inhabitants of the earth otherwise than under an appearance like ours' (*Quod unus sit Christus*, 718d; see 721c–d; 723e; 761e).

A few years later Leo the Great used the same 'invisible/visible' scheme in affirming that the Son of God, 'invisible in his own nature', became 'visible in ours'. This 'self-emptying, whereby the invisible made himself visible', was 'a condescension of compassion, not a failure of power' (*Letter* 28. 3 = *Epistola dogmatica ad Flavianum*). What was divinely invisible would have remained unrevealed. The self-revelation of the Son of God called for the compassionate condescension of the incarnation. Believers' experience of the divine revelation in Christ implied his having become genuinely human as well as being truly divine. To have mediated revelation and salvation, Christ needed, so to speak, a foot in both camps.

2. Our second query concerned the way Christians, from the second century on, went about interpreting Jesus through their inherited Scriptures. The christological interpretation of the biblical texts would need at least a book-length excursus. Here let me call attention to several relevant points which emerged in the second century and beyond.

A second-century heretic, Marcion, who was expelled from the Christian community of Rome in 144 and died around 160, justified his antithesis between the powerful but evil God in the OT and the merciful Father of Jesus Christ in the NT by rejecting all the Jewish Scriptures and accepting only a version of the Gospel of Luke and ten Pauline letters (also emended). Justin and other orthodox Christians disallowed Marcion's truncated Scriptures. They continued to cherish the Jewish bible, their inherited, sacred Scriptures, which Justin cited extensively as books of divine origin to support his christological faith. To understand Christ, the OT patrimony and its Scriptures were essential. Justin's surviving authentic writings also show him drawing on what he called the 'memoirs of the apostles' (*Dialogue with Trypho*, 105–7, *passim*), the Gospels, in particular those of Matthew and Luke, for their decisive witnesses to Christ.

The existence of four Gospels, and especially the differences between all four Gospels and between the Synoptic Gospels and John (with the blatantly explicit self-presentation of Jesus in John over against the largely implicit Christology of the other Gospels), also provided a challenge. Justin's student Tatian met the problem by producing around 155 a history of Christ compiled from all four Gospels. This *Diatessaron* or harmony of the Gospels witnessed to their authority—a fourfold authority vigorously defended by Irenaeus. His loyalty to the four Gospels he received from the tradition helped to assure their acceptance and continued use for liturgy and teaching.

Irenaeus had in fact to fight on two fronts: both against those who wanted to reduce the authoritative Scriptures and against those who were trying to expand them. In opposition to Marcion and any others (especially some Gnostics) who truncated the Bible, he reaffirmed the Christian and christological value of the OT and its sacred writings. He emphasized that the Creator-God of the OT was/is identical with the Father of Jesus Christ (*Adversus haereses*, 5. 15–24). He faced also the work of Gnostic leaders who were busy composing new 'gospels' and other works—on the basis of alleged fresh communications received from the risen Jesus.[4]

Irenaeus himself illustrates the possibilities for development and misunderstanding in the christological use of both OT and NT themes and the Scriptures. We have already noted (in Chapter 2) how Irenaeus in presenting the story of salvation, with its centre in the redemptive and revelatory 'recapitulation' effected by Christ, successfully developed the possibilities of Paul's contrast between the first (disobedient) and the second/last (obedient) Adam. The case proved somewhat different with a phrase that has a broad range of significance in the Gospels: 'Son of man' (see Chapter 3 above). Even before Irenaeus, Ignatius of Antioch in his *Letter to the Ephesians* (20. 2) used the phrase simply to denote the humanity of Christ over against his divinity: he was not merely 'Son of man' but also 'Son of God'. Through

---

[4] See M. A. Donovan, 'Irenaeus', *ABD* iii. 457–61. On Marcion see J. J. Clabeaux, 'Marcion', ibid. iv. 514–16.

Irenaeus[5] this dyad became and remained common currency, with 'Son of man' simply expressing Christ's humanity or human nature. Origen, Tertullian, Gregory of Nazianzus, Cyril of Alexandria, and further Church Fathers followed suit; Thomas Aquinas and other medieval theologians maintained the usage and kept 'Son of man' as a standard way for denoting the human nature of Christ.

With the second century an inevitable shift of Christian language began setting in: from the first-order, pre-philosophical language of the Gospels, the NT generally, and the liturgy there came a change to the second-order, somewhat 'philosophical' language of doctrinal debate. In this move from narrative to theological Christology, apparent or real differences of meaning between particular biblical texts fuelled a great deal of sharp and even fierce discussion.

In the *Contra Arianos* (1. 37–64) Athanasius recorded many of the scriptural passages up for debate in the Arian controversy over Christ's divinity (e.g. Heb. 1: 4; 3: 1; Acts 2: 36). In 1 Cor. 15: 24–8 the Arians found justification for their thesis of the inferiority of the Son to the Father. In Col. 1: 15 they read the 'image' and 'first-born' language ('He is the image of the invisible God, the first-born over all creation') as meaning, respectively, that the Son was an inferior copy as contrasted with the original (God) and that he was a created being. After Justin Martyr in the second century identified Christ with the figure of wisdom in Prov. 8: 22 ('the Lord created/begot/possessed me at the beginning of his work'), this became a key OT text for christological thinking. In a letter of AD 262 written to Dionysius the Great (bishop of Alexandria), St Dionysius (bishop of Rome) rejected a subordinationist exegesis of this verse, and expounded it in terms of the Son being 'begotten but not made' (DS 114). In the following century the Arians naturally pounced on the same verse to support their thesis of the Son being only a creature, albeit the most perfect of creatures.

Both at the time of the Arian controversy and later, orthodox teachers in their turn could put opponents on the defens-

---

[5] See from the third book of his *Adversus haereses*, 16. 3, 7; 17. 1; 18. 3, 6; 19. 1, 2, 3; 22. 1.

ive by insisting on other such texts as 1 Cor. 8: 6 and Phil. 2: 9–
11. Cyril of Alexandria quoted the first text (which expresses
Christ's involvement in creation) and asked: 'How is everything created by a man' (*Quod unus sit Christus*, 749c–d)?
Given that creation is a divine prerogative, Paul's language
implied that Christ was/is more than merely human. Appealing to the second Pauline text and its picture of 'every knee
in heaven, on earth and under the earth bending' at the name
of the crucified and exalted Jesus, Cyril remarks that believers
are forbidden to adore a mere man. The apostle indicates
Christ's divine status (ibid. 771b).

Cyril's major opponent was, of course, Nestorius (d. *c*.451),
whose liking for Heb. 1: 1–3 and Phil. 2: 6 meant that Cyril
gave considerable attention to those texts. At the same time,
a fascination with John's Gospel led Cyril to wrestle in particular with the sense of the 'Word becoming flesh' (John 1:
14). He understood the 'becoming' not as a change of nature
(as if the Word of God could cease to be what he was/is and
change into flesh) but rather as an assumption of something
(humanity) for a function (salvation), while remaining what
he is as divine. In support Cyril cited Ps. 94: 22 ('the Lord
has become my stronghold'), where there is no question of
the immutable God literally changing into something else
(ibid. 718b); it is rather that God 'becomes' something (a
saving refuge) for me/us (ibid. 717e). In short, the Word's
becoming flesh meant adding or assuming a human existence
for our salvation. In a brief christological dialogue, *Quod unus
sit Christus* (written between 434 and 437), Cyril over and
over again recalled this point by speaking of 'the economy of
the Saviour', 'the economy of the flesh', 'the economy of the
incarnation', or, simply, 'the economy'.

That same dialogue not only constantly cited passages from
the OT and NT to support and illuminate its argument but
also repeatedly appealed to 'the sacred scriptures', 'the holy
scriptures', or 'the inspired scriptures'. Only rarely was any
claim based on post-NT teaching (e.g. 'the orthodox and
genuine dogmas of the Catholic church' in 716a). In this
dialogue Cyril never appealed to the authority of philosophers, even if he frequently used such popularized philosophical terms as 'nature' (*physis*). In the fifth century, as in

the fourth, the struggle was to interpret rightly the scriptural testimony (in the light of the Church's living tradition and present experience). Philosophy played a role in clarifying and interpreting biblical texts and Christian beliefs. But the development of second-order, philosophical language remained at the service of that central authority, the biblical text. The decisive normativity of the Scriptures shows through any study of the Arian, no less than the Nestorian, controversy.

Against Arius and his followers, Athanasius and the orthodox quoted Johannine texts that set Christ on a par with God: e.g. 'I and the Father are one' (John 10: 30; see 10: 38; 17: 21–2). In arguing for Christ's subordinate position the Arians retorted by quoting John 14: 28, 'The Father is greater than I' and explained away John 10: 30 as pointing only to Jesus' always acting and speaking in harmony with the Father and his will. The orthodox dealt with the 'subordination' in John 14: 28 by referring it simply to Jesus in his incarnate life on earth. But for both sides the central question remained: what did/does a faithful interpretation of the Scriptures—and, in particular, of John's Gospel—say about Christ's being?

This is not the place to indulge a huge excursus on patristic methods of exegesis. In any case others have described and evaluated at length their methods.[6] Here I simply wish to note the central role which the Scriptures played in christological developments and debates. From Justin Martyr in the second century to Cyril of Alexandria in the fifth and beyond into later centuries, church writers used and appealed to the Scriptures as the decisive norm in their expositions and arguments.

3. The inspired texts were read in contexts affected by a wide variety of cultural, political, and pastoral concerns. Debates with Jewish and pagan thinkers, as well as the defence of Christians' existence and civil rights before the imperial court, shaped for instance much of Justin's christological reasoning. Two hundred years later, after Con-

---

[6] See P. R. Ackroyd and C. F. Evans, *The Cambridge History of the Bible*, i: *From the Beginnings to Jerome* (Cambridge: Cambridge University Press, 1963); R. Grant and D. Tracy, *A Short History of the Interpretation of the Bible* (Philadelphia: Fortress Press, 2nd edn., 1989); J. W. Rogerson and W. G. Jeanrond, 'Interpretation, History of', *ABD* iii. 424–43.

stantine the Great (d. 337) had granted toleration and then imperial favour to the Christian faith, Athanasius suffered banishment in 336 from the emperor who a decade earlier had convened and personally opened the Council of Nicaea (325) to settle the Arian dispute and introduce into the creed the controversial language about Christ being 'of one substance' with the Father.

A section of Athanasius' *De incarnatione Verbi* (7. 33–40) illustrates how christological debates with Jews, if obviously less important than in Justin's day, still mattered—at least to a bishop of Alexandria, which had enjoyed one of the largest Jewish communities in any city of the ancient world. The philosophical presuppositions of contemporary culture unmistakably continued to prove an even greater challenge to Athanasius and other church leaders and writers. How could the Word of God, a divine being by nature eternal, incorruptible, and incorporeal, appear in a mortal, human body? For the cultured Greek mentality of Alexandria and elsewhere the divine attributes ruled out the very possibility of an incarnation. God could not take on and be revealed in the existence of a human being; this was simply incompatible with the perfection of God (ibid. 1. 1–2; 8. 1–9; see Athanasius, *Contra Arianos*, 2. 8). Alongside the debate with Jews and cultured pagans, Athanasius' greater concern was a pastoral one: the unity of Christians around the faith in Christ's divinity expressed at Nicaea. Before his peaceful death at home in Alexandria (May 373), that inner-church struggle had caused Athanasius much suffering, not least through five separate periods of banishment from his diocese.

Where the philosopher Justin had spoken out for Christians threatened with martyrdom, Athanasius dedicated his episcopal energies to resolutely combating the Arian heresy and reconciling dissidents to the faith of Nicaea.

I have used Justin and Athanasius to exemplify four major factors that helped to constitute the context in which the scriptural witness to Christ was heard and interpreted: the debate with Jews, the political climate (of toleration and imperial involvement in church affairs replacing active persecution), doctrinal and other inner-church controversies, and the influential presence of various philosophical and wider cultural currents. As regards this last factor, from the time of Justin Christian teachers repeatedly confronted, dialogued with, and drew on various forms of Platonism. Justin himself struggled to interpret the message of Christ to a culture affected by Middle Platonic, as well as by Stoic, thought. This brings us to the language of christological interpretation.

4. Three Greek terms played key roles in the development of christological interpretation: *ousia*, *hypostasis*, and *physis*. *Prosōpon* also enjoyed its importance in the fifth century. But it will be simpler to examine these terms later: in the contexts through which they moved into christological vocabulary.

Ambiguities and Intimations

To have some further perspectives on what follows from Justin to Constantinople I, it seems useful to remark on two features in the development of thinking and teaching about Christ. We can call them, respectively, linguistic ambiguities and early intimations.

The ambiguities come from ways of describing the incarnation as (1) an appearing, (2) a being clothed (with flesh), (3) a dwelling within (the humanity of Jesus), and (4) a mixing or blending of divinity and humanity. (1) The NT itself refers to Christ's coming as an 'appearing' (Tit. 2: 11; 3: 4). This description could be distorted into a Docetic view according to which Christ merely appeared to be human; his body seemed to be earthly but that was only an illusion. At the same time, an orthodox Church Father like Cyril of Alexandria could speak of the Son of God 'in his human appearance', without wishing to undercut the full reality of the incarnation (*Quod unus sit Christus*, 770c).[7] (2) The same bishop illustrates unwittingly the ambiguity latent in the language of the Word of God being 'clothed' with a human nature. He writes of the Word 'putting on the flesh' (in the biblical sense of a full humanity) through which he could

---

[7] More than 200 years earlier than Cyril, Tertullian, precisely in a work aimed at affirming the reality of the Son of God's human body and birth, wrote of his 'appearing' and 'clothing himself' as a human being (*De carne Christi*, 3. 1, 4).

suffer (ibid. 766d), and 'putting on our likeness' (ibid. 775d–e), only to denounce a few pages later the Nestorian view that, according to Cyril, turned the genuine incarnation of the Word into 'a kind of clothing thrown over him' (ibid. 774d). 'Putting on the flesh' and 'wearing a body', for all this ambiguity, was language already employed by Athanasius (*Epistola ad Serapionem*, 4. 14) and before him by Tertullian (*Adversus Praxean*, 27. 6). Even earlier Melito of Sardis in his homily 'On the Pasch' stressed the reality of the incarnation against spiritualizing Gnostic tendencies. Nevertheless, he spoke of Christ 'clothing himself with a human nature' and 'appearing in our midst as a man'. In the event, Melito removed the ambiguity from the notions of 'clothing' and 'appearing' by adding that Christ not only appeared 'with a body capable of suffering' but also 'took upon himself the suffering of those who suffered' (66).

3. When employing the language of 'indwelling', the NT pointed at times to the gift of the Holy Spirit which turned Christians into God's temple (e.g. 1 Cor. 3: 16–17; 6: 19) and at other times to Christ himself in whom 'the whole fullness of deity dwells embodied' (Col. 2: 9; see 1: 19). Athanasius perpetuated the imagery of Colossians by writing of the Word of God 'dwelling in the flesh' as in a temple (*Epistola ad Adelphium,* 7). In the following century his successor in the see of Alexandria sensed, however, the imprecision of this language. In the context of his criticism of Nestorius, Cyril argued against the image of the Word indwelling a human being (DS 262). That could confuse the incarnation with the condition of baptized Christians who are 'the temple of God' in which the Holy Spirit dwells (*Quod unus sit Christus*, 737e, 738b).

4. A fourth ambiguity comes from the habit which began in the second century of explaining as a 'mingling' the union of divinity and humanity in Christ. By 'his advent in the flesh', Irenaeus saw 'effected the mingling and uniting of God and man' (*Adversus haereses*, 4. 20. 4). A few years later, when arguing for a genuine incarnation against Marcion, Tertullian wrote of the Son 'mingling in himself man and God' (*Adversus Marcionem*, 2. 27). Yet the same Tertullian insisted

that the union of humanity and divinity in the one person of Christ did not entail a 'mixture' (*Adversus Praxean*, 27. 8–9). Later in this chapter we will see, however, the Cappadocian Fathers in the fourth century using the language of 'mingling' and 'blending' when attempting to account for the relationship between Christ's two natures. In the following century Cyril of Alexandria explicitly rejected this terminology as a way of accounting for the incarnation (*Quod unus sit Christus*, 737a–b). Our next chapter will recall the way Eutyches finally paid the price for the ambiguous inadequacy of the 'mingling/blending' language.

Alongside early christological ambiguities research also turns up 'early intimations'—themes which surfaced early and bore fruit later. At least four such early intimations deserve mention.

1. One phrase which eventually came into its own at the Council of Chalcedon expressed the double generation of the Son: in his divinity born of the Father 'before the ages' and in his humanity born of the Virgin Mary 'in the last days' (DS 301). Prefigured in a kerygmatic fragment cited by Paul (Rom. 1: 3–4) and almost articulated as such by Ignatius of Antioch (*Epistola ad Ephesios*, 7. 2), this theme of the double, eternal/temporal generation of the Son flowered with Irenaeus (*Adversus haereses*, 2. 28. 6; 3. 10. 2) and a century later even more clearly with Lactantius (*Divinae institutiones*, 4. 8. 1–2).

In a passage listing various dyads attributable to Christ, Cyril of Jerusalem (*c.* 313–386) included the double 'nativity': 'his birth is twofold: one, of God before time began; the other, of the Virgin in the fullness of time' (*Catecheses*, 15. 1). Before the Council of Chalcedon met in 451, Cyril of Alexandria cultivated the theme of the Word's double generation: the first, eternal and divine, the second in history and 'according to the flesh' (e.g. *Quod unus sit Christus* 721e, 731e, 734b, 740d, 746c, 747a, and 752e). The same theme of the Word's double generation figured prominently in Cyril's second letter to Nestorius (February 430). In his *Tome* or dogmatic letter of June 449 to Flavian, bishop of Constantinople, Leo the Great endorsed the language of Christ's double birth, eternal for his divine nature and temporal for his human nature. Two years later this language passed into the Chalcedonian definition of faith.

2. A scheme of double 'consubstantiality' matched the dyad of eternal/temporal generation.[8] In his *Adversus Praxean* Tertullian wrote of Christ's two 'substances' (*substantiae*), a twofold mode of being which made him both divine and human (27. 10–11). This early intimation marked the start of a trajectory, which led through the Council of Nicaea's teaching on the Son being 'of one substance (*ousia*) with the Father' (DS 150) to Chalcedon's profession of faith in Christ as being 'of one substance (*homoousios*) with the Father in his divinity and of one substance (*homoousios*) with us in his humanity' (DS 301). Chalcedon's teaching on Christ's double consubstantiality did little more than unpack the language of 'double substance' fashioned by Tertullian more than 200 years earlier.

3. A third early intimation concerned the unity of Christ as subject. Against Gnostic attempts to misinterpret the Fourth Gospel and 'divide' the Son of God, Irenaeus insisted that he was/is 'one and the same' (*Adversus haereses*, 3. 16; 2. 8). A few years later Tertullian rejected any division of the Word into 'Son, Christ, and Jesus', insisting that he is 'one person' (*Adversus Praxean*, 27. 2, 10, 11). In what almost seemed glosses on Irenaeus' text, Gregory of Nazianzus and Gregory of Nyssa consistently repudiated any talk of Christ as two sons. Gregory of Nazianzus set his face against 'anyone who introduces two sons, one derived from God the Father and the second from his mother, instead of being one and the same' Son (*Epistola* 101. 18). The trajectory of this theme of Christ being 'one and the same' continued through Cyril of Alexandria (e.g. in his second letter to Nestorius and almost *passim* in his *Quod unus sit Christus*) to the Chalcedonian definition of faith, which three times confessed Christ as 'one and the same Son' (DS 301–2).

4. The fourth example of early intimations concerns something essentially based on the unity of subject in Christ: the 'communicatio idiomatum' (interchange of properties). Since

---

[8] See B. Studer, 'Consubstantialis Patri—consubstantialis Matri', *Revue des études augustiniennes*, 18 (1972), 87–115; reprinted in id., *Dominus Salvator, Studia Anselmiana* 107 (Rome: S. Anselmo, 1992), 29–66.

they believed that divinity and humanity were/are united in the one person of the incarnate Son of God, Leo the Great and other Church Fathers predicated of Christ attributes of one nature even when he was being named with reference to his other nature: e.g. 'the Son of God died on the cross', and 'the Son of Mary created the world' (see DS 251). Obviously this method of attribution called and calls for certain distinctions, so as not to confuse the two natures. The Son of God precisely as divine did not die on the cross, nor did the Son of Mary precisely as human create the universe. The emergence of a sense of the interchange of properties is often associated with the Council of Ephesus (431) and the work of Cyril of Alexandria. But my point here is that this method of predication had in fact shown up much earlier, even if its full implications were not yet grasped.

Back in the late second century, in his homily 'On the Pasch', Melito of Sardis spoke of Christ's crucifixion in a way that named him as divine Creator but predicated of him his shameful human death: 'He who hung up the earth is himself hung up; he who fixed the heavens is himself fixed [on the cross]; he who fastened everything is fastened on the wood; the Master is reviled; God has been killed' (96). Even before Melito the NT itself had initiated this method of predication, by naming the one who was crucified and died not only as 'Jesus of Nazareth' (e.g. Mark 16: 6) but also as 'the Lord of glory' (1 Cor. 2: 8; see Gal. 6: 14) and 'the Son of God' (Rom. 8: 32). Shortly after the NT period Ignatius of Antioch wrote of the Son of God being truly born and crucified (*Epistle to the Smyrnaeans*, 1–2).

A few years after Melito, Tertullian's acceptance of Christ as 'one person' allowed him to speak of the 'crucified God' (*Adversus Marcionem*, 2. 27; *De carne Christi*, 5. 1) and declare: 'the Son of God died' (*Adversus Praxean*, 29. 1; *De carne Christi*, 5. 4). Origen offered some 'explanation' of why human attributes could be predicated of 'the God-man' even when named in terms of his divinity, and of why divine attributes (e.g. coming in divine glory) could be predicated of 'the God-man' even when named in terms of his humanity.

The Son of God by whom all things were created is called Jesus

Christ, the Son of man. For the Son of God is said to have died in respect of that nature which was certainly capable of death; and he is called the Son of man who is proclaimed about to come 'in the glory of God the Father' . . . the divine nature is spoken of in human terms, and at the same time the human nature is accorded the distinctive epithets proper to the divine. (*De principiis*, 2. 6. 3)[9]

But a fully deployed notion of 'person' was still lacking, as was the realization that attributes are predicated of the subject and not properly speaking of the nature(s). Nevertheless, even before the work of Cyril of Alexandria and Leo the Great helped to lay out clearly how his personal unity justified the interchange of properties between the natures of Christ, an instinctive sense of his being one acting subject encouraged fourth-century theologians to keep practising this way of predication. Thus Gregory of Nazianzus spoke of the 'birth of God' and of the 'crucified God' whom we should 'adore' (*Orationes*, 45. 39; *Epistola*, 101. 17, 22).

Divinity and Humanity

After sketching some basic queries, persistent ambiguities, and early intimations that characterize christological thought in the patristic period, we will spend the rest of the chapter on major efforts to clarify Christ's humanity and divinity— through to the First Council of Constantinople in 381.

NT faith set the terms of the challenge. Drawing on traditional formulations, Paul wrote of Christ as both Son of God and 'born of woman' (Gal. 4: 4) or as both Son of God and 'descended from David' (Rom 1: 3). John's prologue presented the Word both as 'God' (John 1: 1) and as becoming 'flesh' (John 1: 14). How could believers maintain this new faith without introducing a radical rupture with their belief in the one and only God which they had drawn from their Jewish heritage? How could they interpret these parallel affirmations about Christ's divine sonship and his humanity without tampering with the integrity of either element?

Heterodox solutions reduced or simply sacrificed either

[9] H. Bettenson, *The Early Christian Fathers* (Oxford: Oxford University Press, 1969), 217.

Christ's divinity or his humanity. As we saw in Chapter 1, the Ebionites dropped his divinity, while the Docetic tendency questioned the genuine bodily and historical reality of Jesus. Since they dismissed his body as only apparent or really 'heavenly', Docetists in effect excluded Christ's true incarnation and death. To eliminate every link between the evil demiurge (or creator of the material universe) and Jesus the Saviour, Marcion attributed to him a merely heavenly body. Valentinian Gnostics admitted that the Saviour had assumed only what was to be saved and hence no physical body.

With the work of Justin, Irenaeus, Tertullian, and Origen, a page began to be turned in exploring the humanity and divinity of Christ without sacrificing a truly monotheist faith. In his *Dialogue with Trypho* Justin explained that 'God has begotten of himself a rational Power' that was called in the Scriptures by various titles: 'sometimes the Glory of the Lord, at other times Son, or Wisdom, or Angel, or God, or Lord, or Word' (61. 1; see 61. 3). To interpret the generation of the Word, Justin appealed to the sun sending forth its rays or a fire kindling other fires. Just as in these analogies, the begetting of the Son did not mean an 'amputation, as if the essence (*ousia*) of the Father were divided' (ibid. 128. 3, 4). Here Justin touched a question which was to be long debated in the fourth century, the consubstantiality of the Father and the Son (or Word) in sharing the same essence or *ousia*. By that time, thanks to Tertullian, Justin's image of 'Light from Light' had entered the Creed (DS 125).

A further approach threatened either to destroy monotheism or at least to reduce Christ's divinity. Justin spoke of him as 'another God' alongside the Creator (*Dialogue*, 50. 1; 56. 1, 11): Jesus Christ who is 'the Son of the true God' and whom Christians honour as 'the second in order, with the Spirit of prophecy in the third place' (*First Apology*, 13. 3). This subordination of the Son (and the Holy Spirit) to 'the Creator of all things' (ibid.; see *Dialogue*, 56. 4) did not, however, lead to any denial that the pre-existent Logos was the universal mediator of creation (and revelation). This universal mediation, according to Justin, meant that the 'seeds of the Word' are everywhere and in every person (*Second Apology*, 8. 1, 10; 13. 5). Although 'the whole human race shares' in the Logos (*First Apology*, 46. 2), some people live only 'according to a fragment of the Logos' (*Second Apology*, 8. 3; see 10. 2; 13. 3); Christians live 'according to the knowledge and contemplation of the whole Logos, who is Christ' (ibid. 8. 3; see 10. 1, 3).

As Logos, the Son mediated creation. As 'Angel', he was the one who spoke to Abraham, Jacob, Moses, and others in OT theophanies. Since 'the Creator of all things' is so utterly transcendent and ineffable, this 'Author and Father of all things' has 'never appeared to anyone and never spoken in person'. It was 'a God and Lord' different from 'the Creator of all things' who spoke to the OT patriarchs and others, and who is therefore 'called Angel' because 'he announces' and brings about the will of God (*Dialogue*, 56. 1, 4).

In his concern to protect the absolute transcendence of the 'Author and Father of all things', Justin developed the theme of the intermediary roles of the Son as 'another' or 'second' God. As Logos he mediates and is present in all creation; as Angel he reveals the divine will in the OT theophanies, which in effect become Christophanies. When the Neoplatonic notion of intermediaries became popular a century or more later, the stage was set for Arius' full-blown subordination of the Logos. Justin's subordinationism, however, did not lead him to anticipate Arius and deny the genuine divinity of the Logos. He disagreed with Greek philosophy's insistence that God's eternal immutability was not to be compromised by talk of a true incarnation and death. Trypho spoke not only for Jews but also for cultured pagans when he challenged Justin's faith in the incarnation: 'You are attempting to prove what is incredible and practically impossible, namely, that God deigned to be born and to become man' (*Dialogue*, 68. 1). In his *First Apology* Justin acknowledged the continuing scandal of the crucifixion for the cultivated non-Christians of his time: 'They accuse us of madness, saying that we attribute to a crucified man a place second to the *unchanging* and *eternal* God, the Creator of all things' (13. 4; italics mine).

More a biblical theologian than the philosophically trained Justin, Irenaeus, as we have already recalled earlier in this chapter, developed a number of themes that maintained the integrity of Christ's humanity and divinity: (1) the salvific (and revelatory) reasons for humanity and divinity being united in Christ; (2) the value of his prehistory (in the OT) and human history (in the four Gospels); (3) the Adam/Christ antithesis in which the new head recapitulated the unified divine project of creation and redemption in one great history of salvation; (4) Christ's double generation, the ineffable and eternal generation from the Father and the temporal generation from Mary.

In passing, Irenaeus upheld the Son's eternal pre-existence with the Father (*Adversus haereses*, 2. 30. 9; 3. 18. 1), but he was much more concerned with the economy of salvation. Against the Gnostics he insisted on the Word becoming real flesh and on salvation being effected through the flesh (ibid. 3. 10. 3; 3. 19. 1). The genuine incarnation postulated the real resurrection of the flesh for Christ and others. Thus the struggle with the Gnostics encouraged a certain shift of interest from Christ's death and resurrection back to his incarnation.

We will see how in the fifth century the Nestorian and Monophysite controversies also contributed to this shift. In his own immediate context Irenaeus' major contribution lay in his countering the anti-incarnational teaching of Marcion and the Gnostics. Against them he defended the real humanity of Christ, the Word become flesh (John) and the new Adam (Paul) whose history was told by the four Gospels.

The next pair of writers, Tertullian and Origen, take us into the third century. In exploring the real divinity and humanity of Christ, they anticipate something which will develop even more towards the end of the fourth and in the first half of the fifth century: the application of trinitarian thought and terminology to Christology.

The targets of his criticisms helped to give a direction to Tertullian's contributions to trinitarian and christological thought. On a first front, he wished to maintain his faith in one God and not lapse into pagan polytheism. The defence of Christ's divinity could not mean abandoning monotheism. On a second front, Tertullian fought to maintain and clarify the truth against Christians who developed modalist monarchianism. This is an umbrella term for different forms of a rigid monotheism which claimed that any 'trinitarian' interpretation of the story of creation and salvation (1) referred only to the several ways (or 'modes') in which God acts externally and (2) did not describe anything about the inner divine life. The aim of these heterodox Christians was to exclude any distinctions within the divinity and safeguard at all costs the unique 'mon-archy' (one principle) of God (the Father). Thus Noetus and Praxeas taught the 'patripassian' doctrine, according to which it was the Father and not a distinct Son who was born in the incarnation, suffered, and died (Tertullian, *Adversus Praxean*, 2. 1). Slightly later in the third century Sabellius (see DS 105) and the Sabellians brought the Holy Spirit into their version of modal mon-archianism. The 'Father' in the OT, the 'Son' in the incarnation, and the 'Holy Spirit' at Pentecost were interpreted as being merely three manifestations of the one God, three different relationships which the one God assumed successively in creation, redemption, and the sending of the Spirit. The Sabellians treated the terms *ousia* and *hypostasis* as synonyms for an individual substance. The more moderate among them were ready to speak of God's three *prosōpa*, the three roles played by one and the same divine *hypostasis*.

Faced with pagan polytheists and Christian modalists, Tertullian wrestled with the question: is the divinity of the Son (and the Holy Spirit) compatible with genuine monotheism? Against the patripassians Tertullian wrote of God's one unique 'substance' (*substantia*) and three distinct but undivided 'persons' (*Adversus Praxean*, 2. 4; 12. 1, 3, 6, 7). The distinction (not separation) of persons does not destroy the unity of substance and the true divine 'monarchy'.

The invaluable asset of Tertullian's linguistic skills made him the first Christian writer to exploit the term 'persona' in theology, the first to apply 'Trinitas' (Trinity) to God (*De pudicitia*, 21. 16), and the first to develop the formula 'one substance in three persons'. This creator of theological Latin pulled in various (material) analogies to suggest how the Word (or *Sermo*) and the Holy Spirit could be derived from the Father without a real separation taking place. He wrote of a root producing a shoot, a spring giving rise to a river, and the sun sending forth its ray.

The Spirit makes the third from God [the Father] and the Son, as the fruit from the shoot is the third from the tree, the canal from the river the third from the source, the point of focus of a ray third from the sun. But none of these is divorced from the origin from which it derives its own properties. Thus the Trinity derives from the Father by continuous and connected steps. (*Adversus Praxean*, 8. 5–7)[10]

This way of looking at the 'derivation' of the Son and Spirit, Tertullian argued, did not subvert the unity of the one divine substance or 'monarchy'.

Right in the same *Adversus Praxean* Tertullian went on to apply to Christology his trinitarian terminology of 'substance' and 'person'. First, he recognized Christ's divinity and humanity as 'Word (*Sermo*) and flesh', 'Spirit and flesh', 'God and man', or 'Son of God' and 'Son of man' (27. 7–10). Far from merely appearing in a human form, the Word undergoes a genuine incarnation; through the flesh he can be truly seen and touched. Against Marcion and the Gnostics, Tertullian emphasized that it was for the sake of our salvation that the Word becomes flesh and takes on a real human existence.[11] In the incarnation two distinct 'substances' are joined in one 'person', without the substances being mixed to form some impossible *tertium quid* (ibid. 27. 7, 10–11). Instead 'the property of each substance remains intact' (*salvaque est utriusque proprietas substantiae*) (ibid. 27. 11)— a phrase that was to resurface more than two centuries later in Leo's *Tome* and get incorporated in the christological teaching of Chalcedon. Tertullian insisted on the one person and rejected any separation between the Son, Christ, and Jesus (ibid. 27. 2), without, however, exploring how 'person' offered the right key for interpreting the union between Christ's two substances.

We can sum up Tertullian's contribution. Against Praxeas and the modalist monarchians he upheld the true divinity of the distinct person, the Word or Son of God. Against Marcion and the Gnostics he stressed Christ's complete human substance, in particular, his genuine bodiliness. Tertullian can

---

[10] Translation (corrected) from Bettenson, *Early Christian Fathers* 120–1.

[11] In Tertullian's lapidary phrase, 'the flesh is the hinge of salvation' (*caro cardo salutis*) (*De resurrectione carnis*, 8. 2).

be seen to have ruled out in advance four major aberrations to come: Arianism by maintaining that the Son is truly God ('Light from Light'), Apollinarianism by defending Christ's integral humanity,[12] Nestorianism by insisting on the unity of Christ's one person, and Eutychianism by excluding any mixture of divinity and humanity to form some *tertium quid*.

The last writer we will look at before moving to Arius and the Council of Nicaea is Origen. As with his theology in general, he developed his reflections on Christ's humanity and divinity largely in response to heterodox views of the time. Against the adoptionists, who excluded Christ's divinity and held that he was merely a creature adopted by God, Origen insisted on the eternal generation of the Son and repudiated the notion that 'there was a time when he was not' (*De principiis*, 1. 2. 9; 4. 1. 2; 4. 4. 1). Against the Valentinian Gnostics he maintained that this eternal generation did not involve a division of the divine substance.

Although he would not call the Son and the Holy Spirit inferior in power, Origen favoured a certain 'sub-ordinationism' which highlighted the place of the Father as the ultimate principle: 'We say that the Saviour and the Holy Spirit are incomparably superior to all things that are made, but also that the Father is ever more above them than they are themselves above created things' (*In Ioannem*, 13. 25). Origen's conception of the Father as the ungenerated source of the Son's mission encouraged him to develop a picture of the 'subordinate' Mediator, somewhat along the lines of Middle Platonism. As Logos, the Son brings about creation and reveals the divine mysteries.

As regards the humanity of Christ, Origen became notorious for maintaining the Platonic view that the human soul of the Logos existed prior to the incarnation, being created with other human souls who likewise pre-existed their historical, earthly lives. In the incarnation his utterly sinless human soul (*De principiis*, 2. 6. 5) effected the union between the Logos and 'the flesh' (ibid. 2. 6. 3).

---

[12] When Tertullian argued against Marcion and the Gnostics that the Word had assumed both a soul and a body (ibid. 34.10), the critical point at issue was the taking of a body and real flesh. Apollinarius was to tamper with faith in Christ's integral humanity by denying that the Word assumed a rational soul.

Sympathetic specialists rightly interpret Origen's Christology as keeping within the bounds of Christian orthodoxy of his day.[13] Nevertheless, his stress on the transcendence of the Father left questions about the real divinity of the Son and the Spirit. If Christ's being divine seems somewhat 'levelled down', his humanity seems 'lifted' beyond what is normal. Origen deserves, of course, credit for breaking new ground by attending to Christ's human soul and its theological significance. However, his picture of a pre-existent soul and of its impeccability being already decided in that pre-incarnation state (rather than in the context of Christ's human history) makes it difficult to recognize Christ's genuine humanity. The problem, one should admit, is a wider, anthropological one. Origen's version of the human condition, with his scheme of pre-existent souls coming to inhabit their bodies, represents a Platonic dualism which has long ago been rejected.

Like Tertullian, Origen approached Christology in the light of his trinitarian doctrine. What he held about the Logos' eternal existence with God the Father largely shaped what he would say about the Son's incarnation and incarnate life.

Born shortly after Origen died, like others in Alexandria Arius (*c*.260–*c*.336) inherited Origen's trinitarian teaching: the Father, Son, and Spirit as three *hypostaseis* or distinct subsistent realities who share in the one divine nature but manifest a certain subordination (of the Son and the Spirit to the Father).[14] Arius apparently wanted to push this subordination much further. The Father is absolutely beyond the Son and, being unbegotten, is the only true God. A generation 'from the substance (*ousia*)' of the Father would misinterpret the divinity in physical categories and wrongly suggest the divine substance being divided into two or three parts. Like the Sabellians, Arius and his followers wanted to

---

[13] See H. Crouzel, 'Origen', in *Encyclopedia of the Early Church*, ii. 619–23; J. W. Trigg, 'Origen', *ABD* v. 42–8.

[14] On Arius and Arianism, see D. E. Groh, 'Arius, Arianism', *ABD* i. 384–6; M. Simonetti, 'Arius–Arians–Arianism', and C. Stead, 'Athanasius', both in *Encyclopedia of the Early Church*, i. 76–8, 93–5; R. Williams, *Arius: Heresy and Tradition* (London: Darton, Longman & Todd, 1987).

preserve the absolute, transcendent 'mon-archy' of God, but unlike the Sabellians they held on to the real difference of identity between the Father and the Son. (Arius had practically nothing to say about the Holy Spirit.) Where Sabellianism asserted a strict unity of the divine essence without any real distinction of subjects, Arianism distinguished the subjects while denying their unity of essence. As Athanasius reported the Arian position, they considered the Son strictly inferior to and, in fact, infinitely different from the Father (*Contra Arianos*, 1. 6).

In an incoherent statement ridiculed by Athanasius, Arius described the Son/Logos as being created before the beginning of the world, out of nothing and by the will of the Father, but not created 'like one of the creatures'. Using a phrase repudiated by Origen in the previous century, Arius denied that the Son was co-eternal with the Father: 'there was a time when he was not.' Since Arius apparently understood 'eternal' and 'unbegotten' as synonymous, he had to deny the Son's eternity. The Son must be 'later' than the Father; otherwise he would be 'unbegotten' like the Father.

After initially speaking of the Son as created out of nothing, Arius subsequently allowed for the Son being 'generated' by the Father but persisted in considering this act of generation to be in effect a creation. The only creature directly created by the Father, the Son carried out the will of the Father by creating everything else and so acting as a kind of demiurge, a Logos exercising divine power between God and the universe. Hence the One who became incarnate was not truly divine but less than God. Christ was also not truly and fully human. According to Arius, the Logos took the place of the human soul in Christ. The Council of Nicaea (325), however, concerned itself with rebutting only Arius' challenge to Christ's divinity.

Nicaea I, speaking of 'the Son' and never of 'the Word', confessed in its creed that the Son is 'of the substance (*ousia*) of the Father, God from God, Light from Light, true God from true God, begotten, not made, of one substance (*homoousios*) with the Father' (DS 125). The Council anathematized those who said of the Son that 'there was a time when he was not', and that 'he was created from nothing and is of different *hypostasis* or *ousia* from the Father' (DS 126). This was to hold that the Son is truly Son of God and not less than God: in the generation (not creation) of the Son, the substance of the Father has been fully communicated, and the Son is co-eternal with the Father.

Nicaea spoke out clearly for Christ's divinity, but three terms continued to run into difficulties well after the Council: *ousia*, *homoousios*, and *hypostasis*.

Ousia ('being', 'reality', 'essence', or 'substance') had a chequered background in Gnostic and Christian circles before it came to be adopted in Nicaea's teaching about the Son being 'of the same substance' (*homoousios*) as the Father. In the second century Valentinian Gnostics taught a triple consubstantiality: the human spirit was 'consubstantial' (*homoousios*) with God, the soul with the demiurge, and matter with the devil. In the third century the term came up when Paul of Samosata was deposed in 268 as bishop of Antioch. In speaking of the Logos as *homoousios* with the Father, he was apparently suspected of using the term in a modalist or Sabellian sense and holding that the unity of the *ousia* was such that there was no personal distinction between Father and Son/Logos. When Nicaea pressed *homoousios* into service, the Council almost inevitably recalled a bogy-figure (Paul of Samosata) and caused some to fear a lapse back into Sabellianism. As we shall see in a moment, the use of *hypostasis* as synonymous with *ousia* compounded this fear.

The other question for *homoousios* was the meaning of 'homo-'. In what sense are the Father and the Son 'of the same/one substance'? Numerically the same individual substance which they share as two particular subjects? Or is the adjective to be understood in an 'abstract' way as denoting the substance or essence common to different individuals (e.g. siblings in a human family)? The former meaning won through but, as we will recall shortly, not without a struggle.[15]

As used both in the NT and in (Platonic and Stoic) philosophy, the relevant range of meanings for *hypostasis* clusters under two headings: the *hypostasis* (1) as the primordial

[15] On this problem see Athanasius, *De synodis*, 28; *Contra Arianos*, 1. 18; 3. 5; *Ep. ad Serapionem*, 2. 3.

essence, or (2) as the individuating principle, subject, or subsistence. This basic ambiguity in the term surfaced in 262 when Pope Dionysius condemned those who divided the one divine 'mon-archy' into three *hypostaseis* (*hypostasis* being understood in sense (1)). To do that would obviously be to split the one divine essence into three divine essences and come up with 'three gods' (DS 112). Shortly before Dionysius' condemnation, however, Origen had been confronting Sabellian modalism by speaking of the triune God as three individual *hypostaseis* (= meaning (2) of the term). The terminological problem was bedevilled by the fact that Western (Latin) Christians, ever since the time of Tertullian, understood the Greek *hypostasis* to correspond to their Latin term *substantia*: that is to say, they took *hypostasis* in sense (1) above. Hence when Eastern (Greek) Christians acknowledged the three *hypostaseis* of God, Westerners were easily shocked as they interpreted such a statement to mean three separate divine substances—in a word, tritheism. However, from their point of view, the Greeks could misunderstand Latin talk about the one divine *substantia* as lapsing into the modalist position of one *hypostasis* in sense (2) of the word and hence as a denial of any personal distinctions in God.

The upshot for Nicaea of this inherited ambiguity about *hypostasis* was that taking *ousia* and *hypostasis* as equivalents ran the risk of *homoousios* being understood in a Sabellian way. Father and Son are not only of the same *ousia* but also of the same *hypostasis*—in sense (2) of *hypostasis*. Then there would be no real distinction between Father and Son; they would not be distinct, individual subsistences. Fortunately Nicaea did not encourage this false conclusion by coining in anticipation a sixth-century adjective, *homohypostatos*, and using it in sense (1) of *hypostasis* as a straight synonym for *homoousios*.

After Nicaea some bishops, while opposed to Arius, continued to prefer a term which had been discussed and rejected by the Council: *homoiousios*, in the sense of the Son 'being of like substance' with the Father. The supporters of Arius rejected both *homoousios* and *homoiousios*. Eventually, from around 355, extreme Arians like Aetius and Eunomius even developed the Anomean ('dissimilar') doctrine, according to which the Son is not only the first creature but also in essence simply 'unlike' the Father and radically inferior.

Then there were many bishops and others who simply remained uneasy about or antagonistic to the term *homoousios*. (1) It was not biblical. (2) It had been condemned in the controversy over Paul of Samosata back in 268. But, as Athanasius insisted, the term had been used then in a different setting and against a different error (*De synodis*, 41, 43–5). (3) We have seen how *homoousios* could be interpreted in a Sabellian sense, as if the Father and the Son were identical not only in substance/nature but also as personal subjects. (4) Furthermore, in itself *homoousios* was ambiguous. Did it merely have that 'specific' meaning whereby individual beings of the same species, which quite separately exemplify the same nature, can be said to share in the same substance (e.g. a brother and a sister who are 'of the same substance' as their parents)? (5) The term could also have the broader, 'generic' meaning whereby beings of the same genus (e.g. different animals) or things which show natural similarities can be grouped together as being 'of the same substance'. (6) Finally, *homoousios* might be applied to material substances like a whole mass of bronze that can be cut up into parts and made into such particular, separate objects as coins. Some at least of the older 'material' illustrations for the relationship between the Father and the Son were open to this misunderstanding.

Everything depended on what was meant by 'the same' in *homoousios*. It was easier to deal with some misinterpretations. Thus Basil of Caesarea could sweep aside (6): orthodox faith was not talking materialistically of one divine substance (*ousia*), as if it were some 'stuff' out of which Father, Son, and Spirit were made. It was possibilities (3) and (4) that mattered more for Basil's analysis of various misunderstandings of *homoousios*. Those who failed to acknowledge in God the real community of essence (4) were lapsing into polytheism and in effect believing in three gods. Those who forced *homoousios* to the extreme of disallowing any personal distinction within the godhead (3) were returning to Judaism or its Christian equivalent, Sabellianism. In a letter written in 375 to the leading Christians of Neocaesarea (Pontus), Basil stated:

It is indispensable to clearly understand that, as he who fails to confess the community of the essence (*ousia*) falls into polytheism, so he who refuses to grant the distinction of the *hypostaseis* is carried away into Judaism. . . . Sabellius . . . said that the same God . . . was metamorphosed as the need of the moment required, and spoken of now as Father, now as Son, and now as Holy Spirit. (*Epistola*, 210. 5)

By that time the battle, led by Basil, St Hilary of Poitiers (*c.* 315–67), and (from around 350) by Athanasius in support of *homoousios* and its right interpretation, had almost been won. The term *homoousios* pointed to the numerical identity of essence between the three divine persons. In particular as regards the 'substance' of God, the Father and the Son are the 'same one'.

The letter from Basil just cited signals both the triumph of Nicaea's teaching on the common essence or *ousia* shared by Father and Son (and Holy Spirit) and also a switch away from the Council's terminology. No longer are *ousia* and *hypostasis* being used as synonyms. Like Gregory of Nazianzus, Basil writes of one *ousia* (numerically identical essence) and three *hypostaseis* (individual personal subsistences with their particular properties) in God.

Seven years later this trinitarian terminology was officially adopted after the First Council of Constantinople. In its letter to Pope Damasus a post-conciliar synod confessed 'one divinity, power, or substance (*ousia*)' in 'three most perfect *hypostasesin*, that is, in three perfect *prosōpois*'.[16] Basil, Gregory of Nazianzus, and, even more, Gregory of Nyssa had been using interchangeably *hypostasis* and *prosōpon* (= the 'face' or visible manifestation and characteristics of the *hypostasis*). Although ready to talk of three *hypostaseis* in God (*Tomus ad Antiochenos*, 5–6), Athanasius had preferred *prosōpon* to *hypostasis*. Building on Origen, the Cappadocians, and Athanasius, Constantinople I put trinitarian language firmly in place: three *hypostaseis* or *prosōpa* and one *ousia* or *physis* in God. Origen, Athanasius, the Cappadocians, and

[16] Tanner, 28.

the post-conciliar synod of 382 (in its letter to Pope Damasus) spoke of God's *physis* (the essence seen as a principle of activity) interchangeably with the divine *ousia*.

We saw above how Tertullian led the way in fashioning a trinitarian vocabulary in Latin which he then applied in Christology. Eastern (Greek) theology followed the same path in using christologically their trinitarian terms. Gregory of Nazianzus (*Epistola*, 101. 19) and then Gregory of Nyssa (*Oratio catechetica*, 10. 1, 3–4) wrote of Christ's two *physeis* (natures or principles of activity). Gregory of Nyssa distinguished between the two *physeis* and the one *prosōpon* of Christ (*Contra Eunomium*, 6. 1, 2, 4). The fourth-century trinitarian vocabulary was fully taken over in Christology when (the one) *hypostasis* began to be attributed to Christ after the Council of Ephesus (431).[17] By that time debate had shifted to the question of the union of/in Christ. Fifty years earlier Constantinople I had, at least officially, put an end to controversy about Christ being truly divine and fully human.

At the trinitarian level Constantinople I reaffirmed the Nicene confession of faith that the Son was 'of one substance' with the Father, as well as teaching the divinity of the Holy Spirit (DS 150). In its letter to Pope Damasus (quoted above) the post-conciliar synod of 382 confessed 'the uncreated, consubstantial (*homoousios*) and coeternal Trinity'. At the purely christological level, Constantinople I (DS 151) rejected the teaching of Apollinarius of Laodicea (*c*.310–*c*.390) and the post-conciliar letter to Damasus called Christ 'perfect' or 'fully man' (Tanner, 28).

Intent on defending against the Arians the Nicene faith in Christ's divinity, Apollinarius had taken 'Logos/sarx' Christology to an extreme. Paradoxically, this meant following Arius in holding that in the incarnation the Logos assumed a body (with its life-giving soul or *psychē*) but took the place of the higher (spiritual and rational) soul or *nous*. The difference lay in the fact that, where Arius underinterpreted the condition of the Logos, Apollinarius underinterpreted the condition of Christ's *sarx* ('flesh'). A friend of Apollinarius,

---

[17] According to Epiphanius (*Adversus haereses*, 73), however, the Semi-Arian Synod of Ancyra (358) acknowledged the Son as particular *hypostasis*.

Athanasius developed a 'Logos/sarx' Christology in which a human soul was irrelevant for any interpretation of Christ's being and work. In a few texts (e.g. *Tomus ad Antiochenos*, 7) we find Athanasius apparently acknowledging an intelligent, human soul in the incarnate Word. Athanasius stopped short of essentially undercutting the full humanity of Christ, as did Apollinarius, out of a desire to defend the incarnate Word's real divinity and strict unity. This made Apollinarius an easy target for Gregory of Nazianzus (*Epistola*, 101), Gregory of Nyssa (in his *Antirrheticos*), and others.

Nevertheless, even after (or especially after?) Constantinople I, the Apollinarian question remained. Granted that Christ is truly divine (Nicaea I and Constantinople I) and perfectly human, how is the union between his divinity and humanity to be understood and interpreted?

8

Ephesus, Chalcedon, and Beyond

❧ ☙

> There was equal danger in believing the Lord Jesus
> Christ to be God only and not man also, or man only
> and not God.
>
> (St Leo the Great, *Tome*)

Differences between what have been called the 'schools' of
Antioch and Alexandria set the stage for the christological
controversies of the fifth century and beyond. Unlike the
followers of Arius and Apollinarius, the groups who remained
unreconciled to the teaching at Ephesus in 431 and Chalcedon
in 451 still have their followers—known, respectively, as the
Nestorians (who call themselves 'Assyrians' or 'the Church of
the East') and Monophysites (now generally called 'Oriental
Orthodox'). 'Logos-anthropos' (Word-man) and 'Logos-
sarx' (Word-flesh) have often been used as convenient labels
to distinguish the Antiochenes, whose Christology may be
summarized as 'the eternal Word assuming the man Jesus',
from the Alexandrians, whose Christology highlighted the
Johannine theme of 'the Word becoming flesh'.

From the late fourth century, as heirs of the teaching from
Nicaea I and Constantinople I, the two schools faced a
common challenge. In defending Christ's true divinity
(against the Arians) and his perfect humanity (against the
Apollinarians), how were they to conceive the unity in Christ
without stating it weakly, on the one hand, or, on the other
hand, maximalizing it to the point of eliminating the real
distinction between the two natures? Decades passed before
it became clear that the union should be seen as taking place
in the person and not in the natures.

In the last chapter we noted how the Cappadocian Fathers

contributed to the clarification of christological terminology. But they also exemplify the problem created by presuming that Christ's unity is to be explored at the level of natures. The Cappadocians presented his unity by using Stoic language about the 'mixing' (*krasis*) and 'blending' (*synkrasis*) of two natural substances which completely permeate each other without losing their characteristic nature.[1] The obvious problem with this doctrine of mixture is that it makes Christ out to be a kind of amalgam, a divine-human hybrid, as well as moving too much in the area of material categories. It would take time to go beyond such attempts to interpret Christ's unity in terms of his natures, no matter whether this nature–nature relationship was explained through categories of 'mingling' or in other ways.

The analogy with the union between the human body and soul provides another example of failing to get the question right. In his *Contra Celsum* (3. 41) Origen presents Christ's personal union in a way that recalls the Aristotelian theory of the union between matter and form. Somewhat nuanced but still clearly affirmed, this analogy turns up in a letter by St Augustine of Hippo: 'just as in any man (except for that one who was uniquely assumed) soul and body form (*est*) one person, so in Christ the Word and the Man form (*est*) one person' (*Epistola* 169. 2. 8 = *Ad Evodium*). A few years later Cyril of Alexandria twice used the same analogy in his third letter to Nestorius (Tanner, 52, 55). The extra difficulty about this analogy is that, in the case of the body (matter) and soul (form), we are dealing with incomplete substances that together make up one complete substance (a human being). In the case of Christ two complete substances are united. The inadequacy of any appeal to the body–soul analogy illustrates once again how accounts of Christ's unity should be addressed to the personal level; his two natures form his duality.

---

[1] See e.g. Gregory of Nazianzus, *Orationes*, 30. 8; 37. 2; 38. 13; *Epistola* 101. 21.

The Councils of Ephesus and Chalcedon

The dramatic differences between the schools of Antioch and Alexandria came to a head at Ephesus in 431. As an Antiochene, Nestorius (patriarch of Constantinople from 428) aimed at defending Christ's integral humanity or, as he put it in his second letter to Cyril of Alexandria, at not 'destroying the distinctive character of the natures (*ta tōn physeōn*) by absorbing them into the one title of "Son"' (Tanner, 46). Hence he taught the 'conjunction' (*synapheia*) of Christ's two complete natures in one 'prosōpon' (ibid.), this latter term being intended as someone's or something's concrete form of existence and particular 'appearance'. Using *prosōpon* to cover the sum total of individual properties that manifest themselves, Nestorius could not only speak of the Christ's one 'prosōpon' but even, as Cyril accurately reports, of the union between the 'prosōpa' (plural) in Christ (ibid. 43). Each nature can be said to enjoy its own (natural) *prosōpon*. In presenting Christ's distinction at the level of natures (*physeis*) and unity at the level of *prosōpon*, Nestorius stressed more the natures over the one subject of these two natures and the one manifestation of the natures.

Although, as we have just seen, Nestorius could also write of Christ's unity (*henōsis*), he preferred the term 'conjunction' (*synapheia*). What did this 'conjunction' signify? His critics interpreted Nestorius' language about the man Jesus being 'assumed' (*homo assumptus*) and about the Word being present in him as in a temple to mean the mere 'conjunction' of two separately existing subjects, Jesus and the Word of God (who did not truly become flesh). In effect, they accused Nestorius of turning the distinction between Christ's two natures into a separation and proposing a merely moral unity between the eternal Son of God and Jesus as adopted son. Later Nestorius was to defend himself vigorously against such charges.

The conflict which led to the Council of Ephesus was a practical and a political one, but it suggests where the heart of the problem lay. Nestorius could not find a theological basis for the traditional *communicatio idiomatum*, which for centuries had justified the Christian practice of saying that

'the Son of God died on the cross'. He refused to attribute to
the Word of God the events of Jesus' human life: in particular,
his human birth from Mary. Hence, at least at first, Nestorius
declined to call Jesus' mother the 'Mother of God'
(*Theotokos*). This Marian title (see Luke 1: 43) had probably
been used by Origen and had been commonly used by Athanasius, Gregory of Nazianzus, and other fourth-century
figures. Nestorius at first proposed 'Mother of Christ'
(*Christotokos*) and eventually was ready to accept *Theotokos*.
But by then it was too late. His role as patriarch of Constantinople had been fatally jeopardized by his insistence on
the integrity and distinction of Christ's two natures and his
failure to appreciate the unity of the one acting subject which
justified calling Mary the mother of the Son of God.[2]

The controversy between Nestorius and Cyril dragged on
for more than two years before the Council of Ephesus met
in June 431. Cyril's defence of Christ's unity was notoriously
bedevilled by his appeal to a formula which he believed to
come from Athanasius but in fact originated with Apollinarius: 'mia physis tou (Theou) Logou sesarkōmenē(ou)'
(the one *physis* of the (God) Word become flesh); 'become
flesh' agreed grammatically with either *physis* or Word. To
Antiochene and other ears this sounded like a heretical fusion
of Christ's two natures. Cyril's thirty-ninth letter, written to
John of Antioch in April 433, showed him anxious to rebut
the charge of 'blending' or 'mixing up' Christ's divinity and
humanity (Tanner, 72). A year or two later he came back to
answer the same accusation in *Quod unus sit Christus*, insisting
that it was 'without mixing up and change' that the divinity
and humanity were united in Christ (736a), and that his
formula of 'the one *physis* of the enfleshed Son' does not
mean a 'confusion and mixing up', as if the human *physis*
disappeared in the face of the divine greatness (ibid. 737a, b).
If Nestorius switched from singular to plural in his use of
prosōpon, Cyril did the same with *physis*. It could mean the
individual subject of activity (as in his classical or notorious
phrase about 'the one *physis* of the Word become flesh').

---

[2] On Nestorius see A Grillmeier, *Christ in Christian Tradition*, trans. J. Bowden
et al., 2 vols. (London: Mowbrays, 1975 and 1995), i. 443–72, 501–19.

But Cyril was also ready to speak of Christ's two 'physeis' (natures), as we see both in his second letter to Nestorius (Tanner, 41) and in his letter to John of Antioch (ibid. 72).

On 22 June 431, without waiting for the papal legates or the Syrian bishops led by John of Antioch, Cyril opened the Council of Ephesus. It condemned Nestorius' teaching, excommunicated him, and proclaimed Cyril's second letter to Nestorius as consonant with the faith of Nicaea (DS 250–68).

1. A reading of that letter yields at least seven points of significance for the development of christology. Cyril points to the Nicene Creed (Tanner, 41), which attributes to the same subject both divine and human attributes. This implies the appropriateness of appealing to 'the exchange of properties' and confessing that the eternal Word of God was born, suffered, died, and rose from the dead.[3] Cyril made this appeal to a liturgical profession of faith without explicitly justifying his argument by invoking the *lex orandi lex credendi* (the law of prayer is the law of belief) principle. By a curious coincidence St Prosper of Aquitaine (*c.*390–*c.*463), when composing a year or so later the *Indiculus* or a dossier on grace drawn from the writings of Augustine, created that theological axiom in the fuller form of 'legem credendi lex statuat supplicandi' (let the law of prayer establish the law of belief) (DS 246). Prosper's theme is the doctrine of grace, Cyril's is Christology. But their major (but not exclusive) theological justification ('the law of prayer') is, in effect, the same.

2. In his second letter to Nestorius Cyril states that the Logos 'united to himself hypostatically (*kath hypostasin*) flesh enlivened by a rational (*logikē*) soul' (Tanner, 41; DS 250). The insistence on a 'rational soul' is directed, of course, against the Apollinarian heresy. The new element here is the phrase that recurs four times in Cyril's second letter to

---

[3] Apropos of liturgical usage—that is to say the baptismal confessions in use—J. N. D. Kelly points out that both in the East and in the West the old baptismal creeds were not at once replaced by the Nicene Creed. Its fuller form after 381, in the Niceno-Constantinopolitan Creed, however, seems to have been quickly employed as a baptismal confession: Kelly, *Early Christian Creeds* (London: Longman, 3rd edn., 1972), 254–62, 344–5.

Nestorius: 'kath'hypostasin'. Where it occurs with the verb 'unite', as in the words just quoted above, the Tanner translation renders the phrase as 'hypostatically united' (Tanner, 41, 42, 44); where the phrase is linked to the noun 'union' (*henōsis*) (ibid. 43), it is translated as 'the hypostatic union'. The Bologna edition of the decrees of the ecumenical councils, from which the Tanner edition takes over the original (Greek and Latin) texts, in its translation shows more sensitivity to the ambiguity in Cyril's use of *hypostasis*: it renders 'kath'hypostasin' once as 'substantially united' (*unito sostanzialmente*), twice as 'union of person' (*unità di persona*), and once as 'hypostatically' (*ipostaticamente*).[4] Cyril has the merit of introducing 'union by *hypostasis*' as a christological formula, which after the Council of Chalcedon will be understood as 'personal union' or 'union in the person'. But Cyril himself still thinks somewhat more in terms of substance when he uses *hypostasis*, even if, as his third letter to Nestorius indicates, he is also ready to use *hypostasis* and *prosōpon* as synonyms (Tanner, 56). A few years later he employs the same pair of terms synonymously in *Quod unus sit Christus* (758a). But Nicaea's coupling of *ousia* and *hypostasis* as equivalents still has its long-term effect on Cyril. The phrase 'united *kath'hypostasin*', as Alberigo and his Italian translator rightly recognize, can also mean 'substantially united' when used by Cyril himself.

3. As we have already seen, Cyril's second letter to Nestorius showed that he was ready to admit the terminology of the incarnate Word's 'two natures (*physeis*)'. Just over twenty years later this language was to be endorsed by the Council of Chalcedon. The same thing was to happen to the letter's (4) scheme of Christ's double 'generation' (from the Father in eternity and from Mary in time), (5) insistence on Christ's being (in Irenaeus' language) 'one and the same', and (6) use of *Theotokos*, the popular Marian title based theologically on the 'interchange' of her Son's divine and human properties. (7) By endorsing Cyril's second letter, the Council of Ephesus joined him in rejecting any Nestorian talk either of 'two Sons'

---

[4] G. Alberigo *et al.*, *Concilium oecumenicorum decreta* (Bologna: Edizioni Dehoniane, 1991), 41–4.

or of a union of *prosōpa* (persons in the plural). Chalcedon was to say practically the same thing by teaching that the one, only-begotten Son, as one *prosōpon*, is not 'separated or divided into two *prosōpa*' (DS 302).

The whole controversy with Nestorius, like that with Eutyches twenty years later, continued to shift theological attention away from Christ's death and resurrection to his incarnation and the relationship between his human and divine natures. The particular impact of the Council of Ephesus was to emphasize that the humanity and divinity of Christ were not to be understood as separated. With different nuances that rejection clearly came through points (1), (2), (5), (6), and (7) of Cyril's second letter to Nestorius. Yet, if the two natures were not separated, were they really to be distinguished? And how were they united? Those questions remained to set the agenda for the Council of Chalcedon twenty years later.

The central terminology for that later council was already coming into wider use, even if it was not yet firmly in place. Cyril's second letter distinguished 'two' natures (*physeis*). Even more than his second letter (in which some ambiguity, as we noted above, still clung to the phrase *kath'hypostasin*), his third letter to Nestorius (which was not, however, officially approved and proclaimed at the Council of Ephesus) helped to give *hypostasis* a personal meaning in christological and not merely trinitarian usage. By coupling *hypostasis* more or less interchangeably with *prosōpon*, Cyril encouraged the move towards dissociating *hypostasis* from *ousia* (with which it had been synonymously linked at Nicaea I) and allowing the term to express more the sense of subsistence than that of substance.

Prevented by Cyril's peremptory impatience from being present when the Council of Ephesus opened in June 431, John of Antioch and his followers produced a formula of union (August 431) which helped to reconcile differences in christological teaching (DS 271–2). In this document the Antiochenes maintained their particular way of excluding Arianism, on the one hand, and Apollinarianism, on the other, by calling Christ 'perfect God and perfect man', maintaining his double generation (in eternity from the Father

and in time from his mother Mary), and teaching a double
consubstantiality (divine with the Father and human with his
mother). They abandoned support for Nestorius by endorsing the Marian title of *Theotokos* and confessing Christ to be
only one *prosōpon* and two natures (*physeis*) in an 'unconfused
union (*henōsis*)'. Here they dropped the term Nestorius preferred for the link between Christ's humanity and divinity:
'conjunction' (*synapheia*). They also left Nestorius behind
when they wrote of the 'union of the natures' (*henōsis tōn
physeōn*).

In a letter to John of Antioch in April 433, Cyril accepted
the formula of union. In doing so, however, he wrote of 'the
difference' of Christ's natures 'from which' (*ex hōn*) came the
union (Tanner, 72). Shortly after Cyril's death in 444, this
language was being pushed to extremes by the head of a large
monastery in Constantinople, Eutyches. His 'monophysite'
position illustrated spectacularly the failure to appreciate that
Christ's human nature was assumed by the person of the
Word and not as such by the divine nature. In looking to
interpret in terms of the two natures the union effected by
the incarnation, Eutyches apparently argued that after the
union the human nature is absorbed by the divine nature.
Hence Christ is 'from' two natures but not 'in' two natures.
Only one 'nature' (*physis*) remains after the union, and Christ
cannot be said to be and remain 'consubstantial' with human
beings.

Condemned in 448 at a home synod in Constantinople,
Eutyches was rehabilitated the following year at a synod
which was held in Ephesus and dubbed by Pope Leo the
Great the 'Latrocinium' (brigandage). In his *Tome* to Flavian,
the patriarch of Constantinople, Leo maintained a classical
balance when describing the undiminished duality of Christ's
perfect natures and the unity of his person. Borrowing language from Tertullian, he wrote of 'the distinctive character
of each nature remaining intact and coming together into one
person' (*salva ... proprietate utriusque naturae et in unam
coeunte personam*) (*Epistola* 28. 3; DS 293). Here Leo acknowledged Christ's one person as the key to his unity.[5] A year

---

[5] On the *Tome* see H. Arens, *Die christologische Sprache Leos des Grossen* (Freiburg:
Herder, 1982).

earlier, at the home synod of 448, Flavian spoke of the one 'hypostasis' or 'prosōpon' of Christ, apparently using them as equivalents, as did Cyril of Alexandria in his third letter to Nestorius (see above).

When it met in 451, the Council of Chalcedon first confirmed four texts: the Nicene Creed in its fuller form from Constantinople I, Cyril of Alexandria's second letter to Nestorius, Cyril's letter to John of Antioch in 433, and Pope Leo's *Tome*. Then the Council added its own christological confession, the first part of which (DS 301) drew on the Antiochene formula of union from 431. This first part of the Chalcedonian confession changed somewhat the order of phrases and terms from the 431 formula but added nothing, apart from two phrases ('true God and true man' and 'like us in all things apart from sin').

The second part of the confession (DS 302) broke new ground by affirming Christ's one person ('prosōpon' and 'hypostasis') 'in' his two natures, human and divine. It specified that 'the one and the same Christ, Son, Lord, and Only Begotten' had been made known in these two natures which, without detriment to their full characteristics, continue to exist 'without blending or change, and without division or separation', while belonging to only one and not two 'persons' (*prosōpa*). In other words, the unity of Christ exists on the level of person, the duality on that of natures. Through the unity of subject in Jesus Christ, the eternally pre-existent Son of the Father is also the Son of the Blessed Virgin Mary. 'Without blending or changing' aimed to exclude the current error of Eutyches in merging Christ's two natures, 'without division or separation' to exclude the error attributed to Nestorius of separating the two natures.

Apropos of the position of the Chalcedonian definition on the subject in Christ, I made the following comments some years ago:

[the definition] did not literally describe Christ as a 'divine person'. It spoke of the one *hypostasis* uniting two natures, but did not in so many words declare this to be the pre-existent divine person of the Logos. (It was left to the Second Council of Constantinople to uphold and interpret the unity of subject in Christ by identifying the principle of union as the pre-existing Logos.) Nevertheless,

Chalcedon got very close to identifying the one *hypostasis* when it moved straight from affirming the oneness of person to talk of 'one and the same Son and *only-begotten God the Word*, Lord Jesus Christ.'[6]

In an article challenging my interpretation of Chalcedon, Anthony Baxter rightly follows E. Schwartz's edition of the Greek text and translates the last phrase from the definition as 'one and the same Son, Only-begotten, divine Word, the Lord Jesus Christ'.[7] If one wants to be rigidly 'correct', however, the translation should be: 'one and the same Son, Only-begotten, God [the] Word, Lord Jesus Christ.' Baxter's highly detailed arguments against my interpretation do not strike me as convincing. Essentially my difficulties with his rebuttal are twofold. First, the definition names Christ once as 'true God', once as 'God [the] Word', four times as 'Lord' (presumably in the strong sense of *Kyrios* or divine Lord), and three times as 'Son'. Since the Son is named as being 'of one essence' with God the Father and as 'Only-begotten', Son should be understood as the (Only-begotten) Son of God the Father. Given these ways of naming Christ, Chalcedon clearly implies that the one *hypostasis* it confesses is a divine *hypostasis*. Second, Baxter's own interpretation leaves me puzzled. He acknowledges that Chalcedon both excludes two *hypostaseis* (one divine and the other human) and does not propose that Christ is a merely human *hypostasis*.[8] Surely one can only conclude then that Chalcedon recognizes (albeit implicitly) that the *hypostasis* in question is divine? Yet Baxter is reluctant to accept this conclusion.

After Chalcedon

In confessing that the unity of Christ exists on the level of person and the duality on that of his natures, the Council of Chalcedon proved a lasting success in regulating language about Christ. Its terminology of 'one person in two natures'

---

[6] Interpreting Jesus, (London: Geoffrey Chapman, 1983) 182.
[7] 'Chalcedon and the Subject in Christ', *Downside Review*, 107 (1989), 1–21, at 9.
[8] Ibid. 12.

became normative down to the twentieth century. Its teaching effected a brilliant synthesis between the Alexandrians, who highlighted Christ's unity, and the Antiochenes, who championed the duality of Christ's distinct natures. The subject who acts is one (divine) person; in what he does he reveals the two natures through which he acts.

In synthesizing the concerns and insights of the Alexandrian and Antiochene schools, Chalcedon provided a 'logical' conclusion to the first three ecumenical councils. Against Arianism, Nicaea I used the term *homoousios* to reaffirm 'Christ is divine'. Against Apollinarianism, Constantinople I affirmed 'Christ is human'. Against Nestorius, Ephesus professed that Christ's two natures (his divine being and his human being) are not separated. Against Eutyches, Chalcedon confessed that, while belonging to one person, the two natures are not merged or confused. One can appreciate the way the first four councils became acknowledged as representing the essential and orthodox norm for understanding and interpreting the christological (and trinitarian) faith of the NT. Five months after his election to the papacy, St Gregory the Great in a circular letter of February 591 to the five eastern patriarchs declared that he received and venerated the first four councils just as he received and venerated the four Gospels (DS 472).

For all of its proving a logical conclusion, Chalcedon obviously left some, even much, unfinished business. To begin with, it did not define the key terms it used when distinguishing in the innovative part of its confession 'nature' (*physis*), on the one hand, and 'person' (*prosōpon/hypostasis*), on the other. In any case, rather than being the proper work of an ecumenical council, the analysis and definition of such terms belong rather to philosophers and theologians. Half a century after Chalcedon, Boethius (*c.*480–524) influenced all subsequent Christology in the West by his definitions. In his *Contra Eutychen et Nestorium* (also called *Liber de persona et duabus naturis Christi*), he defined nature as 'the specific difference informing anything' (1), and person as 'an individual substance of a rational nature' (3). Boethius also grasped the soteriological motivation of Chalcedon by arguing that, if Christ were not one divine person in two complete but distinct natures, he could not have acted as Saviour.

Boethius' desire to rebut both Nestorius and Eutyches reflected the way the differences between an Antiochene Christology of distinction or even separation (represented by Nestorius) and an Alexandrian Christology of union (pushed to an extreme by Eutyches) had not been laid to rest by the achievement of Chalcedon. The Second Council of Constantinople (553) interpreted Chalcedon in a way that represented a return to the Alexandrian triumph at Ephesus, whereas the Third Council of Constantinople (680/1) swung the pendulum in the Antiochene direction. The Second Council of Nicaea (787) reached back behind the Alexandrian–Antiochene controversies to reassert in a new context (the iconoclastic controversy) the truth of the incarnation taught by Nicaea I and Constantinople I. Let us review in turn these post-Chalcedonian developments.

In a synodical letter (February 591) written to the five oriental patriarchs a few months after his election to the papacy, Gregory the Great, as we recalled above, expressed his veneration for the first four ecumenical councils by comparing them to the four Gospels (DS 472). Even so late in the day, his endorsement of the second council, Constantinople I of 381, was important. Before recognizing that council, in which none of its bishops had taken part, the Western Church had shown some resistance. In his letter, as often elsewhere, Gregory also indicated his unqualified acceptance of the fifth council. But this endorsement of Constantinople II was motivated by its fidelity to the first four councils. They remained the touchstone for essential christological and trinitarian orthodoxy.

The Emperor Justinian promoted Constantinople II in an unsuccessful attempt to win over the hard-line followers of Cyril of Alexandria. For a century they had expressed their dissatisfaction with the Chalcedonian formula ('in two natures'). In a swing back to the Council of Ephesus' condemnation of Nestorius, Constantinople III, through its 'Three Chapters', posthumously condemned three authors for supposedly favouring Nestorianism. The condemnation touched the works and person of Theodore of Mopsuestia (c.350–428), some writings by Theodoret of Cyrrhus (c.393–c.466), and a letter by Ibas of Edessa (from 433) (DS 434–7). By (1) using Cyril's 'one nature' and Chalcedon's 'two natures' as equivalent expressions (DS 429) and (2) presenting the union between 'God the Word' and 'the flesh' as taking place 'by way of synthesis' and 'hypostatically' (DS 424–6, 429–30), Constantinople II highlighted the unity of Christ's person over the distinction of his natures. This also came through noticeably when Chalcedon's 'in' two natures was replaced by Cyril's 'from' two natures (DS 429). Its high, Alexandrian Christology also led the Council to remove any possible, lingering ambiguity about his divine identity by calling 'our Lord Jesus Christ' 'one of the holy Trinity' (DS 424, 426, 432). In line with its stress on the union of divinity and humanity in Christ, the Council anathematized those who would not 'venerate in one act of worship God the Word made flesh together with his flesh' (DS 431).

With still no peace in sight between the 'monophysites' (who championed Cyril's language) and the 'diphysites' (who followed Chalcedon's teaching on 'two natures'), Sergius (patriarch of Constantinople from 610 to 638) proposed a compromise with his formula of two natures but 'one energy' in Christ. In a correspondence with Sergius, Pope Honorius I (d. 638) spoke of there being only 'one will' in Christ. Defenders of Honorius I may explain how he did not lapse into heresy: he was not talking 'ontologically' (as if Christ's human nature literally lacked a will) but merely 'morally' (in the sense that Christ's human and divine wills worked in such perfect harmony that it was if they were one). Nevertheless, one can hardly acquit Honorius of the serious charge of being gravely imprudent in his two letters to Sergius. His 'monothelite' (one will) language threatened belief in Christ's full humanity, as if the human nature of Christ lacked an essential faculty, its will. The monothelite view transposed 'monophysite' reductionism from the level of human nature as such to that of human faculties, and represented Christ's human will as being 'absorbed' by his divine will. Patriarch Sergius' 'one energy' formula, in effect, did the same. It slipped over the fact that Christ's 'energy' or modes of activity come from his natures and not as such from his person.

Hence to assert 'one energy' was tantamount to asserting 'one nature'. It amounted to a 'monophysite' view of Christ's activity, as if his human action were absorbed by the divine principle of activity.

The Third Council of Constantinople (680/1) took a firmly Chalcedonian line by distinguishing the two natures of Christ in terms of their willing and activity. It taught that Christ enjoyed a human and a divine will (the two wills being in perfect harmony with each other) and two 'energies' or 'natural operations'. Applying Chalcedonian terminology to the issue it faced, Constantinople III insisted that the two wills and 'natural operations' were neither separated from each other nor blended together (DS 556–8). Thus, at the level of Christ's will and 'natural' activities, the Council upheld the Chalcedonian balance between a 'Nestorian' separation and a 'Eutychian' blending.

The vindication of Christ's complete humanity was motivated by soteriological considerations. Without a human will not only would his true 'consubstantiality' with us have been defective but also the reality of the salvation he mediated would have become suspect. Lacking a human will, Christ could not have freely accepted also on our side (and for our sake) his redemptive mission and have carried it through.

The Second Council of Nicaea (787), called to put an end to the iconoclastic heresy, formed an epilogue to the previous six councils. St John of Damascus (*c*.675–*c*.749) had prepared the way for this seventh council by defending images of Christ and the saints. In particular, he argued that icons of Christ were a necessary consequence of the incarnation: they visibly expressed faith in the Word of God taking 'flesh' and assuming a human existence in our material world. At a practical level, by endorsing iconic expression of belief in the incarnation, Nicaea II summarized and drew to a close the christological teaching of seven ecumenical councils.

Into the Middle Ages

The first major contribution from the Middle Ages which calls for attention is the theory of satisfaction from St Anselm of Canterbury (*c.*1033–1109).[9] But before examining his approach to soteriology and its enduring influence, something must be said about the patristic background.[10]

The last chapter devoted its opening pages to the way Irenaeus and many others interpreted the experience of salvation as a 'wonderful exchange' in which the Son of God's incarnation brought our divinization. Along with this interpretation of redemption, Irenaeus, Basil, Leo, and others introduced further soteriological language that also enjoyed a basis in the Scriptures: through his battle with and victory over the forces of evil, Christ destroyed the tyranny of sin, death, and the devil. In such hymns as 'Vexilla regis prodeunt' and 'Pange lingua gloriosi' Venantius Fortunatus (*c.*530–*c.*600) classically expressed for Western Christianity this image of redemption as a victory in battle. Since the resurrection turned the crucifixion into a victory, Venantius Fortunatus represented the cross as a trophy erected on the site of the triumph. The *Exultet* or Easter Proclamation, which goes back at least to the seventh century, celebrates the two redemptive victories of light over darkness: in the crossing of the Red Sea and in the night of Christ's resurrection from the dead. The Easter sequence 'Victimae paschali laudes' (of the eleventh century) symbolically proclaims the same victorious deliverance in which life triumphed over death. The (sixth-century?) Anglo-Saxon poem *The Dream of the Rood* extols Christ as the heroic young champion who went into battle on the cross and saved humanity from the powers of evil.

Along with this language of victorious conflict, some Fathers extended the NT metaphor for salvation as 'buying back', 'redeeming', and 'setting free by paying a ransom' (e.g. 1 Cor. 6: 20; Gal. 3: 13; 4: 5; 1 Pet. 1: 18). From the third century we begin to hear of a ransom paid to the devil and even of 'the rights of the devil'. Thus Origen wrote of Christ's

[9] On Anselm and *Cur Deus homo* see G. R. Evans, *Anselm and Talking about God* (Oxford: Clarendon Press, 1978), 126–93; R. W. Southern, *Saint Anselm and his Biographer* (Cambridge: Cambridge University Press, 1963), 77–121; id., *Saint Anselm: A Portrait in a Landscape* (Cambridge: Cambridge University Press, 1990).

[10] On various post-NT theologies of redemption, see B. Sesboüé, *Jésus-Christ l'unique médiateur: essai sur la rédemption et le salut*, 2 vols. (Paris: Desclée, 1988–91).

blood being the price paid to the devil who had held power over enslaved sinners (*In ep. ad Romanos*, 2. 13). This 'business' transaction turned into a fight in which the devil, expecting to receive the soul of Christ, was disappointed and defeated. Overcoming the power of death, Christ offered life to all those who wished to follow him (*In Matthaeum*, 16. 8). In the following century Gregory of Nyssa notoriously developed this language. Since human beings had voluntarily sold themselves into his hands, the devil was their legitimate owner. By concealing his divinity under the veil of humanity, Christ tricked the devil into 'swallowing the hook of divinity along with the bait of flesh' and so losing both his 'rightful' ransom and his captives (*Oratio catechetica*, 21–4). Some Fathers like John Chrysostom (*Homiliae in Johannem*, 67. 2) and Augustine (*De Trinitate*, 13. 12. 16; 13. 13. 17; 13. 14. 18) qualified this theory of the devil's rights by adding that he had abused these rights in putting to death the innocent Christ. For his part, Gregory of Nazianzus vigorously contested the whole idea of divine redemption as a ransom paid to the devil (*Oratio*, 45. 22), but his protests failed to carry the day.

These two theories of redemption, whether kept distinct or merged, largely held the field prior to Anselm. To highlight Christ's victorious combat and/or ransom paid to the devil was to take very seriously both the powers of evil and what redemption cost Christ. These pre-Anselmian approaches also held together the crucifixion and resurrection in the paradox of this violent and atrocious death being the moment of victory. Repelled especially by talk of the rights of the devil, Anselm turned elsewhere to elaborate a more 'reasonable' version of salvation.

'Satisfaction', a non-biblical term drawn from Roman law and applied by Tertullian to penitential practice, took pride of place in Anselm's theology of redemption as developed in *Cur Deus homo* (1098). 'Every sin', he argued, 'must be followed either by satisfaction or by punishment' (1. 15). God does not wish to punish but to see the good project of creation 'completed' (2. 5). Satisfaction requires from human beings not only that they should stop sinning and seek pardon but also that they do something over and above existing obligations, a work of supererogation. However, since all sin offends the honour of the infinite God, the reparation made must have infinite value—something of which finite human beings are incapable. Moreover, they have nothing extra to offer God, as they already owe God everything. Thus Anselm concludes to the 'necessity' of the incarnation. Only the *God*-man can offer something of infinite value; the hypostatic union confers such value on the human acts of Christ. Only the God-*man* has something to offer; being without sin, Christ is exempt from the need to undergo death and hence can freely offer the gift of his life as a work of reparation.

Although Anselm's context was primarily monastic, he aimed to present a rational case for the coherence and even 'necessity' of the incarnation to a non-Christian—in particular, a Jewish—audience. In doing so, he laid a fresh stress on the humanity and human freedom of Christ, who spontaneously acts as our representative and in no way is to be construed as a penal substitute who passively endured sufferings to appease the anger of a 'vindictive' God. Anselm's theory, for all its originality, puts him with those like Irenaeus, Basil of Caesarea, and Leo the Great who, as the previous chapter reported, understood redemption to be brought about *also* from within the human scene.

Anselm's theology of satisfaction has often been criticized for being juridical and Roman. In fact, its cultural roots were found rather in the feudal society of northern Europe. So far from being a legal and private matter, the 'honourable' service owed by vassals to their lords was a social factor that guaranteed order, peace, and freedom. Denying the honour due to lords meant chaos. Anselm's 'inculturation' of the theology of redemption was more vulnerable on other grounds: its non-biblical version of justice and sin. Rather than expressing God's fidelity to all creatures and, especially, to human beings, Anselm's commutative notion of justice seemed to picture God as so bound to an abstract order of things that it would be 'unthinkable' simply to grant forgiveness without requiring reparation. Likewise, instead of interpreting sin very clearly as an infidelity and disobedience which bring a break in personal relationship with a loving God, Anselm understood it more as an infinite dishonour that upset the just order of things. Although elsewhere he richly recognized the role of God's merciful love, *Cur Deus homo* contained only a brief closing reference to the divine mercy. Other notable omissions in this theology of satisfaction included (1) the resurrection (with the gift of the Holy Spirit, and that major patristic theme, the divinization of the redeemed), and (2) the full significance of Jesus' life and public ministry. For the scheme of satisfaction it was enough that the incarnation occurred and that Christ freely gave his life to make reparation for human sin. Anselm turned Christ's life into a mere prelude to death.

Despite his common ground with notable predecessors among the Greek Fathers over the essential role of Christ's human will in redemption, Anselm stands for a Western parting of the ways with Eastern theology. He opens the christological development which will take us through the medieval period to our own times.

9
Medieval and Modern Christology

⊰⊱ ⊰⊱

The offence is cancelled only by love.

(St Thomas Aquinas, *Contra gentiles*)

Any account of medieval Christology cannot ignore three lines of development, which may be labelled academic, monastic, and popular. Anselm's younger contemporary Peter Abelard (1079–1142) had an important impact on the scholastic method of debate to be used in the emerging European universities and other theological centres. Rather than pursuing Anselm's thesis about satisfaction, he stressed the revelation of divine love communicated by the passion and death of Christ. This example inspires our response, a response which is made possible by the interior help of the Holy Spirit.[1] It has been conventional to criticize Abelard's view of redemption as unilaterally subjective and 'merely' exemplary. At all events he rightly appreciated love as the key to the story of salvation, a theme which will be developed later (in Chapter 12).

Abelard's relentless opponent St Bernard of Clairvaux (1090–1153) developed his Christology in a spiritual, mystical way. He had a major influence on the devotion to the human Jesus (as friend and lover) that grew stronger in the twelfth century and flourished through St Francis of Assisi (1181/2–1226), the popular piety inspired by the Franciscan movement, and new developments in liturgy, painting, sculpture,

---

[1] See Peter Abelard, *Commentaria in Epistolam Pauli ad Romanos*, Corpus Christianorum, Continuatio Mediaevalis 11, 210–28. On medieval soteriology, see J. Pelikan, *The Christian Tradition: A History of the Development of Doctrine*, iii (Chicago: Chicago University Press, 1978), 106–57; and on Abelard see R. E. Weingart, *The Logic of Divine Love: A Critical Analysis of the Soteriology of Peter Abelard* (Oxford: Clarendon Press, 1970).

and architecture. Anselm, Cistercian writing, St Hildegard of Bingen (1098–1179), and Julian of Norwich (c.1342–after 1413) helped to encourage, in particular, the use of the motherhood metaphor in Christology and trinitarian theology. Christ was understood to act like a mother in loving, feeding, and instructing the individual soul. This fresh use of feminine language for Christ was encouraged by a widespread interest in the Song of Songs and a return to Jesus' own image of himself as a hen with her chickens (Matt. 23: 37 par.), an image which had already drawn comments from Clement of Alexandria, Origen, John Chrysostom, Ambrose, Augustine, and Anselm.[2]

Christology as such, however, was to flourish less in the spiritual, liturgical, and monastic setting of Bernard and his successors than it did in the academic setting of the European universities which emerged from the twelfth century on. We take up Thomas Aquinas, the classic protagonist of the new, university-style Christology. For the sake of convenience, let me concentrate on the third part of his *Summa theologiae*, while recognizing that a full-length account of his Christology would include other such works by him as his *Summa contra gentiles* and biblical commentaries.[3]

Thomas Aquinas

In his Christology 'from above', Aquinas argued that the primary motive for the incarnation was to remit and remedy human sins. Hence 'if there were no sin, the incarnation would not have taken place' (1. 3 *resp.*). Nevertheless, he also endorsed a principle from Dionysius the Pseudo-Areopagite ('good diffuses itself') to anticipate twentieth-century theology[4] and expound the incarnation as God's supreme self-

[2] See C. W. Bynum, *Jesus as Mother* (Berkeley, Calif: University of California Press, 1982).

[3] On Aquinas' Christology see B. Catao, *Salut et rédemption chez S. Thomas d'Aquin: l'acte sauveur du Christ* (Paris: Aubier, 1965); G. Lohaus, *Die Geheimnisse des Lebens Jesu in der Summa theologiae des heiligen Thomas von Aquin*, Freiburger theologische Studien 131 (Freiburg: Herder, 1985); E. H. Wéber, *Le Christ selon saint Thomas d'Aquin* (Paris: Desclée, 1988). Intertextual references will be made to the third part of the *Summa theologiae*.

[4] See my *Retrieving Fundamental Theology* (London: Geoffrey Chapman, 1993), 52–4, 98–107.

communication (1. 1 *resp.*). In a way that almost anticipated
the lines along which Karl Rahner was to develop an evolutionary christological view that owed something to Pierre
Teilhard de Chardin (1881–1955),[5] Aquinas also represented
the personal union between the Word of God and a human
nature as the 'fitting' consummation of human perfection
(3. 8 *resp.*).

Several christological analyses in the third part of the
Summa theologiae took a triple shape. These concerned the
grace, the knowledge, and the 'offices' of Christ. (1) Through
the grace of union his humanity enjoyed the highest imaginable gift, that of being 'assumed' by the person of God's Son.
Habitual or supernatural grace sanctified and perfected his
human nature in the fullest possible way. The grace of 'head-
ship' endowed Christ with the power to sanctify others as the
head of the Church or Mystical Body.

2. Like other medieval theologians Aquinas pushed the
principle of perfection—or supposition that Christ's
humanity must have the absolute best of everything—to its
limit. Among other things, this meant that, during his earthly
life, right from the first moment of his conception, Jesus'
human mind was credited with the beatific vision of God.
Along with his knowledge (in which he knew all things in a
full vision of God in the divine essence), Aquinas recognized
that Jesus' human knowledge included 'ordinary', exper-
imental knowledge but simultaneously attributed to him the
special, 'infused' knowledge of angels and prophets (9. 1–12.
4).

3. When dealing with its OT background and sources, we
treated in Chapter 2 the triple scheme of priest-prophet-king.
Aquinas pressed this scheme into service when examining
Christ's saving role as mediator between God and human
beings. Christ fulfilled this role not only through his priesthood (22. 1), but also as prophet (7. 8) and king (22. 1 *ad* 3;
31. 2 *ad* 2; 2. 59. 4 *ad* 1).

A further significant feature in Aquinas' Christology came
in his attention to the 'mysteries' of Jesus' life (especially

[5] See K. Rahner, *Foundations of Christian Faith*, trans. W. V. Dych (London:
Darton, Longman & Todd, 1978), 178–203; id., 'Christology within an Evolutionary
View of the World', *Th. Inv.* v. 157–92.

those presented by the Synoptic Gospels (e.g. his baptism, temptations in the desert, miraculous activity, teaching, and transfiguration on the mountain. Like Bernard of Clairvaux (and Bonaventure) and unlike Anselm of Canterbury, Aquinas showed an appreciation for the concrete historical Christology—the identity of Christ's person and his redemptive work—mediated through the story of his ministry. After Francisco de Suárez (1548–1619) a theological interest in the 'mysteries' of Christ's life—in particular, his public life— largely disappeared and has returned again to Christology only in our century.

Later in this chapter we will hear the classic remarks from Albert Schweitzer (1875–1965) about the way nineteenth-century 'lives' of Christ read and interpreted the data about Jesus in the light of personal and cultural interests and pre-suppositions. Aquinas himself at times reads the gospel story in the light of his own religious vocation. He looks down the well of history and sees Christ almost as a Dominican in anticipation. Christ handed on the fruits of his contemplation ('contemplata tradere': 40. 1. *ad* 2; 40. 3 *ad* 3), by acting as a preacher of 'the Word of God' (40. 3 *resp.*; 41. 3 *ad* 1) and combining the contemplative and active life (40. 1 *ad* 2 and 3).

Before he reaches the passion and death of Jesus, Aquinas has already taken up the Anselmian notion of satisfaction (1. 2), but does not endorse its 'absolute' necessity. In detailing reasons for the 'fittingness' of the incarnation, Aquinas high-lights the destruction of sin and the 'repairing' of human beings themselves more than the 'repairing' of sinful offences against God (1. 2; 1. 4). He mitigates Anselm's soteriological thesis by maintaining that God could pardon sin even though adequate satisfaction was not made and stressing the way love makes satisfaction valid: 'In satisfaction one attends more to the affection of the one who offers it than to the quantity of the offering' (79. 5).[6] Christ's passion is expounded as a meritorious sacrifice, being undergone by Christ and truly accepted by God as being inspired by love (48. 3 *resp.*).

---

[6] In his *Contra gentiles* Aquinas states in an unqualified way: 'the offence is cancelled only by love' (3. 157).

Unfortunately Aquinas understood the specific point of sacrifice to be that of 'placating' God (49. 4 *resp.*): 'In the proper meaning of the term one calls sacrifice that which is done to render God due honor with a view to placating him' (48. 3 *resp.*). In general, Aquinas dealt with Christ's passion and sacrifice in the light of satisfaction as the act of a particular form of justice—namely, penance which involves a penal or punitive element (an element expressly excluded by Anselm). This helped to open the way, sadly, to the idea of Christ propitiating an angry God by paying a redemptive ransom. Aquinas himself denies that Christ's work of reconciliation means that God began to love us again only after the ransom was paid. God's love for us is everlasting; it is we who are changed by the washing away of sin and the offering of a suitable compensation (49. 4 *ad* 2).

After his treatment of Christ's passion and death, Aquinas added a substantial section on the resurrection (53–6), interpreting it, above all, in terms of exemplary and efficient causality (56. 2). As exemplary causes, Christ's death and rising to glory have their corresponding effects in the work of redemption. His glorified humanity can produce results superior to itself precisely because it is 'moved' and applied by a higher, principal cause (God).

Any summary of Aquinas' christological achievement should include at least five items. (1) Far from picturing Christ as a mere passive victim, Aquinas followed the lead given by Constantinople III, and integrated into his doctrine of redemption the essential role played by the graced but free and loving consent of Christ in his human will to the passion and cross. Salvation came not only from the outside (from the initiative of the transcendent God) but also from within the human race. (2) Although one may well wonder whether Aristotelian thought (e.g. about efficient causality) really shaped and structured Aquinas' Christology or simply remained a useful language and surface terminology, nevertheless, he followed the Church Fathers in doing theology by combining two 'bests': the best biblical exegesis of his time and the best philosophy he could find. (3) In unfolding the different facets of Christ's mediatorship, Aquinas endorsed that serviceable scheme of priest-prophet-king. (4) His attention to the 'mysteries' of Christ's life stood in judgement over many subsequent Christologies and their neglect of Jesus' human story. His attention to the Synoptic Gospels contrasted with the approach of F. D. E. Schleiermacher (1768–1834), who rightly turned to the historical life of Jesus but in doing so one-sidedly privileged John's Gospel. (5) Aquinas' Christology 'from above' inevitably highlighted the incarnation. At the same time, however, he did not allow an all-absorbing theology of the incarnation to take over. He stood apart from many of his predecessors and successors in treating Christ's resurrection at considerable length.

His less fortunate christological impact comprised at least three points. (1) An alternative scenario question ('would the Word have become incarnate if Adam and Eve had not sinned?') kept apart the orders of creation and redemption. Here the christological vision of St Irenaeus, Blessed Duns Scotus (*c.* 1265–1308), and Teilhard de Chardin rests on good NT grounds (e.g. Col. 1: 15–20). Creation and redemption (together with its future consummation) form three moments in one great act of salvation through Christ and his Holy Spirit. The redemption should not be taken as a divine rescue operation, mounted subsequently after an original plan of creation went astray. (2) Aquinas encouraged the subsequent Catholic theological tradition to hold that in his human mind the earthly Jesus enjoyed the beatific vision and hence lived by sight, not by faith. Notable difficulties can be brought against this view. For instance, the comprehensive grasp of *all* creatures and *all* they can do (which Aquinas attributed to the beatific vision) would lift Christ's human knowledge so clearly beyond the normal limits as to cast serious doubts on the genuineness of his humanity, at least in one essential aspect. In Chapter 11 we will take up the question of Christ's knowledge and faith. (3) Despite some improvements (e.g. the stress on Christ's *loving* acceptance of his passion), the way Aquinas adjusted Anselm's theory of satisfaction helped open the door to a monstrous version of redemption: Christ as the penal substitute propitiating the divine anger.

To the Reformation

Anselm's classic thesis on salvation both expressed and encouraged a concern which was to remain dominant right through to the time of the Reformation and beyond: the saving work of Christ. Some medieval developments fed into this soteriological concern.

Renewed devotion to the Eucharist, along with the specific initiative of Blessed Juliana of Liège (1192–1258), secured the establishment of the Feast of Corpus Christi in 1264. Thomas Aquinas himself was probably the author of a sequence for the feast ('Lauda Sion'), a hymn ('Pange lingua'), and other texts composed for the newly instituted feast. Besides celebrating Christ's eucharistic presence, the feast supported a sense of the Mass as an expiatory sacrifice for sins. That also meant fostering faith in the sacrificial and expiatory death of Christ on the cross. The infinite merits of that death, made available pre-eminently through the Eucharist, could supply the penance which living and dead sinners have failed to perform.[7]

A further feature, which evolved in the life of the Western Church from the eleventh century, also promoted belief in the infinite merits of Christ's sacrificial death: the doctrine and practice of indulgences. Understood as the remission before God of temporal punishment required by sins for which repentance had already been expressed and pardon received, indulgences were granted by the official Church out of the heavenly 'treasury' of the merits of Christ and his saints. The history of indulgences is also a sad story of grave abuses, which very late in the day the Council of Trent decided to stop (DS 1835). Rooted in the penitential practice of the first Christian millennium, indulgences, while calling for human 'works' (e.g. prayer, almsgiving, and pilgrimages), rested on the conviction that Christ's own redemptive 'work' was infinitely valuable.

The arrival of Europeans in the Americas raised with new rigour the issue of universal participation in the benefits of

[7] See M. Rubin, *Corpus Christi: The Eucharist in Late Medieval Culture* (Cambridge: Cambridge University Press, 1991); for a useful review of this important book see R. Kieckhefer, *Journal of Religion*, 73 (1993), 255–6.

Christ's redemption. The discoveries initiated by Christopher Columbus in 1492 revealed the existence of millions of human beings in societies which had gone on for many centuries without the slightest chance of hearing the gospel and joining the Church. How could Christ have been Saviour for the indigenous peoples of the Americas? How could they have shared in his redemptive grace without even hearing his name?[8] In the long run, Columbus' discovery raised questions about Christ's salvific 'work' for those 'outside' which were at least as important as those raised 'inside' by the theology and practice of the Eucharist and indulgences.

At the heart of the Reformation initiated by Martin Luther (1483–1546) was the question of grace ('Where/how do I find a gracious God?'), which amounted to the question of the sinner's justification. Luther maintained that the justice or saving work of Christ is imputed (for the remission of sins) through faith which arises from hearing the word of the gospel. He based his doctrine of justification on a fourfold 'only': 'solo Christo' (by Christ alone), 'sola gratia' (justification by God's grace alone), 'sola fide' (by faith alone and not by good works), and 'sola scriptura' (by the authoritative word of the Bible alone and not by human traditions). Luther's great collaborator Philip Melanchthon disliked the ontological christology of Thomas Aquinas and other scholastic theologians. His soteriological concentration, which fitted well into Luther's doctrine of justification, was summed up in the dictum: 'To know Christ means to know his benefits and not ... to reflect upon his natures and the modes of his incarnation.'[9] In subsequent editions of his *Loci communes* Melanchthon dropped this remark. But it expressed well the intense soteriological interest and concern over our union with Christ consistently developed by his colleague Luther. Human beings are lost, enslaved by sin, and utterly guilty. It is Christ who redeems them (from sin,

---

[8] See F. A. Sullivan, *Salvation outside the Church?* (London: Geoffrey Chapman, 1992).

[9] See Ch. 1 n. 15 above. For Reformation Christology see M. Brecht *et al.*, 'Luther', *TRE* xxi. 513–94, esp. 542–4; H. Kessler, 'Christologie', in T. Schneider (ed.), *Handbuch der Dogmatik*, i (Düsseldorf: Patmos, 1992), 190–2, 366–70; W. Nijenhuis, 'Calvin', *TRE* vii. 568–92, esp. 582–3.

death, and the devil) and reconciles them with God.

Luther was averse to metaphysical Christology and the speculations of the medievals. At the same time, he maintained the doctrine of Chalcedon, stressing the soteriological character of the two-natures teaching. He emphasized the *communicatio idiomatum* and the omnipresence of the risen body of Christ. Even more than Luther, Calvin respected Chalcedonian Christology, criticizing vigorously any Nestorian tendency to separate Christ's two natures or any Monophysite tendency to confuse them. As we saw in Chapter 2, Calvin exploited Christ's threefold office (as prophet, priest, and king) in his Christology.

Two years after it finally opened in 1545, the Council of Trent took up the question of justification, which—as in the case of Luther's teaching—necessarily involved some interpretation of Christ's work as redeemer. In its 1547 decree on justification the Council, when explaining the various causes of human justification, repeated the medieval doctrine on Christ's merit and satisfaction.

The meritorious cause [of justification] is the beloved, only-begotten Son of God, our Lord Jesus Christ who, 'while we were sinners' (Rom. 5: 10), 'out of the great love with which he loved us' (Eph. 2: 4), merited for us justification by his most holy passion on the wood of the cross and made satisfaction for us to God the Father. (DS 1529; see 1523, 1690)

Without offering any definition of 'merit' and 'satisfaction' and without introducing the term 'sacrifice', Trent here interpreted the saving impact of Christ's passion with language that reached back, as we have seen, to Aquinas and Anselm.

The Reformation disputes about the nature of the Eucharist also required taking some stand on the salvific meaning and efficacy of Christ's death (and resurrection). The Council of Trent dedicated its twenty-second session (1562) to the sacrifice of the Mass. It repeated traditional Catholic teaching: the bloody sacrifice Christ offered once and for all on 'the altar of the cross' (DS 1740) is represented 'in an unbloody manner' (DS 1743), but not repeated, 'under visible signs' to celebrate 'the memory' of Christ's 'passage from this world' (DS 1741) and to apply 'the salutary power' of his sacrifice 'for the forgiveness of sins' (DS 1740). It could not recognize the Mass as sacrificial and salvific without linking it to the once-and-for-all, historical sacrifice of Christ on Calvary. The Council did not, properly speaking, define the term 'sacrifice', but it did have some things to say about its characteristics. Christ's 'clean oblation' was 'prefigured by various types of sacrifices under the regime of nature and of the law'; as 'their fulfillment and perfection', it included 'all the good that was signified by those former sacrifices' (DS 1742). This very open view of Christ's sacrifice was followed by statements which offered a penal description (not definition). As 'truly propitiatory', the eucharistic sacrifice serves to 'appease' (*placare*) God who 'grants grace', the 'gift of repentance', and 'pardon'. Hence the sacrifice of the Mass is rightly offered 'for the sins, punishments, satisfaction, and other necessities' of the faithful, both living and dead (DS 1743; see 1753).

By aligning 'satisfaction' with 'punishments' and speaking of God being 'appeased', the Council of Trent signalled penal elements which Aquinas and others had introduced into Anselm's theory of satisfaction. Quite against Anselm's explicit intention, satisfaction was now depicted as involving punishment. The Council of Trent went that far, but did not go further to speak (in its decree on the Mass) of the divine anger being discharged against Christ as the one who literally carried the guilt of the world's sins. Others did that. In place of Anselm's commutative version, God's justice was being interpreted as vindictive—with the divine anger venting itself on Christ, the penal substitute for sinners, whose suffering on the cross was the rightful punishment imposed on human sin.

Protestant reformers did not accept Trent's teaching on the sacrificial character of the Mass, but they had no difficulty in using (and expanding) the language of punishment and propitiation for Christ's sacrificial death on the cross. Luther and John Calvin (1509–64) wrote of a war between God (the Father) and God (the Son). They understood Christ to have literally taken upon himself the guilt of human sin, just as if he had personally committed all these sins himself. He suffered as our substitute on the cross, and his atrociously

painful death placated the anger of God and so made justification available for us. This view of redemption as penal
substitution was 'supported' by misusing and mis-
interpreting various texts from Paul (e.g. Gal. 3: 13 and 2
Cor. 5: 21) and elsewhere in the Bible (e.g. Ps. 22; Isa. 53;
Lev. 16).

The changes made in Anselm's theory did not remain a
Protestant monopoly. Catholic preachers like J. B. Bossuet
(1627–1704) and L. Bourdaloue (1632–1704) spoke of God's
vengeance and anger being appeased at the expense of his
Son. As victim of the divine justice, Christ even suffered the
pains of the damned. French religious eloquence, both in the
seventeenth century and later, turned God into a murderer
who carried out a cruel vendetta before being appeased and
exercising the divine mercy. Paul's sense of the loving initiative of God as the key to human redemption (e.g. Rom. 5: 6;
8: 31–2) had slipped right out of the picture.[10]

The Background for Today

In setting the stage for my own contribution to current Christology, I could leap straight ahead to von Balthasar, Barth,
Kasper, Moltmann, Pannenberg, Rahner, and other major
figures in twentieth-century Christology. Instead of dealing
so much with individual figures, however, it seems preferable
to plot some major shifts which have affected both the questions Western Christology raises and the ways it goes about
its arguments and use of evidence. In particular we need
to attend to developments in philosophy, history, and other
academic disciplines.

With his principle 'cogito ergo sum', René Descartes
(1596–1650) symbolized and encouraged the 'anthropological turn'—that switch to a concern for the conscious
subject which has deeply affected modern Christology and
other branches of theology. The consciousness of individual

---

[10] On the Council of Trent, as well as on Calvin, Luther, and others who developed
a soteriology of penal substitution, see B. Sesboüé, *Jésus-Christ l'unique médiateur*,
2 vols. (Paris: Desclée, 1988, 1991), i. 67–83, 238–47, 280–7, 360–5; and J. Wicks,
'Justification and Faith in Luther's Theology', *Theological Studies*, 44 (1983), 3–29,
esp. 21–2.

subjects and their experience of themselves and the world have at times become the sole focus of attention and have been turned into the major and even exclusive criterion for christological argument. At a popular level, A. N. Wilson recently typified again the conviction that the divinity of Jesus is to be accepted or rejected only on the grounds that during his earthly life he did or did not experience himself and/or believe himself to be such.[11] The anthropological turn has included such one-sided emphases on human subjectivity as well as happier versions of the Cartesian heritage.

The anthropocentric theology of Schleiermacher showed a massively subjective switch in the way he systematically set out to base all Christian truth on the experience and self-consciousness of the individual. Eventually he came to interpret faith in terms of a human 'feeling of absolute dependence' (*Gefühl der schlechthinnigen Abhängigkeit*) from God. Hence his Christology revolved around, or was practically reduced to, Jesus' unique God-consciousness. By making the subjective experience of the earthly Jesus dominate at the expense of post-NT Christian reflection and teaching, Schleiermacher in effect turned Christology into Jesuology. But in this his followers, both within liberal Protestant circles and beyond, have been legion.[12]

Like Descartes and John Locke (1632–1704), who was very influenced by Cartesian thought, John Henry Newman (1801–90) took as his starting-point the 'I' and one's consciousness of oneself. Rather than arguing, for instance, for God's existence on the basis of the external world, Newman grounded his case on one's personal existence and the presence of God in the voice of conscience. My subjective consciousness, according to Newman, makes my own existence and that of God 'luminously self-evident'.[13]

From Descartes's questions about the subject who asks and seeks to know, the anthropological turn was mediated to

[11] A. N. Wilson, *Jesus* (London: Sinclair-Stevenson, 1992), pp. xvi, 235.

[12] On Schleiermacher see J. Moltmann, *The Way of Jesus Christ* (London: SCM Press, 1990), 59–63; on Schleiermacher and many major figures in modern Christology, see J. Macquarrie, *Jesus Christ in Modern Thought* (London: SCM Press, 1990), 175–335.

[13] *Apologia pro vita sua* (Oxford: Clarendon Press, 1990).

the twentieth century via the transcendental philosophy of Immanuel Kant (1724–1804) and his successors. Kant challenged classical metaphysics in the sense that whoever makes claims about such matters as God, the immortality of the soul, and its liberty must first inquire whether such an enterprise is at all possible. What we call 'external' reality may be shown to be (at least in part) the product of our own mind. In its extreme (Kantian?) form, the anthropological turn attends only to the subject of knowledge. Like Joseph Maréchal (1878–1944) before him, Karl Rahner (1904–84) defended a theistic realism by arguing that human beings and their (metaphysical) questions reveal a drive which leads them beyond the immediate data of the subject's sense perception towards the Absolute. Rahner's Christology of human self-transcendence within an evolutionary view of the world interpreted the incarnation not only as the divine self-communication in the person of the Son but also as *the* limit-case in what is possible to humanity in its dynamic openness to the Absolute.[14]

In his role as mathematician and natural scientist, Descartes stands for another quite different development that has modified modern Christology and, indeed, theology in general: the quest for scientific objectivity. Besides looking inward, as founder of modern optics, Descartes also looked outward, as did Galileo Galilei (1564–1642) in using his telescope to unlock the secrets of the universe. The physicist and mathematician Isaac Newton (1642–1727) built on both of them to develop a picture of the world as a machine or closed continuum of causes and effects. This model of the universe reached its high point with the mechanistic determinism of P. S. Laplace (1749–1827) and others. The remarkable progress in physics and the natural sciences in general encouraged many scholars in other disciplines to endorse the search for absolute objectivity. The ideal frequently became a dispassionate, neutral, and value-free version of reality (often conceived in merely physical terms), which reduced or even eliminated personal participation and could establish conclusions in a mathematical way.

[14] See Rahner, *Foundations of Christian Faith*, 176–321.

This one-sided search for utter 'objectivity' created a 'prejudice against prejudice',[15] which reversed Augustine's axiom 'believe in order to understand' (*crede ut intelligas*) and made it read 'if you believe, you will not understand'. More and more the quest for dispassionate objectivity meant forgetting that the subject shares in reality 'out there', and we cannot eliminate the thinking, acting, and believing subject. Truth is something to be known also by contemplating it, dwelling in it, and living it.

The twentieth century had hardly begun when the natural sciences themselves began to modify the dream of absolute 'objectivity', and accept the fact that pure objectivity does not exist, not even in physics. By rehabilitating the observer's viewpoint and arguing that there are no absolute markers for time or space, the General Theory of Relativity presented in 1905 by Albert Einstein (1879–1955) spelt the end of classical, Newtonian physics, built as it was on the objective measurability of causes and effects.

Other theoretical physicists helped to demolish further the mechanistic image of the world as a closed and measurable continuum of causes and effects. With his Uncertainty Principle Werner Heisenberg (1901–76) stated that we cannot know accurately, at the same time, both the position and the velocity of any of the particles which make up an atom. When we measure very accurately the velocity, we cannot measure the position very accurately, and vice versa. The corollary is that many subatomic processes cannot be 'explained' by the traditional laws of causality but only by statistical laws. We have only a statistical knowledge, for example, of where a given subatomic particle might be at any given moment.

The work of Einstein, Heisenberg, Max Planck (1858–1947), and many other scientists (and philosophers) has fostered the sense that all knowledge is also properly subjective. The role of observers and of the 'instruments' chosen by them is in no way to be disqualified. The results of observations and experiments inevitably depend upon the observers' point of

---

[15] On this see Hans-Georg Gadamer, *Truth and Method* (London: Sheed & Ward, rev. edn., 1989), 269–72; also see my *Fundamental Theology* (London: Darton, Longman & Todd, 1981), 5–14, and M. G. Brett's reflections on Gadamer in *Biblical Criticism in Crisis?* (Cambridge: Cambridge University Press, 1991), esp. 135–48.

view; we get answers only to the questions we put. As forms of our knowledge, scientific laws put together the many observations we have made.

As the twentieth century moved on, specialists in different fields came to agree that the personal viewpoint and—more broadly—personal questions, values, and faith help rather than hinder knowledge. A natural scientist turned philosopher, Michael Polanyi (1891–1976), argued authoritatively that the personal component is a necessary, and not undesirable, element in all human knowledge. The opening pages of Chapter 3 above assumed, rather than attempted to argue for, the subjective nature of all knowledge, in particular our knowledge of other persons.[16]

The dream of a Cartesian-style, scientific objectivity has been rightly abandoned by many scholars in various disciplines. Curiously it remains alive in certain biblical quarters: specifically, among some who do their research into the history of Jesus. The importance of John Meier's *A Marginal Jew: Rethinking the Historical Jesus*, for instance, is somewhat reduced by his attempt, which naturally cannot always be maintained, to do his work as a 'neutral' historian—by merely describing the 'facts' and declining to explain and evaluate the purpose of Jesus' life.[17]

Other developments which were often intertwined and have affected the christological climate in the twentieth century included the enlightenment, deism, and the theory of evolution. The enlightenment, with its stress on the use of human reason, generally opposed divine revelation, religious tradition, and their authority. God was to be known by reason alone or else, as in the case of Kant, reduced to a postulate of practical reason. As a doctrine inaccessible to reason, belief in the Trinity was either denied or marginalized. This rationalism excluded the notion that one of the three divine persons assumed a human existence. It handed on its interpretation of Jesus as the teacher of wisdom, and the perfect example of moral perfection. This sapiential vision of Jesus fed into the work of Albrecht Ritschl (1822–89), Adolf von Harnack

[16] M. Polanyi, *Personal Knowledge* (London: Routledge, 1962).
[17] See the review by R. Fisichella in *Biblica*, 74 (1993), 123–9.

(1851–1930), and many others. The neo-Kantian, liberal theology of Ritschl understood Jesus' preaching of the kingdom as a call to join an ethical community whose achievements would help to establish the coming reign of God. One can identify as neo-Ritschlians those contemporary writers who play down Jesus' eschatological message and turn him into a kind of countercultural, Cynic-style philosopher.[18]

Leaders of the enlightenment in the British Isles, continental Europe, and North America often coincided in fact with those who came to be known as 'deists'. An umbrella term for many writers from the seventeenth century on, deism stressed the role of reason in religion and rejected special revelation, miracles, and any providential involvement in nature and human history. After creating the world, the God of the deists left it to be governed by natural, immutable laws that Isaac Newton led the way in discovering. This image of the universe denied any direct divine interactions subsequent to the original act of creation. The logic of deism excluded the possibility of any such special subacts of God as miracles, an incarnation, a virginal conception, and any resurrection from the dead. Deist presuppositions and tendencies continue to turn up in contemporary Christology: for instance, in some of Edward Schillebeeckx's reflections on Christ's virginal conception and bodily resurrection.[19]

Deists and others welcomed the theory of evolution developed by Charles Darwin (1809–82) to explain the origin and appearance of new and higher forms of life. The species evolved through natural selection and survival in the struggle

[18] See J. D. Crossan, *The Historical Jesus* (Edinburgh: T. & T. Clark, 1991); F. Gerald Downing, *Christ and the Cynics: Jesus and Other Radical Preachers in First-Century Traditions* (Sheffield: Sheffield Academic Press, 1988); B. L. Mack, *The Lost Gospel* (San Francisco: HarperCollins, 1993); id., *A Myth of Innocence: Mark and Christian Origins* (Philadelphia: Fortress, 1988). In 'Jesus and the Cynics: Survey and Analysis of an Hypothesis', Hans Dieter Betz (who names Downing and Mack but not Crossan) remarks: 'the presumed presence of Cynics in the Galilean society in which Jesus lived is mostly fanciful conjecture. The evidence for Cynicism is limited to Gadara and Tyre, Hellenistic cities outside Galilee' (from a paper, 'Jesus and the Cynics: Survey and Analysis of an Hypothesis', delivered at the August 1993 meeting of the Studiorum Novi Testamenti Societas and published in *Journal of Religion*, 74 (1994) 453–75, at 471.

[19] See my comments in *Interpreting Jesus* (London: Geoffrey Chapman, 1983), 20–4 and 195–6, on Schillebeeckx's *Jesus: An Experiment in Christology*, trans. H. Hoskins (Collins: London, 1979).

for existence. Darwin's theory, biological in its intent, has been applied to other fields, even to the evolution of the whole cosmos itself. Darwin's *On the Origin of Species by Means of Natural Selection* (1859) aroused bitter opposition from many Christians, who believed it to be irreconcilable with the biblical accounts of creation in Genesis. In our own century Teilhard de Chardin, however, embraced and extended Darwin's key insights by interpreting in the key of evolution the whole cosmological and human story from creation to the final consummation. His scheme of cosmogenesis, anthropogenesis, and christogenesis detected an evolving spiritualization of matter, in which humanity and the entire universe move towards the final consummation in Christ as the omega-point. Teilhard's evolutionary Christology recognized Christ as the intrinsic goal and purpose of the entire cosmic-historical evolution.[20]

A further development in the modern world, which at least in the Western world has complicated christological (and more generally, theological) work, has been the emergence of a new philosophic pluralism. Up to the Reformation and beyond, Greek philosophy, even if we insist on the differences between Platonic and Aristotelian modes of thought, helped and in various ways held together theological reflection. To a degree European scholars all shared in the one perennial philosophy deriving ultimately from the Greeks. But from the sixteenth century philosophical thought has split up into different and new systems. From Descartes to Martin Heidegger (1889–1976) and Ludwig Wittgenstein (1889–1951), philosophers have stood back from their culture, surveyed centuries of intellectual history, and quite consciously tried to take philosophy and human thought in new directions. The upshot is that the practitioner of Christology must choose today between philosophies (which often must be distinguished according to different authors, schools, and stages) such as analytic philosophy, existentialism, idealism, neo-Thomism, phenomenology, philosophical hermeneutics, pragmatism, process philosophy, and transcendental phil-

[20] See C. F. Mooney, *Teilhard de Chardin and the Mystery of Christ* (London: Collins, 1966).

osophy. Influences from these philosophies turn up constantly in twentieth-century Christologies.

Let me take one example, the speculative idealism of G. W. F. Hegel (1780–1831), who interpreted all history as the process through which the Absolute Spirit expands dialectically and comes to itself in the other (humanity). In the short term, left-wing Hegelian thought led to the denial of Christ's divinity and eventually, as in the case of Ludwig Feuerbach (1804–72) and Karl Marx (1818–83), to the denial of God. Hegelian dialectic opened the way for David Friedrich Strauss (1808–74), who named orthodox supernaturalism as the thesis which asserted the historicity of the events recounted in the Gospels. The antithesis became the rationalist attempts to explain 'naturally' the miracles and all other events in the life of Jesus. Strauss himself proposed the synthesis by interpreting all inexplicable gospel events as 'myths', by which he meant the non-historical, culture-conditioned 'clothing' of Christian ideas that alone possess validity.

In the twentieth century, either by their acceptance or rejection, the lasting legacy of Hegelian themes shows in the christological thought of writers like Hans Urs von Balthasar (1905–88), Eberhard Jüngel (b. 1934), Jürgen Moltmann (b. 1926), and Wolfhart Pannenberg (b. 1928). Pannenberg, for instance, has taken over from Hegel such themes as the horizon of universal history and truth being found in the whole (= the totality of history). For Moltmann's political-eschatological approach, in the passion and death of Jesus the whole story of human suffering becomes the suffering of the triune God.[21]

Faced with contemporary philosophical pluralism, it is no solution to ignore dialogue with philosophy, as Karl-Josef Kuschel largely does in his long study *Born before All Time? The Dispute over Christ's Origin*.[22] Yet where should Christology look for the kind of philosophical help outlined in

[21] See W. Pannenberg, *Jesus: God and Man* (London: SCM Press, 1968); id., *Systematic Theology*, ii, trans. G. W. Bromiley (Edinburgh: T. & T. Clark, 1994); J. Moltmann, *The Crucified God*, trans. R. A. Wilson and J. Bowden (London: SCM Press, 1974); id., *The Way of Jesus Christ*.

[22] London: SCM Press, 1992.

Chapter 1 above? This challenge which the next four chapters must face will become even more acute for the final chapter's christological synthesis in terms of presence. Given the fact that, apart from some existentialists and phenomenologists, philosophers have more or less ignored that theme, we will need to clarify for ourselves the conceptuality of presence. Nevertheless, even when relevant philosophical notions and theories are available, they can never be simply taken over. Theologians may have to modify, at times significantly, what philosophers tell them, for example, about divine and human attributes. All in all, theologians need to be constantly on the alert to evaluate, choose, and modify what philosophers offer them. My modest hope for the chapters which follow is that I remain at least clear and self-consistent in writing on such themes as nature, person, freedom, time, and eternity— themes over which theologians ignore at their peril what their philosophical colleagues have to say.

Changes in and the emergence of disciplines other than philosophy have also deeply affected the christological milieu. At least some of these other disciplines should be mentioned before tackling the major systematic issues in Christology. Even while the perennial Greek philosophy began losing its monopoly as various (more or less) new philosophies emerged, another new force came into existence, at least in the Western world: historical consciousness. It is certainly exaggerated to claim proudly or admit sadly that historical thinking has replaced metaphysical thinking or that truth is no longer seen as ontological but only as historical. But the rise of historical consciousness and the development of criti- cal research into history have obviously profoundly influ- enced theology and, what is more directly pertinent to this book, contemporary Christology.

His deeper sense of how Christian doctrines had developed over the centuries stirred John Henry Newman to write and publish in 1845 his *Essay on the Development of Christian Doctrine*. Decades before that, Schleiermacher had been the first modern academic to offer lectures on the life of Jesus. He aimed to help his educated contemporaries (the 'cultured despisers') find a new path towards faith in Jesus or at least come to share in Jesus' own 'God-consciousness'. Throughout the nineteenth century, 'liberal' Christians or straight non-believers produced their lives of Jesus, representing him as a moral reformer or merely human teacher of wisdom. They used historical data to undercut orthodox, dogmatic faith in the divine-human Christ of the Church's creeds. In *The Quest of the Historical Jesus* (German original 1906), Albert Schweitzer brilliantly told the story of *Leben-Jesu-Forschung* and put his finger on its fatal flaw: 'it was not only each epoch that found its reflection in Jesus; each individual created Him in accordance with his own character.'[23]

Apropos of von Harnack, George Tyrrell (1861–1909) made the same point but even more brilliantly: 'the Christ that Harnack sees, looking back through nineteen centuries of Catholic darkness, is only the reflection of a Liberal Protestant face, seen at the bottom of a deep well.'[24] In other words, without being critically aware of what they were doing, the writers who published during the 130 years surveyed by Schweitzer projected on to Jesus their own preconceptions and beliefs.

By endorsing Schweitzer's judgement on his predecessors, I do not intend to take back what was maintained in Chapter 3 and reiterated above: it is only through our subjective involvement that we know reality and, above all, the reality of other persons, whether they live now or like Jesus lived in the past. Our preconceptions, interests, and value-systems are necessarily at work in our historical research and judgements. At the same time, we need not only to be critically aware of this 'pre-comprehension', but also to be ready to let evidence revise our prior judgements.

On both scores one can wonder what Schweitzer would say about recent attempts to play down Jesus' Jewishness, bypass the apocalyptic, eschatological elements in his message, and turn him into a wandering, Cynic-style preacher of peasant wisdom.[25] What would Schweitzer have to say about the 'dogmatic' reasons which seem to play a major role in a recent refusal to allow that any of the gospel 'sayings which identify

---

[23] *The Quest of the Historical Jesus* (London: A. & C. Black, 2nd edn., 1936), 4.

[24] G. Tyrrell, *Christianity at the Cross-Roads* (London: Longmans, Green & Co., 1909), 44.

[25] See Mack, *The Lost Gospel*; and n. 18 above.

Jesus as the son of man are genuine sayings of Jesus'? At the end of a long and learned article on 'Son of Man', G. W. E. Nickelsburg explains the final grounds for his reluctance to attribute to Jesus sayings about the Son of man:

To accept them as genuine more or less in their present form, one must posit that Jesus cast himself in the role of the suffering prophet or sage and, more important, that he believed that his vindication from death would result in his exaltation to the unique role of eschatological judge.[26]

As Nickelsburg is unwilling to 'posit' such conclusions, the provenance of the Son of man sayings in the Gospels largely remains an enigmatic puzzle.

Alongside shifts in philosophical and historical thinking, many other new factors have emerged to help set specific agenda, influence methods, and affect the use of sources in christological studies. Some classical disciplines like archaeology and literary criticism have gone through dramatic changes. Other disciplines have been born: one thinks of cultural anthropology, the history of religions, psychology, and sociology. Some of these disciplines have made solid contributions to Christology: archaeological finds have shed much light on the historical setting of Jesus' life. Other disciplines have at times overplayed their hand. Psychology can prove useful for research into our well-documented figures from modern times. But the lack of the necessary data turn psycho-biographical studies of Jesus (and, for that matter, of his first followers) into ingenious speculations. When we come to the question of the virginal conception, we shall see how forced some parallels taken out of the history of religions prove to be.[27]

The best research on the socio-historical context of Jesus and the first Christians coming from such scholars as John Elliott, Martin Hengel, Bruce Malina, Jerome Neyrey, and Gerd Theissen adds information and insight. But the worst of such research reduces the story of the first Christians to an imaginative reconstruction of their social history, with

---

[26] 'Son of Man', *ABD* vi. 137–50, at 149.
[27] On alleged but artificial parallels to Jesus' resurrection see my *Jesus Risen* (London: Darton, Longman & Todd, 1987), 102–3.

little or no attention to their religious faith. The religious dimension in the activity even of Jesus himself is submerged by talk about his social critique and countercultural behaviour.[28] In the case of some christological contributions from other disciplines, it may still be too early to make a balanced assessment. I think here, for example, of the work of the literary critic René Girard about scapegoating and social order being based on victims. Some find that his ideas unlock the NT doctrine of redemption.[29]

To draw this chapter to a conclusion, let me briefly recall several other modern influences which feed into the making of Christology today. (1) Different forces were deployed in the development of the liturgical movement. One force at work was a renewed contact with Eastern Christianity, which has encouraged 'doing' Christology in an ecclesial and sacramental (especially a eucharistic) context. We will return to the sacramental nature of Christology in the final chapter. (2) Questions raised by and insights coming from the feminist movement have already left their mark on the present and earlier chapters of this book and will continue to do so (e.g. when we deal with the humanity of Christ). (3) Over 100 million men and women have so far been killed in the twentieth century. Violent deaths have always played an enormous role in human affairs. Our own century has increased the ways men and women have been prone to seek out and destroy each other—even to the point of straight genocide and the use of nuclear weapons. Auschwitz and Hiroshima have set Jesus' own violent death in a ghastly new context of interpretation. After the Second World War, killing fields have kept turning up—in Cambodia, the Sudan, Bosnia, and elsewhere. Even so, no later atrocities raise the question posed for believers by the Holocaust: what does the systematic attempt to eradicate his Jewish brothers and sisters mean for contemporary faith in Jesus Christ and the theology that flows from it?

[28] For a recent example of such distortion see Mack, *The Lost Gospel*.
[29] For a convenient introduction and some bibliography on Girard's thought see J. Alison, *Knowing Jesus* (London: SPCK, 1993).

IO

Divine and Human

❖ ❖

And is it true? And is it true
This most tremendous tale of all ...?

(John Betjeman, 'Christmas')

Earlier chapters (especially Chapters 7 and 8) have documented, from the NT to date, those Christian beliefs in Jesus
Christ which bear on his being (1) divine and human, and (2)
an eternally pre-existent, divine person. We have looked at
various struggles to maintain intact these beliefs and to clarify
them, to the extent that clarification is possible. Contemporary journals and books overflow with systematic questions that could be faced here.[1] This chapter will limit itself
to four issues: what is it for Christ to be divine? What is it
for him to be human? Can we even entertain the notion of
someone being simultaneously divine and human? What is it
to be an eternally pre-existent, divine person?

Divinity

What makes God to be God? What makes the infinite to be
infinite? What conditions need to be met for some individual
to be divine and what are some essential ways for describing
divinity? Before we ask what 'God' means, we need to ask:
where and how does 'God' get its meaning—at least for those
in the Judaeo-Christian tradition?

---

[1] The longest (441 pages) and best survey of current issues in Christology that
I know is G. Iammarrone (ed.), *La cristologia contemporanea* (Padua: Edizioni
Messaggero, 1992). That book—and, I hope, this present chapter—shows clearly the
distance between the idiom of any present-day Christology and older formulations
modelled closely on Chalcedon's language.

Biblical history, Jewish-Christian thought and teaching, and religious experience provide a rich quarry of notions about 'God'. First, we know the attributes of divinity from what has been revealed and interpreted about God through the experience of the community and individuals (e.g. prophets) in the OT and NT history. Any adequate biblical dictionary will summarize the characteristics of the God who was the God of Abraham, Isaac, and Jacob and the Father of our Lord Jesus Christ.[2] This is to know God and the traits of God from below or 'from the bottom up'.

In her creeds, liturgy, and teaching the Church has, for the most part, simply repeated the firmly held biblical attributes of God as one, all-powerful, eternal, all-good, and so forth. But from the second century strains of Platonic, Stoic, and Aristotelian thought have provided more exact analysis. 'From the top down', in a style that is more conceptual than experiential and historical, the God of the philosophers has turned up in theological writing (e.g. Anselm's notion of the greatest possible/conceivable, thinking Being), especially in all kinds of attempts to develop theodicies, 'natural' the-ologies, and philosophies of religion.[3] Philosophical analysis has also left its mark on church teaching about God and the divine attributes.[4]

Lastly, 'God' gets its meaning not only from the biblical and philosophical tradition, but also from personal religious experience. This is the word used to denote the 'object' of explicit and implicit religious experiences. The believed characteristics of the God who is thus personally known 'within', especially through prayer, can increase and be modi-fied a great deal in the course of our lives. Yet the One to whom our personal religious experience is referred remains the same God. This name expresses the 'content' of experi-

[2] Exod. 3: 6, 15, 16. See J. J. Scullion and J. M. Bassler, 'God', *ABD* ii. 1041–55; J. M. Byrne (ed.), *The Christian Understanding of God Today* (Dublin: Columba Press, 1993).

[3] A convenient historical introduction to the God of the philosophers is provided by K. H. Weger and K. Bossong (eds.), *Argumente für Gott: Gott-Denker von der Antike bis zur Gegenwart* (Freiburg: Herder, 1987). Much bibliographical and further information is provided by G. Lanczkowski *et al.*, 'Gott' and 'Got-tesbeweise', *TRE* xiii. 601–784.

[4] See DS 800, 3001–3.

ences, which differ from 'other' experiences, and in which we are somehow conscious of the Being who is both infinitely beyond us and yet intimately related to us.[5]

Our account of God could take two forms: either biblical, experiential, and concrete, or more philosophical, precise, and abstract. The first version names divine characteristics of two kinds. (1) On the one hand, God is supremely mysterious, indefinable, or even unknowable. God dwells beyond our sense experience 'in approachable light', without beginning or end (= eternal). The deity is beyond the material world (= utterly spiritual) and all its categories of gender and class: infinitely wise, holy, apart, untouchable, and yet necessarily the 'object' of our adoration. (2) Along with these transcendent attributes, God is also, on the other hand, 'within' or immanent: personal, relational, perfectly loving, and intimately compassionate; the creator of all things and lord of history, who is, nevertheless, 'closer' to us than we are to ourselves.[6]

A philosophical version would express more abstractly the truths about God which have been experienced historically and personally. It highlights all 'omni-properties' and 'total' characteristics as being essential for divinity: God is omnipotent, omniscient, omnipresent (yet beyond all space and time with their limits), the creator and sustainer of everything, perfectly free and perfectly good (as being personal and of the highest perfection), the ground of all being and of all life. God is subsistent Being itself, the uncaused cause or unmoved mover, the one necessary, infinite Being who is utterly self-sustaining, self-determining, and therefore totally self-explanatory. In every way complete, ultimate, and unconditioned, God is infinitely simple and profoundly uncomplicated—unlike spatial and temporal beings who are divided or separated into parts. The absolute source of all that is true, good, and beautiful, God is not only absolutely self-fulfilled but also absolutely self-giving—as a hymn cited by St Paul

---

[5] See e.g. J. E. Smith, *Experience and God* (New York: Oxford University Press, 1968); H. Wissmann *et al.*, 'Erfahrung', *TRE* x. 83–141, esp. 109–36.

[6] In his *Confessions* Augustine wrote of God, or rather said to God: 'Tu autem eras interior intimo meo' (but you were more inward than my inmost self) (3. 6. 11).

appears to suggest. Precisely because he was divine, Jesus gave himself away (Phil. 2: 6–7).

The doctrine of the incarnation means that in this man, Jesus of Nazareth, we recognize characteristics (whether we express them philosophically or more biblically and experientially does not ultimately matter) that enable us to identify him as divine, God-with-us. His human life was the human life of God or God's human way of being and acting.

'Soft' accounts of the incarnation or alternative accounts that simply drop the language of incarnation have enjoyed a fresh resurgence since the Second World War.[7] They declare that in a new and final way God has been disclosed in Jesus. He has decisively opened the way to God or focused faith in God more than anyone else has or ever will. As God's fully empowered 'representative', he 'embodied' the divine purpose and plan for our salvation. The choice then becomes: is Jesus only a fully empowered representative who tells us about God (albeit in a unique way) or is he God's self-gift? Is he merely a window (or, to change the metaphor, someone who mirrors God perfectly) or is he the reality of God? Does he simply reveal God and 'embody' divine purposes (as the leader of a nation might reveal his/her people and embody their ideals), or is he the divine Mystery that is beyond but comes from the beyond to be with us and for us, as the fully immanent divine Gift-in-person? The full doctrine of the incarnation acknowledges in Jesus not just epistemological transcendence (which portrays him merely as God's revealer, embodiment, or representative), but also a genuine ontological transcendence. He is 'beyond', and comes to us 'from the beyond'.

'Soft' (or should we call them neo-Arian?) versions of the incarnation likewise reduce or deny the qualitative difference between the divine presence in Jesus and the divine presence through grace in other human beings. Jesus is portrayed as mediating salvation by being the normative revealer of God. But to say that God was present and active in Christ could be said equally of others, or at least of those of heroic, shining virtue.

---

[7] See e.g. H. Küng, *Credo* (London: SCM Press, 1993), 58–61.

Could Christ, in any case, fully and finally reveal God to us unless he were himself a 'divine Insider'? Could we find in him the absolute Representative of God, Someone in whom we can know, experience, and meet God, unless he were personally divine? Could we acknowledge in him the absolute Saviour (who brings redemption for the whole human being and for all human beings, 'divinizing' us through grace—to use the language of the Greek Fathers), without also acknowledging in him the genuine characteristics of God? Could he give us eternal life without being himself eternal? An affirmative answer to these questions is, in effect, asking us to accept a Jesus who functions for us as God, without actually being God. This position seems at least as strange as asking others to accept someone who acts in every way as the President of the United States without actually being the American President.

By recognizing in Christ truly divine characteristics, Christians are justified in drawing a consoling conclusion from their belief in the incarnation: God so valued us and our historical, space-time world that the Son of God entered it in person. By assuming a human existence, the second person of the Trinity showed what we mean and meant to God. The alternative, a Jesus who is not truly divine, means that God was really unwilling to become human and did not after all set such a value on us. Someone else (who was not divine) was sent to do the job of mediating to us final revelation and salvation.

By recognizing in Christ truly divine characteristics, Christians are justified in doing what the vast majority of them have done from the first century and continue to do today: namely, adore him and give him the worship appropriate only to God. The alternative view, espoused by a number of contemporary, revisionist Christologies, that no one should adore and worship Christ, cannot explain away this worship as a mere, unfortunate 'mistake' which has persisted since the origins of Christianity. The bulk of Christians have been and still remain guilty of idolatry in the full and proper sense of the term. For 2,000 years such an appalling sin has underpinned Christianity, or so revisionists would lead us to believe.

Before moving to the question of Christ's humanity, we should note the two-directional nature of our thinking about his divinity. We can and should do what has been done above—namely, offer some account of divine characteristics and then acknowledge that those characteristics are to be found in Christ. Yet there is some feedback here. In the light of Christ we understand God afresh; above all, we come to appreciate the tripersonal being of God. What we make of Jesus and his Spirit ultimately shapes what we make of God.

Humanity

Apropos of Christ's humanity there is no great difficulty about identifying the two central questions: what is it to be human? Why is it supremely important that Christ was/is truly and fully human? After replying to those questions, we will be in a position to face the crucial issue of making some sense of a person who is simultaneously divine and human.

What then are the set of properties which are necessary and sufficient to be human?[8] We would probably be quick to name five essential characteristics: organic, bodily existence, coupled with rationality, free will, affectivity, and memory. In other words, we would require a living body with all its functions; an intelligence with which to know, reason, judge, and interpret things; the ability to make autonomous choices and commitments; the capacity to feel and express emotions; and a conscious continuity with the past through memory.

'Dynamic' and 'social' could be the next themes to come to mind. Human beings are open-ended projects, called to develop dynamically, discover meaning, follow up insights, actualize potentialities, deepen their self-understanding as well as their relationships with others, and through experience to grow continually from cradle to grave. In a very real sense, we are not yet human; we are always becoming human. 'Social' points to the fact that we are trans-individual, as sexual, linguistic, traditional, cultural, and political beings

---

[8] For an introduction see W. Pannenberg, *Anthropology in Theological Perspective* (Philadelphia: Westminster Press, 1985); T. Weinandy, *In the Likeness of Sinful Flesh: An Essay on the Humanity of Christ* (Edinburgh: T. & T. Clark, 1993).

who live in relationship with one another, with the world, and with God. Human beings, for all their capacity to live autonomously and savour silence and solitude, are through and through beings in community.

The polarity of limited/unlimited catches essential aspects of the human condition. As Chinese, Japanese, Sicilians, or Samoans, men and women lead specific lives, limited to a particular slice of space and time. They are corporeal and intelligent, but do not possess infinite bodily strength, infinite intellectual power, or an infinite store of knowledge. Their social nature entails a massive dependence on one another and the world. From moment to moment they depend on God to sustain them in their very existence. As female or male they are human in a specific and hence limited way. In death, the great and inevitable limit, we shall all eventually be laid to rest. On every side finiteness puts its stamp on our human nature and destiny.

At the same time, however, transcendence shows itself to be central to our condition. Human beings go beyond themselves not only in their openness to the mystery of one another but even more in their openness to the infinite. Made in the divine image and likeness (Gen. 1: 26–7), they remain restlessly open to God. The question of this dynamic openness has exercised many great thinkers, in particular such transcendental Thomists as Joseph Maréchal, Johannes Lotz (1903–92), and Karl Rahner. Judgements and tastes differ here. My own preference is to develop insights from Graf von Dürckheim and interpret the human condition as an incessant search for the absolute fullness of life, meaning, and love which is only to be found in God. In their various forms we constantly experience death, absurdity, and isolation/hatred. But hope lifts us beyond such present circumstances and lets us imagine that things could be very different. We yearn for Life, Meaning, and Love (all in upper case). However we express it, a dynamic openness to the infinite shapes our human condition just as much as our obvious finiteness, contingency, and limits.

The pastoral case is strong and obvious for recognizing the importance of Christ being truly and fully human. Through the incarnation the Son of God experiences at first hand what it is to be human—with all our limits, including death. As one of us he can experience and love us. Second, he can represent us before/to God because he belongs to us by completely sharing our condition in life and death. Could someone appropriately represent us human beings while being an alien who does not authentically share as an insider in our condition? Third, by being truly and fully one of us, Christ can communicate very concretely and show us how to live, act, suffer, and pray—in short, show us what a human life before God should really be. Fourth, the fact that Christ has genuinely shared our experience from the inside can persuade us that God personally understands and loves us. Thus we can be convinced that we are uniquely worthwhile and lovable. The true assumption by the Word of a full humanity assures us of that in a way which no amount of messages from and about God could, so long as God remained personally an outsider. Fifth, we can lovingly identify with and follow Christ with faith and hope because we know he shares our human condition. Sixth, if his genuine humanity means effective revelation, it indicates something crucial as well about our redemption. God also heals and saves us from the inside and not simply by a kind of divine fiat from the outside. Our Saviour is one of us.

Before progressing to the thorny question of Christ being simultaneously divine and human, something should be said about his maleness and the 'feedback' from his life for the question of what is takes to be truly human. First, as has been alluded to above, the specific quality of human existence also entails being limited in gender—that is to say, being either male or female. Neither here nor elsewhere can anyone be a human being in general, exhibiting merely universal characteristics. Both women and men completely express human nature and both are made in the image and likeness of God. Yet being human means being specific: male or female, Jew or Gentile, of the first century or of the thirteenth, and so forth. To deny such specific characteristics of Jesus as his maleness and his Jewishness would be tantamount to denying his genuine humanity.

An earlier paragraph listed nine essential traits of human existence: we are bodily, rational, free, emotional, remembering, dynamic, social, and limited/unlimited beings. We find this assemblage of traits amply illustrated in Christ's life; we may and should declare him to be fully human. Along with this recognition, however, his history can prompt a reappraisal of what it is to be human. This point has already been hinted at when we spoke two paragraphs back of Christ revealing through his humanity what a human life before God should really be. In other words, just as with the question of Christ's divinity, so the question of his humanity produces a certain feedback. We reflect on his being divine and human in the light of prior notions about the properties necessary and sufficient for someone to be divine and/or human. Yet Christ's particular story should lead us to revise our notions of divinity and humanity. Here, in particular, he should make us reappraise those themes that recur almost universally when we tell the story of other men and women, or (even especially) when we tell our own story: desire, power, and achievement. The 'ecce homo' of John's passion (John 19: 5) and the abandoned Jesus in Mark's crucifixion story (Mark 15: 34) might prompt us to look very hard again at suffering and what we might have to allow for when calling human existence 'finite'. Such finitude can include dying in horrendous failure and disgrace as one in whom friends have lost faith, whom enemies are quite free to treat with sadistic brutality, and who appears even to have been abandoned by the God whom he has called 'Abba'. In brief, Christ's cross should feed into and revise our account of what it is to be human.

Further, Christ's way of being human should trigger a reappraisal of sin as a characteristic of our actual finite condition. If he was 'without sin', could he be like us 'in every respect' (Heb. 4: 15)? Does it necessarily belong to an unimpaired humanity to be concretely open to sin? We take up this question in the next chapter. Lastly, his limit-case reveals that one can be fully human without being merely human. How is that possible? How is it possible for the Letter to the Hebrews to affirm simultaneously (1) the divinity of Christ (Heb. 1: 2–3, 8–13), and (2) his human growth (Heb. 1: 4; 5: 9–10) and radical link with the whole human race in that he suffered and experienced death for everyone (Heb. 2: 9–10)?

Divine and Human

What would it be like for someone to exist who would be both divinely infinite and humanly finite? How could Christ simultaneously possess these properties? Schleiermacher long ago framed the question this way and decided against the possibility: 'One individual cannot share in two quite different natures.'[9] In his anti-incarnational position Schleiermacher enjoys his contemporary followers. They argue that Christ's being truly divine would threaten the integrity of his humanity, and dismiss the incarnation as incoherent.

One general and one specific observation serve at least to mitigate the difficulty. In general, not only the dyad infinite/finite but also the dyads matter/spirit, time/eternity, divine/human, and transcendent/immanent present us with a huge ontological gap. But the divide cannot be so great that we are faced with entities or properties that are mutually self-exclusive in a total way. There must be something spiritual about matter; otherwise the totally spiritual God could not create the material world, nor in the Eucharist could bread and wine become the 'spiritual body' of the risen Christ. Eternity must have something of time about it and vice versa. Otherwise the eternal God could not create time, nor—and this is our case—could the eternal Son of God assume life in time. If human beings are made in the image and likeness of God (Gen. 1: 26–7), there must be something divine about every human being. If, and this is our case, the divine Logos could assume a humanity, there must be something human about God. Thus, in Schleiermacher's language, infinite/finite and these other dyads may be 'poles apart' but not necessarily mutually exclusive.

When we face the particular case of Christ, his being simultaneously divine and human appears to be a contradiction in terms. Human beings are limited in various ways. God is

---

[9] *The Christian Faith* (Edinburgh: T. & T. Clark, 1928), 393. From around 1970 D. Cupitt, J. Hick, M. Wiles, and others have been raising a series of objections to incarnational Christology. T. V. Morris in *The Logic of God Incarnate* (Ithaca, NY: Cornell University Press, 1986), R. Sturch in *The Word and the Christ* (Oxford: Clarendon Press, 1991), and others have shown how these contemporary difficulties (some of which go back to Schleiermacher or earlier) are either unfounded or misdirected.

such as to be unlimited in virtually every way: for example in knowledge and power. (Doing or deciding to do what is in itself impossible like producing a square circle are among the very few divine limits which come to mind.) Hence someone who is both divine and human would have to be both limited and unlimited with respect to many properties. Christ would be all-knowing or omniscient through his divine nature but limited in knowledge through his human nature. He would be unsurpassably powerful with regard to his divinity but limited in power with regard to his humanity. We seem to be faced with a contradiction in terms, the same subject being credited simultaneously with pairs of essential characteristics that are simply incompatible.

However, as they used to say in Prussia, the situation is serious but not desperate. It would be a blatant contradiction in terms to attribute to the same subject at the same time *and under the same aspect* mutually incompatible properties. But that is not being done here. With respect to his divinity Christ is omniscient, but with respect to his humanity he is limited in knowledge. Mutually exclusive characteristics are being simultaneously attributed to him but not within the same frame of reference. The personal union of divinity and humanity entailed by the incarnation exceeds our conceptuality, and cannot be clarified in plain descriptive language in such a way as to be positively intelligible. If we cannot imagine and describe what it would be like to be God, we cannot imagine and describe what it would be like to be God and man. Nevertheless, for the reasons given, the incarnation does not present itself as clearly incoherent.

One Divine Person

We have just been looking at difficulties that arise from recognizing in Christ two natures, two distinct principles of activity. From the question of divine and human natures (which answers the question *what* was/is Christ?), we pass to the subject or self *who* acts and experiences, and *to whom* things are attributed.

The explicit doctrine of Christ as one (divine) person begins with the Chalcedonian definition of his being one *prosōpon* or *hypostasis*. Karl Rahner's now classical observation about Chalcedon being more a beginning than an end,[10] if it holds true about anything, bears on the notion of person. It was to evolve for many centuries: from Boethius (*c*.480–*c*.524) through Richard of St Victor (d. 1173), Descartes, and Kant, down to the present.[11] One can synthesize all that progress and describe a person as *this* rational and free individual, who is the subject and centre of action and relationships and who enjoys incommunicable identity, inalienable dignity, and inviolable rights. The interconnectedness of all things, which tends to relativize the weight we attribute to things in themselves, may give new vigour to one aspect of the description of personhood which we have just offered. How significant is relationship for personal identity? In constituting personhood are relationships just as primary as being an individual and autonomous centre of action? When interpreting Christ's personhood, we would be unwise to concentrate on the individual subject and play down his being person-in-relation to the God whom he called 'Abba'. As subject-in-relation he acted/acts through his two rational and volitional principles of operation, his divine and human natures.

Consciousness and sense of identity come into close association with our account of personhood. It is easy of course to rebut those who wish to define persons through their consciousness. If consciousness and personhood are the same, do we declare to be non-persons those who are asleep, knocked unconscious, in a coma, or not yet born? What then is the link between being a person and consciousness of one's distinct existence? The cases just recalled illustrate that personal identity as such cannot simply depend upon

[10] K. Rahner, 'Current Problems in Christology', *Th. Inv.* i. 149–200, at 149.
[11] On 'person' and 'personhood' see M. Fuhrmann *et al.*, 'Person', in J. Ritter and K. Gründer (eds.), *Historisches Wörterbuch der Philosophie*, vii (Basle: Schwabe Verlag, 1989), cols. 269–338; A. I. McFadyen, *The Call to Personhood: A Christian Theory of the Individual in Social Relationships* (Cambridge: Cambridge University Press, 1990); A. Milano, *Persona in teologia* (Naples: Edizioni Dehoniane, 1984); A. Pavan and A. Milano (eds.), *Persona e personalismi* (Naples: Edizioni Dehoniane, 1987); A. Thatcher, *Truly a Person, Truly God* (London: SPCK, 1990). For a perceptive review of McFadyen's book see N. Lash, *Journal of Theological Studies*, 43 (1992), 332–4.

conscious awareness of oneself. Yet our sense of identity does depend upon our awareness of ourselves. Through my awareness of my one self, I know myself to be this 'I'. In brief, self-identification depends on self-consciousness.

Through our experience of other persons and the whole world, our self-consciousness and hence our self-identification develop and take a firm shape. Our experience of the world beyond the borders of our bodily self also mediates our conscious sense of our own self and its unity. Thus we know our personal identities not only in ourselves but also in our relationships. It is especially through our experience of the world that our sense of ourselves grows and changes. Here a clear parallel emerges between personhood and sense of personal identity. Persons are not only (rational and free) subjects but also subjects-in-relation. Likewise through our conscious sense of personal identity we know ourselves to be social as well as individual selves.

We can proceed to apply these reflections to Christ. His personal identity (as Son of God) did/does not depend upon his human awareness of himself—that is to say, upon the self-consciousness mediated through his human mind. Yet his (human) *sense* of his own identity did depend upon his awareness of himself and his experience of the world. (Other, opposing views of his self-consciousness and sense of distinct identity jeopardize our recognition of Christ's full and complete humanity.) His self-identification depended upon a self-consciousness of the world 'out there'. Through his (human) awareness of his own personal identity, Christ knew not only his distinct identity in himself but also his identity-in-relationship (his 'social' self) as subject-in-relation to the God whom he called 'Abba'.

Memory has a role in maintaining our sense of personal identity but overemphasis on memory could lead us astray. A person enjoys diachronic identity. Yet there is no future in trying to define our personhood and explain our diachronic identity simply through memory. One's enduring personhood cannot simply depend upon one's memory. Otherwise loss of memory could entail loss of personhood. As a starter the case of amnesia rebuts any attempts to promote memory as the (sole?) means for constituting personal identity. Nevertheless, the sense of continuity provided by memory obviously feeds into and affects our awareness of personal identity, both as subjects-in-ourselves and in our interaction with the world and the human community.

In the case of Christ there is no reason to doubt that the sense of his personal identity mediated through his human mind was shaped in part by his memory. But his memory in no way constituted his personal identity. This must be said firmly, whenever one scents the temptation to found his eternal, personal pre-existence on a memory of that pre-existence or at least to derive it from such a memory. Christ's human memory began to take shape only with his conception and birth (around 5 BC). Through that memory he could not recall his eternal pre-existence.

Personal Pre-existence

Orthodox Christian faith believes that Jesus of Nazareth was personally identical with the eternally pre-existent Son of God or Logos. Here Christians hold the pre-existence of a divine person, something distinct from other such notions as the pre-existence of the Jewish Torah or Plato's scheme of pre-existing ideas that provided the pattern for the demiurge in fashioning the world.

The christological doctrine of pre-existence maintains that Christ's personal existence is that of an eternal Subject within the oneness of God, and hence cannot be derived from the history of human beings and their world. His personal being did not originate when his visible human history began. He did not come into existence as a new person around 5 BC. He exists personally as the eternal Son of God. To adopt tensed language from Nicaea I ('there never was a time when he was not' (DS 126)) and state that Christ 'always existed' could easily be misleading. Through sharing in the divine attribute of eternity he exists timelessly, given that eternity is in itself timeless. Even the classical definition of eternity left by Boethius, 'interminabilis vitae tota simul et perfecta possessio' (the all-at-once, complete, and perfect possession of endless life) (*Consolatio philosophiae*, 5. 6), could misrepresent matters. 'All-at-once' (*simul*) positively and 'endless'

(*interminabilis*) negatively point us towards time and temporal
duration. Eternity and eternal life, however, are not to be
reduced to any such temporal duration. The eternal now of
the divine existence means perfect union and simplicity in un-
changeable fullness of life, with no parts and with no relations
of before and after, no having-been and going-to-be.

These considerations also show up some dangers in the
very term pre-existence. To speak of Christ as pre-existing
his incarnation and even the very creation of the world (when
time began) could be (wrongly) taken to imply a 'before' and
'after' for his personal, divine existence. An addition that
Constantinople I made to the Nicene Creed, 'begotten from
the Father *before all ages*' (DS 150; addition italicized), might
mislead us into thinking here of temporal succession as if
Christ merely anteceded or 'antedated' everything that later
began (in/with time). Pre-existence means rather that Christ
personally belongs to an order of being other than the created,
temporal one. His personal, divine existence transcends temporal (and spatial) categories; it might be better expressed
as trans-existence, meta-existence, or, quite simply, eternal
existence. None of this is intended to take back the claim
made above that 'eternity must have something of time about
it and vice versa'. After all Plato could define time as 'the
eternal image of eternity, moving according to number'
(*Timaeus*, 37d). Eternity transcends time but without being
apart from it; eternity and time should be considered
together. Through the attribute of eternity God is present
immediately and powerfully to all times. But here, if anywhere in Christology, we need to 'watch our language', and
be sensitive to the points which have emerged in the renewed
debate about eternity that has followed a 1981 article of
Eleonore Stump and Norman Kretzmann.[12]

In his *Christology in the Making* J. D. G. Dunn has argued
that, while early Christians and NT authors borrowed the
relevant terms from their predecessors and although pre-
Christian Jewish thought envisaged intermediaries between
God and the world, there are no demonstrable antecedents

[12] For details of the debate and his own contributions see B. Leftow, *Time and Eternity* (Ithaca, NY: Cornell University Press, 1991).

in Jewish or Gentile thought to account for the fully personal pre-existence of Jesus as the Son of God and Logos who 'descended' from heaven to earth. No evidence establishes clearly a pre-Christian notion of an individual heavenly figure who pre-existed and really took human form and flesh. The NT doctrines of Christ's personal pre-existence and incarnation remain unique and unparalleled in religious beliefs up to the first century AD. In pre-Christian Judaism, as divine Wisdom and Logos are vivid metaphors for God's own attributes and activities, they strengthen rather than 'weaken' Jewish monotheism. As personifications, not distinct persons, they 'protect' the absolute divine transcendence.[13]

Dunn's other major thesis that it is only in John's Gospel and letters that we unambiguously find Christ's pre-existence as Son of God and Logos has been widely criticized and rejected. The sending language of Rom. 8: 3 and Gal. 4: 4 may not be fully clear. But 2 Cor. 8: 9 and Phil. 2: 6–8 suggest a pre-existent, divine state, contrasted with his 'subsequent', humble, human existence. Being 'in the form of God', Christ took on human form and did not exploit the right to be recognized for what he was. Col. 1: 15–17 presents Christ as being, like pre-existent Wisdom, the very agent of creation. It seems reasonable to conclude that Paul thought of the Son as coming into the world from the Father and as having been active in the creation of the world (see 1 Cor. 8: 6). Heb. 1: 1–3, 6; 9: 26; and 10: 5–10 likewise tell against Dunn's claim that the notion of Christ's eternal pre-existence first emerged fully with John's Gospel.[14] Admittedly John's prologue and

---

[13] See J. D. G. Dunn, *Christology in the Making* (London: SCM Press, 2nd edn., 1989), 168–76, 215–30. As Dunn also demonstrates, there was no notion of a pre-existent Messiah, still less of a pre-existent Son of man, in pre-Christian Judaism (ibid. 67–82). For the discussion of Dunn's views see K.-J. Kuschel, *Born before All Time?*, trans. J. Bowden (London: SCM Press, 1992), 597 n. 6.

[14] It seems forced exegesis to 'explain' Heb. 1: 6 and 10: 5–10 as pointing to nothing more than the predetermined, eternal, divine choice of one who had a particularly prominent place in the fulfilment of God's purposes. Dunn is so intent on establishing his thesis that 'the Fourth Evangelist was the first Christian writer to conceive clearly of the personal pre-existence of the Logos-Son' (*Christology in the Making*, 249) that he strains credulity in explaining away texts such as 1 Cor. 8: 5–6 (merely a way of speaking of divine agency, not of a divine agent distinct from God, ibid. 179–83), and the creation 'in him' of Col. 1: 16 (may be simply '*the writer's way of saying that Christ now reveals the character of the power behind the world*', ibid. 190; italics his).

other Johannine passages attribute special importance to the change from heaven to earth, whereas in such Pauline passages as Phil. 2: 6–11 Christ's divine pre-existence is 'only' the point of departure. But, all the same, it is affirmed and that as early as the hymn Paul quotes here.

The Christology 'from above', which goes back through Thomas Aquinas and Cyril of Alexandria to John's affirmation that 'the Word became flesh and dwelt among us' (John 1: 14; see 1 John 4: 2; 5: 6; 2 John 7), clearly involves the personal, eternal pre-existence of the Logos who 'descended from above' to be incarnated and assume a human existence. The pre-existent Son of God entered the world and revealed himself in human history. Thus believers acknowledge in Jesus Christ the one who already as eternal, divine person existed before his earthly life. They claim his personal pre-existence, and do not merely hold that some prior divine purpose was focused and defined in his life.

The exercise of Jesus' human consciousness, affectivity, memory, and freedom shaped his earthly life. A christological approach 'from below', which has in various ways been developed by Kasper, Küng, Pannenberg, Schillebeeckx, Jon Sobrino, and others, has raised the question: was Jesus (humanly) conscious of his divine identity? Back in Chapters 3 and 5 we gathered evidence that supports the conclusion that the earthly Jesus was aware of his divine identity. But then there is the further question: through his human consciousness was he also aware of his personal pre-existence as the Son, Word, and Wisdom of God?

In its 1981 document, 'Theology, Christology and Anthropology', the International Theological Commission asserted that, 'at least in an indirect fashion', Jesus Christ showed that he was conscious of 'his eternal existence as Son of the Father'. The second proposition of the Commission's 1985 document, 'The consciousness of Christ concerning Himself and his Mission', went even further in maintaining the following questionable claim: 'The consciousness Jesus has of his mission also involves ... the consciousness of his 'pre-existence'. The mission (in time), in fact, is not essentially separable from his (eternal) procession; it is its prolongation.' Hence Jesus' 'human consciousness of his own mission "translates", so to speak, the eternal relationship with the Father into the idiom of a human life'.

The first (more cautious) proposition of the 1981 document endorses the view of many NT scholars that in his words and works the earthly Jesus claimed divine authority and showed that he was aware of standing in a unique relationship to the God whom he called 'Abba'. Jesus lived out his ministry radically conscious of being sent as *the* Son. Granted that he showed himself to be aware of his divine status, was he also conscious—at least implicitly and in an indirect fashion—of existing eternally before his human conception and birth? Much depends here on how one understands 'implicitly' and 'indirectly'. Yet I find no solid evidence in the Synoptic Gospels supporting the conclusion that, in any recognizable sense of the words 'indirect' or 'implicit', Christ's consciousness showed that kind of awareness of his eternal pre-existence. Such a position would come very close to alleging that through his human memory he half-remembered such a pre-existence.[15]

It is interesting to note that in a long 1984 document on Christology the Pontifical Biblical Commission did not even address the question: was the earthly Jesus in any way aware of his personal pre-existence from all eternity? Its closest approach to that issue came when it recalled (with apparent approval) the view that 'the christology *implicit* in the words of Jesus and in his human experience forms a certain continuum and is profoundly united with the different christologies that are *explicitly* found in the New Testament'. Among those NT Christologies we find the belief that Jesus was (personally) identical with the eternally pre-existent Son of God.[16]

From a theological point of view, it is important to note that Christ's personal pre-existence is in itself compatible with his having, during his earthly life, a limited (human) understanding of his divine identity and no consciousness at

---

[15] For those texts of the International Theological Commission, see M. Sharkey (ed.), *International Theological Commission: Texts and Documents 1969–1985* (San Francisco: Ignatius Press, 1989), 207–23, at 217; 305–16, at 310.

[16] See J. A. Fitzmyer, 'The Biblical Commission and Christology', *Theological Studies*, 46 (1985), 407–79, at 418.

all of his eternal pre-existence. Furthermore, a Christology 'from above' does not necessarily entail Christ enjoying a *full* knowledge of his divine identity and any conscious awareness of his personal pre-existence. Alternatively, a Christology 'from below' certainly does not as such exclude belief either in Christ's divine identity or in his personal pre-existence. In both christological approaches, no matter whether they begin 'from above' or 'from below', issues about the personal being of Christ should be sharply distinguished from those concerned with his human knowledge and consciousness of himself.

Confusion both about what personal pre-existence is and about what the Council of Chalcedon taught has led recent authors to explain away or simply deny Christ's pre-existence. John Macquarrie argues that 'the belief that Jesus consciously pre-existed in "heaven"' would 'threaten the genuineness of his humanity'. Hence he pre-existed only in the sense of (1) his being elected for his role and preordained from the beginning in the mind or purpose of God, as well as (2) being previously 'there' in the evolving cosmos, the history of the human race, and the particular history of Israel. Macquarrie assures us that (1) is 'a very high degree of reality', but it is almost indistinguishable from our form of pre-existence in the eternal purposes of God (Eph. 1: 4–5; see Gal. 1: 15). The (2) form of pre-existence is an illusion if Macquarrie thinks that it says anything special which would set Christ apart. We could say of any human person whatsoever that he or she had been 'there' in the evolving cosmos, the history of the whole human race, and the particular history of his or her race and culture. The pre-existent Christ of John's prologue, Phil. 2: 6–8, and Col. 1: 15–20 is not to be reduced to mere divine intention. He personally pre-existed everything that was created. He was not a mere possibility or idea which became actualized as a person with the incarnation and redemption. Besides being incompatible with Christian faith, that would be trivial because true of all of us.[17]

Macquarrie's proposal proves itself inadequate because he

---

[17] J. Macquarrie, *Jesus Christ in Modern Thought* (London: SCM Press, 1990), 121, 390–2; see 57, 145.

fails to see that personal pre-existence does not mean that Jesus eternally pre-existed *qua Jesus*. His humanity first came into existence as such around 5 BC. The human consciousness of Jesus did not pre-exist 'in heaven'. To claim that would be to threaten the genuineness of his humanity. The consciousness which did pre-exist was the divine consciousness of the eternal Logos, Wisdom, or Son of God. By assuming a full human existence and history, the person of the Logos came also to be known as Jesus of Nazareth and to be also humanly conscious of himself.

Roger Haight has argued that 'a notion of the preexistence of Jesus' is 'incompatible with the doctrine of Chalcedon that Jesus is consubstantial with us'. He states: 'One cannot think in terms of the preexistence of *Jesus*; what [*sic*!] is preexistent to Jesus is God, the God who became incarnate in Jesus. [The] doctrine [of Chalcedon] underscores the obvious here, that Jesus is really a creature like us, and a creature cannot preexist creation.'[18] The problem with all this is a real confusion over Chalcedon's teaching, in particular, its distinction between Christ's person and his two natures. First, Chalcedon did not say that Jesus *tout court* was/is consubstantial with us, but rather that he is consubstantial with us *in his humanity*. Any notion of the pre-existence of Jesus' humanity or human nature would be incompatible with Chalcedon. The pre-existence of the person who came to be named historically as Jesus is quite another issue. Chalcedon most emphatically did not teach that the person (Jesus) as such was/is consubstantial with us. The deep confusion between person (who?) and nature (what?) becomes thoroughly apparent in Haight's claim that '*what* is preexistent to Jesus is God, the God who became incarnate in Jesus'. Haight should rather speak of the One *who* is pre-existent to Jesus' human history (= pre-existent to the creation of his humanity and its story) and who is the Son of God. The God who became

---

[18] R. Haight, 'The Case of Spirit Christology', *Theological Studies*, 53 (1992), 257–87, at 276. In a footnote Haight claims that 'the point of the doctrine of preexistence is that salvation in and through Jesus comes from God' (ibid. 276 n. 37). 'Point' is ambiguous. One can agree, if Haight uses 'point' as equal to underlying motive. But if he alleges that 'point' = meaning, this is a travesty of what the teaching of Nicaea I and Chalcedon intended. Motivation must not be confused with meaning.

incarnate in Jesus is not 'God' as such but the second person of the Trinity, the One whom Chalcedon called 'Lord', 'Christ', 'Word', and 'Son of God'. Jesus is 'a creature like us' through his humanity, and, being created, that human nature cannot pre-exist creation. But the doctrine of the eternal pre-existence, based on Chalcedon's teaching, addresses itself to Christ's *personal* pre-existence, and is not making blatantly false claims about the eternal pre-existence of his created humanity.

This chapter set itself to reflect systematically on Christ's divinity, humanity, and eternal, personal pre-existence. These systematic reflections need to be completed by dedicating a further chapter to other questions: his faith, sinlessness, and virginal conception. But before doing that, we can attend to some matters that arise immediately out of what has just been dealt with.

Further Issues

It is one thing to expound a contemporary version of the Chalcedonian doctrine about Jesus Christ as one (eternally pre-existent, divine) person in two natures. It is another thing, however, to deal with spin-off questions which inevitably arise here. Christ was/is not a human person. What kind of a human nature is his if it lacks human personhood? It would seem to be an essentially deficient humanity. Then the obvious corollary of his two natures is that he had/has two consciousnesses, both a divine and a human one. But can one and the same person possibly have two distinct minds? How could we account then for Christ's sense of identity, his sense of being *this* 'I', responsible for *these* actions? Lastly, what were the causal powers Christ used during his earthly history? Did he also act through his divine nature or was his human nature his sole principle of activity? Without being comprehensive this list at least samples the range of questions that have emerged for present-day 'Chalcedonian' Christologies.

First, a reluctance to ascribe to Christ a humanity without human personhood, because it would seem radically deficient,[19] leads some to speak of him as a divine-human person or even to state that he was simply a human person. The latter view, even when we allow for all the post-sixth-century development in the notion of 'person', seems incompatible with the orthodox Christian belief that follows Chalcedon. The former view could, in principle, be understood as shorthand for 'one person with divine and human natures', just as the traditional phrase about Jesus as 'God-man' pointed to one subject (Jesus) who was/is both divine and human by nature. However, those who champion a 'divine-human personhood' probably intend by this a double personhood through which Christ 'has' both human and divine personhood. This position, so far from advancing the discussion, rests on a confusion between nature (which one 'has') and person (which one does not 'have' but 'is'). No one has laid his finger better on the confusion than Daniel Helminiak:

Current insistence that Christ was a human person generally does not appreciate the classical meaning of the term, person, and as a result does not really appreciate the change in that term's meaning. ... [T]o suggest that without being a human person Christ would not be fully human is to misunderstand the distinction between nature and person. Nature is what makes one human or not. Christ has a completely human nature. Therefore, Christ is completely human. One indication of the misunderstanding is reference to person, hypostasis, as something we have: 'Did Christ have a human hypostasis? We do. Then, if he did not, how can we claim he is fully human?' But hypostasis is not something someone has. The hypostasis is the someone who has whatever is had. If the divine hypostasis, the Word, has all the qualities that constitute someone as human—a human nature—then the Word, a divine hypostasis, is a human being, and fully so, period.[20]

Perhaps some of the trouble in accepting Christ as only divine person stems from the unarticulated sense that this would be to deny him a genuine human personality, if we agree to distinguish personality from personhood and person.

[19] Thus J. Moltmann names as a first 'impasse' for the 'two-nature' Christology of Chalcedon the way it 'dehumanizes' and 'degrades' the 'non-personal human nature' of Christ (*The Way of Jesus Christ*, trans. M. Kohl (London: SCM Press, 1990), 51).

[20] *The Same Jesus: A Contemporary Christology* (Chicago: Loyola University Press, 1986), 292.

The one personal subject is God the Son, but this does not exclude the existence of a particular, distinctive assemblage of traits and habits that made up the human personality of Jesus of Nazareth. In this sense Jesus did not lack a human personality. On the contrary, his human historical existence entailed an assemblage of individual traits and habits which in the concrete made him the uniquely striking personality that he was. In this way we may distinguish his human personality from the one (divine) person that he was/is.

Then we have to face a corollary of the Chalcedonian teaching on Christ's two complete natures: his double set of cognitive powers—that is to say, his having both a divine and a human mind or both a full divine consciousness and a full human consciousness. For some people this raises particularly troublesome, even simply knock-down, difficulties against this Chalcedonian corollary and finally against the logical coherence of the whole two-natures doctrine. Some of these difficulties arise from picturing Christ's two minds as if they were psychological subsystems, along the lines of profoundly disturbed patients who suffer from 'divided minds'. This way of tackling the issue gets things wrong from the start. Talk of two psychological subsystems forgets that in the dyad, divine/human mind, we are not faced with members that are equal and on the same level. The divine mind simply does not think in the propositional and discursive way a created, human mind does. The divine mind's unlimited knowledge sets it quite apart from the limited knowledge of any human mind. There exists an infinite epistemological gap between the divine mind and any human mind, including that of Christ.

Further difficulties arise here from failing to remember that it is the person, not the nature, who is the subject of actions. Awareness and knowledge are acts of the person—in and through a divine and/or a human nature. In a review of Richard Sturch's *The Word and the Christ: An Essay in Analytical Christology*, Timothy W. Bartel in the same paragraph slips from correctly attributing actions to the person of Jesus to such statements as 'the divine mind does not have perceptual experiences which are caused by changes in Jesus' body' (surely he should say, 'the person of Jesus through his

divine mind' etc?), and 'Jesus's body is subject to the direct
voluntary control of the divine mind'.[21] Surely he should put
it this way: 'Jesus' body is subject to the direct voluntary
control of the divine person of God the Son'? With 'the divine
mind' shared equally by the three persons of the Trinity,
Bartel's language suggests that the three persons have been
incarnated, which is neither the case nor the Christian claim.

Even if we can eliminate some false problems and misleading language about Christ's two minds, we cannot ignore
the *unity of consciousness* with which a person is endowed: in
the 'I think' of the theoretical reason, the 'I act' of the practical reason, and the 'I should' that characterizes the moral
sphere of responsible freedom. In the case of Christ, surely
the ontological unity of his person requires some psychological unity or one self-aware centre of reference for his
actions and experiences? Can that only be his divine person,
the 'ego' of the Word operating through the divine human
consciousnesses? Could we make anything of his human self-
consciousness as such a centre, if there is in Jesus Christ
no human personhood? Given that he had a full human
consciousness, self-consciousness, and sense of identity, we
have the conditions for a human psychological centre of reference, a human 'I' or ego. In all other cases one 'I' cor-
responds to and expresses one self or one subject. Here,
however, the human ego of Jesus is not such an autonomous
subject. The ego of his human consciousness is also the Word
of God as humanly conscious and self-conscious, that is, as
operating in and through *this* human awareness. God the Son
takes as his own this human self-consciousness, self-identity,
and centre of reference.

What, however, of the man Jesus? Does and how does his
human ego know that he is a divine subject, God the Son?
Can we hazard any suggestions here? The next chapter will
discuss and refute one traditional answer: his divine identity
was made known through the beatific vision which Christ's
human mind enjoyed from the moment of his conception.
Another possibility opens up if we recognize a feature of our
experience of what is finite and infinite (or temporal and

---

[21] *Religious Studies*, 28 (1992), 123–5, at 124.

eternal). Whenever we experience finite things, we experience simultaneously the infinite that lies within them. Our perception of anything finite (and temporal) depends upon our intuition of the infinite (and eternal). The totality of the infinite (and eternal) manifests itself in the specific things of our experience. Without co-experiencing the infinite we could not experience the finite.

Applying this account of our experience of the finite/infinite to Jesus' self-awareness, we might suggest that, in knowing what was finite and temporal through his human consciousness, he co-experienced the Infinite and Eternal as One to whom he stood in the intimate, personal relationship of Son to Father. This co-experience of the Infinite differed from ours, inasmuch as it essentially involved the sense of a unique personal relationship to the God whom Jesus named as 'Abba'.

Alternative explanations speak of Jesus, in and through his human consciousness of his own finite and temporal existence, intuiting himself as infinite and eternal. Or else it has been suggested that in his human consciousness he enjoyed infused knowledge of (or even an immediate, not beatific, vision of) the Father and his own intimate personal relationship to the Father. My own proposal has, I think, the advantage of building a little more clearly upon the general human co-experience of the infinite.

Lastly, there is the issue of the set of causal powers Christ used during his earthly history. The miracles he undoubtedly worked and the supernatural predictions he was alleged to have made raise the question: on the scene of his human history did he also use the powers of his divine nature? The message of his genuine humanity and the 'kenotic' state of his historical existence (see Phil. 2: 7–8) might suggest otherwise. In his earthly history, was the sole principle of activity of the incarnate Word his human nature? His earthly acts were all human acts, yet at times divinely empowered in a special way (the case of the miraculous deeds), given that the acting subject was the incarnate Son of God. In a manner that was appropriate to his historical mission and 'kenotic' state on the earthly scene, the Word always operated through his human nature but not always in a merely human way. The One acting was the Word of God, whose divine powers could come into play to achieve salvific and revelatory purposes.

Faith, Holiness, and Virginal Conception

❖ ❖

> Praising is all a poet understands,
> The only giving is with empty hands.
>
> (Peter Steele, 'XXI')

> We might begin by going back to the mystics; if there is
> some guidance to Jesus' mind in their experience, we
> can profitably consult St Teresa of Avila on the difficulty
> she had in expressing what she received from God.
>
> (Frederick Crowe, 'The Mind of Jesus')

Previous chapters have often operated at the interface
between exegesis and theology. This will also hold true of
this chapter, which takes up two questions which bear on
Jesus' historical life after he came to 'the age of reason' (his
faith and holiness) and one which bears on his human origin
(the virginal conception).

The Faith of Jesus

Past christological thinking did not normally even raise the
question of the existence and nature of faith exercised by
Jesus during his earthly life.[1] It seems to have been widely
taken for granted that his divine identity and his human
knowledge of God were such as to rule out the possibility of
genuine faith. This unwillingness to entertain any attribution
of faith to Jesus has obviously affected the translation of
certain NT passages which might be construed as presenting

---

[1] The first part of this chapter is based on G. O'Collins and D. Kendall, 'The
Faith of Jesus', *Theological Studies*, 53 (1992), 403–23.

Jesus as a model for our faith. Thus the Revised Standard
Version translated a key phrase from Heb. 12: 2 as 'Jesus the
pioneer and perfecter of our faith', even though the original
Greek text does not include 'our'.[2] The 1989 New Revised
Standard Version has kept the same translation. The 1985
New Jerusalem Bible makes a similar addition and impression
by translating the phrase as 'Jesus, who leads us in our faith
and brings it to perfection'.

At the same time, where the New American Bible originally
rendered the phrase from Heb. 12: 2 as 'Jesus, who inspires
and perfects our faith', its 1988 revised NT version shifted
to calling Jesus 'the leader and perfecter of faith'. A number
of theologians have recognized exemplary faith in the life of
Jesus. He is 'the witness of faith' for Gerhard Ebeling.[3] James
Mackey calls Jesus 'a man of faith', qualifying his faith as
'extraordinarily radical'.[4] Jon Sobrino dedicated a chapter of
his Christology to 'The Faith of Jesus'.[5] Karl Rahner and
Wilhelm Thüsing, in their interdisciplinary study, explore
the theme of Jesus as 'believer'.[6] Hans Urs von Balthasar
argues that we cannot take the genitive in the Pauline phrase
'the faith of Jesus Christ' as simply an objective genitive,
although he hesitates to attribute to the earthly Jesus the

---

[2] The 1978 New International Version followed suit, by rendering the phrase
'Jesus, the Pioneer and Perfecter of our faith'.

[3] G. Ebeling, *The Nature of Faith* (London: Collins, Fontana Library, 1966), 44–
57. In Ebeling's 'Jesus and Faith' (*Word and Faith* (Philadelphia: Fortress Press,
1973), 204–46) *the* witness of faith, Jesus, became the source and ground of our
faith. On the passage from the faith *of* Jesus to faith *in* him, see also E. Fuchs, 'Jesus
und der Glaube', in *Zur Frage nach dem historischen Jesus* (Tübingen: Mohr, 1960),
238–57.

[4] J. Mackey, *Jesus the Man and the Myth* (London: SCM Press, 1979), 171.

[5] J. Sobrino, *Christology at the Crossroads* (London: SCM Press, 1978), 79–145.

[6] K. Rahner and W. Thüsing, *Christologie: Systematisch und Exegetisch*, Quaestiones Disputatae 35 (Freiburg: Herder, 1972), 211–26. This was translated as *A
New Christology* (London: Burns & Oates, 1980), 143–54. C. Palacio ('A Comparative Study of the Treatment of Jesus' Obedience in Some Modern Christologies', *Concilium*, Nov. 1980) treats this same material under the rubric of
obedience. He maintains that the NT gives 'a threefold description of Jesus' obedience; in the first place, it is the mode of being characteristic of his *earthly life* (Heb.
5: 7 ff.; Phil 2: 8; Heb. 10: 7); in the second, it denotes Jesus' intrinsic and total
reference to God, to the extent of not being able to live or understand himself
except standing before the Father; finally, it delineates the unique and unrepeatable
character of *Jesus' way*: leading in faith and bringing it to perfection (Heb. 12: 2),
the principle and source of all salvation (5: 9; see 10: 10, 14; 12: 1–2) for those who
obey him' (74).

same faith required of all humans. He concedes that problems about not recognizing in Jesus the paradigm of biblical faith arose in the history of theology.[7]

Yet serious limitations affect the way these and other[8] defenders of Jesus' faith have so far tackled the question. Some do not distinguish clearly enough between the confession and the commitment of faith—a distinction which is vital for the discussion of Jesus' faith. Others do not analyse sufficiently the range of relevant New Testament texts. None of them sees the possibility of recognizing in the earthly Jesus a commitment and confession that are *analogous* to ours.

Any attempt to discuss the faith of the earthly Jesus and reach solidly founded conclusions (either for or against attributing faith to him) requires reflection in at least three areas: the nature of faith, the question of Jesus' human knowledge, and the NT data that bear on claims about Jesus' faith. Let us begin with some working account of faith.

1. Thomas Aquinas described faith as the assent of the intellect to that which is believed.[9] Two qualities necessary for faith, he maintained, are that a person be willing to believe, and that the contents of belief be proposed to that person.[10] Aquinas, therefore, held that faith involves both a voluntary commitment and a cognitive content. His scheme ('credere Deum, credere Deo', and 'credere in Deum')[11] developed first, two aspects of (*a*) the cognitive side of things—that is to say, the way faith is oriented towards meaning and truth. While (*a¹*) 'credere Deum' refers to believing *that* God exists, (*a²*) 'credere Deo' entails believing *what* God has revealed. (*b*) 'Credere in Deum' is believing *in* God or self-commitment *to* God. Dimension (*a*) concerns the content or object of faith (the *fides quae*), whereas (*b*) concerns the act of faith or the *fides qua*. It is a distinction between (*a*) firmly holding to be meaningful and true the Christian message as revealed by God, and (*b*) entering a loving, obedient, and trusting relation-

---

[7] H. U. von Balthasar, 'Fides Christi', *Sponsa Verbi* (Einsiedeln: Johannes Verlag, 1961), 45–79.

[8] See e.g. J. Guillet, *La Foi de Jésus-Christ* (Paris: Desclée, 1980).

[9] *Summa theologiae*, 2a. 2ae. 1. 4 *resp.*: 'Fides importat assensum intellectus ad id quod creditur.'

[10] Ibid. 1a. 111. 1 *ad* 1.

[11] Ibid. 2a. 2ae. 2. 2.

ship with the God who graciously forgives us and gives us life. We could distinguish two aspects of (*b*): on the one hand, faithful commitment here and now (*b'*); on the other hand, a persevering confidence that entrusts our future to God's hands (*b²*). Just as the cognitive content of faith (*a*) can be seen to have two aspects, so also with faith's voluntary commitment (*b*). At the same time, a working account of faith can follow Aquinas' general lines by distinguishing between 'believing that/what' and 'believing in', while recognizing how the content of faith (*fides quae*) and the act of faith (*fides qua*) belong together. In these terms faith is (*b*) an obedient and trusting response to God, who is (*a*) acknowledged as revealed to us as having acted on our behalf.[12] In a lapidary statement on faith the First Vatican Council taught what is equivalent to the same doctrine by calling faith 'the full homage of intellect [= *a*] and will [= *b*] to God who reveals' (DS 3008).

This version of faith could obviously be further nuanced and expanded to much greater length. There is, for example, the issue of grace and freedom. How can faith be simultaneously a gift from God and the free act of a human being? How can it be 'inspired and assisted by the grace of God' (DS 3008) and yet remain our free act? Second, granted that there is a cognitive content of faith, it focuses on a physically invisible goal (2 Cor. 5: 7; Heb. 11: 1; see also Rom. 8: 24). 'Seeing' is normally, but not always, understood to exclude 'believing'.[13] Conversely, believing is usually under-

---

[12] Standard accounts of faith, with somewhat different emphases, include both dimensions: the trusting, personal relationship and the confession of (revealed) truth. See e.g. A. Dulles, *The Survival of Dogma* (Garden City, NY: Doubleday, 1971), 17–59; H.-J. Hermisson and E. Lohse, *Faith* (Nashville: Abingdon, 1981); J. Pelikan, 'Faith', in M. Eliade (ed.), *The Encyclopedia of Religion*, v (London: Collier Macmillan, 1987), 250–5; R. Swinburne, *Faith and Reason* (Oxford: Clarendon Press, 1981), 104–24.

[13] Aquinas calls faith 'that habit of mind by which eternal life begins in us, making the intellect assent *to things that are not evident*' (*Summa theologiae*, 2a. 2ae. 4. 1 *resp.*; italics mine). Raymond Brown, *The Gospel According to John* (Garden City, NY: Doubleday, 1966), analyses five verbs used to express 'seeing'. In most cases these verbs express only physical seeing, although occasionally they can mean seeing a sign and coming to seemingly adequate sight (501–3). In commenting on John 20: 15–16, Brown mentions that Mary Magdalene saw Jesus but did not recognize him. He concludes that the 'mere sight of the risen Jesus does not necessarily lead to understanding or faith' (1009). 'Necessarily' is important here, as John's Gospel sometimes does present seeing as an occasion for belief (1: 14; 11: 40; 14: 8–9; 20:

stood to imply some element of not-seeing.[14] How does that not-seeing qualify 'believing that' and 'believing in'? Third, what of those believers who sin gravely? How does their option against God affect their 'believing that' and 'believing in'? These are merely some of the issues that could be developed at considerable length. The question of seeing/knowing or believing will turn up later in this chapter. But for our discussion a distinction between 'believing that' (confession; see Rom. 10: 8–10) and 'believing in' (commitment)—or, in Paul's terms, 'the obedience of faith' (Rom. 1: 5; 16: 26)—should be enough to let us raise questions about the existence and nature of faith exercised by the earthly Jesus. To do that we need first to reflect on Jesus' human knowledge.

Aquinas and the subsequent Catholic theological tradition held that in his human mind Jesus enjoyed the beatific vision and hence lived by sight, not by faith.[15] Aquinas expressed classically this thesis: 'When the divine reality is not hidden

8; 20: 29). See also Ferdinand Hahn, 'Sehen und Glauben in Johannesevangelium', in H. Balthensweiler *et al.* (eds.), *Neues Testament und Geschichte* (Tübingen: Mohr, 1972), 125–41.

[14] 'Some element' is important here. Entailing a personal knowledge of God and oneself or a new understanding of God and oneself, faith means 'seeing in a mirror dimly', 'knowing in part' (1 Cor. 13: 12), and even 'the light of the knowledge of the glory of God in the face of Christ' (2 Cor. 4: 4–6). See P. Rousselot, 'Les Yeux de la foi', *Recherches de science religieuse*, 1 (1910), 241–59 and 444–75, and various converts (e.g. Arnold Lunn, *Now I See* (New York: Sheed & Ward, 1933)) who describe their move to faith as coming to see, even if faith's knowledge remains a *cognitio obscura* (a shadowy knowledge).

[15] On the issue of Jesus' human consciousness and knowledge see E. Gutwenger, *Bewusstsein und Wissen Christi* (Innsbruck: Rauch, 1960); P. Kaiser, *Das Wissen Christi in lateinischen (westlichen) Theologie* (Regensburg: Pustet, 1981); H. Riedlinger, *Geschichtlichkeit und Vollendung des Wissens Christi*, Quaestiones Disputatae 32 (Freiburg: Herder, 1966); L. Ullrich, 'Der Glaube Jesu Christi', in W. Beinert (ed.), *Lexikon der Katholischen Dogmatik* (Freiburg: Herder, 1987), 197–9; J. H. P. Wong, 'Karl Rahner on the Consciousness of Jesus: Implications and Assessments', *Salesianum*, 48 (1986), 255–79. There is much to be said in favour of predicating non-conceptual, infused knowledge of Jesus—a knowledge which bears on his mission and identity. B. McGinn's account of mysticism as 'the consciousness of, and the reaction to what can be described as the immediate or direct presence of God' (*The Presence of God: A History of Western Christian Mysticism*, i (New York: Crossroad, 1991), p. xvii) fits what we saw of Jesus in Chs. 3 and 5; we should then call Jesus a mystic and even the greatest of the mystics. But the question here is rather that of the beatific vision: as Aquinas rightly argued, to attribute the beatific vision to the human mind of Jesus during his earthly existence rules out faith. Their infused, non-conceptual knowledge did not and does not exempt mystics and prophets from faith.

from sight, there is no point in faith. From the first moment of his conception Christ had the full vision of God in his essence ... Therefore he could not have had faith' (*Summa theologiae*, 3a. 7. 3 *resp.*).[16] Along with this knowledge of vision, Jesus' human knowledge was recognized to include 'ordinary', experiential knowledge but was credited with embracing special, 'infused' knowledge (ibid. 3. 10–12).

Notable difficulties can be brought against the thesis which holds that Jesus' human knowledge embraced the beatific vision. First, how could he have genuinely suffered if through his human mind he knew God immediately and in a beatifying way? Second, to put it mildly, such a vision raises problems for the free operation of Jesus' human will. Despite the way Aquinas qualifies somewhat Jesus' knowledge of vision (ibid. 3. 10 *ad* 2), such an immediate, beatifying vision of God in this life would seem to rule out the possibility of human freedom in the conditions of earthly history. Here and now the exercise of freedom requires limited knowledge. Third, Jesus was remembered to have remained obedient towards his Father, despite trials and temptations (e.g. Mark 1: 12–13; 14: 32–42; Luke 22: 8; Heb. 2: 18; 4: 15). The steady possession of the beatific vision would seem to rule out any genuine struggle on the part of Jesus. His 'trials and temptations' could not have been real threats but only a 'show' put on for our benefit and edification. Fourth, how can one reconcile the knowledge of vision (which Aquinas interprets as also including a comprehensive grasp of all creatures and everything they could do) with Jesus' human knowledge of the world? As human, such knowledge grows and develops through experience, but always remains limited. We recalled in the previous chapter how such limitations belong to the very nature of humanity. A knowledge in this life which entailed (right from conception itself) a comprehensive grasp of all creatures and everything they could do appears to be so superhuman that it casts serious doubts on the genuine status of Jesus' human knowledge. Fifth, the Synoptic Gospels contain passages that suggest ordinary limits in

[16] In the Middle Ages the view that Jesus had no faith was common teaching: see e.g. Peter Lombard, *Sent.* 3. 26. 4; Alexander of Hales, *Summa theologica*, 3, *inq.* 2, *tr.* 1, *art.* 4, 694.

Jesus' human knowledge (e.g. Mark 5: 30–2; 13: 32). Sixth, in the previous chapter we noted how such limitations belong to the very nature of humanity.

The Council of Chalcedon's insistence on Christ's human nature preserving the 'character proper' to it (DS 302) should make one cautious about attributing special properties (in this case, the quite extraordinary knowledge of the beatific vision) to his human mind. Christ's human mind and knowledge were maintained and not made superhuman through the hypostatic union. The comprehensive grasp of *all* creatures and *all* they can do (which Aquinas holds to belong to the beatific vision) would lift Christ's knowledge so clearly beyond the normal limits of human knowledge as to cast serious doubts on the genuineness of his humanity, at least in one essential aspect.

For these and related reasons it is hard to endorse Aquinas' thesis that the earthly Jesus' knowledge included (surely one would have to say was dominated by?) the beatific vision. We need to insist on what was implied for the human knowledge of the eternal Word in our nature as a second principle of activity. Inasmuch as and so long as the divine subject operated through a human nature in this earthly life, the Logos acted through a nature and a mind limited in knowledge. Otherwise the genuine status of that human nature would be suspect, and Jesus would not have been 'truly' human in the terms classically defined by the Council of Chalcedon.

Once we pull back from the maximalist position which holds that Jesus enjoyed the beatific vision during his earthly existence, should we go to the other extreme and maintain that his human mind enjoyed no special, divine knowledge whatsoever? Or was he humanly conscious of his unique personal identity as Son of God and of his absolute revealing/redemptive mission for others? To recognize such a consciousness in the earthly Jesus will obviously affect our conclusions about the existence and nature of his faith. Knowing and 'seeing' such divine realities would seem to exclude believing in them or taking them on faith. Let us examine first the question of Jesus' self-consciousness of his divine identity and develop further some points already handled in the last chapter.

Two methods are available in tackling the issue of Jesus' consciousness of his personal identity and mission: the deductive and the inductive. Rahner argues deductively from the principle that the higher the level of being, the more it is conscious of itself. In the case of Jesus, through the hypostatic union his human nature received the highest possible grade of being open to something created. Hence we would expect the mind of that human nature to be immediately conscious of its situation as assumed by the person of the eternal Word. Reflexively and progressively Jesus articulated that primordial, direct knowledge of his own divine identity.[17]

Instead of this deductive, intra-christological approach which argues from the relationship of Christ's human nature to the divine Logos, the Synoptic Gospels yield a historical, trinitarian picture of his fundamental epistemological condition: that of being constantly oriented in the power of the Spirit to the God whom he called 'Abba'. In and through that unique relationship, Jesus was humanly aware of his divine sonship and salvific mission—an awareness that was progressively expressed, developed, and acted upon. Such an inductive argument for Jesus' core-knowledge of his identity and mission can appeal to the data from Jesus' ministry gathered in Chapter 3. Once we agree, either inductively or deductively, that Jesus was humanly 'in the know' about his divine identity and revealing/redemptive mission, these two affirmations will affect what we can now say about the existence and nature of Jesus' faith.

'To believe' (*pisteuein*) and 'faith' (*pistis*) are among the commonest words in the NT, the verb occurring 241 times and the noun 243 times. But nowhere do we find the Gospels or any other NT books explicitly saying that during his earthly life 'Jesus believed'. The phrase 'faith of Jesus' occurs only once (Rev. 14: 12), while the phrase 'faith of Jesus Christ' and similar expressions turn up eight times in the Pauline letters (Rom. 3: 22, 26; Gal. 2: 16a, 16b, 20; 3: 22; Eph. 3: 12; Phil. 3: 9). The 'faith of Jesus' (Rev. 14: 12) has been interpreted as an objective genitive: 'faith in Jesus' or '*our*

[17] K. Rahner, 'Dogmatic Reflections on the Knowledge and Self-Consciousness of Christ', *Th. Inv.* v. 193–215.

faith in Jesus'. The possibility of translating the phrase as 'the faith exercised by Jesus' does not seem to be an issue for commentators on Revelation.

As regards the 'faith of Christ', James Mackey makes much of the grammatical possibility offered by Gal. 2: 16 and understands the passage to mean that we are justified not through believing *in* Jesus Christ (as the object of our faith) but through (being infected by) the faith *of* Jesus (the personal subject of his own faith).[18] Here Mackey has ignored the priority of context over mere grammar. Paul is writing, at least primarily, of *our* faith *in* Jesus Christ. Every contemporary translation I have checked (the New American Bible (both the original edition of 1970 and the revised NT version of 1988) the New International Version, the New Jerusalem Bible, the NRSV, and the REB) takes the passage in that sense.[19] So too the standard commentators.[20]

In a presidential address to the Society of New Testament Studies Morna Hooker summed up the main lines in the modern debate about the Pauline 'faith of Christ'. She added further bibliography on the issue and concluded that the phrase 'must contain *some* reference to the faith of Christ himself', understanding the phrase 'as a *concentric* expression, which begins, always, from the faith of Christ himself, but which includes, necessarily, the answering faith of believers, who claim that faith as their own'.[21] Despite the support from Hooker and others,[22] the tide does not seem to have seriously turned in favour of those like Mackey who take the Pauline 'faith of Christ' to mean the 'faith exercised by the earthly Jesus'.[23]

[18] Mackey, *Jesus the Man and the Myth*, 163, 188.
[19] For all eight occurrences in Paul, however, footnotes in the NRSV leave open the possibility of understanding 'the faith of Jesus Christ' as the faith exercised by Jesus.
[20] See e.g. H. D. Betz, *Galatians* (Philadelphia: Fortress, 1979), 115–19; J. A. Fitzmyer, 'Galatians', *NJBC* 784–5; F. F. Bruce, *The Epistle to the Galatians* (Grand Rapids: Eerdmans, 1982), 137–48; H. Schlier, *Der Brief an die Galater* (Göttingen: Vandenhoeck & Ruprecht, 1965), 94.
[21] M. D. Hooker, 'Pistis Christou', *New Testament Studies*, 35 (1989), 321–42, at 341.
[22] R. B. Hays, *The Faith of Jesus Christ* (Chico, Calif.: Scholars Press, 1983), 140–2, 157–76.
[23] This matter is covered by J. D. G. Dunn (*Romans* (Dallas: Word, 1988), 174–

As further scriptural warrant for recognizing that Jesus exercised faith, Mackey appeals to two passages from Hebrews: 5: 8 ('as Son, he learned obedience through what he suffered'), and 12: 2 (he is the 'pioneer and perfecter of our [!] faith'). Mackey interprets these texts as saying that, just as we human beings '*learn* faith or obedience through what we suffer', so did Jesus. His 'faith was perfected, and he was freed from the fear of death which makes us slaves, and he thus became the pioneer and perfecter of faith, the one we follow when we have faith like his'.[24]

Mackey is right in turning to Heb. 5: 8 and 12: 2, even if he misses the fact that the original Greek of Heb. 12: 2 does not have the adjective 'our' qualifying 'faith'. With the notable exception of C. Spicq, exegetes support Mackey's appeal to Hebrews and interpret Heb. 12: 2 in terms of Jesus' exemplifying faith in its highest form and leaving the perfect model to be imitated.[25] By also speaking of Jesus' prayer and obedient suffering 'in the days of his flesh' (Heb. 5: 7–8), Hebrews encourages us to accept what we might glean from the Gospels, above all from the Synoptic Gospels, about Jesus' faith and what it involved.

Repelled by unfounded speculations about Jesus' inner life, some scholars, however, refuse to make any claims about Jesus' interiority and experience of God. David Tracy, for example, dismisses the possibility of saying anything at all about Jesus' inner life: the 'psychology of Jesus is unavailable to modern scholarship'.[26] But not all modern theologians and exegetes agree with this flat statement.[27] Beyond question, the Synoptic Gospels do not aim at presenting the inner life

---

6, 182–3) in his comments on Rom. 3: 21–6. See the debate between Dunn and Hays over the 'faith of Christ' in E. H. Lovering (ed.), *Society of Biblical Literature 1991 Seminar Papers* (Atlanta: Scholars Press, 1991), 714–29 (Hays) and 730–44 (Dunn).

[24] Mackey, *Jesus the Man and the Myth*, 168–9.

[25] For details see O'Collins and Kendall, 'The Faith of Jesus', 413–15.

[26] D. Tracy, *The Analogical Imagination* (New York: Crossroad, 1981), 326.

[27] See e.g. some statements on the earthly Jesus which the Pontifical Biblical Commission made in a 1984 document, translated by J. A. Fitzmyer in his 'The Biblical Commission and Christology', *Theological Studies*, 46 (1985), 407–79, at 424, 436–8. The cautious and nuanced claims made here about Jesus' awareness of his filial relationship and redemptive mission obviously involve some claims about his 'psychology'.

of Jesus. Nevertheless, both from what they let us know about his characteristic attitudes and actions and from authentic sayings they preserve, we can reach some modest, yet important conclusions about his interior dispositions. It is clear that Jesus spoke repeatedly of the divine kingdom and his Father, showing an awareness of his own relationship to both. By reflecting on that awareness we can uncover something of what Jesus thought about himself in this relationship. Not to know much about the 'psychology of Jesus' is not equivalent to knowing nothing at all.[28] Let me turn now to the evidence from the Synoptic Gospels.

It is easy to recognize that during his earthly existence Jesus exemplified a 'believing in', a 'credere in Deum' which expressed itself in a totally obedient self-commitment to the God whom he called 'Abba' (Mark 14: 36). Publicly this 'believing in' was lived out in Jesus' total openness to and unconditioned trust in the divine kingdom that was breaking into the world. We could hardly sum up better his public ministry than by describing him as being utterly at the service of God's reign. Not only Jesus' actions but also some of his sayings reflect this dimension of his faith: e.g. 'if you had faith as a grain of mustard seed, you could say to this mulberry-tree, "be rooted up and be planted in the sea", and it would obey you' (Luke 17: 6).[29] Through those whose faith truly puts them at God's disposition, extraordinary results (like the healings and other miracles of Jesus) would happen. J. Gnilka reflects on this logion: 'As Jesus' word this [saying] can hardly be interpreted in any other way than as a statement about his own faith.' Gnilka continues:

For the miraculous healings not only the faith of the one who received help but also the faith of Jesus is relevant. . . . In that Jesus was open to God in a unique way he showed his unique faith. . . . When Jesus according to Mark 9: 23 says to the father of the

---

[28] In explaining the virtue of faith Aquinas distinguishes between (1) its principal act, believing, and (2) its secondary, external act, which is to confess, witness, and give testimony; see *Summa theologiae*, 2a. 2ae. 3. 1. In these terms we might think of arguing from the secondary, external testimony of faith communicated through Jesus' words and deeds back to the principal act of his inner belief.

[29] Like others J. Gnilka holds that 'mulberry-tree' goes back to Jesus, and that 'mountain' (Mark 11: 23; Matt. 17: 20) is a secondary development (*Jesus von Nazaret* (Freiburg: Herder, 1990), 134).

epileptic boy, 'All things are possible to him who believes', that is an invitation to share in his faith.[30]

In this episode Jesus complains of his contemporaries as being 'a faithless generation' (Mark 9: 19). They have 'little faith' (Matt. 6: 30 = Luke 12: 28) and should learn to trust in divine providence. He reproaches his disciples as a group and Peter in particular for having 'little faith' (Matt. 8: 26; 14: 31; 17: 20). He promises that those who keep asking in prayer will be heard (Matt. 7: 7–12 = Luke 11: 9–13). Some, or probably much, of this language goes back to Jesus himself. He speaks about faith as an insider,[31] one who knows personally what the life of faith is and wants to share it with others (see 2 Cor. 4: 13).[32]

The 'private' side of Jesus' faith 'in' God showed itself through (and presumably was fed by) the life of prayer he assiduously practised (e.g. Mark 1: 35; 6: 46; 14: 12–26; 32–42; Matt. 11: 25; Luke 3: 21). Praying like that expressed a deep sense of dependence and trust—in other words, a strong relationship of faith in God.[33]

Not only authentic sayings of Jesus, but also NT writings themselves (and their traditional sources) witness to his *fides*

[30] Ibid. 135 (translation mine).

[31] As regards 'little faith', however, J. A. Fitzmyer commenting on Luke 12: 28 (= Matt. 6: 30) doubts that the word goes back to Jesus. In *The Gospel According to Luke* (Garden City, NY: Doubleday, 1985), 979, he writes: 'A Greek compound adj. *oligopistos*, added to the tradition already in "Q", lacks any real equivalent in the Semitic languages, and hence is scarcely traceable to Jesus himself.' U. Luz understands 'person(s) of little faith' (in Matt. 6: 30; 8: 26; 14: 31) as coming from the tradition, but does not discuss whether it goes back to Jesus himself (see *Matthew 1–7: A Commentary*, trans. W. C. Linss (Edinburgh: T. & T. Clark, 1990), 406).

[32] Paul may be applying to Christ the words of a psalm 'I believed and so I spoke' and imagining that he (Christ) speaks here. If this interpretation is correct, Paul would be claiming to share in Christ's *own spirit of faith*: 'Paul in all probability takes the verse from Ps. 116 as an utterance of the Messiah, an utterance of faith in God's salvation' (A. T. Hanson, *Studies in Paul's Technique and Theology* (Grand Rapids: Eerdmans, 1974), 17–18; see ibid. 213; id., *The Pioneer Ministry* (London: SCM Press, 1961), 76–8).

[33] Mackey speaks of Jesus' faith having 'its deepest roots in the most ordinary experience of everyday life', but not in prayer (*Jesus the Man and the Myth*, 171). L. Boff does better by recognizing the role that 'prayer and meditation' with 'the reading of the scriptures' played in Jesus' life of faith: *Passion of Christ, Passion of the Word* (New York: Orbis, 1987), 61.

qua in its trusting (Mark 14: 25),[34] persevering (Heb. 10: 36; 12: 1–2), developing (Luke 2: 52; Heb. 5: 9; 7: 28), and obedient (Rom. 5: 19; Phil. 2: 8; Heb. 5: 8) characteristics. The difficulties arise much more with the dimension of *fides quae* or 'believing that/what'.

Not only in the past (with those who followed Aquinas in attributing the beatific vision to the earthly Jesus) but also today, some 'special' aspects of Jesus' consciousness can seem to rule out any recognizable kind of 'believing that/what'. Jean Galot, for instance, finds no basis for claiming that Jesus enjoyed the beatific vision during his mortal life,[35] but soon modifies this position. He states that Jesus had 'other knowledge that could not have resulted from his experience or from the normal exercise of his intellect, and which can be explained as stemming from a higher source'. Jesus possessed 'certain pieces of infused information, but he did not possess infused science [knowledge] *per se*'.[36] These 'pieces of infused information' included the awareness on Jesus' part that he was divine. Galot concludes that, even if he experienced ordeals closely resembling the trials of faith, 'since Jesus is the Son of God' and possessed 'the [human] consciousness proper to this sonship, it is impossible to attribute faith to him in the strict sense of the word'.[37] A case can be made for attributing to Jesus a certain endowment of infused knowledge. The great OT prophets enjoyed some special experience of God and divine things. Their knowledge of the divine may be compared with the profound awareness of God found in later, Christian mystics. If a special endowment of divine knowledge was granted to the prophets before him and the mystics after him, why not credit Jesus with some similar endowment?

---

[34] The authenticity of this saying is affirmed by V. Taylor, *The Gospel According to St. Mark* (London: Macmillan, 2nd edn., 1966), 547; also by J. Jeremias, *The Eucharistic Words of Jesus* (London: SCM Press, 1966), 192. Jeremias believes that Jesus is effectively saying: 'I would very much have liked to eat this passover lamb with you before my death. (But I must deny myself this wish.) For I tell you I do not intend to eat of it again until God fulfils (his promises) in the kingdom of God' (211).

[35] J. Galot, *Who is Christ?* (Chicago: Franciscan Herald Press, 1981), 354–6.

[36] Ibid. 360, 362.

[37] Ibid. 380, 382.

At the same time, however, is it possible to reckon with some limitations in Jesus' 'believing that/what' caused by his 'special' knowledge and still recognize in him faith in an analogous sense? Let us take up the difficult question of the possibility and scope of a *fides quae* for Jesus.

Certain very important convictions did not and could not enter Jesus' confession of faith. The evidence from the Synoptic Gospels encourages the conclusion that he had a primordial awareness of being the unique Son of the God whom he addressed as 'Abba' (Mark 14: 36), and of being the final agent of salvation for human beings (e.g. Mark 8: 38; Luke 11: 20; 12: 8–9). Jesus *knew* God, his own divine identity, and redemptive mission. He did not and could not *believe* that God existed and that he himself was the Son of God and Saviour of the world.

Further, since his crucifixion and resurrection had not yet taken place, he could not confess his redemptive death and resurrection in the way Christians began to do (e.g. Rom. 1: 3–4; 4: 24–5; 10: 8–10; 1 Cor. 15: 3–5). Here, however, one might argue that a historical nucleus behind the passion predictions (Mark 8: 31; 9: 31; 10: 33–4; see also 12: 1–11; 14: 25) shows us Jesus confidently confessing his coming passion and vindication. But leaving aside for the moment this question, we can reasonably claim that some essential convictions, above all, his own divine identity (and with that the very existence of God) and saving mission, were matters of knowledge and not of faith for Jesus.

What then was left to make up his *fides quae*? Without distinguishing and speaking of 'the *confession* of faith', Mackey tells us that Jesus' faith

had its deepest roots in the most ordinary experience of everyday life. The man Jesus—apart from his tradition, of course, which had already tried to verbalize this faith—had no more 'information' about God than could be gleaned from the birds of the air, the farmers in their fields, kings in their castles, and merchants in the market-place.[38]

This is to privilege the confession of faith in God the Creator, the God revealed for everyday in the world and in the experi-

---

[38] *Jesus the Man and the Myth*, 171.

ences of everybody's life. The revelation of God, communicated through the history of Israel and (under the
inspiration of the Holy Spirit) recorded and interpreted by
the Hebrew Scriptures, becomes a mere parenthesis and not
even that. In Mackey's version Israel's 'tradition' had 'tried
to verbalize *this* faith' (italics mine), that is to say a faith
rooted, not in the history of the people, but in 'the most
ordinary experience of everyday life'. Surely Jesus' faith,
while rooted in creation, was also (even more?) rooted in the
special history of God's call of and dealings with the chosen
people? Mackey is right in drawing attention to the present
'object' of Jesus' faith, that *fides quae* in God the loving and
provident Creator, which the opening words of the Creed
express and which Jesus expressed in terms of the Shema
(Mark 12: 28–34; see Deut. 6: 4). Nevertheless, the past and
future could also have constituted Jesus' *fides quae*.

Creeds of Israel confessed not so much God revealed in
creation as God revealed through the divine acts in the history
of the people:

A wandering Aramean was my ancestor; he went down into Egypt
and lived there as an alien, few in number, and there he became a
great nation, mighty and populous. When the Egyptians treated us
harshly and affected us, by imposing hard labour on us, we cried to
the Lord, the God of our ancestors; the Lord heard our voice and
saw our affliction, our toil and our oppression. The Lord brought
us out of Egypt with a mighty hand and an outstretched arm, with
a terrifying display of power, and with signs and wonders; and he
brought us into this place and gave us this land, a land flowing with
milk and honey (Deut. 26: 5–9; see 6: 20–5, Josh. 24: 2–13).

These historical creeds made up the typical confessional
element for Jewish faith, and, one can reasonably argue, for
the *fides quae* of Jesus. He quotes the Shema (Mark 12: 29–
30), which in its original setting (Deut. 6: 1–25) drew its
meaning and support from the way God fulfilled promises to
the people by delivering them from Egypt and giving them
'a land flowing with milk and honey' (Deut. 6: 3, 10–12, 20–
3).
    The Synoptic Gospels do not contain any suggestion that
Jesus had special sources of knowledge about the religious

history of his people. Nor do they contain any suggestion that Jesus refrained from confessing the old creeds with his fellow Jews. In short, the credal summaries found in the OT point us to the confessional content of Jesus' faith, the traditional faith he shared with devout Jews.

In the Apostles' Creed not only the present and the past but also the future ('I believe in ... the resurrection of the body, and life everlasting') figure among the objects of *faith*. The Niceno-Constantinopolitan Creed, admittedly, articulates matters rather in terms of *hope*: 'We look for the resurrection of the dead, and the life of the world to come.' We might speak here of the *spes quae* (hope that), and recall Paul's words about waiting in hope for the invisible blessings of the future: 'now hope that is seen is not hope. For who hopes for what is seen? But if we hope for what we do not see, we wait for it with patience' (Rom. 8: 24–5). Nevertheless, this relationship to the invisible blessings of the future can be thematized in other ways. Echoing Isa. 64: 4, Paul puts *love* at the heart of the relationship: 'what no eye has seen, nor ear heard, nor the human heart conceived, what God has prepared for those who love him—these things God has revealed to us through the Spirit' (1 Cor. 2: 9–10). Finally, as in the Apostles' Creed, *faith* is applied to those who obey God and trust the divine promises, without seeing (Heb. 11: 1) the future rewards, or seeing them only 'from afar' (Heb. 11: 13). The future can be listed among the objects of our faith. According to Aquinas, faith like the other theological virtues orders human beings toward the future beatific vision. Through faith we assent not only to the way of salvation prescribed by God but also to God as our end.[39] In the case of Jesus, if we agree that he did not yet have the beatific vision, could his faith have ordered him towards it? Did his faith lead him to assent not only to the way of salvation which the divine kingdom involved but also to his Father as his last end?

Once again the question of Jesus' knowledge is decisive. Was his knowledge of his own destiny and of the parousia such as to rule out his confessing 'resurrection and life ever-

---

[39] *Summa theologiae*, 1a. 2ae. 62. 3.

lasting'? Here one walks into a minefield of problems that have been exploding at regular intervals for a century or more. How much of Mark's chapter about the signs of the end and the day of the Son of man, for example, goes back to Jesus himself (Mark 13: 1–37)? If we are satisfied that we can establish some sayings from Jesus himself, what did he mean by his eschatological language? Does it indicate claims to some special knowledge of the future or rather limits in his knowledge of the future (Mark 13: 32)?

Without entering into detailed debate and the immense literature on the eschatological knowledge and expectations of Jesus,[40] it seems that a reasonable case can be made for holding that Jesus believed and hoped for what he did not yet see. As with the heroes and heroines of Heb. 11: 1–40, the as yet invisible blessings of the future formed part of Jesus' confession of faith.

Such then is my thesis about the *fides quae* of Jesus, in its past, present, and future dimensions. This position means holding that the content of faith, even within the special, biblical history of revelation and salvation, can be analogous. The *fides quae* of Jesus did not coincide perfectly with that of later Christians. Even in comparison with that of his contemporary Jews, some differences were there, inasmuch as, for example, he knew and could not, in the technical sense of the word, confess the existence of God. At the same time, Jesus' confession of faith could coincide substantially with that of contemporary and earlier Jews. An analogous approach to the content of faith allows for similarities and differences between the faith of devout Jews, Jesus' faith, and subsequent Christian faith.

This position means parting company with those who argue for a more or less uniform content of faith. Aquinas, for example, held that, even though the gospel had not yet been proclaimed, the Israelites had essentially the same faith as Christians, since the real object of their confession was the same. On the basis of Heb. 11: 6 ('whoever would approach him [God] must believe that he exists and that he rewards

[40] See R. E. Brown, *Jesus: God and Man* (New York: Macmillan, 1967), 59–79; A. Harvey, *Jesus and the Constraints of History* (Philadelphia: Westminster, 1982), 87–97; and the closing section of Ch. 3 above.

those who seek him'), like others Aquinas maintained that belief in God's existence and rewards constituted the primary, essential content of faith. By holding this faith, the Israelites implicitly grasped the entire revealed mystery of God and hence could be seen to have already had essentially the same faith as (later) Christians.[41] Instead of thus 'levelling' the content of faith down to the lowest common denominator, I am proposing the alternative of allowing for variations in the confessional *fides quae*. In what they confessed about God in creation and history, there are similarities and differences between devout Israelites, Jesus, and early Christians. There is no need to argue, for instance, that the faith of the Israelites was essentially, if implicitly, the same as that of early Christians responding to the good news of Jesus' death and resurrection.

As well as acknowledging an analogy between Jesus' *fides quae* and that of Jews and Christians, we should also reckon with an analogy at the level of his commitment or *fides qua*.[42] We have seen above how the NT evidence clearly supports conclusions about his 'believing' or obedient self-commitment to the God whom he called 'Abba'. Along with this, we should also recall the NT's insistence on the perfect quality of that obedience (e.g. John 8: 46; 2 Cor. 5: 21; Phil. 2: 8; 1 Pet. 2: 22–4; 1 John 3: 3–5). The radicality of Jesus' unconditional commitment means that we must recognize analogy also at the level of his *fides qua*.

To conclude this section. We have seen how, with the exception of Heb. 12: 2, the NT never explicitly makes the earthly Jesus the subject of the verb 'to believe' or clearly characterizes him by using the corresponding noun 'faith'. Faith in the NT Church was very much associated with

---

[41] *Summa theologiae*, 2a. 2ae. 1. 7.

[42] To use 'faith' analogously is no startling innovation. Any large-scale NT dictionary will illustrate how the usage and meaning of *pistis* and *pisteuein* vary between Paul, the Synoptic Gospels, Hebrews, and John—not to mention the different nuances to be found in other NT books. Paul holds Abraham up as the great model of faith (Rom. 4: 1–22). 'Our father in faith', however, even if he obeys God's commands and trusts God's promises in an exemplary way, can only have a *fides quae* which is radically less than and very different from that of later Jews and Christians. Given Abraham's place at the very beginning of salvation history, when we speak of the content of his faith, we do so in a thoroughly analogous way.

believing the proclamation of Christ's resurrection from the dead (e.g. Rom. 10: 9–10), with baptism in the name of Jesus himself (Acts 2: 38; 8: 16; 10: 48; 19: 5) or 'in the name of the Father and of the Son and of the Holy Spirit' (Matt. 28: 19), and with faith *in* Christ (e.g. Acts 20: 21; Gal. 3: 26; Col. 1: 4). These associations undoubtedly made it harder to draw from the memory of Jesus' ministry the conclusion (drawn by Hebrews) that Christians were called not only to believe in the risen Christ but also to believe like the earthly Jesus. Despite the tension, there was no contradiction here. To find in Jesus the supreme exemplar for the life of faith in no way excluded believing in him as the risen Lord of their lives.

The Sinlessness and Grace of Christ

The obedient self-commitment of Jesus moves us naturally to the next question: how perfect was his *fides qua*? Did he ever sin? Was he immune from sin—sinless not merely *de facto* but also *de jure*? Such an absolute impeccability in principle would have to be intrinsic; a merely extrinsic impeccability seems like a contradiction in terms. But how could we reconcile an absolute, intrinsic impeccability with Christ's complete humanity—in particular, with his genuine human freedom? If Jesus could not have sinned under any circumstances whatsoever, was he truly free? Furthermore, sin seems an all-pervasive presence. If, absolutely speaking, Jesus could not have disobeyed the divine will, how could he then have identified with the human condition? Add too the fact that the NT recalls Jesus as having been tempted and tested (e.g. Mark 1: 13 parr.; Heb. 4: 15). If he truly felt temptation— and that must mean feeling tempted inwardly—how could this be coherent with his being intrinsically and absolutely impeccable?

The NT clearly affirms the fact of Jesus' radical obedience (Phil. 2: 8; Heb. 5: 8) and sinlessness (John 8: 46; Heb. 7: 26; 1 Pet. 1: 19; 2: 22; 1 John 3: 5). The Council of Chalcedon appeals to Heb. 4: 15 in teaching the same (DS 301). The eleventh Council of Toledo (DS 533) and the Council of Florence (DS 1347) taught that Jesus was born without original sin. Constantinople II affirmed that any inclination to sin or 'concupiscence' was absent in Jesus (DS 434), while Constantinople III affirmed a perfect harmony between his divine and human wills (DS 556). Neither the NT nor the post-NT teaching takes us beyond merely *de facto* sinlessness to any clear claim about Jesus' *de jure* sinlessness. What of this latter question?

First, the status of Christ's moral goodness is not to be examined simply and solely in terms of his human nature. We sin or refrain from sinning as persons; it would be incorrect to excuse oneself on the grounds that 'it wasn't me but only my (human) nature that sinned'. The question under discussion must then be phrased: was Christ personally impeccable *de jure*? The answer should be yes. Otherwise we could face the situation of God possibly in deliberate opposition to God; one divine person would be capable (through his human will) of committing sin and so intentionally transgressing the divine will. The possibility of Christ sinning seems incompatible with his personal divine identity and the absolute holiness of God. He was incapable of sinning because he was not only human but also divine.

Second, it is obvious that being human does not necessarily mean being virtuous. But does being human inevitably and necessarily mean the possibility of being non-virtuous? Here we can introduce the distinction between truly essential and merely common or universal properties. Until recently all human beings were conceived within their mother's body. With the advent of *in vitro* fertilization, we now know that being conceived within our mother's body is a common property but not an essential one. Can we apply this distinction to the all-pervasive presence of sin, and speak of sin as a common but not an essential human property? In general human wills are prone to sin and are not *de jure* sinless. But the case of a human will which belongs to that particular human nature assumed by the Son of God is different, in fact unique. That particular will is necessarily and *de jure* without sin. One might also add here that the possibility of sin is not always a common human property. New-born babies (like Francesco whom I baptized some months ago) are fully human but, at least here and now, incapable of sinning.

Furthermore, as a deliberate transgression of the good

God's loving will for us, sin makes us less than fully and perfectly human. Hence to allow for the possibility of Christ sinning would be tantamount to allowing for the possibility of his being less than fully and perfectly human. When the Council of Chalcedon followed Constantinople I in affirming Christ's perfect humanity (DS 301), it did so only in a general way and entered into few details, certainly not taking up the issue of whether sin is or is not consistent with being fully and perfectly human. We can, however, confront Chalcedon's blanket affirmation of Christ's perfect humanity with the possibility of his sinning. It seems reasonable to hold that to be fully human is to be fully and in principle virtuous.

We can move this conciliar teaching back to its source, the human history of Jesus reported by the Gospels. His activity comes across as that of someone utterly oriented towards God and unconditionally committed to the cause of the kingdom. The more we agree that such an orientation and commitment accurately summarize the data, the more we should be inclined to accept that Jesus was sinless in principle. If he could have sinned, that orientation and commitment were not after all total and unconditional. We would have to modify seriously our previous judgements about Jesus' activity for the kingdom being totally in tune with the divine will.

Third, the greatest difficulty with acknowledging Jesus to be *de jure* sinless often comes from convictions about freedom as essentially a choice, often a difficult choice between good and evil. To equate freedom with such a choice would entail denying the freedom of the blessed in heaven, which is perhaps our closest analogue to Christ's human freedom. They live in the freedom of the choice they have made. In their total communion with God, they no longer have the ability to choose between good and evil, but this freedom from sin can be seen as freedom at a higher level. Whatever we say of the blessed, identifying freedom with choice between good and evil must mean denying the freedom of God (namely, the freedom to choose to share the divine goodness). Directly choosing evil is utterly impossible to God.

How then should we describe and define freedom? As the exercise of choice is often bedevilled with the sense of choosing between good and evil, it could be more helpful here to speak of conscious self-determination as the essence of freedom.[43] To be free is to be personally determined from within and not by some compulsion either from without or from within. At its best, freedom means consciously going beyond oneself in love and living in communion, the supreme example being the free communion of life and love enjoyed by the Trinity. Through his human will Jesus acted with a free self-determination that entailed perfect, loving conformity with the divine will which excluded the possibility of sin. To put this position positively, the utterly loving relationship of the man Jesus to the Father transposed into human conditions the eternal relationship of the Logos to the first person of the Trinity. At both levels the free and loving relationship ruled out even the possibility of offence and breakdown.

Fourth, the fact of Jesus having been tempted poses its special problems for those who argue for his *de jure* sinlessness. How could he have been really tempted and yet all along have been in principle immune from sin? A distinction between the order of being and that of knowledge can help us here. Jesus could be truly tempted and tested, provided that he did not know that he could not sin. If he had known that he could not sin, it would be difficult, if not impossible, to make sense of genuine temptations; they would be reduced to make-believe, a performance put on for the edification of others. It was quite a different situation to be incapable of sin but not to know that.

Reflection on Christ's sinlessness and human freedom inevitably brings us to the question of the grace with which his humanity was graced. In the third part of his *Summa theologiae* Aquinas elaborated an inherited scheme of Christ's threefold grace: the grace of the hypostatic union itself, habitual grace, and that 'capital' grace bestowed on Christ inasmuch as he is the head of the Church (*qq.* 7–8). This threefold scheme remains useful, provided we leave behind Aquinas' abstract and scholastic language.

Grace may be described as the gratuitous self-com-

---

[43] See H.-W. Bartsch *et al.*, 'Freiheit', *TRE* xi. 497–549.

munication of God which elevates human beings and makes possible their new loving relationship with God and a share in the divine life.[44] Because of Augustine and his influence, it was with reference to the doctrine of grace that the theological conception of liberty was principally elaborated. The relationship between grace and freedom became a primary theological issue for the Protestant Reformation. Before describing briefly Christ's graced state, let me state two relevant convictions.

1. Just as Christ's particular human will and action are not competing at the same level with his divine will and action (DS 556–8), so in general divine action and human freedom are not competing at the same level. Hence, although God is directly involved in the determination of everything that happens in the world, a given effect can be completely the work of human freedom no less than completely the work of God. Like others at the human level Jesus could act freely and responsibly, even though divine providence is actively present in everything which happens within the world. (2) Apropos of divine grace and human freedom, it is wrong to take them to be opposed or in inverse proportion, as if more grace entailed less freedom. The truth is quite the opposite: free self-determination grows in direct proportion with nearness to and graced union with God.[45]

In the case of Christ's grace, the hypostatic union or personal assumption of a complete human nature by the second person of the Trinity constitutes a unique divine self-communication, the closest imaginable union between God and a human being. Then the humanity through which Christ lives out his loving union with the Father is supernaturally graced by the Holy Spirit to perfect his human activity, bring it to participate in the divine life, and enhance its freedom in line with his unique nearness to God.

Aquinas described the third dimension of Christ's grace as follows:

Grace was bestowed upon Christ, not only as an individual but also

---

[44] See K. Berger *et al.*, 'Grace', in K. Rahner *et al.* (eds.), *Sacramentum mundi* (6 vols.; London: Burns & Oates, 1968–70), ii. 409–24.

[45] See K. Rahner, 'Grace and Freedom', ibid. 424–7.

inasmuch as he is the head of the church, so that it might overflow into his members. Therefore, Christ's works are referred to himself and his members in the same way as the work of another human being in a state of grace are referred to himself ... Christ by his passion merited salvation not only for himself, but likewise for all his members. (*Summa theologiae*, 3a. 48. 1 *resp.*)

Two things call for adjustment in this account of Christ's grace as 'head'. First, while pride of place may be accorded to Christ being the source of grace for members of the Church, as the last Adam he is also the head of all humanity and 'recapitulates' the whole human story (see Irenaeus in Chapters 2 and 7 above). Grace is bestowed on Christ for all men and women. Second, more personal language can replace the talk about Christ's 'works' and his grace that 'overflows'. Through his incarnation, life, death, and resurrection, Christ has come into the human story as the divine self-communication in person. He manifests in our history God's gracious love, delivers from evil, and through the gift of the Holy Spirit empowers men and women to share in the divine life. Such personal terms do more justice to Christ's grace as 'head'.

The Virginal Conception

The last section of this chapter will move back from the faith and holiness which characterized Christ's life to consider the traditional doctrine about his human origin: the virginal conception or Mary's conceiving Jesus through the power of the Holy Spirit and without the co-operation of a human father. This belief maintains that Christ's incarnation did not follow the ordinary, innerworldly laws of procreation but was the fruit of a special intervention by the Holy Spirit.

Philosophical, historical, hermeneutical, and theological difficulties have been raised against the virginal conception. Deists and others who reject in principle any special subacts of God subsequent to the act of creation itself exclude the virginal conception along with such other items as the miracles of Jesus and his bodily resurrection. The debate with them goes far beyond the virginal conception and concerns questions of divine causality that the closing section to

Chapter 4 examined. Second, students of comparative religion and others have proposed that pagan stories about male deities impregnating human women to produce extraordinary children encouraged Christians to construct a legend of his virginal conception. They already believed Jesus to be of divine origin and so they created a story like that, for instance, of the origin of Romulus and Remus.[46] But these alleged parallels are by no means close. In the legend of Romulus and Remus, a vestal virgin conceived the twins when she was violated by the god Mars. Whether or not rape was involved, sexual intercourse regularly features in the supposed parallels, and that alone (apart from the very dubious historicity of Romulus, Remus, their mother (Rhea Silvia), and the other protagonists of such legends over against Jesus and his mother) makes these legends quite different from the non-sexual virginal conception reported in the infancy narratives of Matthew and Luke.

A third challenge to the virginal conception has come from those who, albeit in different ways, think that Christians have misinterpreted the intentions of the infancy narratives of Matthew and Luke. These evangelists did not want to communicate some historical truth about the miraculous way Jesus was conceived, but merely aimed to express and arouse faith in his unique role and status as Son of God and Messiah. Edward Schillebeeckx, for example, maintains that the tradition about the virginal conception preserved (in their different ways) by Matthew and Luke did not intend 'to impart any empirically apprehensible truth or secret information about the family history, but a truth of revelation'. This tradition offered 'a theological reflection, not a supply of new informative data'. Here Schillebeeckx allows only for the alternative: either some 'informative data' which would have constituted an 'empirically apprehensible truth', or 'a truth of revelation' to serve 'theological reflection'.[47] But must it have been an either/or? Could not the tradition preserved by the two evangelists have intended to embody both

---

[46] This is the parallel suggested by J. Moltmann, *The Way of Jesus Christ*, trans. M. Kohl (London: SCM Press, 1990), 81.

[47] E. Schillebeeckx, *Jesus: An Experiment in Christology*, trans. H. Hoskins (London: Collins, 1979), 554–5.

informative data (about the virginal conception) and some truth of revelation (about Jesus' divine filiation)? A similar either/or approach turns up in Hans Küng's *Credo*: the virginal conception is not a historical reality but a symbolic interpretation.[48] Yet why should we rule out the possibility of our being confronted with an historical truth (the bodily reality of the virginal conception), which yielded and yields a great depth of symbolic interpretation? Küng would hardly want to propose in general that historical events and symbolic interpretation are mutually exclusive, or that a thoroughly bodily event cannot also be a deeply symbolic event.

A fourth difficulty comes from those who believe that a virginal conception would involve a serious diminishment in Christ's true and full humanity. Would the lack of a standard origin to his historical existence, inasmuch as he has a human mother but no human father, leave him no longer complete in what is ours (*totus in nostris*)—to use Leo the Great's words (DS 293)? Two considerations seem pertinent here. First, once again we might distinguish between common and essential human properties. Obviously enjoying a biological father as well as a mother is a common property. But can we establish that it is also an absolutely essential property? Second, as experience often illustrates, mere biological paternity does not automatically guarantee appropriate human fatherhood, whereas many men can prove excellent fathers to children who are not biologically their own offspring. Although Jesus did not have a biological human father, the infancy narratives of Matthew and Luke encourage us to think that he enjoyed fine fathering from Joseph.

The two evangelists refer to the virginal conception from different standpoints—Matthew from that of Joseph, Luke from that of Mary. The traditions on which they draw, the ways in which they develop them, and the OT language and motifs that they adapt for their infancy narratives differ markedly. We simply cannot harmonize into a unified account the opening chapters of these two Gospels. Nevertheless, Raymond Brown seems correct in holding that 'both

---

[48] H. Küng, *Credo* (London: SCM Press, 1993), 44. An either/or approach to the virginal conception turns up likewise in Moltmann's *The Way of Jesus Christ*, 78, 82–5.

Matthew and Luke regarded the virginal conception as historical', even if 'the modern intensity about history was not
theirs'.[49] In other words, the two evangelists presented the
conception of Jesus as actually taking place not through
normal sexual intercourse but through a special intervention
of the Holy Spirit.

I strongly suspect that it has been difficulties at the level
of meaning which have led many people to doubt or reject
the fact of the virginal conception. In early Christianity
apocryphal gospels developed further biological aspects of
Jesus' conception and birth, so that their readers increasingly
lost sight of the deep religious significance of those events. In
modern times, I believe, many reject the virginal conception
because they share the difficulties indicated above or else
react against a caricature of an explanation: because of his
unique holiness, Jesus had to be originally conceived, since
sexual intercourse is impure. What religious and saving significance then does the miraculous manner of Jesus' conception convey?

Traditionally the major value of his virginal conception
has been to express Jesus' divine origin. The fact that he was
born of a woman pointed to his humanity. The fact that he
was born of a virgin pointed to his divinity. This interpretation should be fitted into the wider and developing pattern
provided by the NT.

Christians began by recognizing the personal identity and
saving function of Jesus Christ as Son of God in his resurrection from the dead (Rom. 1: 4). When Mark composed
his Gospel he included a 'baptism Christology': at the beginning of his ministry Jesus is declared by God to be 'my
beloved Son' (Mark 1: 11). Matthew and Luke moved matters
further back to add a 'conception Christology': the unique
divine intervention in the conception of Jesus revealed that
there never was a moment in his history when Jesus was not
Son of God. Finally, other NT authors went even further
back to add a 'pre-existence Christology' (John 1: 1–18; Heb.
1: 1–3). Without saying anything about the manner of Jesus'

⁴⁹ R. E. Brown, *The Birth of the Messiah* (London: Geoffrey Chapman, 1977),
517.

conception, they acknowledged in his coming on the human scene the incarnation of One who was 'previously' 'with God' and now was 'made flesh'. Thus the event of the virginal conception provided a further link between what began at the end with his risen 'post-existence' and finished at the beginning with his eternal 'pre-existence'.[50]

We can spot other patterns of significance to which the event of the virginal conception contributed. Matthew names the newly conceived Jesus 'Emmanuel, which means God with us' (1: 23). Right from his conception and birth Jesus fulfilled and expressed the presence of Yahweh with his people. Then at the end of the same Gospel the risen and exalted Christ met his disciples as the One to whom 'all authority in heaven and on earth has been given', and who promised: 'I am with you always to the close of the age' (Matt. 28: 18, 20). What Jesus became through the resurrection he had already been from the start: the fulfilled expression of Yahweh's presence with his people.

To name Christ's divinity is to speak of his relationship to the Father in the Spirit. Hence the event of the virginal conception can be expected to yield meaning not only about Christ's divine filiation but also about his relationship with the Holy Spirit. Christians experienced the outpouring of the Spirit in the aftermath of Jesus' resurrection. They came to recognize that the Spirit sent to them by the risen Christ or in his name (e.g. Luke 24: 49; John 14: 26) had been actively present in the whole of his life—not only at the start of his ministry (Luke 3: 22; 4: 1, 14, 18) but even right back to his conception. In other words, the risen Jesus actively blessed his followers with the Spirit. But in his entire earthly existence he had been blessed by the Spirit—right from his very conception when he came into this world through the Spirit's creative power.

Thus the event of the virginal conception plays its part in revealing and clarifying that central truth: from the beginning to the end there is a trinitarian face to the story of Jesus

---

[50] This pattern, however, is not perfect. As we have seen, pre-existence texts surface early in the formation of the NT and are to be found already in Paul's letters (e.g. 1 Cor. 8: 6; 2 Cor. 8: 9; Phil. 2: 6).

Christ. His total history discloses the God who is Father, Son, and Holy Spirit.

Finally, in his *Quod unus sit Christus* Cyril of Alexandria would encourage us to read the story of the virginal conception in its significance not only for divine self-revelation but also for human salvation (724c–d). Christ's conception, in initiating the saving drama of new creation, shows that redemption comes as divine gift. Human beings cannot inaugurate and carry through their own salvation. Like the original creation of the world, the new creation is divine work and pure grace—to be received on the human side, just as Mary received the new life in her womb.

These concluding thoughts usher in the large issue which has repeatedly surfaced in early chapters but which must be treated in proper detail: Christ's work as Saviour.

12
Redeemer

❧ ❦

Love makes us give ourselves as far as possible to our
friends.

(St Thomas Aquinas, *Summa theologiae*)

As was noted back in Chapter 1, the salvific work of Christ
('Christ for us') is not properly separable from his person and
being ('Christ in himself'). Considerations about that salvific
work have repeatedly surfaced in the intervening chapters.
Nevertheless, soteriology invites our undivided attention. A
problem is created, however, by our Jewish-Christian
sources.

Both the OT and the NT abound with salvific terms,
themes, and images. Either directly or indirectly, almost every
page of the Bible has something to say about salvation and/or
the human need for it. Post-NT liturgical texts of all kinds are
shaped around redemptive language. Whereas controversies
and official teaching about Christ's person helped to establish
clear terminology in Christology, such conciliar clarification
has never taken place in soteriology. Nevertheless, theological
debates and official teaching over original sin, grace, the salvation of the non-baptized, justification, the Eucharist, and
the other sacraments naturally raised questions about
Christ's salvific work or at least about its appropriation.
Yet no period of Christianity can claim to have produced a
truly unified systematic soteriology. It could be argued that
variety in this sector is even more appropriate than it is in
Christology.

The pages that follow will present a brief account of the
human need for salvation, expound several major positions
on Christ's salvific work, and conclude by developing the

theme of love as the most promising key to salvation.[1]

The Human Need

Views of Christ's redemptive work obviously depend upon the way we understand the evil that affects the human condition (what we are to be saved from), as well as the possibilities of the divine–human relationship (what we are to be saved for).

The evil from which human beings suffer can be assessed as (1) alienation: all kinds of alienation from oneself (the divided self), from other human beings, from the world (lack of harmony with nature), and from God. At any level and in any relationship a painful and inappropriate separation or alienation calls for some remedy. (2) Death in all its forms can be named as a second way of expressing the evil which we endure. Not only biological death itself but also sickness, war, bondage in many shapes, losses of all kinds, and further evils function as 'deadly' forces from which we long to be saved. (3) We can group together ignorance, false beliefs, and a feeling of absurdity as a third way in which evil plagues the human condition. Meaning and truth can be painfully absent.

Thus evil can be cast in terms of (1) deficient or even ruptured relationships, (2) loss or even annihilation of being, and (3) absence of meaning and truth. Naturally the realities from which human beings suffer are far more complicated and painful than these labels. Yet we need some such labels whenever we want to give an account of the evil that Christ's redemptive work saves us from. We may even fall back here on the classic notion of evil as the absence of good: the absence of appropriate relationships, of life, and of meaning and truth.

The basic evil from which Christ delivers human beings is, of course, sin, which has often been defined as a personal

---

[1] See F. W. Dillistone, *The Christian Understanding of Atonement* (London: Nisbet, 1968); C. E. Gunton, *The Actuality of the Atonement* (Edinburgh: T. & T. Clark, 1988); A. J. Hultgren, *Christ and his Benefits: Christology and Redemption in the New Testament* (Philadelphia: Fortress, 1987); G. Lanczkowski *et al.*, 'Heil und Erlösung', *TRE* xiv. 605–37; J. McIntyre, *The Shape of Soteriology* (Edinburgh: T. & T. Clark, 1992); K. Rahner *et al.*, 'Salvation', in K. Rahner *et al.* (eds.), *Sacramentum mundi* (6 vols.; London: Burns & Oates, 1968–70), v. 405–38.

and intentional transgression of the divine will. Just as with
evil, we can interpret sin in terms of broken relationships,
lost being, and absence of meaning. (1) Divine love bestows
on us our personal value and identity, so that each of us can
say, 'I am the person God loves.' Sin then constitutes the most
critical alienation from God, self, and others. In Augustine's
language, it signifies a disordered love for oneself which
excludes love for God (*De civitate Dei*, 14. 28). One of Jesus'
most memorable parables begins by representing sin as a
younger son leaving his father's home and going away into a
far country (Luke 15: 13). Alienated from his father, he is
also alienated from himself; he must first 'come to himself'
(Luke 15: 17) before he can return to his father and family.
In the opening pages of the Bible sinful alienation quickly
reaches a climax of indifference and hatred when Cain
murders his brother Abel. Sin entails a rupture in relationship, above all with God. (2) The Scriptures record a variety
of insights about death, including, not surprisingly, the recognition that it can be the natural, normal end of a long and
fruitful life (e.g. Gen. 25: 7–11).[2] They also understand death
to have become the consequence and sign of sin (e.g. Gen. 2:
17; 3: 19; Wis. 2: 23–4; Rom. 5: 12; 6: 23). Paul identifies sin
as an enslaving force which also 'works death' in human
beings here and now (Rom. 7: 10–11, 13). (3) Lastly, sin
can be evaluated as culpable meaninglessness, falsity, and
injustice in action. What is meaningful and truthful is swept
aside when sin disturbs the proper balance of rights and
duties. Some sins like those of pride and avarice stand out
easily for their inherent absurdity, while others like racism
stand out for their sheer untruthfulness. All sins are simply
not right and rise up against the just order of things.

Apropos of evil and sin a great deal more could be added.[3]

---

[2] See K. H. Richards and N. R. Gulley, 'Death', *ABD* ii. 108–11; U. Vanni,
'Dalla morte "nemico" alla morte "guadagno" (lo sviluppo della concezione della
morte in Paolo', *Studia missionalia*, 31 (1982), 37–60.

[3] See R. C. Cover and E. P. Sanders, 'Sin, Sinners', *ABD* vi. 31–47; J. B. Hygen,
'Böse, Das', *TRE* vii. 8–17; W. E. May, 'Sin', in J. Komonchak *et al.* (eds.), *The
New Dictionary of Theology* (Wilmington, Pa.: Michael Glazier, 1987), 954–67; P.
Ricœur, 'Evil', in M. Eliade (ed.), *Encyclopedia of Religion*, v (London: Collier
Macmillan, 1987), 199–208; P. Schoonenberg and K. Rahner, 'Sin', in *Sacramentum
mundi*, vi. 87–94.

A comprehensive treatment would include, for instance, the issues of collective evil and sin, original sin, and structural sin, as well as the evil and sin from which nature suffers. At the same time, at least some points of reference have been offered about the basic human need for deliverance from evil and sin. Images, themes, and elaborated positions on the deliverance effected by Christ can largely be seen to match the three approaches to evil and sin outlined above.

Christ's Saving Work

Despite the rich variety in biblical, liturgical, and other traditional language for salvation, a triple classification covers much of what is offered. (1) Pauline and Johannine theology converges in pronouncing the divine love to be the major key to redemption. Whether thought of collectively (e.g. John 3: 16–17; Rom. 5: 8; 2 Cor. 5: 14–15; 1 John 4: 9–10) or more personally (e.g. Gal. 2: 20), God's initiative of love clarifies the story of salvation. Even though some classical NT passages on redemption do not explicitly appeal to the divine love (e.g. Luke 15: 3–32), they remain unintelligible if that love is ignored.

The same point applies to various relationships which supply the NT with salvific images: parents/children (e.g. Luke 15: 11–32; John 11: 52; see Luke 13: 34 = Matt. 23: 37), bridegroom/bride (e.g. Eph. 5: 25–7; Rev. 21: 2, 9–10), friends (e.g. John 15: 13, 15), and the teacher who wishes to found a new family by turning his students into his brothers, his sisters, and even his mother (Mark 3: 35). None of these images for the redemptive process can be properly appreciated if we neglect the divine love revealed and at work in Christ. We also need to recall love when expounding other salvific relationships invoked by the NT: for instance, the high priest in deep solidarity with those he represents (Heb. 4: 15), the merciful 'doctor' at table with the sinful 'sick' (Mark 2: 15–17), and the dedicated shepherd who knows all his sheep by name and is ready even to die for them (John 10: 1–16).

It is at our peril that we reflect on central biblical versions of redemption as reconcilation, adoption, and covenant without appealing to the divine love. The context for Paul's two classic passages on God's reconciling activity (Rom. 5: 10–11; 2 Cor. 5: 18–20) evokes the love which has moved God to seek reconciliation with sinners (Rom. 5: 5, 8; 2 Cor. 5: 14). God's desire to introduce adopted sons and daughters (e.g. John 1: 12–13; Rom. 8: 29; Gal. 4: 4–6) into the divine life and family cannot be appreciated so long as we leave love out of the picture. Lastly, only those who play down its profound intimacy will fail to acknowledge how 'the new covenant' effected by Christ's redemptive death and resurrection is nothing if not a covenant of love (e.g. 1 Cor. 11: 25; Heb. 9: 15).

My first major christological work, *Interpreting Jesus*, was constructed around its longest section, the chapter on redemption. That chapter highlighted the divine love, but a re-examination shows me how much more there is to say. Such biblical notions of redemption as the gift of the Holy Spirit, deification, and transformation into the divine image, for example, fail to yield their full meaning whenever the divine love is left out of consideration. If we make only a perfunctory nod towards love, the 'extraordinary exchange' (*admirabile commercium*) that the Greek and Latin Fathers cherished as the key to salvation remains less than adequately interpreted.

2. As was recalled in Chapter 8, the theme of victorious conflict established itself from the beginning as a major interpretative key for redemption. This was hardly surprising, since Christ's death and resurrection took place during the days when Jews celebrated their exodus from Egypt, God's delivering them from slavery to freedom. During his ministry Jesus himself had already presented his exorcising activity as a victorious conflict with satanic powers (e.g. Mark 3: 27). In the post-Easter situation various NT authors followed suit by expounding Christ's salvific work as a triumph over and deliverance from the forces of evil: sin, death, and diabolic powers (e.g. John 16: 33; 1 Cor. 15: 24–6; Col. 2: 14–15; Rev. 19: 11–16). In place of slavery and death, Christ brought freedom and life. A sense of the paradoxical nature of this triumph emerged already in the NT imagery about the victory of the lamb who was slain (Rev. 5: 6–14; 17: 14).

Traditional language—especially, liturgical language—in the post-NT Church cherished the theme of Christ's redemptive victory and its paradoxical nature. Augustine of Hippo declared: 'slain by death, he slew death' (*In Ioannem*, 12. 10–11). The classical hymns of Venantius Fortunatus and even more the Easter sequence of Wipo, 'Victimae paschali', celebrated Christ's salvific battle, that 'wonderful duel in which death and life fought'. In the Anglo-Saxon poem *The Dream of the Rood* and other medieval religious poetry, Christ appeared as the heroic warrior who fell in seeming defeat but whose gallant resistance carried the day. For many Christians the image of redemption as victory stays alive in the *Exultet* or Easter Proclamation, sung or recited every Holy Saturday night: 'This is the night in which Christ, breaking the bonds of death, rose victorious from the tomb.'

3. A third version of redemption is built around Christ as priest and victim who, in the last supper, death, and resurrection, offers, once and for all and as our representative ('for us'), the sacrifice which expiated sin and brought the new covenant between God and the human race. The Letter to the Hebrews develops massively this version of redemption. Some of its elements, perhaps surprisingly few of them, are found elsewhere in the NT (e.g. Mark 14: 22–5; John 1: 36; Rom. 3: 24–5; 1 Cor. 5: 7; 11: 23–6).[4]

Sacrifice, a key term here, can bear a broader, non-cultic meaning: the obedient self-sacrifice in life (Rom. 12: 1) which involves personal loss and even violent death. The Suffering Servant of Isaiah 53 exemplifies that heroic obedience to the divine will of an innocent person whose sufferings can expiate the sins of others. In its strict sense sacrifice is a cultic action, which takes place in a sacred place (e.g. the Jerusalem temple) and through which some pure victim or offering is 'made holy' and transferred to God (e.g. by being burnt or poured out, or—as in the case of a bloody sacrifice—by being slain). Through such cultic sacrifice something is symbolically

---

[4] See G. A. Anderson and H.-J. Klauck, 'Sacrifice and Sacrificial Offerings', *ABD* v. 871–91; J. Henninger, 'Sacrifice', in *Encyclopedia of Religion*, xii. 544–57; R. H. McLean, 'The Absence of an Atoning Sacrifice in Paul's Soteriology', *New Testament Studies*, 38 (1992), 531–53; O. Semmelroth and L. Scheffczyk, 'Sacrifice', in *Sacramentum mundi*, v. 388–94.

'given' to God, even though human beings cannot, properly speaking, confer a benefit upon God. In fact, it is God and only God who can truly make things holy and sacred (*sacrum facere*). Furthermore, we should not take a narrow view of cult, forgetting that cultic worship goes beyond sacrifice. Even if the liturgy of sacrifice is the high point of cult, liturgy is not necessarily and always sacrificial in its nature. Sacrifice itself may, as in the case of Christ, expiate sins, and inaugurate a new covenant. Despite the importance of these effects, however, sacrifice can include other such features as adoration, praise, thanksgiving, and intercession.

These clarifications can serve to introduce hard questions inevitably raised by this third version of redemption. Did God directly mandate the violent death of Christ? Was the bloody sacrifice on Calvary necessary to placate the divine anger? What gave Christ's death and resurrection its sacrificial value and its power to expiate sins?

Here there should be no tampering with what we recalled above: the central NT conviction that the whole project of redemption derived from the loving, reconciling forgiveness of God. Paul does not write: 'when we were still sinners and enemies, God was angry with us and wanted retribution before forgiving us' (see Rom. 5: 8, 10). The apostle stresses rather the divine love in that the Son of God came/was sent and died for those who were not yet reconciled. The NT does speak of the divine anger, for instance, in terms of the destructive consequences of sin (Rom. 1: 18–32), but never in the context of Jesus' passion and death. Only a determined 'eisegesis' can read God's anger into the cry of abandonment on the cross (Mark 15: 34). Rather than allowing that God directly willed Christ's atrocious suffering and death, we should think of the passion and crucifixion as the inevitable consequences of Jesus' loving fidelity to his mission which he lived out for us in a cruel and sinful world (see Gal. 1: 4). Centuries earlier in his *Republic* Plato anticipated what human beings would do to an imaginary 'saint'—a perfectly just person: 'the just man will have to be scourged, racked, fettered, blinded, and, finally, after the most extreme suffering, he will be crucified' (361e–362a). With Christ there came among us not merely a perfectly just person but also one who was perfectly loving and good. His complete and conspicuous dedication to the divine will and the redemption of humanity inevitably put him on collision course with murderous men and made his violent death in that sense 'necessary'.

It is not that the atrocious suffering Christ underwent simply has value in and of itself. Being tortured to death just as such redeems no one. The issue changes, however, since it was loving and obedient self-giving which put Christ into the hands of his killers. His total innocence and his divine identity gave unique value to his self-sacrifice, which he had interpreted in advance at the last supper. By raising him from the dead and glorifying him, God accepted and 'made holy' this victim, the high priest who thus entered into the heavenly sanctuary (Heb. 8: 2; 9: 24).

All said and done, there is no excessive difficulty in recognizing how Christ mediated representatively a new and final covenant between human beings and God. That his death and resurrection expiated sin on our behalf is, however, much more resistant to any explanation. How could Christ have expiated and made reparation for sins on our behalf?

Before offering some answer, we should first ask: what does sin do to us, our world, and God? As an offence against God, sin does wrong to God. It cannot literally harm God, except in the sense of harming the incarnate Son of God. Over and above hostility to God, sin does harm to others, to the world, and to ourselves. At the human level situations damaged by sin need to be set right even after sinners have repented and received pardon. Between human beings matters of injustice call for reparation. Wrongdoers may have to transfer some truly costly good to their victims. Within ourselves recovery after sin can involve a painful and long readjustment. God is always ready to forgive but does not do violence to our human condition by abruptly rehabilitating us through overpowering grace.

But what of sin precisely as guilty alienation from God? What sense does it make to talk of Christ on our behalf making reparation for the sins we have committed against God? Any idea that God 'needs' reparation either from us or from our representative should be banished, as should the idea that there is some kind of moral order which is above

God and to which God must conform by requiring reparation. Christ expiates and makes reparation for sin in the
sense of definitively 'dealing with' sin and the sinful world.
As victim of our wrongdoing he provides us wrongdoers with
the means of rising above our sins, being made righteous
and sharing as adopted sons and daughters in God's own
existence. The life, death, and resurrection of Christ (with
the gift of the Spirit) inaugurate the new world that promises
to take us beyond sin and all its power.

This powerful dealing with sin occurs paradoxically
through the 'weakness' of the cross (2 Cor. 13: 4). The self-
giving love with which Christ accepted his passion prevails
over the worst of human malice. He conquers sin through
the powerful 'weakness' of love. Yet, as Eberhard Jüngel
warns, given the 'weakness' of love and the apparently
'superior force of lovelessness', one 'can only believe in this
victory of love ... over everything which is not love'.[5]

This brings us back to the primary key to Christ's salvific
work: love. We should not let ourselves be intimidated by
rightful criticism of inadequate accounts of love. A mod-
erately far-reaching analysis of love will illuminate the
redemption effected by Christ.[6]

Saved by Love

The reality of love is far more complicated than any instant
labels might suggest. A detailed analysis must be expected
from those who claim the centrality of love in God's salvific
project. At least eight themes will enter into that analysis.
Before examining these various aspects of divine love,
however, two relevant prolegomena should be indicated.

First, the Johannine proposition, 'God is love' (1 John 4: 8,
16), represents love as constituting God's being. The classic
axiom about activity following being (*operari sequitur esse*)

---

[5] E. Jüngel, *God as the Mystery of the World* (Grand Rapids: Eerdmans, 1983),
339–40.
[6] On love see P. Gerlitz *et al.*, 'Liebe', *TRE* xxi. 121–91; Jüngel, *God as the
Mystery of the World*, 299–343; E. McDonagh, 'Love', in *The New Dictionary of
Theology*, 602–16; G. O'Collins, *Retrieving Fundamental Theology* (London:
Geoffrey Chapman, 1993), 120–8.

would suggest that love also constitutes then God's redemptive doing. Second, the Johannine literature (John 1: 3–4, 9–18), along with other NT witnesses (e.g. Col. 1: 15–20; Heb. 1: 2–3), associates redemption with creation. As Hans Hübner interprets the christological hymn in Colossians, creation is there 'for the sake of redemption'.[7] The incarnate Logos who mediates the divine revelation and redemption was already the agent of creation. Paul led the way in identifying the One through whom the world was created in the beginning (1 Cor. 8: 6). The mystery of love that was creation reaches its climax at redemption, with both creation and redemption coming through the same agent.

   1. Let me begin my analysis of love by highlighting love's unconditional approval. Love accepts, affirms, and approves whatever or whoever it loves. It delights in and agrees to the beloved being there: 'it is good that you exist. I want you to exist.' Love's approval entails the firm desire that the beloved should never go out of existence. To say to someone 'I love you' is, in terms of the classic insight from Gabriel Marcel, to say to that person: 'you must not die; you must live forever.'[8] Love's profound approval cannot tolerate the idea of the beloved no longer being there.

   According to the priestly account of creation, God saw the goodness of everything that was made—above all, the goodness of human beings made in the divine image and likeness (Gen. 1: 26–7). In and through love God deeply approved of us and our world, saying, in effect, to all humanity: 'it is good that you exist. I want you to exist.'

   The loving approval of God brings with it even more, something that human love alone can never achieve: the fullness of life forever. The divine love, deployed in creation and redemption, is more powerful than death (Cant. 8: 6–7). It not only delivers us from death but also holds out a new, transformed, and definitive life to come.

   2. My second observation concerns the way reason alone

---

   [7] H. Hübner, *Biblische Theologie des Neuen Testaments*, ii: *Die Theologie des Paulus und ihre neutestamentliche Wirkungsgeschichte* (Göttingen: Vandenhoeck & Ruprecht, 1993), 352.

   [8] See G. Marcel, *The Mystery of Being*, trans. G. S. Fraser and R. Hague, ii (London: Harvill Press, 1950–1), 153.

can never fully account for the choice and intensity of love, either at the divine or at the human level. Of course, love is never unmotivated. We can always point to reasons which help to explain the choice, for example, of one's marriage partner or one's profession. But by themselves rational motives can never completely explain and justify love and its activity. Being a supremely free act, love is never compelled but always has something gratuitous about it. It is a mysterious act of freedom which is creatively self-determining and cannot be purely commanded, coerced, or simply controlled by other factors—not even the force of reason. Unquestionably we run up against a mystery here. How can a loving action be rational and yet not be fully clarified or at least justified by reason? What happens when love leads someone to do things that go beyond the merely reasonable?

There is mystery in this vision of the interplay of reason and love. Nevertheless, the alternative—love being simply and totally controlled by reason alone—would obviously rob love of that spontaneity which we associate with it and which is suggested by the parable of the labourers in the vineyard (Matt. 20: 1–16). In that story the way in which the owner is more generous to the latecomers is not unjust, but it illustrates a divine generosity that reason by itself could not fully justify. Love is a self-gift which goes beyond reason and the sheerly reasonable.

One can assign some reasons for God's original act of creation. Yet mystery remains when we attempt to answer the question: why did God create? It was and is a mysterious act of loving, divine freedom to create and from moment to moment sustain in existence all the things that have been created. Still less can we account in a merely rational way for the mystery of God's love that promises us resurrected life with the new heaven and the new earth. Reason alone cannot explain the love already shown in creation and in the mystery of redemption and its coming consummation.

3. A third major feature of love, whether human or divine, is its creative and re-creative activity. To begin with, love is creative: it gives life and brings into existence that which has not yet existed. The procreation and raising of children offer the classic example of this generative characteristic of love.

But the medical and teaching professions, the pastoral ministry, and the work of artists, writers, and architects also
provide rich insights into the life-giving, creative force of
love. Love creates new being. Without love nothing would be
at all. In the beginning God showed infinite love by creating
the universe and its centre, human beings. God's overflowing
goodness gave birth and gives birth to everything that is. All
created reality is the fruit and expression of the divine love.
In Augustine's words, 'because God is good, we exist'.[9]

If God's love is the key to the creation and conservation of
the world, all the more should it be seen as the key to the new
creation of all things in redemption and its final consummation. Divine love lay behind the original creation when
God gave life to what had not yet existed. *A fortiori* love lies
behind the new creation in which God gives and will give
new, transformed, and definitive life to what once existed but
has died.

From the classic OT prophets on, love has proved a central
theme for expressing God's redeeming activity on our behalf.
The divine love sets us free from the forces of evil; it heals
and transforms us.[10] Christians agree that redemption will
reach its consummation in the world to come. That is equivalent to saying that the activity of God's redeeming love will
reach its climax at the eschaton.

4. Love's activity, at its authentic best, is other-directed at
whatever cost to itself. This disinterested concern makes
those who love vulnerable. Fidelity to their love, or rather to
those whom they love, can prove costly, painful, and even
deadly. The sorrow brought by such faithful love comes
through what the merciful father says in the parable of the
prodigal son: 'this my son was dead' (Luke 15: 24; see 15:
32).

We may want to interpret creation itself in terms of love's
vulnerability. God put at least some of the works of creation
at risk by entrusting them to our stewardship. Christ's presence for human redemption involved him in his 'passion', a

[9] Augustine, *De doctrina cristiana*, 1. 32.
[10] In *God as the Mystery of the World* Jüngel expresses this way the transforming
power of God's love towards sinners: 'it makes what is totally unloveworthy into
something worthy of love. And it does that by loving it' (329).

word that in English and other modern languages signifies
not only suffering but also intense love. The term 'passion'
suggests how Christ enacted his own injunction about loving
one's enemies (Matt. 5: 44). His love even for his enemies
made him utterly vulnerable and weak; he died at their hands
and on their behalf.

5. Some words attributed to Jesus in John's Gospel point
us toward a fifth characteristic of love, its revelatory power.
First, Jesus says: 'he who loves me will be loved by my Father,
and I will love him and manifest myself to him' (John 14:
21). Then, a little later in the same final discourse, Jesus adds:
'I have called you friends, for all that I have heard from my
Father I have made known to you' (John 15: 15). Love means
self-manifestation and self-revelation. Here I am not referring to self-indulgent, endless chattering about one's sayings,
doings, and successes. Real love is different. When it breaks
out of itself to reveal itself, it does so with a self-sharing style
that is oriented towards and centred on other persons. We
constantly come across and experience the way love opens up
in marriage and deep friendship. Friends make known much
or even everything to other friends. We manifest ourselves to
those whom we love. In an unpretentious manner love is
always self-disclosive and self-communicative.

This fifth point closely attaches itself to the third, since
authentic self-revelation is always transforming and redemptive. Just as Jesus' own loving self-manifestation changed the
human situation for all, so disclosing oneself in love serves to
heal and save others. At the individual level of our interpersonal relationships, revelation is redeeming. To adapt St
John, our loving and freely manifested truth about ourselves
sets us and others free (see John 8: 32). At the universal
level of Jesus himself and his salvific 'work', revelation and
redemption are two sides of the same coin. God's self-revelation is essentially redemptive; and, vice versa, redemption
through the divine love must be known, in order to be effective or at least fully effective.

The Letter to Titus catches beautifully the deep relation
between revelation and salvation when it declares, 'the grace
of God has appeared for the salvation of all human beings'
(Tit. 2: 11). A few verses later this letter expresses the same

thought but in a way which attends more explicitly to the role of love in the divine self-revelation that has already occurred: 'when the goodness and loving kindness of God our Saviour appeared, he saved us' (Tit. 3: 4–5). Love has prompted the divine self-manifestation, a self-manifestation in Christ that has saved us.

Like other books of the NT the Letter to Titus associates revelation even more with the future, with what it calls 'the appearing of the glory of our great God and Saviour, Jesus Christ' (Tit. 2: 13). At the end no one will have to look hard to find God. Through the divine love we have already been made children of God. When Christ comes again, through the divine love both redemption and revelation will be consummated. As First John states, 'it does not yet appear what we shall be. But we know that when he appears, we shall be like him, for we shall see him as he is' (1 John 3: 2). The divine love which has already initiated the process of salvific self-disclosure will definitively complete its work at the end.

6. *Love reconciles and unites*. This sixth characteristic of love gets perfectly represented in the parable of the prodigal son, which would be more accurately called the parable of the merciful father (Luke 15: 11–32). The love of the father reaches out not only to welcome home the prodigal but also to cope with the bitterness of the elder son. Of its very nature love is a reciprocal force, and remains incomplete so long as its sentiments are not returned and there is not yet a full giving and receiving. During the first centuries of Christianity, the redemptive reciprocity of divine love, as we saw in Chapter 7, was expressed through the theme of the *admirabile commercium*: God became human so that we might become divine. In this century no one has done more to emphasize the essentially reciprocal nature of love than Maurice Nédoncelle (1905–76). For me to love someone necessarily means to hope that my feelings will be reciprocated. As Nédoncelle has argued well, this is not a question of selfishly trying to manipulate or coerce others into loving me. It is a matter of the very nature of love itself as reciprocal.[11]

---

[11] See M. Nédoncelle, *La Réciprocité des consciences* (Paris: Aubier, 1942); F. J. van Beeck, *God Encountered* (San Francisco: Harper & Row, 1989), 84–8.

The full communion of life which love entails does not mean a smothering union, still less a union that reduces or simply absorbs one of the parties. Love unites without being destructive. The greater the loving union, the more personal identity is safeguarded and the more our true selfhood is enhanced. In a striking way Jüngel describes the union of love that brings us to ourselves and does not destroy us: 'the beloved Thou comes closer to me than I have ever been able to be myself, and brings me to myself in a completely new way.'[12] Here the particularly happy example is the Blessed Trinity. The communion of love between the divine persons is supremely perfect; in no way does this union lessen the distinction of three persons within one godhead. They live together for each other and with each other, without disappearing into each other.

Love's reciprocity will be perfected when Jesus comes again. That will be the final home-coming, the welcome home which never ends. We recalled above the parable of the merciful father to illustrate the reconciling, reciprocal nature of love. We may use the same parable in an extended sense and speak of heaven as our finally coming home from a 'far country'. According to John's Gospel, Jesus puts it this way: 'when I go and prepare a place for you, I will come again and will take you to myself, that where I am you also may be' (John 14: 3).

This final, mutual, loving union with God through Christ will not destroy our individuality. God is going to be 'all in all' (1 Cor. 15: 28) but not in the sense of swallowing us up into the deity. On the contrary, our personal identity with its bodily history will be safeguarded and our true selfhood enhanced. At the end love will mean the highest possible union but not our disappearance back into the divine source from which we came.

7. The parable of the merciful father ends with those lovely words to his eldest son: 'it was fitting to make merry and be glad, for this your brother was dead, and is alive; he was lost, and is found' (Luke 15: 32). Joy inevitably accompanies love and all those occasions which in a particular way celebrate

---

[12] *God as the Mystery of the World*, 324.

and express interpersonal love: a baptism, a bar mitzvah, a wedding, an ordination, even a funeral. Joy is woven into the very texture of love. We happily join our special friends and joyfully take part in family reunions. There is no more obvious spin-off from love than joy.

The boundless joy that God's love holds out to/for us in redemption's consummation at the eschaton is expressed by the NT through two characteristic images: a marriage or a banquet. (Sometimes the images merge into a marriage banquet.) Jesus pictures the coming kingdom as a final feast: 'many will come from east and west and sit at table with Abraham, Isaac, and Jacob in the kingdom of heaven' (Matt. 8: 11). His parable of the watchful slaves contains the amazing reversal of roles: when he returns, their master himself will serve them at a late-night feast (Luke 12: 35–8). The Book of Revelation portrays our heavenly home, the new Jerusalem, as a beautiful bride coming to meet her spouse, Christ, the Lamb of God (Rev. 21: 2, 9–10). Those who 'are invited to the marriage feast of the Lamb' can only rejoice and be glad (Rev. 19: 9). Both now and even more at the end, God's redemptive love brings with it real joy.

To express the utterly joyful change which Christ and his love have brought and will bring, the NT uses the language not only of spousal relationship but also of friendship (e.g. John 15: 15) and filiation (e.g. Rom. 8: 29; Gal. 3: 26; 4: 5–7). Love and the joy of love run like a golden thread through all three kinds of relationships: the loving joy of spouses, of friends, and of children with their parents.

8. Finally, let me recall a theme especially associated with Augustine of Hippo: the connection between beauty and love. Beauty rouses our love; we love what is beautiful.[13] That theme, made familiar by Augustine's *Confessions* (10. 27), leaves us, however, with some important questions. Is the formal object of love not goodness but beauty? Can something be truly good without also being beautiful, or truly beautiful without also being good? Thomas Aquinas did not explicitly include beauty in his list of transcendentals—that is to say,

---

[13] See C. Harrison, *Beauty and Revelation in the Thought of Saint Augustine* (Oxford: Clarendon Press, 1992).

concepts which apply to all being. Nevertheless, he did argue that goodness and beauty, if logically distinguishable, coincide in fact.[14] His position encourages us to keep endorsing Augustine's conviction about our loving what is beautiful.

At present the divine beauty of the risen Lord redemptively stirs our love, even though it remains mysterious—visible only indirectly through sacramental and other signs, which include in a particular way human beings who suffer. In the world to come we shall see God as God is and shall live face to face with the divine beauty which is, as Augustine put it, 'the beauty of all things beautiful' (*Confessions*, 3. 6; see 9. 4). Contemplating the infinite beauty of God, we will freely but inevitably love God and others in God. The divine beauty will see to it that we are definitively redeemed by finally and fully obeying the commandment to love the Lord our God with all our heart and our neighbours as ourselves (see Mark 12: 30–1). The end of all things will vindicate the truth of Dostoevsky's dictum that 'beauty will save the world'.

This chapter has attended to Christ's saving work and has proposed love as the richest key for its interpretation. Undoubtedly one could say much more about salvation, love, and their interrelatedness. At least one theme, however, deserves special attention: Christ's saving work for those who have not accepted his message and very often have not even heard his message.

[14] On transcendentals see P. Sherry, *Spirit and Beauty: An Introduction to Theological Aesthetics* (Oxford: Clarendon Press, 1992), 43–5.

13
Universal Redeemer

⁂ ⁂

In a real sense, only one human being will be saved: Christ, the head and living summary of humanity.

(Pierre Teilhard de Chardin, *Le Milieu divin*)

That which is called the Christian religion existed among the ancients . . . from the beginning of the human race until Christ came in the flesh, at which time the true religion which already existed began to be called Christianity.

(St Augustine, *Retractationes*)

From its earliest to its later books, the NT does not waver in acknowledging Christ as the one Saviour for all people. The first Christians recognized his redemptive role to be universal (for all without exception), unique (without parallel), complete (as One who conveys the fullness of salvation), and definitive (beyond any possibility of being equalled, let alone surpassed, in his salvific function). In particular, his universal role means that through him sin is forgiven, the life of justification and grace is imparted, and the new existence as God's adopted children made available. This NT sense of Christ's indispensable and necessary role for human salvation could be summarized by a new axiom: *extra Christum nulla salus* (outside Christ no salvation). His all-determining place in the whole redemptive drama is suggested by the fact recalled in Chapter 6 above: the NT gives the title 'Saviour' only to God and Christ.

Paul insists that Christ died 'for all' without introducing any exception (2 Cor. 5: 14–15). Hence he can say that 'God was in Christ reconciling the world to himself' (2 Cor. 5: 19). In sharp contrast with the collective figure of Adam who brought sin and death to all human beings, the obedient Christ has led all to justification and life (Rom. 5: 12–21; 1 Cor. 15: 20–8, 45–9). In fact, this redemption will have its impact on the whole of creation (Rom. 8: 18–23). An early christological hymn quoted by a Deutero-Pauline letter emphatically expresses Christ's universal role, in both creation and redemption, through its refrain of 'all things' or its equivalent (Col. 1: 15–20). The conclusion of Matthew's Gospel attributes to the risen Christ the same all-embracing impact for human salvation: 'Jesus came and said to them, "All authority in heaven and on earth has been given to me. Go therefore and make disciples of all nations"' (Matt. 28: 18–19). Perhaps the classic NT verse in this regard comes from Peter's reiterated and exclusive claim about Jesus: 'there is salvation in no one else, for there is no other name under heaven given among human beings by which we must be saved' (Acts 4: 12). A (later) book of the NT highlights Jesus' unique mediatorship for all: 'there is one God, and there is one mediator between God and human beings, the man Christ Jesus who gave himself as a ransom for all' (1 Tim. 2: 5–6; see Mark 10: 45).

The Johannine literature uses its characteristic terms to affirm the universal relevance of Christ for revelation ('light', 'way', and 'truth') and salvation ('life'). He is 'the true light that enlightens every human being' (John 1: 9; see 9: 5). In his last discourse Jesus declares: 'I am the way, and the truth, and the life; no one comes to the Father, except through me' (John 14: 6). First John endorses the absolute nature of this claim ('*the* way, *the* truth, and *the* life . . . *no one*') in terms of Christ being the sole source of eternal life: 'God gave us eternal life and this life is in his Son. He who has the Son has life; he who does not have the Son of God does not have life' (1 John 5: 11–12).

Beyond question, the NT assertions about Christ's universal and unique function for salvation may seem arrogant and even outrageous. How can the particular Jewish Messiah of the first century prove eternally determinative as the way of salvation for all people of all times and places? How is Jesus of Nazareth *the* Word of God, *the* new/final Adam, and *the* Mediator of creation and redemption for everyone? Yet

without any embarrassment the Greek and Latin Fathers of
the Church maintained and elaborated these universal claims.
Back in Chapter 2 we recalled, for instance, Irenaeus'
development of a Pauline theme: as the second Adam, Christ
'recapitulated' human history in its entirety. Two centuries
later, in his *Oratio catechetica* (*magna*) Gregory of Nyssa saw
our 'deification' rooted in the fact that through his individual
human nature Christ entered into a kind of physical contact
with the whole human race. This was to acknowledge an
ontological unity of all humanity in Christ.

Both in the NT and subsequently, this vision of Christ's
universal significance left room, however, for a genuine
appreciation of the religious situation of those who did not
or could not consciously accept him as their saviour. A list of
heroes and heroines of faith, which reached its perfect climax
with Christ (Heb. 11: 1–12: 2), did not simply begin with
Abraham and Sarah (who set going the covenanted history
of the Jewish people), but reached back to Abel, Enoch, and
Noah (Heb. 11: 4–7). Thus this cloud of witnesses who were
to inspire Christian faith included also some who did not
share in the special history of promise that Christ brought to
its completion and consummation. In Paul's speech on the
Areopagus the NT left a further classic example of esteem
for religious traditions 'before' and 'outside' Christ (Acts 17:
22–31). The speech announced that, while the end of 'the
times of ignorance' had come with the message of Christ's
resurrection, this did not invalidate the Athenians' prior quest
for and experience of 'the unknown God'. In upholding the
fact of Christ's universal impact as Saviour without deni-
grating those who were not (or were not yet) aware of how
salvation worked, the NT followed a large-minded fairness
which had repeatedly surfaced in the OT. The subsequent
covenants with Abraham and Moses, so central to the special
salvation history of the Jews, did not nullify or abrogate the
universal covenant made through Noah not only with all
humanity but also with all living creatures (Gen. 9: 1–17).
That covenant with Noah remained firmly in place in a late
list of seven covenants that ended with David (Sir. 44–7).
The OT theme of such 'good pagans' as Melchisedek (Gen.
14: 18–20), the Queen of Sheba (1 Kgs. 10: 1–13), Ruth, and

Job laid the ground for holding together a universal call to faith in Christ as Saviour (Acts 4: 12) and a recognition of how the Holy Spirit also operates before that call can be effectively received (Acts 10: 1–11: 18). The Book of Jonah had already witnessed powerfully to God's loving concern for all people.

The rest of this chapter must grapple with the two questions that have already been introduced. How may one justify naming Jesus of Nazareth as universal redeemer—with all grace coming from him as head of humanity?[1] How then can one interpret redemption for those who did not or have not (yet) heard and accepted the NT message of light and life coming through Christ?

Universal Saviour

On any showing, claims about Jesus as the mediator of salvation for all people emerge from faith in him as risen from the dead. His resurrection has inaugurated the general resurrection to come at the end (Rom. 8: 29; 1 Cor. 15: 20–8). The passage in 1 Corinthians to which reference has just been made could hardly be clearer about the universal impact of the risen Christ and his saving work; repeatedly it speaks of what he will effect for 'all', for 'all things', and for 'everyone'. In his universal lordship he is present 'always'—right to the close of history (Matt. 28: 20). At the end he will be the saving goal for all men and women: as the universal judge (Matt. 25: 31–46) and the 'light' of the heavenly Jerusalem (Rev. 21: 23). Their ultimate destiny leads all human beings towards Christ. They are called to be raised like him, know him, and through him share in the divine life forever. In his glorified humanity he will remain the means by which the blessed know the Trinity and enjoy the fullness of salvation.[2] There can be no bypassing Christ when we come to the goal

---

[1] See the remarks on the *gratia capitis* in Aquinas' scheme (Ch. 9).

[2] See J. Alfaro, *Cristología y antropología* (Madrid: Ediciones Cristiandad, 1973), 170–82; K. Rahner, 'The Eternal Significance of the Humanity of Jesus for our Relationship with God', Th. Inv. iii. 35–46; B. Hebblethwaite, 'The Resurrection and the Incarnation', in P. Avis (ed.), *The Resurrection of Jesus Christ* (London: Darton, Longman & Todd, 1993), 155–70, at 162–3.

of salvation (and revelation). He will be there for everyone as Saviour (and revealer).

The teleological conviction that 'the end commands everything' goes hand in hand with a strong sense of Christ's universal salvific role here and now. To profess faith in his redemptive function for everyone at the end necessarily entails faith in his acting redemptively for all even now. Not only in the world to come but also in this present world Christ mediates salvation universally. It will be true and is already true that 'outside Christ there is no salvation'. We are all part of his saving story. At least five considerations serve to illuminate what might seem little more than a deduction from a teleological conviction.

1. In a central exposition of redemption Paul celebrates the Holy Spirit who delivers 'from the law of sin and death' and communicates life here and hereafter (Rom. 8: 1–27; the apostle invokes the Spirit sixteen times in this passage). 'The Spirit of Christ' (Rom. 8: 9) is there for all, Jews and Gentiles alike (Gal. 3: 2–6: 8), to lead them to 'eternal life' (Gal. 6: 8). One cannot 'have' the Spirit without being *in Christ* a son or daughter of God (Gal. 4: 4–7). More clearly than Paul, Luke (e.g. Acts 2: 33) and John (e.g. John 7: 37–9; 19: 30, 34; 20: 22) present the Spirit as given by the crucified and risen Christ (and his Father). As the Cornelius episode illustrates in Acts 10, the Spirit of Christ operates beyond the community of baptized believers to bring others to Christ. The universal presence and impact of the Spirit enacts the universal relevance of Christ's redemptive work. Active everywhere, the Holy Spirit relates the whole history of humanity to Christ and vice versa. To share in the Spirit is to share in the new sonship and daughtership effected by Christ.[3]

Some theologians have developed what amounts to the same argument but have done so through the themes of grace, divine self-communication, or justification. They argue, for

---

[3] See G. D'Costa, 'Christ, the Trinity and Religious Plurality', in G. D'Costa (ed.), *Christian Uniqueness Reconsidered* (Maryknoll, NY: Orbis Books, 1990), 19; K. Rahner, *Foundations of Christian Faith*, trans. W. V. Dych (London: Darton, Longman & Todd, 1978), 316–18. In *Grace: The Gift of the Holy Spirit* (Sydney: Catholic Institute of Sydney, 1979), David Coffey develops the thesis that it is precisely because of the relationship to Jesus that the Holy Spirit is the Spirit who brings about graced sonship and daughtership.

instance, that since God's grace is offered to all and since all grace comes from (and leads to) Christ, through the universal offer of grace Christ is redemptively present to all. The argument is almost tautological. Since Christ is the prototype of our grace and since grace means a new likeness to Christ that turns human beings into God's sons and daughters in the Son, grace necessarily entails the presence of Christ. Thus the universality of grace bespeaks the universal role of Christ as Saviour here and now. Once we agree that there is no grace apart from the grace of Christ, even as there is no Holy Spirit apart from the Spirit of Christ, we must draw the universal conclusion: no one can experience the offer of salvation without experiencing, however obscurely, the presence of Christ as redeemer. Any and every acceptance of saving grace and the Holy Spirit, whenever it takes place, is an acceptance of Christ. There is no zone 'outside Christ', since there is no zone 'outside' grace and the Holy Spirit. All experience of salvation is christological.[4] Jesus' preaching of the kingdom also underpins this conclusion.

2. Chapter 3 mustered evidence to show that during his earthly ministry Jesus linked with *his own person* the presence and coming of God's kingdom. The same chapter also pointed to the universal dimension that emerged in Jesus' preaching of the kingdom. His immediate audience was found in 'the lost sheep of the house of Israel', but he also looked beyond them to all those who would come 'from east and west' into God's kingdom (Matt. 8: 11). The resurrection, as Chapter 4 argued, among other things authenticated Jesus' claims. Here we should not fail to advert to the fact that this vindication validated his claim to be in person the agent of a divine kingdom that is and will be all-inclusive—or, in other words, the agent of universal salvation.

3. The incarnation also bears on this issue. Through his incarnation Christ moved into historical solidarity with all human beings, as well as with the created world. He entered history to become, in a sense, every man and every woman. Hereafter to receive divine grace through other men and

---

[4] Thus Rahner calls Christ 'absolute Saviour': see his *Foundations of Christian Faith*, 193–5, 204–6, 279–80, 318–21.

women and through the world would be to receive divine grace through the incarnate Christ. The story of the last judgement in Matthew 25 singles out strangers, hungry and thirsty people, the naked, the sick, and prisoners to support the point: not only in meeting and caring for those who suffer but also in being graced by them, we meet and are graced by Christ. By his incarnation 'the Son of God has in a certain way united himself with every human being' (*GS* 22)—to quote a key passage from the Second Vatican Council. Hence to experience and receive God's grace through other human beings is to experience and receive that grace through the incarnate Christ.

4. Unlike the O T, the N T does not have much to say about creation. But in the little that is said Christ, identified as the Son or the Word, takes over the role attributed by Jewish theology to the divine word and wisdom. He is acknowledged to be the agent of creation: 'all things were created *through* him and for him. He is before all things, and in him all things hold together' (Col. 1: 16–17; see John 1: 1–4, 10; Heb. 1: 3; 1 Cor. 8: 6). Despite their different nuances, these texts agree that through Christ all things were created. They confess him as the universal and exclusive agent of creation. This belief underpins a conclusion about Christ's universal role in salvation. Wherever the created world and its inner and outer history mediate God's grace, those who receive this saving grace are in fact receiving it through Christ. As divine agent of creation, Christ also brings the grace of God through the external world and the inner experience of human beings. Christ's agency, through his sharing in the divine nature (and not, as I insisted several times in Chapter 10, through his humanity (which came into existence around 5 BC)), is as broad and old as creation itself.

The sense of Christ as the creative Word, who is present from the beginning, sustains all things, and permeates all things, almost became a normative theme for the Greek Fathers from Justin to Athanasius of Alexandria and beyond (see Chapters 2 and 7 above). They followed and expanded the N T teaching by appreciating the revealing and redeeming presence of the Word or *Logos spermatikos* in the whole cosmos and all history. In their version of things, the salvation offered to those living before Christ came through the Word of God who was to be made flesh in the fullness of time. As agent of creation the Word was and is always present, at least as a seed (*spermatikōs*), in every human being. Thus those who lived before the incarnation were nourished by the divine truth and set on the way of salvation by the Word of God.

5. Talk of the divine Word brings us to what forms the ultimate ground for maintaining Christ's universal role as the life of salvation (and the light of revelation). As divine, Christ is universally present, actively influencing the mediation of redemption to all. Those who profess faith in his divinity have no choice but to acknowledge also his universal role for salvation.

Christ and Non-Christians

What then of the religions of the world and, even more broadly, the situation of those many millions of people who did not and have not (yet) heard and accepted the message of salvation through Christ?[5] We can extend Luke's language of the 'unknown God' (Acts 17: 23) to speak of the unknown Christ who has been and is effective everywhere and in all history, albeit often hiddenly. He mediated the fullness of revelation and salvation through particular historical events. Yet he is more than a simple reality of the temporal and spatial order. He is effectively present in all creation and history, yet not in a way that depersonalizes him and reduces him to being a mere 'Christ idea' or universal principle. Salvation and revelation come personally—through the divine person who became incarnate as Jesus of Nazareth.

---

[5] See D'Costa (ed.), *Christian Uniqueness Reconsidered, passim*; M. Dhavamony, 'The Cosmic Christ and World Religions', *Studia missionalia*, 42 (1993), 179–225; J. Dupuis, *Jesus Christ at the Encounter of World Religions*, trans. R. R. Barr (Maryknoll, NY: Orbis Books, 1991); P. Phan, 'Are there Other "Saviors" for Other Peoples? A Discussion of the Problem of the Universal Significance and Uniqueness of Jesus the Christ', in P. Phan (ed.), *Christianity and Wider Ecumenism* (New York: Paragon House, 1990), 163–80. On Christ and non-Christians see K. Rahner's many relevant chapters in different volumes of Th. Inv.: e.g. in v–vi, ix–x, xii–xiv, xvi–xviii, xxi; and G. D'Costa, 'Other Faiths and Christianity', in A. E. McGrath (ed.), *The Blackwell Encyclopedia of Modern Christian Thought* (Oxford: Blackwell, 1993), 411–19.

The universal presence of Christ has been thematized in three ways, which have their deep OT roots (see Chapter 2). He is present through the Spirit, as Word, and as Wisdom. The function of the Holy Spirit as vital principle or 'soul' of the Church (see 1 Cor. 6: 19) in no way excludes the presence and activity of the Spirit beyond the Christian community. While being the primary agent in carrying out the mission of the Church, the Holy Spirit's influence extends everywhere. The mysterious working of the Spirit offers everyone the possibility of sharing in the saving grace brought by Christ's dying and rising (*GS* 22), as Vatican II observes. Earlier chapters and point (4) above have developed some lines of thinking about Christ's role as creative and redemptive Word before and beyond Christianity. In the present ethos we might gain more by clarifying that role through another image which Christians drew from their Jewish origins: the image of Lady Wisdom. At the end of three millennia of a strongly masculine consciousness reflected in the Bible, what might this feminine, nurturing image convey about Christ's salvific function for all people?

Chapter 2 recalled the NT and post-NT identification of Christ with Lady Wisdom. This partially neglected, feminine image helps to suggest the universal role of Christ, who invites and draws all to share in the divine banquet—like Lady Wisdom in Proverbs and other OT sapiential books. The Christian community has long been identified as 'Holy Mother the Church'. Within this visible, feminine community Christ has been primarily identified by his masculine qualities—as the 'Spouse' of the Church (e.g. Eph. 5: 21–33; Rev. 19: 7, 9; 21: 9). But the feminine image of Lady Wisdom catches his role beyond the visible community—in drawing, healing, and receiving, albeit anonymously, human beings around the world.

An obvious advantage about interpreting Christ's role of universal Saviour through the image of wisdom comes from the fact that the Jewish-Christian Scriptures and religion do not have a monopoly on wisdom. In one form or another, at least some wise teachings and ways of life turn up in all cultures, societies, and religions. Being found everywhere, sapiential modes of thought make an obvious bridge between

the adherents of Christianity and others. Christian faith can
see in all genuine wisdom the saving and revealing presence
of Christ: *ubi sapientia ibi Christus* (where wisdom is, there is
Christ). To recognize in Christ the full revelation of God and
the Saviour of all is not, then, to deny to other faith any true
knowledge of God and mediation of salvation. The unique
and normative role of Christ in the history of salvation
extends to the numerous and varied ways he works as divine
Wisdom in the lives of people who follow other religions and
receive salvation through them.

A persistent challenge for any efforts to correlate Christ,
the Church, and non-Christians comes from the conviction,
even if it is not always fully articulated, that some unfair
element lurks in the background. It is all too clear that life's
lottery does not distribute evenly life's blessings. There can
be no denying that public fact. But if we move our focus from
the merely human scene to our relationship with God, is it
fair that only a minority of the world's population consciously
know and accept Christ as their Saviour, while the majority
experience only his anonymous presence? Is it tolerable to
think of the incarnation as the full and explicit manifestation
of divine Wisdom in person at a particular point in human
history, while 'other' times and places have to be content
with partial and implicit manifestations of that Wisdom? In
response we might call attention to the mysterious freedom
of God's saving love (see the previous chapter). That love
discloses its presence in an endless variety of choices, ways,
degrees, and intensities. Love constitutes, as we have maintained, the heart of redemptive Christology. Active presence
is its mode. To that we dedicate our closing chapter.

14
The Possibilities of Presence
❖ ❖

For Christ plays in ten thousand places,
Lovely in limbs, and lovely in eyes not his
to the Father through the features of men's faces.

(G. M. Hopkins, 'As Kingfishers Catch Fire')

Unquestionably the notion of presence recalls and even sum-
marizes many significant items which have surfaced in this
book. Much of what was handled, for instance, in the first
part (Chapters 2 to 9) involves this notion.

As the last Adam (Chapter 2), the head of a new humanity,
Christ is present wherever there are men and women. He is
priest-prophet-king for the whole world. Identifying him as
the divine Logos and Wisdom entails acknowledging his
all-pervasive presence in the universe. There neither is nor
can be any situation outside or without Christ. By creating
and sustaining the world, the Logos-Sophia intimately
accompanies everyone and everything.

Chapter 2 explored something of Jesus' Jewish background
and some topics in the OT Scriptures that fed into NT
christological thinking. We could have chosen further
themes: for example, God's fatherly/motherly love in repeatedly *delivering a suffering people* and the great public sign of
the divine nearness, *the Jerusalem temple*. Both in the OT
and when related to Christ, these two themes involve a deep
sense of his universal presence. Through the new temple of
his risen existence (John 2: 20–1), Christ functions as the
Saviour not only for his own people but also for the entire
world (John 4: 42).

The incarnation and then his public ministry (Chapter 3)

communicated Christ's presence (the divine presence) in a new way which went beyond his self-communication in the creation of the world and history of the chosen people (see 1 Cor. 10: 1–5; John 12: 39–41). Both in his preaching and in his further activity, Jesus showed himself inseparably connected with the inbreaking of the divine kingdom. With his person, God's rule had come and was coming. His powerful presence brought the divine kingdom close to all.

The message of the kingdom, as we also saw in Chapter 3, led to the mystery of Christ's passion. His trial and crucifixion, among other things, dramatized a striking feature of the ministry: his healing presence to sinners and the suffering. His death on Calvary between two criminals symbolized for all time his close solidarity with those who suffer and die, an anonymous identification with human pain expressed also by Matthew's parable of the last judgement (Matt. 25: 31–46).

Chapter 4, in dealing with the redemptive impact of Christ's resurrection, noted the NT conviction about the universal nature of the salvation mediated through the crucified and risen Christ. It is not simply a mission that must go out to all nations (Matt. 28: 19; Luke 24: 47). The risen Christ is present to exercise his saving power over 'all' persons and 'all' things (1 Cor. 15: 20–8). The divine Lord, who is present to the whole universe and merits the worship of all (Phil. 2: 10–11), has poured out his Holy Spirit on the whole world (Acts 2: 33). The post-resurrection role of Christ in sending the Spirit, as examined in Chapter 6 above, constitutes a further aspect of his cosmic presence. The Co-sender of the Holy Spirit is present wherever his Spirit is present, and that is everywhere (see Chapter 13).

Chapter 6 also touched the function of the Spirit as the vital principle of the Church. Through the sacraments, Scriptures, preaching, teaching, members, and ministers of this new Easter community, the Spirit mediates the presence of the crucified and risen Christ. With the eucharistic invocation (the *epiclēsis*) and the words of institution, the Spirit descends upon the gifts to change them and bring about the intense and real presence of Christ for the Church and the world. In this way a Christology of presence responds to the concern of Eastern Christians which was endorsed at the end of

Chapter 9: the need to approach Christology in an ecclesial, sacramental, eucharistic, and 'spiritual' (or pneumatic) way. In particular, the Eucharist forms the central sign of Christ's communing presence with his followers in self-gift.

Their ecclesial and personal experience of Christ's saving presence proved the driving force behind the theological debates about his person and natures which issued in the official teaching of the first seven councils (see Chapters 7 and 8). Having experienced Christ in the forgiveness of sins, the gift of the Holy Spirit, and the new life of grace in community, Christians asked themselves: what does this experience imply about Jesus' being and identity? What does he have to be as the cause, in order to save us in the way we have experienced (the effect)? They drew their conclusions about Jesus as the cause who was personally and intimately close to them and not absent elsewhere or far back in the past.

Chapter 9 reviewed medieval developments which would have been unthinkable without a vivid sense of Christ's personal presence: a new relationship to him as friend, mother, and lover; the renewed devotion to the Eucharist demonstrated in the establishment of the Feast of Corpus Christi. The same chapter also paid attention to major debates (at the time of the Reformation) which would have made no sense apart from a faith in and an experience of Christ's presence: where and how can I encounter Christ and his saving grace? What do the Eucharist and his eucharistic presence mean and effect?

The notion of presence weaves through these and other specific topics handled from Chapters 2 to 9. The same notion also entered, explicitly or implicitly, into the systematic treatment of Christology (Chapters 10 to 13). In upholding and reflecting on the divinity of Christ, Chapter 10 was in effect saying that, faced with him, people found and find themselves in the presence of the Holy One (see Mark 1: 24). His presence is numinous; he is holy, in the full sense of Rudolf Otto's 'mysterium tremendum et fascinans' (the fearful and fascinating mystery). Then the interpretation of evil and sin as alienation from oneself, from others, and from God obviously implies a loss of presence in each case. Such a loss of presence comes through the repeated words 'my son was lost' in the parable of the prodigal son (Luke 15: 24, 32). Christ's reconciling work as Saviour entails bringing about an end to this loss and a new presence to oneself, the world, and God (Chapter 12). In the same chapter the exposition of redemption as love would be inconceivable if it were to exclude personal presence. Some express Christ's universal role as revealer/redeemer, as we mentioned in the last chapter, through the theme of grace. This is the mystery of Christ's universal presence in creation, history, and our individual lives. A 'world of grace' is a world of Christ's gracious presence. The history of grace is the history of Christ's saving presence.[1]

To justify, however, the choice of presence as a notion capable of synthesizing a fully deployed Christology, it would not be enough simply to list all the places in this book where this notion appropriately fits in. We need first to analyse the notion and reality of presence. Then we will be in a position to exploit the possibilities of this notion for expounding more coherently faith in Christ as the universal Saviour who is at once truly divine and fully human. The reader can then have the chance of judging how attractive presence might be over against other organizing themes such as the true, the good, and the beautiful. The personal possibilities of presence have encouraged me to follow the line this chapter adopts.

Presence as Divine and Human

A major challenge to be faced in developing a Christology of presence comes from the fact that philosophers offer little help here. Over the centuries theologians have often taken advantage of the way philosophers have clarified a whole range of concepts, which—with the necessary adjustments made—could then be pressed into service to express Christian faith coherently and systematically. With the notion of presence, however, little philosophical analysis is available. This neglect is documented by the fact that major encyclopedias and dictionaries of philosophy rarely carry an entry

---

[1] See L. J. O'Donovan (ed.), *A World of Grace: An Introduction to the Themes and Foundations of Karl Rahner's Theology* (New York: Seabury, 1980).

on 'presence'.[2] From the time of Augustine, when offering a doctrine of God, theologians and philosophers have discussed the question of the divine omni-*presence*. In their theories of knowledge the medievals treated the presence of the object (and of truth) to the mind, the primordial unity between the subject knowing and object known. Edmund Husserl, Martin Heidegger, and other phenomenologists (including French phenomenologists of language) have paid some attention to the theme of presence. But, all in all, the theme has often been left alone by philosophers and handled rather by mystical and spiritual authors, who write of experiencing and cultivating the divine presence.[3] One can puzzle over and speculate about this relative silence from philosophers. Whatever the explanations, we need first to spell out at least some of the essential components of presence before applying the concept christologically.[4]

1. Among the most obvious characteristics of presence is

[2] P. Edwards (ed.), *Encyclopedia of Philosophy*, 8 vols. (London: Collier Macmillan, 1967) has no article on presence; there is no entry on 'Präsenz' (or on 'Gegenwart' for that matter) in H. Krings *et al.* (eds.), *Handbuch philosophischer Grundbegriffe*, 6 vols. (Munich: Kösel Verlag, 1973–4). 'Presenza' receives only one column in the eight-volume *Enciclopedia filosofica* published by the Centro di Studi Filosofici di Gallarate, vi (Florence: Lucarini, 1982), 790–1.

[3] In J. Ritter and K. Gründer (eds.), *Historisches Wörterbuch der Philosophie*, vii (Basle: Schwabe Verlag, 1971), under 'Präsenz' cols. 1259–65, T. Kobusch reports the relatively slight treatment of 'presence' in the history of philosophy; see also J. Hennig, 'Gegenwart', ibid. iii, cols. 136–8. One can add a few items to their treatment and bibliographies: e.g. L. Lavelle, *La Dialectique de l'éternel présent*, 4 vols. (Paris: Aubier, 1945–51); id., *La Présence totale* (Paris: Aubier-Éd. Montaigne, 1935). Postmodern, deconstructionist philosophers have been debating the theme of presence: see P. Gilbert, 'Substance et présence: Derrida et Marion, critiques de Husserl', *Gregorianum*, 75 (1994), 95–133.

[4] Christologies have largely neglected the theme of presence. One of the few exceptions is P. C. Hodgson, *Jesus: Word and Presence* (Philadelphia: Fortress, 1971), a work which interprets God as the primordial word-event and somewhat onesidedly proposes word as *the* medium of presence. Hans Frei (1922–88) touched on the theme of presence but his major contribution came through reading the Scriptures as realistic narrative. The theological neglect of presence is illustrated by the fact that the following standard dictionaries have no entry under 'presence': *Dictionnaire de théologie catholique*, *Dizionario teologico interdisciplinare*, *A New Dictionary of Christian Theology*, *The New Dictionary of Theology*, and *Sacramentum mundi*. Moreover, these reference works do not introduce a treatment of presence in their entries under either 'Christology' or 'Jesus Christ'. 'Presence' turns up, of course, in treatments of the sacraments, especially the Eucharist, and at times also in discussions of the liturgy: see e.g. K. Rahner, 'The Presence of the Lord in the Christian Community at Worship', Th. Inv. x. 71–83.

the way it implies 'presence to'. Being present always means being present to someone, something, or some event. 'I was present at Sabina's wedding'; 'I was present when the Westgate Bridge collapsed and fifteen people died.' In other words, presence entails 'being to' or 'being in relation', not simply 'being in itself'.

This 'being to' covers also one's presence to oneself, 'das Bei-sich-sein' as German philosophers would put it, or that coming to oneself which forms the nub of Thomist interpretations of knowledge.[5] The higher one's being, the more one can come to or return to oneself in knowledge. Self-knowing and being thus form a primordial 'presence to'; consciousness is being self-possessed or present to oneself.

2. Whether we deal with conscious self-presence (a relation of identity) or presence to others (a relation of difference), 'presence' is relational and 'happens' in relationship. That is almost the same thing as naming presence as essentially personal. Only persons can, properly speaking, be present, even if one must admit that faithful dogs can imitate and supply some of the better features of human presence.

In considering personal existence we argued that it should be primarily understood as being constituted by relationship to other persons (Chapter 10). The personal self can be self only in relation to other selves. Being personal means being relational, and here we may add: being personal means being present to other persons. Being in relation and being present express what it is to be personal. 'Presence' picks up two essential aspects of being personal: the togetherness or relationship to the other(s) and, at the same time, the distinction between each other. Without this distinction the communion and proximity would collapse into identity and we would no longer have two or more persons present *to* each other. In brief, presence signifies 'being with' but not 'being identical'.

3. As a (or rather the) form of self-bestowal, presence implies the exercise of personal freedom. We are truly present to those to whom we really wish to be present; in other words,

[5] See J. Maritain, *Degrees of Knowledge*, trans. G. B. Phelan (New York: Scribner, 1959); K. Rahner, *Hearer of the Word*, trans. R. Walls (London: Sheed & Ward, 1969).

we are and remain present to those whom we love.

4. The free self-giving that is interpersonal presence denotes a bringing together which effects a communion of life and love. The relationship of spouses to one another and that of parents to children spring to mind as paradigm examples of the loving communion of life brought about by interpersonal presence. In more or less dramatic ways, such active presence means sharing one's presence and enjoys results that are life-giving and life-enhancing—in a word, salvific. Where death signifies absence, life signifies presence and vice versa. One might adapt John 10: 10 to read: 'I came that they may have my presence and have it abundantly.' To enjoy the Lord's bountiful presence must mean to receive life in abundance.

5. Further, the mediation of presence calls for some attention. Our experience shows how personal presence can be mediated through words, events (e.g. phone-calls, faxes, voyages, meals, and embraces), and things (e.g. photographs, letters, and bodies). Between the divine persons of the Trinity presence is communicated immediately. But where presence involves human beings, it happens symbolically—through the mediation of our voices, our actions, and things which have some special connection with us: that is to say, it is always in some sense a mediated and never a strictly and exclusively immediate presence.

6. As much as anyone else, Gabriel Marcel has highlighted the differing qualities and modes of presence.[6] The relationships involved can be very various. Interpersonal presences can always be closer, more intense, more freely chosen, and productive of an even richer communion of life. An 'infinite variety' characterizes the presences we experience; 'presence' is a radically analogous term and reality. We never face a simple alternative, presence or absence. It is always a question of what kind of presence and what kind of absence, of how someone is present or absent. Room opens up to differentiate,

---

[6] On presence and its varieties see G. Marcel, *Creative Fidelity*, trans. R. Rosthul (New York: Farrar, Strauss & Co., 1964); id., *Homo viator*, trans. E. Craufurd (London: Victor Gollancz, 1951); id., *The Mystery of Being*, trans. G. S. Fraser and R. Hague (London: Harvill Press, 1950–1); id., *Philosophy of Existence*, trans. M. Harari (Freeport, Tex.: Books for Libraries Press, 1969).

for instance, between special and general presence and between indefinitely many kinds of special and general presences.

7. Finally, reflection suggests a feminine dimension to presence. Our primordial experience of presence showed it to be maternal, when we were all umbilically bonded to our mother who harboured and kept us. After birth her presence continued to shelter and nurture us. It is no wonder then that there is a receptive, nurturing, and maternal feel to the presence of God, in whom 'we live and move and have our being' (Acts 17: 28). Inasmuch as it creates a quiet 'space' in which to breathe and grow, human and divine presence wears a feminine face.

This working account of presence comprises then seven elements. As relational, personal, and free, presence creates communion, is mediated symbolically among human beings, bespeaks an infinite variety of possibilities, and, while obviously not exclusively so, comes across as primordially feminine. What light can this account shed on the central christological datum, the world's Saviour who is at once truly divine and fully human?

As Word/Wisdom/Son of God, Christ is eternally and personally related to the Father in the Spirit. To adapt a central denial from Nicaea I, 'there never was a moment when God was not present to/in him' (see DS 126; Col. 1: 19; 2 Cor. 5: 19). This divine 'presence to', which constitutes the triune God's life in communion, is mirrored in Christ's earthly existence—from the trinitarian face of his virginal conception and baptism right through to his 'being exalted at the right hand' of God the Father and jointly 'pouring out' the Holy Spirit on the world (Acts 2: 33). The trinitarian presence takes into account the ultimate reality of Christ's eternal and temporal existence. His addressing God as 'Abba' reflects that 'being related to' which is his eternal life-in-communion transposed into time. This is a 'knowing' which denotes a mutual existence-in-the-other's presence: 'no one knows the Son except the Father, and no one knows the Father except the Son' (Matt. 11: 27 par.). In Chapter 11 (text at n. 15) we pointed out Jesus' mystical consciousness of and reaction to God's immediate and direct presence.

The Q-text just quoted ends by saying, 'no one knows the Father except the Son and anyone to whom the Son chooses to reveal him'. How then does the notion of presence illuminate not only Christ's intratrinitarian being-in-relationship but also his revealing and saving 'work' for human beings? How serviceable is 'presence', once we move from a christological consideration of Jesus 'in himself' (*in se*) to a soteriological consideration of his being 'for us' (*pro nobis*)?

We might well describe soteriology as the multiform ways (see (6) above) in which Christ's presence (or God's unique, foundational presence in/to Christ) mediated and mediates itself to human beings and their world, so as to communicate revelation and redemption. Here what was brought up under (5) above proves peculiarly important. On the basis of some spatio-temporal nearness a vital, personal 'presence to' can develop. A bodily presence allows the interpersonal relationship with Christ to emerge and grow as *the* revealing/saving presence *pro nobis*. Justifiably Irenaeus and other Church Fathers upheld, against the Gnostics and Marcion, the goodness of creation and the christological relevance of the Jewish story and indeed of all human history (Chapter 7 above). By vindicating the material world and Christ's corporeal humanity, they were in fact defending the essential point of departure for our redemption: his full, spatio-temporal presence. Here we could fairly adapt Tertullian's lapidary phrase (Chapter 7 n. 11) 'caro cardo salutis' and make it read: 'presentia corporea cardo salutis' (bodily presence is the hinge of salvation). From this point of view let us explore the christological/soteriological mysteries—from creation to the end.

As Justin and other Greek Fathers appreciated, through creating and sustaining the universe the Logos permeated the body of the world. No place or person lay or lies far from God's creative Logos or Wisdom. The Logos was and is universally present. The incarnation, when the Logos became flesh, brought a new revealing and saving presence. This mystery put Christ in a material solidarity with all human beings and their world. Present now in a bodily, human fashion, he offered and offers new possibilities for mutual, interpersonal relationships. The words and deeds of his public ministry made present God's saving kingdom. Christ drew near to all human beings and, in a particular way, to their sufferings. His own body on the cross expressed for all time his mysterious but truly redeeming presence to those who suffer. Pascal's reflection ('He is in agony to the end of the world') has classically articulated the crucified Christ's enduring presence in the mystery of all human suffering.[7]

One group which has remained together and whose history has constantly re-enacted that passion is the Jews, the chosen people who could also be called God's suffering people. Around AD 58 St Paul reflected on how this people, his own brothers and sisters, spoke to him of God's mysterious plan for the whole world (Rom. 9–11). The apostle wrote of the Mosaic law, the covenants, the promises, the future salvation of Israel, and the rest. But from his vantage-point in the first century he could hardly be aware of one overwhelming reality, the appalling history of suffering which his race would continue to undergo. In the twentieth century, as in Paul's day, the chosen people communicate many messages to those who care to look, pray, and think. Among other things they serve as a living reminder of Jesus the Jew, God's suffering servant who rose from the dead. In a special way, their agony has embodied and symbolized his. The painful story of God's chosen people should enter into any adequate Christology, particularly one that focuses on the presence of the crucified and risen Christ.

His resurrection from the dead ushered in a dramatically new, life-giving sharing of his presence, or—to put it another way—a situation in which his loving, reconciling activity remains definitively and universally present. This post-Easter presence is reflected in Luke's liking for the language of life when speaking of the resurrected Christ (e.g. Luke 24: 5, 23; Acts 1: 3), and in John's subsequent identification of Jesus with life (e.g. John 11: 25; 14: 6). Risen from the dead, Christ is actively present as the source of eternal life. This new presence meant that Christ was not only merely with us (through creation and the incarnation) and for us (through

[7] Listed as *Pensée* 552 in such editions as W. F. Trotter's trans. (New York: E. P. Dutton, 1958), which follow the standard Brunschvicg edition, this *pensée* is numbered 919 in A. J. Krailsheimer's trans. (Harmondsworth: Penguin Books, 1966), which adopts the order of the *Pensées* as Pascal left them at his death.

his ministry and crucifixion), but also was/is now in us, inviting us to respond to his presence (e.g. Col. 1: 27). His personal self-bestowal, made possible through a glorious transformation that lifts him beyond the normal limits of space and time, has effected a presence which John typically describes as 'Christ-in-us and we-in-Christ' and Paul as 'we-in-Christ'. Where John's Gospel represents this new presence as mutual indwelling, Paul usually depicts it as our dwelling 'in Christ' as in a corporate personality.[8] The risen Christ and his Holy Spirit bring about a divine presence in the lives of believers that reflects the perfect union with and presence to God in the life of Christ.

The first Easter also produced the outpouring of the Holy Spirit and the emergence of the Church, two essential elements in the new, saving presence of the risen Christ. With her sacraments, teaching, members, and whole life, the Church bodies forth the living presence of the risen Jesus. She forms the visible verification of his invisible but actively real presence. He exercises the primary ministry in and through all the sacraments. Whenever the sacraments are administered, the risen Christ is personally and effectively present. In his commentary on John's Gospel, Augustine summed up this sacramental presence and ministry of the risen Lord: 'when Peter baptizes, it is Christ who baptizes. When Paul baptizes, it is Christ who baptizes' (*In Ioannem*, 6. 7). As 'soul' or living principle of the Church, the Holy Spirit mediates the presence of the risen Christ—in an endless variety of ways, not least through the Scriptures, the writing of which was inspired by the Spirit and in the reading of which the same Spirit can witness now to Christ. The invisible Spirit, who gives the Church her identity and permanence, joins believers to Christ in calling God 'Abba' (Gal. 4: 6; Rom. 8: 15) and brings them into that relationship with God as loving parent exemplified by Jesus. The personal Love between Father and Son, the Holy Spirit works to transform the whole world, configure all to the pattern of Christ's dying and rising, and draw all to the presence of and

---

[8] Very occasionally Paul varies his normal usage and writes of 'Christ/Jesus in us/me' (e.g. Gal. 2: 20).

life-in-communion with the Trinity (see Rom. 8: 2–27).

Lastly, the resurrection of Jesus means that he is present as the end of history. His rising from the dead has initiated the presence of the end, the eschatological body of human beings and their world which will be consummated at the 'parousia' (1 Cor. 15: 20–8) or final gathering into the divine presence and 'being with' God through Christ (Rev. 21: 3–4). In the mean time through Christ the story of the world unfolds as a drama of cosmic and human reconciliation (Rom. 5: 10–11; 2 Cor. 5: 18–19; Col. 1: 19–20). By means of its vivid scenarios and apocalyptic images, the Book of Revelation invites its readers to contemplate the victory of the suffering Christ in human history. In 'the signs of the times' Christians note and seek to interpret current indications of Christ's personal presence and influence. Dialogue with non-Christian religions can enrich a sense of the ongoing, universal presence of Christ. Like Justin, Clement of Alexandria, and their successors, we may acknowledge and reverence the risen Christ as, in varying ways and degrees, actively if anonymously there in other religions even before any contact with the gospel message has taken place. These other faiths and their cultures have proved a matrix in which his saving revelation has also been effectively present. His hidden but redemptive presence links the manifest context of Christian life with the wider context of world religions and world history.

To sum up. A Christology of presence displays many attractive features. It ties faith in Christ firmly to the mystery of the Trinity. It provides a thread to link all the soteriological mysteries: from creation, through the incarnation (and its proximate preparation in the OT), the ministry of Jesus, his crucifixion, the resurrection, his self-bestowal in the life of the Church, the activity of the Holy Spirit within and beyond the Christian community, the role of Christ in human history and world religions, and his inauguration of the universal eschaton in which through him God will be unavoidably and publicly there for all.

This Christology of presence, as implied by point (5) above, yields at the horizontal level (between Christ and us rather than 'vertically' between Christ and 'Abba') a bodily vision of things. Christ is there whenever and wherever we encounter the body of creation, suffering human bodies, Jewish bodies, the ecclesial body (indwelt by the Holy Spirit), the 'body' of world religions, and the historical 'body' of humanity. His presence is mediated here and now in an infinite variety of ways and with varying degrees of intensity and clarity—until the consummation of all things in his eschatological body.

The championing of presence in this concluding chapter does not intend to take back anything of what has been argued above: in particular, when Chapter 12 pressed the claims of love to be the key for interpreting Christ's redemptive work. The chapters complement each other. Love is the content of salvation through Christ; his various presences form the mode.

Finally, one can plead three particular advantages for the perspective of presence: its Jewishness, its feminine face, and its spiritual, pastoral, and even mystical possibilities. A central theme of OT theology is provided by the conviction that God is present to Israel and has promised to remain present no matter how unfaithful the people prove to be. The Jews marvel at the unique divine presence which they enjoy (Deut. 4: 7). God's desire to be present constantly to the chosen people manifests itself concretely in the Tent of Meeting (e.g. Exod. 26; 36; 40) and then, of course, through the temple in Jerusalem. More than any other prophet Ezekiel values the divine presence symbolized by the temple, mourns the departure of God's glory (Ezek. 10: 1–22; 11: 22–5), and looks forward in hope to the divine presence returning when the temple is restored (Ezek. 40: 1–48: 35). Such key figures in the OT history as Isaac, Jacob, and Moses receive from God a special promise of presence ('I am with you') in carrying out their divinely authorized mission (e.g. Gen. 26: 24; 28: 15; Exod. 3: 12; 4: 12). The assurance of the divine presence forms a regular feature of these commissioning narratives (see also e.g. Josh. 1: 5, 9; Judg. 6: 12, 16; 2 Sam. 7: 3). Given the persistent importance of the divine presence in OT religious thought,[9] it is not surprising that this theme

[9] See S. Terrien, *The Elusive Presence* (New York: Harper & Row, 1978). On modern Jewish thought see E. L. Fackenheim, *God's Presence in History: Jewish Affirmations and Philosophical Reflections* (New York: New York University Press, 1970).

emerges in Matthew, the most Jewish of the four Gospels. Recognizing that Jesus comes as the climax in the story of a people to whom God has been uniquely present (Matt. 1: 1–17), Matthew calls him 'Emmanuel' or 'God with us' (Matt. 1: 23). It is also only Matthew who appreciates that during his earthly ministry Jesus has already replaced the Jerusalem temple as the visible sign of God's presence: 'greater than the temple is here' (Matt. 12: 6). In his closing missionary mandate the risen Jesus promises to be always with his disciples (Matt. 28: 20), a promise which parallels the promise of divine presence that regularly accompanies OT commissions. Matthew's Jewish sense of presence emerges not only when presenting the public mission to 'all nations' but also when reporting Jesus' instructions for prayer within the Church: 'where two or three are gathered in my name, there am I in the midst of them' (Matt. 18: 20). By praying together, believers will experience the presence of Christ, 'God with us'.

The feminine quality of Jesus turned up early in this book, when we called to mind how he presented himself as a mother hen and how from NT times on Christians identified him with the OT personification of divine activity, Lady Wisdom, who is present and active in all creation.[10] To distinguish nowadays feminine and masculine characteristics is to face controversy almost at every turn. However, it must be done if one is to develop the data from Scripture and tradition. Following Walter Ong and others,[11] I would see masculinity as differentiating, moving outward, set on change, breaking idols, and restlessly earning its identity through struggle. The contrary feminine qualities include being receptive, nurturing, interior, self-assured, self-possessed, and not needing constant contest to earn and maintain one's identity. Being present belongs unmistakably to this list. Both in 'real' life and in literature women are persistently 'there'—from birth (necessarily) to death (by choice) in a way that men do not

---

[10] On some possibilities provided by this identification see E. A. Johnson, 'Jesus—the Wisdom of God: A Biblical Basis for a Non-androcentric Christology', *Ephemerides theologicae Lovanienses*, 41 (1985), 261–94.

[11] See W. Ong, *Fighting for Life: Contest, Sexuality and Consciousness* (Ithaca, NY: Cornell University Press, 1981).

match. Men have often avoided these situations, perhaps through insecurity and a fear of being absorbed by the feminine.

What does the gospel record indicate about Jesus' masculine and feminine qualities? Unquestionably we come across adversarial, masculine language and characteristics. He looks with anger at those who would condemn his healing a handicapped person because they have made an idol of sabbath observance; he challenges them by restoring the man's withered hand (Mark 3: 1–6). He presents his mission in combative and divisive terms: 'you must not think that I have come to bring peace to the earth; I have not come to bring peace but a sword. I have come to set a man against his father, a daughter against her mother, a daughter-in-law against her mother-in-law' (Matt. 10: 34–5 par.). The same sense of masculine divisiveness turns up in another Q-saying: 'he who is not with me is against me, and he who does not gather with me scatters' (Matt. 12: 30 par.). Jesus is set on radically changing the environment he has encountered: 'I have come to set fire to the earth' (Luke 12: 49). His identity as bearer of God's final kingdom emerges in his struggle with the forces of evil (Matt. 12: 22–9 parr.). John's Gospel, while remaining silent about Jesus' exorcisms or delivering people from the grip of demonic powers, expresses this masculine struggle through the theme of light clashing with darkness (John 1: 4–13; 9: 1–41).

Alongside such masculine characteristics we can easily uncover feminine ones. Jesus receives into his presence and nurtures little children (Mark 10: 13–16 parr.; see Mark 9: 33–7 parr.). He is remembered as constantly cultivating the inner life through prayer (e.g. Mark 1: 12–13, 35; 6: 46). The struggle in Gethsemane comes across as the more surprising, since hitherto Jesus has seemed so self-assured about his mission and identity. His sayings include some that seem downright feminine or at least do not find support in male, adversarial logic: for instance, 'whoever wants to save his life will lose it, but whoever loses his life for my sake and for the gospel's will save it' (Mark 8: 35). 'Seek and you will find; knock and the door will be opened to you' (Matt. 7: 7 par.) sounds masculine and the way to win. But letting go and losing because one hopes to be saved converges with the non-violent, feminine strength-in-surrender with which Luke portrays the death of Jesus: 'Father, forgive them ... Father, into your hands I commend my spirit' (Luke 23: 34, 46). A striking testimony to the untroubled, feminine delicacy of Jesus' language emerges when we recall the image of female prostitution used at times by the OT prophets to focus the disobedience of God's people. The vivid, ugly allegories of sexual infidelity developed by Ezekiel (Ezek. 16: 1–63; 23: 1–49) more than hint at the male insecurity and dominance of that priest-prophet. The Jesus of the Synoptic Gospels never needs to indulge in such language. On the contrary, he does not flinch from applying to himself a very homely, female image (Luke 13: 34 par.). He is present like a mother hen to shelter her chickens when they run back under her wings. Like Lady Wisdom he invites his audience: 'come to me, all you who labour and are heavily burdened, and I will give you rest' (Matt. 11: 28). John's Gospel develops its feminine version of Jesus in various ways: for instance, through the discourse on the nurturing bread of life which evokes Lady Wisdom's banquet (John 6: 22–58; Prov. 9: 1–18), and the allegory of the branches that dwell in the receptive vine and bear much fruit through that welcoming presence (John 15: 1–10).

A third advantage offered by a Christology of presence surfaced already in the spirituality and mysticism of the Middle Ages. Anselm, Bernard, women mystics, and others fostered a tender devotion to Jesus as friend, lover, and mother. Alongside such masculine images as the warrior who paradoxically conquers evil through his death, spiritual teachers and mystics developed feminine images of a Jesus who is there to harbour and nurture those who turn to and delight in his presence. 'His presence' climaxes the opening stanza of the classically tender hymn attributed to Bernard: 'Jesu, dulcis memoria | | dans vera cordis gaudia. | | Sed super mel et omnia | | eius dulcis presentia.' Not only centuries ago but also today a Christology of presence offers attractive links to the living world of Christian (and, for that matter, non-Christian) spirituality, mysticism, and pastoral care.

Anyone who works today in the Christian ministry knows

full well what a decisive difference it makes when people enjoy a sense of Jesus' living presence. They can re-enact then the experience of the individuals portrayed in John's Gospel, who by encountering Jesus find meaning in such basic challenges as religious doubt (Nicodemus), an irregular marital situation (the Samaritan woman), and a physical handicap (the man born blind). Jesus' presence engenders meaning and creates life for them.

We have looked at three advantages which the theme of presence promises in Christology: its Jewishness, its feminine characteristics, and its connections with mystical and pastoral spirituality. We could go on to add further advantages: for example, the way such a Christology, by highlighting the new presence of Christ and his Spirit that comes through his dying and rising, maintains the centrality of the Easter mystery. The resurrection of the crucified Christ lifts to a new level the christological presence already there in creation and incarnation, and anticipates the universal, public presence to come at the eschaton. Along these lines christological thinking can satisfy an absolutely essential conviction of Christian liturgy: the pre-eminent place of the paschal mystery in the sacraments and entire life of public worship. A Christology of presence can thus endorse a prime tradition within the community of believers. It can also help to face a challenge coming from without: revelation and salvation for those who do not (yet) believe in Christ. The choice cannot be seen as simply that between Christ's presence and his absence. Respect for the multiform variety of his presences allows us to acknowledge Christ as everywhere present but in an infinite variety of ways.

In this book I have tried as far as possible to refrain from parading my Christian beliefs. Yet they have constantly come through, particularly at decisive points. Several times I have taken issue with those who entertain the ambition of adopting a neutral, non-partisan approach in theology and similar fields. I still endorse strongly what I put forward years ago: that personal commitment and critical reflection can and should mutually support each other.[12] As an esteemed colleague in the United States has stated,

---

[12] See my *Fundamental Theology* (London: Darton, Longman & Todd, 1981), 6–7.

to be confessional is simply to be open about one's historical and religious locatedness, one's specificity, an openness that is essential for serious theological work and indeed for any serious intellectual work that is not in thrall to the myth of the disembodied and unlocated scholarly intellect.[13]

In the particular discipline of Christology, to be confessional involves some claim to 'know' Jesus. St Augustine drew attention to the daunting truth here: 'nemo nisi per amicitiam cognoscitur,' which could be paraphrased as 'you need to be a friend of someone before you truly know him or her'.[14] But who dares to make the claim, 'I am a true friend of Jesus'?

---

[13] P. J. Griffiths, 'The Uniqueness of Christian Doctrine Defended', in G. D'Costa (ed.), *Christian Uniqueness Reconsidered* (Maryknoll, NY: Orbis Books, 1990), 169.

[14] *De diversis quaestionibus*, 83. 71. 5.

SELECT BIBLIOGRAPHY

✤ ✤

DUNN, J. D. G., *Christology in the Making* (London: SCM Press, 2nd edn., 1989).

DUPUIS, J., *Jesus Christ at the Encounter of World Religions*, trans. R. R. Barr (Maryknoll, NY: Orbis, 1991).

——*Who do you Say I am?: Introduction to Christology* (Maryknoll, NY: Orbis, 1994).

FREDRIKSEN, P., *From Jesus to Christ: The Origins of the New Testament Images of Jesus* (New Haven, Conn.: Yale University Press, 1988).

GNILKA, J., *Jesus von Nazaret* (Freiburg: Herder, 1990).

GRILLMEIER, A., *Christ in Christian Tradition*, trans. J. Bowden *et al.*, 2 vols. (London: Mowbrays, 1975 and 1995).

KASPER, W., *Jesus the Christ*, trans. V. Green (London: Burns & Oates, 1976).

KUSCHEL, K.-J., *Born before All Time? The Dispute over Christ's Origin*, trans. J. Bowden (London: SCM Press, 1992).

MACQUARRIE, J., *Jesus Christ in Modern Thought* (London: SCM Press, 1990).

MEYER, B. F., *et al.*, 'Jesus', *ABD* iii. 773–819.

MOLTMANN, J., *The Way of Jesus Christ*, trans. M. Kohl (London: SCM Press, 1990).

MORRIS, T. V., *The Logic of God Incarnate* (Ithaca, NY: Cornell University Press, 1986).

PANNENBERG, W., *Jesus: God and Man*, trans. L. L. Wilkins and D. A. Priebe (London: SCM Press, 1968).

——*Systematic Theology*, ii, trans. G. W. Bromiley (Edinburgh: T. & T. Clark, 1994).

RAHNER, K., *Foundations of Christian Faith*, trans. W. V. Dych (London: Darton, Longman & Todd, 1978).

SANDERS, E. P., *The Historical Figure of Jesus* (London: Penguin Press, 1993).

SCHWEIZER, E., *et al.*, 'Jesus Christus', *TRE* xvi. 670–772; xvii. 1–84.

SESBOÜÉ, B., *Jésus-Christ l'unique médiateur: essai sur la rédemption et le salut*, 2 vols. (Paris: Desclée, 1988–91).

SOBRINO, J., *Christology at the Crossroads* (London: SCM Press, 1978).

STURCH, R., *The Word and the Christ* (Oxford: Clarendon Press, 1991).

THOMPSON, W. M., *The Jesus Debate: A Survey and Synthesis* (Mahwah, NJ: Paulist Press, 1985).

——*Christology and Spirituality* (New York: Crossroad, 1991).

WITHERINGTON, B., *The Christology of Jesus* (Minneapolis: Fortress Press, 1990).

INDEX OF NAMES

BIBLICAL INDEX

⁂ ⁂

1 THE OLD TESTAMENT

2 INTERTESTAMENTAL WRITINGS

3 THE NEW TESTAMENT